Christianity *and* the Culture Machine

Christianity *and* the Culture Machine

Media and Theology in the Age of Late Secularism

by Vincent F. Rocchio

CASCADE *Books* • Eugene, Oregon

CHRISTIANITY AND THE CULTURE MACHINE
Media and Theology in the Age of Late Secularism

Cascade Books
An Imprint of Wipf and Stock Publishers
199 W. 8th Ave., Suite 3
Eugene, OR 97401

www.wipfandstock.com

PAPERBACK ISBN 13: 978-1-4982-0979-3
HARDCOVER ISBN 13: 978-1-4982-0981-6
EBOOK ISBN: 978-1-4982-0980-9

Cataloguing-in-Publication data:

Names: Rocchio, Vincent F.

Title: Christianity and the culture machine : media and theology in the age of Late Secularism / Vincent F. Rocchio.

Description: Eugene, OR: Cascade Books, 2016 | Includes bibliographical references.

Identifiers: ISBN 978-1-4982-0979-3 (paperback) | ISBN 978-1-4982-0981-6 (hardcover) | ISBN 978-1-4982-0980-9 (ebook)

Subjects: LCSH: Mass media criticism. | Cinema and Television. | Mass Media Social aspects. | Theology. | Title.

Classification: P91 R625 2016 (paperback) | P91 (ebook)

Manufactured in the USA. 08/02/16

An earlier version of chapter 3 appears in the *Journal of Culture and Religion* 11:2.

To the women of clan Crowley:
Norma, Patricia, Joan, Serena, and Judy,
each in her own way a model and testament
of what strength truly is.

And to my wife, Margaret:
without her, this book would not have been possible.

In many ways, the work of a critic is easy. We risk very little, yet enjoy a position over those who offer up their work and their selves to our judgment. We thrive on negative criticism, which is fun to write and to read. But the bitter truth we critics must face is that, in the grand scheme of things, the average piece of junk is more meaningful than our criticism designating it so. But there are times when a critic truly risks something, and that is in the discovery and defense of the new.

—Anton Ego, from *Ratatouille* (2007)

Contents

Acknowledgments

This project started off, simply enough, with Lucia Piazza's childhood obsession with *Mary Poppins*. I had not seen the film since my own days as a young child, but her toddler's fascination with it made me take a closer look, and before I knew it, a project was born. As is often the case, my first attempts were crude, but I was fortunate enough to enlist the help of David Miller, who not only persuaded me to delve deeply into the work of Bakhtin, but also to explore the writings of Ernst Bloch, the formidable Marxist critic who tossed away the atheism of Marxism like yesterday's newspapers.

The staff and students at John Cabot University in Rome gave me my first opportunity to develop my ideas about combining media and cultural studies with theology into a full-scale book project. They diligently attended my special topics course and pushed me to do more. Having various staff members sit in on the course and participate not only raised the discussion and sharpened my thinking, but showed the students what an intellectual community really looks like.

As I got to the task of actually writing, my readers, Joshua Bellin, John Champagne, and Roger Simon, were crucial for consistently asking me to go further with my ideas, and to flat out up my game. I was, to say the least, rusty, but they were patient, encouraging, and demanding all at the same time. Theologically, I could have never accomplished this without enormous help. Fritz Bauerschmidt, David Toole, Tim Muldoon, and Joseph Guido, OP were my go-to theologians, always willing to point me in the right direction and clarify my thinking. I also received an enormous amount of help from Stanley Hauerwas, who, despite being so busy, always took the time to answer my queries and provide direction. Likewise, Frank Desiderio, CSP, gave me ample opportunity to informally discuss ideas and concepts I was working through.

Sonia Malpeso and Katrin Schneck kindly provided me with German translations for the films I wrote on. I'm also very grateful to Vivica Pierre,

Library Director at Bunker Hill Community College, who cut through all the bureaucratic red tape to provide a scholar in need with a place to work.

When it came time to actually publish, Rodney Clapp and Matt Wimmer at Wipf and Stock made this daunting process seem easy.

I began writing this book in the quiet of a converted Roman villa many years ago, more years than I like to admit. Along the way, the project, and my family, got derailed many times—the result of traumatic events. I was lucky to get back on track through the loving and material support of my brothers and sisters—A. J., Bob, Gina, Lisa, and John—who never fail to be there for me.

The length of time it took me to finish this book is illustrated by the fact that the last time I was finishing a book, my daughter Antonia was an only child. Now, she not only has Giovanna and Dominic for siblings, but is about to graduate high school and enter college. Clearly, being a prolific writer is not one of my problems, but thanks to my children, neither is lack of motivation to try to make a better world. They will always be my greatest contribution to humanity. And, just like with all my books, I owe the ability to work in the world of ideas to my wife Margaret, who not only keeps me grounded, but encourages me forward. She survived two different cancers and still gets up every day to bring light to the darkness. If this book has any positive impact on the world or the world of ideas, it is due to the inspiration and help that these people and countless others have given me over the years. The limitations herein, however, can only be attributed to me.

1

Introduction

On March 13, 2013, the Vatican greeted the entire world with its traditional phrase "*Habemus papam*," little realizing the ironies that would soon be in play when Jorge Mario Bergolio emerged on the balcony. Dressed in a simple white cassock, the new Pope conducted an unprecedented move, bowing down and asking the crowd to pray over him. The gesture of personal humility was such a dramatic departure from the usual Vatican pomp that journalists reported being able to "hear a pin drop," despite the overflow crowd packing the piazza.[1] The newly elected pontiff deftly used his introduction to signal the end of the imperial papacy and the beginning of a new direction for the Roman Catholic church. Although reluctant to assume the papacy, once he did, Pope Francis immediately began using the office to transform it.

The immediacy with which Francis began instituting change belies a tension within the Roman Catholic Church. The last two popes privileged orthodoxy as a means for the church to maintain its identity and viability in an increasingly dehumanizing and secular world. Pope Benedict XVI saw orthodoxy as a means to "purify" the church, caring little that it made the church seem backward-looking and aloof, especially in light of a worldwide clergy sex abuse crisis and a continually eroding base in the developed countries. With purification as his goal, Pope Benedict was concerned neither that the Roman Catholic Church continued to shrink, nor that the emphasis on orthodoxy had a polarizing effect: dividing the church between progressive Catholics who are oriented towards social justice, and more inward looking conservatives for whom obedience to the church and its Magisterium is tantamount.

In repositioning the focus of the church on the poor, Pope Francis ushered in a seismic paradigm shift that deftly got out from under the temporal dualism that divides Catholics—substituting instead a vision of church deeply rooted in Scripture that all could embrace. From the very beginning of his papacy, Pope Francis acted through and reemphasized the concept of "servant leadership" as fundamental to the church, following the example of Pope John Paul II, but taking it in new directions: he accepted the congratulations of his fellow cardinals by standing (as opposed to sitting on the papal throne), rode the bus back to his hotel with his fellow cardinals, and paid the bill at the hotel out of his own pocket. He continues to live in a guest house rather than the palatial Vatican apartments, and is known to drive his own modest car around Vatican City rather than be driven in a papal limousine.

The significance of Pope Francis's leadership for this book is twofold. First, as the leader of the world's largest Christian denomination, his attempts at reforming the Catholic Church will have profound implications for the rest of the Christian world, which will respond in one way or another to his attempt to reinvigorate Christian theology. Second, and most importantly, the vision and direction Pope Francis is charting for the Roman Catholic Church recognizes that the image of the church—based largely on its conduct—plays a determining role in the church's ability to communicate Christian theology, not to mention a fundamental role in people's relationship to the church. The Pope's privileging of the relationship between theology and communication makes critical communications theory more important than ever.

Pope Francis demonstrates a belief that the crisis of Christianity—its continued erosion in the late twentieth and early twenty-first century—is not a theological failure, but an aesthetic problem. For Francis, the core theology of Christianity is not what people have turned away from, but rather, how theology is enacted and communicated—which, in his view, is not very well at all. In a subtle critique of his predecessors, Francis commented, "The church sometimes has locked itself up in small things, in small-minded rules."[2] Rather than a church in need of a more obedient faithful, Francis sees a church that needs to be more faithful to theology and less concerned with dogma, stating,

> We cannot insist only on issues related to abortion, gay marriage and the use of contraceptive methods . . . . [I]t is not necessary to talk about these issues all the time. The church's pastoral ministry cannot be obsessed with the transmission of a disjointed multitude of doctrines to be imposed insistently . . . . We have

> to find a new balance; otherwise even the moral edifice of the church is likely to fall like a house of cards . . . .[3]

What Francis clearly recognizes is that church is failing to effectively communicate the vitality of its theology—"the freshness and fragrance of the Gospel."[4]

For Pope Francis then, the vitality of Christian theology is being choked off by the message and conduct of the church itself. His vision of reform is a church that can respond to an aesthetic crisis by communicating the ethos of Christianity more compellingly—and the primary way it accomplishes that task is by embodying that ethos more authentically. "I prefer a church which is bruised, hurting and dirty because it has been out on the streets, rather than a church which is unhealthy from being confined and from clinging to its own security," writes Pope Francis.[5] The vivid imagery Pope Francis consistently employs when speaking about the church belies the aesthetic impulse Francis brings to the task of reform.

Francis himself speaks about the image of the church, but not aesthetics, and with good reason. Francis has shown himself to be a practical leader concerned with reforming how the church conducts itself, and *aesthetics* is a slippery term at best. Although it may be difficult to define, aesthetics is anything but an esoteric concept unconcerned with the practicalities of conduct. Rather, as the terms *image, vision, emphasis*, and *leadership style* attest, aesthetics is at the heart of some of the fundamental framework(s) by which Christianity is conceptualized. Traditional concepts of aesthetics, from both theology and art history, are helpful, but have distinct limitations. Theology, for example, has an expansive view on locating aesthetics—it is a matter for all of creation—but limits the concept to a theological concern with beauty and its relationship to the Divine. Following the work of Avery Dulles, Cecilia Gonzalez-Andrieu demonstrates that the importance of theological aesthetics is its focus on "the depth and power of 'the revelatory symbol'"—the signs, whether natural occurrences or produced through artistic virtuosity, which evidence the transcendent.[6] Gonzalez-Andrieu's work makes clear that aesthetics must encompass the world of art and creativity as further ground for theological explication, but art and art history have their own limitations for the concept. Art history, for example, opens out the concept of aesthetics to include concepts of style and stylistic operations. Media studies has built upon that framework, adding the idea that style itself functions as a discourse—a concept that is now foundational in media theory. The problem with an art history and/or media studies approach is the tendency to reduce aesthetics to only a matter of the mind—whether it be the creative mind and its ability to construct artistic arrangements, or the critical mind and its ability to discern the message of the work and its relationship to broader ideological and hegemonic operations.

Some contemporary theorists explore the concept of aesthetics through the affective dimension, analyzing how art, beauty, and for that matter meaning itself, moves an audience. Metaphors abound to describe this level of audience engagement: gripping, tear-jerker, knee-slapper, gut-wrenching, or shaken to the core—all of which point to the body. Here, I am following the lead of Michael Shapiro, but also S. Brent Plate, whose work on theology and aesthetics restores the term to the body as a means of reestablishing all the physical relationships at stake in creative production and reception. Plate argues that, at its very basic level, aesthetics is regulated through perception, an activity that involves both body and mind. Moreover, Plate argues that "perception . . . links the inner world to the outer world, the body to the physical stuff around us, the body to the mind, and bodies to other bodies . . . ."[7] My interest in restoring the body to the concept of aesthetics is twofold. First, reconceptualizing aesthetics to include the body brings focus to the social dimensions of aesthetics (what Plate describes as the relationship of bodies to other bodies). In addition, resituating the body within the concept of aesthetics ushers in those dimensions of aesthetic reception that transcend the mind—reasserting, for example, the relationship between the body and spirit. Gonzalez-Andrieu argues that "revelatory symbols unite spirit and matter"—they provide, if only for a moment—or a glimpse—evidence of the transcendent, an experience that incorporates mind, body, and spirit.[8]

As a concept, then, aesthetics must bring into analysis how discourse—or the discourse of art—relates to being: not just the mind, but rather, the lived experience of its audience. Here, Raymond Williams's concept of a "structure of feeling" is particularly useful. For Williams, always wary of analysis being too reductionist, affective experience can neither be dismissed as too subjective, nor ignored as not having a relationship to the social field. In particular, Williams is interested in how generations or historical periods are defined by forms and styles that "exert palpable pressures and set effective limits on experience and on action."[9] Williams, then, insists on a dialectical model where artistic forms and styles develop in relationship to both art itself and the social field through which it operates.[10]

In analyzing contemporary Christianity through aesthetics, Williams's concept focuses analysis on formal changes that signal a transition from one period to another. He argues: "The idea of a structure of feeling can be specifically related to the evidence of forms and conventions—semantic figures—which, in art and literature are often among the very first indications that such a new structure is forming."[11] The Catholic writer James Carroll describes that structure of feeling as having been resistant to change when it comes to the aesthetic of Christianity. He argues:

> Though born near the middle of the twentieth century, I was initiated, like so many of my kind, into a way of thinking and believing that owed more to the Middle Ages than to modernity. I use myself as an example not because my case is special, but because it is not. My faith was grounded in a common teaching that shaped the views of most Catholics and many Christians. Fewer and fewer people in the contemporary age have experience of such a worldview, yet it was the decisive milieu in which every experience of Jesus could be had.[12]

The medieval concept or aesthetic that was at the heart of faith formation for Carroll, and for most Christians of the twentieth century, is the primary focus of Pope Francis's reform efforts: aimed at moving Christianity from one concept—obedience and toeing the line on sinful acts—to a fundamentally different understanding—acting with mercy.

Moreover, Francis is clearly cognizant that the conduct of the church acts as a discourse. What Pope Francis (and for that matter, modern public relations) emphasizes is the overarching role that image exercises in determining perception, and subsequently, relationship. In this respect, aesthetics encompasses the role of the overarching image, concepts, vision, and discourses that operate to determine an audience's perception of something. Aesthetics functions in the mode of a gestalt to help determine the overall meaning. This is not to downplay, however, the manner in which aesthetics also embodies the means through which overarching images or concepts are conveyed. Aesthetics is deeply involved in elements of style and structure, in the exchange of symbols and symbolic ritual, and with the signifying practices employed to communicate messages. Lastly, as the work of Williams, Plate, and Gonzalez-Andrieu demonstrate, aesthetics is goal driven: producing affect—the movement between perception and relationship.

Pope Francis's efforts to create a new aesthetic for Christianity is, in this respect, a massive undertaking whose goal is nothing short of making Christianity vital again: to make Christian discourse speak in ways that manifest the Divine—that unite the mind, body, and spirit of its followers in the experience of the transcendent. Towards that end Gonzalez-Andrieu argues that art can be helpful to the work of theology "in its role as witness and producer of revelatory symbols, which speak eloquently of the veracity of a communicating mutuality with the Divine."[13] Here, the example of the Roman Catholic Church's Second Vatican Council is particularly instructive.

Vatican II created seismic shifts that reverberated throughout Christendom, creating a paradigm shift for Catholicism in its concept of the church. Whereas prior to Vatican II the church was identified with its clergy, Vatican II boldly asserted that the church was the people of God—a radical shift from a medieval concept of church as hierarchical leadership to a modern concept of the church as a collective—as the body of Christ. This new concept of church required a new aesthetic, but never really forged one. Because so much of the work of Vatican II concerned itself with reconciling the church with modernity, Modernism itself became the default aesthetic, ushered in as an important vehicle for communicating the new vision of church. With its fundamental focus on the relationship between the form of the art itself and the content expressed—the relationship between signifier and signified—modernism served, in general, as a poor aesthetic for communicating the veracity of mutuality with the Divine.

The vitality of Vatican II saw other aesthetic forms emerge as a means of expressing the new concept of church: guitar masses, street priests, nuns eschewing the habit for regular clothing. These all became ways of expressing a collective vision of church—of a church engaged in the world, not hiding from it. The social tumult that surrounded Vatican II—the Vietnam War, wars of liberation in Africa, the civil rights movement, student movements, women's and gay rights movements—all challenged the hierarchical power of established social orders. They all required new aesthetic forms, like rock music, to express their challenge and vision of a new world order. When the backlash to these ideological challenges emerged in the mid-1970s, and continued into the 1980s, the emerging aesthetics were either extinguished or, as in the case of rock music, appropriated by the culture industry and rendered harmless and apolitical.

The aesthetic shortcomings of Vatican II, the profound difficulties in forming a new aesthetic, are an important object lesson for Pope Francis's attempt to create a new vision and concept of church. The institutional church itself, having clung to its medieval aesthetic for too long, is fairly ill-prepared to create a new aesthetic. As a result, Christianity needs to look elsewhere, needs to go outside the church for lessons on how to better communicate its vision. I argue that it should look within the margins of mainstream media to find elements of a new aesthetic—find instances that point to the veracity of transcendence and the Divine.

HOLLYWOOD AND A NEW AESTHETIC FOR CHRISTIANITY

As the capitol of the culture industry where secular humanism is the dominant ideology, Hollywood seems like the last place to look for a new Christian aesthetic. Mass producing media texts disseminated through television and the cinema, Hollywood is engaged in nothing less than mass producing the ideology of secular humanism as a "dominant cultural order," to use Stuart Hall's concept. For Hall, the purpose of this cultural order is to impose its "classifications of the social and cultural and political world"—to map out different areas of social life into hierarchically organized, dominant meanings.[14] At least part of the job of the culture industry in America is maintaining the place of religion: which is heralded as a freedom, but confined as a private practice that should never tempt the allegiance of the citizen (which is, after all, pledged to the flag, and to the Republic for which it stands).

Hall's work on ideology, however, emphasizes that the dominant cultural order "is neither univocal nor uncontested," an argument that cautions treating Hollywood monolithically.[15] Following the work of Hall, several studies demonstrate that counter-hegemonic and ideologically challenging discourses can and do operate through mainstream media—the result of its structure as a collective process and decentralized institution. Social discourses come into Hollywood just as much as they are issued from it. As a cultural producer, Hollywood must respond to social trends and events or find itself obsolete. In maintaining the hierarchical dominance of secular humanism, Hollywood and the culture industry have responded in various ways to the increasing inability of institutional Christianity to impact people's lives meaningfully—to be anything more than quaint discourses that give people comfort, security, and a way to feel good on Sundays. Predominantly, the culture industry has responded to the aesthetic crisis of Christianity by offering ideological substitutions—romantic love in place of sacramental love, as with *When Harry Met Sally* (1989), *Four Weddings and a Funeral* (1994), and *Sense and Sensibility* (1995) (to name a few); righteous violence in place of resistance, Christian nonviolence, or peacemaking, as with the Rambo series, *The Rock* (1996), *Black Hawk Down* (2001), and *Saving Private Ryan* (1998) (a small sampling in this category); and the more recent trend of the workplace as the site of a replacement or better family, where a more caring and functional community can be found, as with TV shows like *ER*, *CSI*, *NCIS*, and *Grey's Anatomy*.

Christian theology is so fundamental to Western civilization, and so irrepressibly dynamic, that institutional lethargy and cultural containment cannot keep it from reasserting itself—and insisting itself—within the margins of popular culture texts. There, under the radar screen, it operates counter-hegemonically and in response to the aesthetic failures of the institutional church. Unauthorized by the church, unorganized by any central idea or institution, a new Christian aesthetic can be found communicating the power and vitality of Christianity: its vision for a totalizing social transformation, its inexhaustible, unquenchable drive for the egalitarian community, and its resolute insistence on the transcendent.

An example of this new aesthetic operating within the margins can be found on television every Christmas season: in *A Charlie Brown Christmas* (1965), Charles Schulz's first attempt to animate his famous comic strip. Although the show became an instant classic, ironically, CBS executives were convinced the show was going to be a flop. Among the many perceived flaws in the final cut were two major violations of the rules of American television comedy. First, there was no laugh track, which television executives of the era were convinced was necessary to guide the audience in their response to a show's humor. Even more troubling to CBS executives than the lack of canned laughter, however, was the program's climactic moment, where the character Linus quotes from the Bible. Rather than riveting, as a climax should be, CBS was certain that the scene would land with a thud, and derail an already troubled story.

CBS was not alone in fearing the scene. Both the show's producer, Lee Mendelson, and its director, Bill Melendez, tried to persuade the creator, Charles Schulz, to take it out.[16] Schulz and his comic strip *Peanuts*, however, were already world famous at the time, so even though he had ceded creative control of the actual program to Melendez, Schulz nonetheless prevailed. From their perspective, Mendelson and Melendez felt they had to trust Schulz's judgment: the animated program was slapped together in the impossible time frame of six months, and Schulz was the creative force behind it.[17]

As a story, *A Charlie Brown Christmas* is loosely bound together, ostensibly under Charlie Brown's disillusionment with the commercialization of Christmas. Because Charlie Brown is depressed about the commercialization of Christmas, he has no real desire that drives the narrative forward. Rather than a main character acting upon the narrative world, here, the narrative world seems to be acting upon the main character, as Charlie Brown moves from vignette to vignette that further confirms the over-commercialization of Christmas.

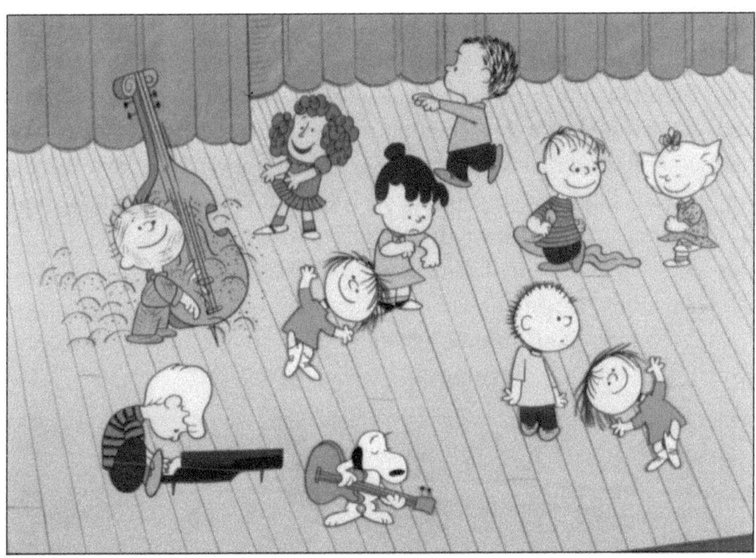

The dance scene before pageant rehearsal is characteristic of the tenuousness of the narrative.

Into this disjointed story line, lacking canned laughter to deliver the punch lines, and voiced, for the most part, by amateur children, Schulz dropped a fifty-second recitation of Luke 2: 8–14 from the King James Bible. CBS executives were fully confident that it would be the first and last time the show would be broadcast. They could not have been more wrong.

What CBS failed to see, but audiences immediately recognized, was that the scene fundamentally rejected Hollywood's dominant style of biblical representation in favor of the message itself. The narrative that Schulz created for *A Charlie Brown Christmas* stripped away every Hollywood convention of biblical representation and replaced it with alternative stylistic features. Instead of lavish period costumes, he had children in ordinary clothes. In fact, the narrative could have easily placed the children in period costumes when it came time for Linus's recitation—they were rehearsing the infancy narrative for the pageant. Instead, the plot remained in a simple, contemporary setting.

The scale of Schulz's narrative is also a core reversal of conventional biblical representation. Rather than an epic scope featuring a cast of thousands, Schulz's narrative is shrunk down to a neighborhood—the cast no bigger than the average *Our Gang* episode. *Shrink* is the operative term here, because not only is the numerical size of the cast decreased dramatically, but so is the physical size of the cast, going from adult A-list, live-action characters to unprofessional children voicing animated child characters. What CBS executives saw as a quirky—and seriously flawed—stylistic choice proved to have enormous impact on the narrative. When the Bible verse is recited in the narrative, it is pronounced by a solitary child, not from the lofty position of authority. The recitation is also absent the preferred Hollywood style for biblical representation: where actors use perfect articulation in a quotation-reciting style that sounds like an imperial mandate for all to hear. Instead, Linus's style is more in line with the core Peanuts charm: "adult" discourse issuing from the mouths of babes. In this respect, it is easy to see why Schulz eschewed adult actors and chose actual children to do the voices. An adult "playing down" could not have brought the same position to Linus's voice—their inflections would have compromised the effect of having little voices say big things.

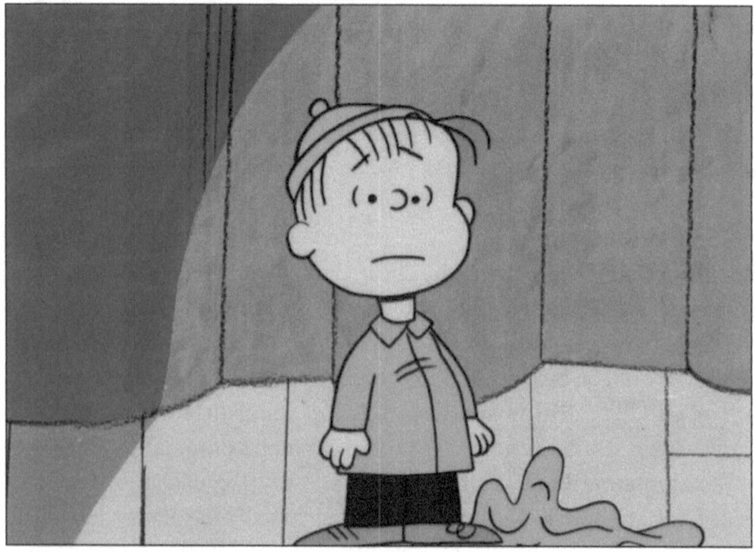

The climax of the story is Linus reciting Luke 2: 8–14 from the King James Bible.

Finally, the scene rejects another stylistic convention of Hollywood's biblical representation: a background music soundtrack. Especially for its time, the soundtrack to *A Charlie Brown Christmas* is very much in the foreground and downright funky—prominently featuring the jazz music of Vince Guaraldi, and the occasional somber tones of Beethoven (Schroeder's hero). When Linus takes to the spotlight to quote from Luke, however, the soundtrack is silent. There is no orchestra or chorus swelling the soundtrack with heightened passion to imbue the character's discourse with regal authority. Instead, Linus is a very small, and at that moment, isolated figure whose only authority—symbolized by his ability to literally take the spotlight—is his understanding that the birth of Jesus of Nazareth is "what Christmas is all about."

In some ways, the argument that *A Charlie Brown Christmas* rejects Hollywood's stylistic conventions of biblical representation is not as accurate as saying that the show replaces them. The difference is not just semantics. Avant-garde filmmakers frequently reject Hollywood's styles and conventions, particularly narrative itself, but often in alienating ways that fail to engage an audience—especially a mainstream or popular audience. Michael Snow's *Wavelength* (1967) is a brilliant rejection of Hollywood style, and Annette Michaelson insightfully lauds the forty-five-minute film as a "masterwork" that redefines "filmic space as that of action," but most audiences would not sit for it.[18] The crucial difference here is that *A Charlie Brown Christmas* is not out to reject Hollywood, the Hollywood style, or even the institution of television. Rather, its agenda is to enhance the core message of the show by adopting stylistic techniques that are in harmony with it—even if that means replacing conventional and dominant stylistic techniques that would work against it.

The harmony—or coherency—of the stylistic techniques, the way they integrate, interact, and impact the narrative, is crucial for understanding the success of *A Charlie Brown Christmas*, and its stature as an enduring cultural legacy. Schulz crafted a narrative with a very alternative (if not subversive) message, but in addition, he created a new aesthetic, both for the genre—children's animation—and the core, or underlying text the narrative draws on—the Bible. *A Charlie Brown Christmas* is a significant site for understanding aesthetics in this way because the story itself illuminates this concept: it builds its narrative around aesthetic experience in a manner that moves its internal audience (the characters of the story). Just as significantly, the narrative restores transcendence—especially spiritual transcendence—as the heart of aesthetic experience.

CBS executives judged wrongly because, for them, the resolution to the climax seemed anticlimatic. The conflict between two opposing views of Christmas—spiritual vs. material—is demarcated when Charlie Brown sets off to purchase a Christmas tree for the pageant. Lucy suggests that Charlie Brown get "a great big shiny aluminum Christmas tree," reinforcing the point in front of the others by saying, "get the biggest aluminum tree you can find, Charlie Brown. Maybe paint it pink!" Charlie Brown, however, does the opposite, purchasing the most pathetic tree on the lot, despite Linus warning him. Charlie Brown is motivated by the fact that it is the only real tree on the lot—in the iconography of the scene, it is the only green tree. In addition, however, Charlie Brown is motivated to purchase the tree more by his feeling that the forlorn tree "needs him."

The conflict between the two opposing views, motivated as it is by Charlie Brown's search for Christmas, operates within the melodramatic structure—not the pop culture sense of melodrama as exaggerated drama, but rather, the melodramatic form that Peter Brooks describes as the search for the sacred in a post-Enlightenment, post-sacral world.[19] The narrative world that Charlie Brown moves through is contemporary American culture—albeit as seen through the eyes of precocious children—a world drained of the sacred and replaced with the comforts and commercialism of modernity: signified by the characters' admiration for shiny aluminum trees. Charlie Brown's choice of a real tree moves the conflict to the climactic scene, where the group ridicules him for obtaining such a paltry specimen of a Christmas tree. As is the case in many narrative and melodramatic climaxes, it all comes crashing down for Charlie Brown. He is humiliated by the group, and his point of view is seemingly vanquished. Charlie Brown chose to attend to the "least of these" and he is resoundingly rejected for choosing that principle over the flashiness of style.

Here, then, is where *A Charlie Brown Christmas* manages to hold on to being an alternative aesthetic with a subversive message—an alternative aesthetic that replaces convention. Though he is personally spurned by the group, Charlie Brown does not take the public humiliation as an assault on his identity—despite the fact that it was intended as just that. Violet, for example, states, "Boy, are you stupid, Charlie Brown," while Patty tells him, "You're hopeless," and Freda emphasizes it by stating, "Completely hopeless." Charlie Brown, however, neither retaliates nor snatches victory from the jaws of defeat—the two standard Hollywood conventions for a main character in this position. Rather, and tellingly, Charlie Brown resignedly accepts his imperfections, stating, "Everything I do is a disaster" and then concluding that he must not "know what Christmas is all about." His demand, then, for someone to tell him what Christmas is all about is not the desire for retribution, but rather, resolution.

Linus then provides that resolution with the aforementioned quote from the Gospel of Luke. The degree to which *A Charlie Brown Christmas* works as an alternative voice with a subversive message is demonstrated by the effects that Linus's moment has on the story. In the immediate aftermath of Linus's monologue, Charlie Brown receives a measure of restoration, and what he thinks is resolution. He takes the tree away, and as he walks outside, begins admiring the stars, reflecting on Linus's message about the true meaning of Christmas. If the story were a classical Hollywood story, then Charlie Brown would have been successful, and the other children shamed for upholding the wrong views. The narrative, however, replaces both those conventions. What the plot makes clear is that while he heard the message, and was filled with the spirit of Christmas, Charlie Brown did the wrong thing with it. Charlie Brown resolves to take the tree home and decorate it so that he "can show them! It really will work in our play." In taking that position, however, Charlie Brown is succumbing to the workings of both classical Hollywood narrative and the melodramatic mode, where one side is right, the other side is wrong (or one side is good, and the other side is evil) and where one side wins, and the other side loses.

A Charlie Brown Christmas, however, replaces that structure with a different one: it moves beyond the melodramatic form without resorting to tragedy or comedy. Charlie Brown's resolve, it turns out, is misplaced. He tries to decorate the tree, but fails: the tree is too frail.

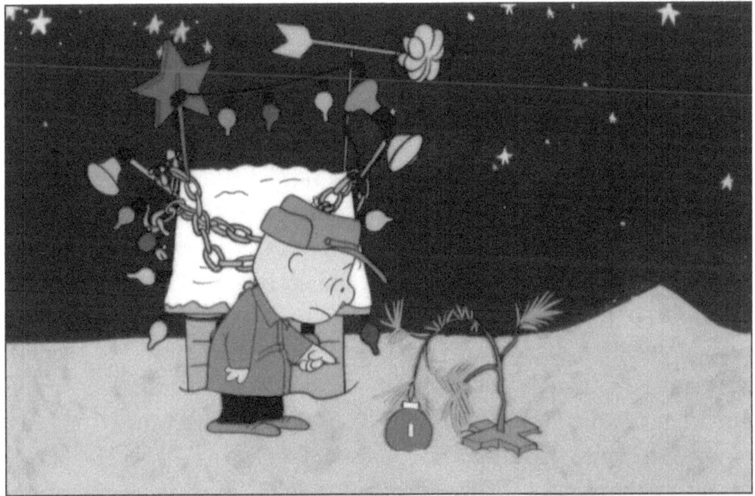

The narrative rejects Charlie Brown's individual determination to make the others see that he was right

Overcome with anguish, Charlie Brown leaves the tree—and the scene. In this respect, he takes on tragic dimensions: he is rejected by the group, and fails in his mission. The narrative, however, rejects a tragic structure and its need for sacrifice, and instead, resorts to transformation. Charlie Brown exits the scene, but the other children enter from offscreen, where they have been silently following Charlie Brown all along because they were moved by Linus's monologue. Coming upon the tree, and filled with the newfound spirit of Christmas, they take the decorations off of Snoopy's dog house, and restore the tree to a vibrance and stoutness that it alone did not possess.[20] The group then begin to wordlessly ("loo loo loo . . .") sing "Hark the Herald Angels." As opposed to the rampant individualism of the jam session on stage, here they move as one, and sing in perfect harmony.

Hearing their collective voice, Charlie Brown returns, sees the tree, and asks what is going on. Their reply is a hearty "Merry Christmas" before breaking into song again. Charlie Brown then joins them.

The narrative resolution, then, brings opposing points of view together as one whole, not awarding victory to one and defeat to another, as in melodrama or with the loss/sacrifice of tragedy. The uniqueness of this resolution is the message it conveys about the spirit of Christmas and the form that it takes. All through the narrative, Charlie Brown struggles to uphold the spirit of Christmas to his community, but they are oblivious—indoctrinated into a commercialized version of Christmas by the materialistic society that surrounds them. While the spirit of Christmas wins out in the end, the plot makes clear that it only wins if it transforms the group, not elevate Charlie Brown. Linus's monologue has a transformative effect on Charlie Brown, but it is the transformative effect it has on the group that is significant. As much as the plot places emphasis on the discourse of Christianity—repeating sections of Linus's monologue to underscore its importance—it elevates even more the effects of the discourse. The story demonstrates that the purpose of the discourse of Christianity, its ultimate goal, is social action, that Christianity cannot realize itself until it achieves social transformation.

The narrative returns the concept, and the image, of the collective back to the form of the story itself. In his discussion of the melodramatic form, Brooks argues that "Melodrama represents both the urge toward resacralization and the impossibility of conceiving sacralization other than in personal terms."[21] *A Charlie Brown Christmas* is a significant departure from melodramatic structure because it favors the collective over the personal. The structure of the plot lies with a collective resolution, not individual triumph. While he functions as the main character within the story, Charlie Brown is not the hero in the narrative, but rather, its moral compass. Likewise Linus, who is able to deliver the plot's message, and leads the group to its collective action, also does not function within the role of hero. Rather, the narrative forgoes an individual hero as a means of de-emphasizing the individual. This de-emphasis lays the foundation for the story's ending, where the individualism of Charlie Brown is rejected for a vision of collective harmony and social action: of Charlie Brown's acceptance into the group, and the group's realization of what "Christmas is all about." The plot's message, then, is that the meaning of Christmas is not about the individual—or in the terms of Christianity, individual salvation—but rather, it is about the collective, the community, and social transformation.

The significance of the aesthetic that Schulz created for *A Charlie Brown Christmas* is the way in which it creates a new generic form—inscribing aspects of both melodrama and tragedy, but transcending each. In its form, the story insists on the collective, and attempts to imagine—however briefly—the sacred in a post-sacred world, without resorting to a return to the past. Rather, in a message similar to Pope Francis, the narrative suggests that attending to "the least of these" can accomplish transcendence. The narrative form of *A Charlie Brown Christmas* is not an attempt to provide Christmas nostalgia—even for the Christ child story—but instead points to the future: hints at the harmony of a transformed community.

TRANSDISCIPLINARY AESTHETICS

An innocuous, heartwarming, children's Christmas classic, *A Charlie Brown Christmas* nonetheless evidences Gonzalez-Andrieu's argument that art and media can bring us into contact with the experience of revelation and the transcendent itself. Moreover, it demonstrates the corollary of Gonzalez-Andrieu's argument: that the affective dimension of art and media can place subjects in the terrain of revelation far more effectively than sound theological or dogmatic argument. The purpose of this book is to analyze media that effectively produces those affective dimensions through their aesthetic virtuosity: to delineate the principles for creating a new aesthetic of Christianity that can reimagine Christian social mandates as viable and necessary alternatives. More than just making Christianity relevant to our era, this study employs critical methods from across disciplines that can enable the radical and transcendent social vision of Christianity to escape the ideological confines of secularism which have marginalized and contained it.

The goal here is to restore both the meaning and subsequent viability of Christianity as an alternative ideology that is just as "real" as secular humanism—indeed, as far more progressive, less contradictory, inherently more comprehensive, and more sustainable. Neither Christianity nor secular humanism are stable ideologies. Christianity, for example, began as small communities trying to reform the theology and practice of Judaism. It then evolved into the religion of the state, conceiving of itself as the universal community—a concept that then led to crusades. Likewise, the secular state wrenched itself out of the medieval church/state alliance and evolved into the nation-states, which led to power politics, colonialism, and frequent wars. Even now, the nation-states are beginning to be eclipsed by the ideology of neoliberal economics and transnational global capitalism, which has dramatically increased the gap between rich and poor, developed and undeveloped nations, and increased, rather than decreased, wars of religion. In short, both Christianity and secular humanism are unstable ideologies whose claims to being objectively real exist only in the minds of their adherents. As the ideology of Christianity evolves away from both its clear opposition to modernism and its comfortable accommodation with both the state and global capitalism, aesthetic theory is a necessary component of articulating a new vision. This study draws on the theoretical models of media and cultural studies, even while it transgresses the self-imposed boundary of those disciplines. Media and cultural studies, especially as practiced in the US, are obsessed with ideological critique, and fundamentally unwilling to move beyond analysis and take the next logical step: theorize solutions based on analysis. Leading scholars such as Fredric Jameson and Meaghan Morris have long ago laid down the gauntlet in trying to move these disciplines past ideological critique and into direct social engagement, but they have been roundly ignored.[22]

Here, too, the work of Stuart Hall is an important guide. John Fiske describes Hall's most important contribution to cultural studies as maintaining openness when methods or theories begin to impose restrictions—and nowhere more, Fiske asserts, than with the rigidity and reductionism of critical theory.[23] For all the influence Hall's work had on cultural and media studies, it was underemployed in examining the disciplines themselves—particularly with respect to critiquing its own ideology. Hall argues, for example, that the mark of a hegemonic view—the ideological beliefs that dominate through structural power—is the "stamp of legitimacy" that render codes and classifications as "'natural' 'inevitable' or 'taken for granted' about the social order."[24] For cultural and media studies the stamp of legitimacy is the ideology of secular humanism. These disciplines are so overdetermined by the ideology of secular humanism that they treat religion and spiritual belief as part of the domain of unreason and irrationality, succumbing to the very kind of binary opposition (rational/irrational) that critical theory warns against. So prevalent is this position that Nick Couldry (who adamantly believes in the value of secularism) describes it as an "automatic assumption" that has become a "fundamental obstacle" to dialogue.[25] Couldry's use of the term "obstacle" describes the core inability of media and cultural studies to recognize that theology—or worse, religious belief—can offer any intellectual contribution, let alone acknowledge that there be transcendent knowledge or knowledge beyond the limits of reason.

Media and cultural studies are not the only academic disciplines with limitations and blind spots, however. Certainly, theology can be just as much disengaged as media and cultural studies—to the point where Rodney Clapp once asked what the effect would be if academic theology were to suddenly disappear. [26] More to the point, theology finds itself unprepared to analyze the complex, polyvocal messages constructed and disseminated in and through culture—primarily, though not exclusively, through the media—an ironic critical limitation for the intellectual discipline that gave exegesis to Western civilization to begin with. Likewise, for all its engagement with textual operations, aesthetics has a pronounced tendency to retreat into abstractions far removed from real audiences. Even worse, aesthetics can very easily ignore actual concern for social issues. The purpose of combining media and cultural studies with theology and aesthetics, however, is to be transdisciplinary: to use the strengths of each discipline to overcome the limitations of the other.

TOWARDS A CRITICAL FRAMEWORK OF AESTHETICS

Media and cultural studies encompass several analytical approaches, but this project focuses on the three foundational theories: semiotics (the science of signs and symbols), psychoanalysis (the science of the unconscious and the operations of identity), and critical theory (the science of ideology). These theories are foundational because their investigations decenter (and destabilize) how society and the individual operate and interact. As opposed to concepts of society (and for that matter "reality") as inherent, fixed, stable, and accessible, these theories—each in a different domain—demonstrate the degree to which society, our experience of identity and of reality itself, is contingent, unstable, and largely inaccessible. Most importantly for a transdisciplinary aesthetics, however, is how the primary implications of these decentering theories intersect and concur with core elements of Christian theology. The brief summaries below point to some of these significant intersections.

Semiotics and the Semiotic Model

The semiotic model developed by Ferdinand de Sassure is generally agreed upon to have laid the foundation for modern linguistics. Rather than historical linguistics and linguistic evolution, de Sassure focused on the structure of language at its most elementary level: the relationship between the linguistic sign (the word) and what it represents (the thing). His work led to one very simple, very obvious, but notoriously overlooked fact: the word has no relationship to the thing it represents. To express this arbitrary relationship, de Sassure constructed the semiotic model:

$$\frac{S}{S}$$

Here, the top "S" designates the "signifier"—the word itself—and the bottom "S" designates the "signified"—the object or the thing that the word comes to represent. The most important part of de Sassure's model is the solid line—the bar—that separates the word from the thing, the signifier from the signified. The bar designates the manner in which the signifier has no access to, no relationship with, the thing it represents. Reality, nature, or the laws of physics have no role to play in determining the meaning of the sign.

The stunning obviousness of de Sassure's model would be ludicrous were it not for the far-reaching and radical implications of his conclusions. The first such conclusion is that the arbitrary and contingent relationship between sign and meaning determines that there can never be any truth in language. Meaning is always the result of pacts and agreements between social groups; it can never be grounded in reality or come out of nature itself. As a result, societies will always struggle over meaning, and signs will invariably take on added dimensions (called "connotations"). The radical implication of this theoretical fact is that truth, as such, is always beyond language, beyond representation, and inherently inaccessible.

De Saussure's model forecloses the possibility of truth, and debunks any sign's truth claims. In so doing, de Saussure's model intersects the fundamental Judeo-Christian concept of the Divine as abstract spirit—as all-powerful, all-encompassing being that cannot be designated and contained by the sign. From the introductory books in the Bible onward, God prohibits an icon, resists even a name, as a means to avoid containment through the signifier. Moreover, the semiotic model insists that truth is beyond human possession. Rather, as beyond representation, truth is on the side of God—outside the boundaries of human grasp. Transcendent experiences can provide glimpses of truth, of divine revelation—but humans as such cannot possess it. De Saussure's model thus provides an analog to reinterpret the relationship between the Divine and the "fallen" nature of humanity: the gap, the separation, can never be traversed, and the truth that is God will never be fully in our grasp.

Even more importantly than the analog that de Saussure's model provides, is the implications the model brings to theology and dogma. When the hierarchy of the Roman Catholic Church, for example, argues that women cannot be allowed into the priesthood because Jesus only called men to be his apostles, the semiotic model demonstrates that they make a false truth claim. In making the act of Jesus choosing male apostles a "sign" the Roman Catholic hierarchy claims to know what Jesus "meant" by that action. They not only make a truth claim about that sign, which Semiotics demonstrates is beyond our grasp, but also, betray a fundamental belief of both Christianity and Judaism: that humanity can never know the mind of God. The Roman Catholic hierarchy, however, claims to know just that when it makes a case over what the choice of male apostles actually designates.

Psychoanalysis and Lacanian Psychoanalytic Theory

Psychoanalysis, the science of the unconscious developed by Sigmund Freud, likewise intersects theology in provocative ways. Much has been written "debunking" the work of Freud, but his fundamental theories of the unconscious and its operations remain indisputable—however neglected they may be. Freud's radical decentering theory is that identity is not a stable "essence" of the self: innate, organic, accessible, and tangible. Rather, identity for Freud is an ongoing operation—a series of identifications and introjections the individual acquires as a means of regulating, displacing, and repressing the driving instincts that maintain life. Because identity is an effect, not an essence, the individual is consistently driven to discourse in a never-ending process of maintaining and confirming identity.

Freud's theory on identity has two significant implications for this study. First, the individual's need for social discourse as a means to maintain and confirm identity provides the economic demand for the media industry—which delivers those discourses in the images and stories it produces. The ability to meet that demand on a mass scale is the basis of any media institution's power. Second, but just as importantly, psychoanalysis, much like semiotics, intersects theology at some of its most basic conclusions regarding human existence. French psychoanalyst Jacques Lacan, explicating Freud's theory of identity, argues that identity dynamics result from an incompleteness or "lack" in being. Lacan tracks the development of human cognition, and emphasizes that the earliest stage of psychical development is characterized by enormous dependency and the lack of an essential identity. The result, argues Lacan, is a primary drive for wholeness that puts into operation identity formation and its maintenance.

Lacanian theory, following Freud, argues that identity is a dynamic operation of identification and introjection that solidifies around certain themes and discourses, but must be continually maintained and reconfirmed. For Lacan, identity will never be "real," will never be at rest and whole. Lacan's theory finds it theological corollary in the theological foundations of Augustine of Hippo. In the opening to his first theological tract, Augustine describes the human condition as a restless heart.[27] At the core of human existence, Augustine argues, is both an incompleteness in being and a striving towards unity—wholeness—with God. Much like Lacan,

Augustine argues that the incompleteness of being will always remain subject to yearning and longing for fulfillment—a fulfillment they will never wholly experience. The experience of grace can provide the individual with a brief glimpse of the salvation experience, but never remain.

Lacan's frequent references to St. Augustine demonstrate that the intersection is far from coincidental. Lacan is the key figure who brought semiotic theory into psychoanalysis. In the work of St. Augustine, Lacan finds one of the earliest theoreticians of semiotics. Augustine not only questions the arbitrary status and contingent function of the signifier, but also its role in the operation of identity. In both his life and his work, Augustine finds that pursuit of passions—drinking, sexuality, popularity, and even intellectual forays whose goal is glory and power—is an attempt to cover over the incompleteness of being. The foundation of Augustine's theology is his discovery that self-denial—mortifying his passions—did not create a prison house of repression, but rather, brought forth enormous freedom. For Augustine, the unrelenting drive to fill the incompleteness of being could only be quelled by turning to the source of being itself, the Divine.[28]

Lacan's work delineates the dialectical dimensions to Augustine's theology. In creating his own dialectical model of the psyche, Lacan emphasized how identification with the signifier functions to repress and displace the instinctual drives of the individual. Drawing on the intellectual foundations of Augustinian thought, Lacan recognized—and described—these identifications as mortification: as a means for the individual to control the continual demands of the instincts. Similar to Augustine, Lacan's anti-idealist model leaves no place of stasis and wholeness: instincts are ruthless and relentless while the identifications and sense of identity that regulates them are external, artificial, and in continual need of maintenance. Lacan's theory underscores what is at stake in Augustinian self-denial. The external and arbitrary discourses that Lacan argues make up the sense of self are, in the Augustinian view, a barrier to a relationship with the Divine: by definition they are not the authentic "self." Only by abandoning the self—letting go of the identifications that make up identity—can the individual create the space to experience being—the Divine.

Conversely, Lacanian theory warns against romanticizing self-denial and mortification for the sake of itself. Lacan describes the signifier as a mortification on being to emphasize its relationship to nonbeing. In Lacan's purview, the signifier is unto death itself. An over-identification with repressive or self-denying practice is nothing less than idolatry and death worship. As an anti-idealist theorist, Lacan argues that the individual's ability to get out from under their identity "themes" or "discourses" can provide a measure—and moments—of psychic freedom. The religious practices and disciplines Augustine advocates can create the kind of detachment from the self that Lacan points to, but only, as Augustine points out, if it is directed to divine being: the soul turned toward God.

The inter-relationship between Lacanian theory and Augustinian theology demonstrates how psychoanalysis can provide theology with analytical tools that delineate the individual's relationship and interactions with the external world: with society, with symbols and discourse, as well as the transcendent and the Divine. Far from being the enemy, it can add complex dimensions to theological analysis and insight.

In a similar manner, another atheistic critique of religion—critical theory—can prove itself far more a friend of theology than foe.

Critical Theory

Critical theory stems from the work of Karl Marx, who theorized about the machinations of ideology and how it operates within specific societies. In developing the concept of ideology, Marx theorized that the structures of power in a social system were in a privileged position to control and regulate the boundaries and the contours of knowledge—what Stuart Hall described earlier as a cultural order mapping out the social order into hierarchically organized, dominant meanings.[29] Fredric Jameson's work emphasizes that far from being an organized conspiracy on the part of the powerful to sow false consciousness throughout the land, ideology is decentralized and dispersed. He emphasizes the concept of "mode of production" to delineate how productive modes within a social system will value ideas that facilitate the specific productive mode and make it prosper. Conversely, productive modes will devalue and denigrate disruptive discourses or ideas that are unproductive. As an abstract process, ideology itself is part of the very structure that makes societies possible: shared ideas that create social organizations with specific productive modes. In this manner, ideology constitutes a web within the entire sphere of social organization—a web that holds specific locations or nodes that produce and reproduce ideology in highly disciplined ways.

Critical theory brings into focus the all-encompassing goal of ideology: to define, categorize, and assign meaning to the entire sphere of social relations, as it does in defining our current globalized society through neoliberal economics. Critical theory brings analytical tools to delineate how ideology operates within the social system: through institutional and educational practices, through professional codes and discourses, bureaucratic organization and operation, and through cultural signifying practices—including, but not limited to, the mass media. Lastly, critical theory reveals the profoundly ambivalent role that religion—and most specifically Christianity—exercises in contemporary culture. Enveloped in institutionalization, the church as such continues to play a role in supporting the status quo of contemporary society. Theologians like Stanley Hauerwas, Ched Myers, and John Howard Yoder, among others, argue that the ideology of Christianity is fundamentally in conflict with the dominant ideological operations of contemporary, secular, consumer-capitalist society. They are not alone. Popes Francis, Benedict XVI, and John Paul II have all leveled stinging criticism of secular humanism *and* the profit motive as a mode of social organization—in other words, they have all been critics of capitalism.[30]

The relative ease with which these criticisms are absorbed—their outright challenge defused or bypassed—demonstrates the necessity of combining critical theory with theology. Christian theology itself is fully capable of recognizing its fundamental conflicts with contemporary culture: it is prepared to contest and resist power—the life work of both Gandhi (influenced by Christianity) and Martin Luther King Jr. prove that. Christianity is less prepared, however, to struggle against its own marginalization. For that, it not only needs critical theory, it needs a new aesthetic. By examining contemporary media and culture, this book attempts to provide Christianity with more effective tools—indeed, with the tools of the master himself: the better to dismantle from within a social mode of organization that perpetuates social hierarchy, maldistribution of power and wealth, and ecological devastation.

Theology is not the only beneficiary of a transdisciplinary approach, however. For all their powerful analytical tools, media and cultural studies are intellectually stuck in a rut: able to identify the complexities of power, but unwilling to actually contest it. As a result, the work of media and cultural studies has become increasingly esoteric and, ironically, apolitical—lost in the search for yet another source of oppression operating through the text. In addition, media and cultural studies are irretrievably locked within a negative hermeneutic: obsessively unmasking the truth claims that circulate through society through the operations of ideology. John Milbank, Slavoj Žižek, and Creston Davis argue that the eradication of truth claims—the result of semiotic theory, psychoanalysis, and critical theory—has so imprisoned postmodern philosophy that only theology can save it. They argue,

> Philosophy is dead because it no longer believes in itself, in truth, in a world in which reflection is supported . . . . This suggests that other theoretical and practical possibilities may

> provide some resources to which philosophy can appeal in order to circumvent its present ill-fated condition. In other words, for philosophy to survive its present conditions it must appeal to other fields of knowledge external to itself.[31]

For Milbank, Žižek, and Davis, theology can offer, at the very least, a model of how a positive hermeneutics can operate. For these theorists, "theology has a positive truth-claim" which allows it to work towards a specific social vision.[32] While the vision of cultural studies is no doubt one of egalitarianism—a world free from race, class, and gender—it stubbornly refuses to leave analysis behind and map a course towards that goal (resulting in the aforementioned critiques of Morris and Jameson). Rather, as I argue, media and cultural studies have become self-satisfied with esoteric microanalyses of texts whose direct political engagement is increasingly lacking.[33]

Conversely, Christianity has very specific discourses on confronting power, resisting the state, fomenting revolution, and creating lasting peace. As Milbank, Žižek, and Davis argue, "Christian theology contains within it an irreducible revolutionary possibility that ruptures with the predetermined coordinates of the world and offers an entirely new kind of political subject altogether."[34] Using the analytical tools of media and cultural studies, this book examines those places in which media provides a glimpse of that irreducible possibility of Christianity—for the way in which that potential for rupturing the predetermined power structures of the world insists itself as a foundational discourse structuring and overdetermining the meaning within specific media texts. Moreover, when this foundational and irreducible potential of Christianity operates within media, there is a consistent restructuring of the media form or genre. Like *A Charlie Brown Christmas* the text offers "a new kind of political subject altogether."

Clint Eastwood's biopic *Invictus* (2010) provides a contemporary example of this restructuring effect. As a biographical film on Nelson Mandela, the generic form for *Invictus* is a plot structured by a "Great Man" theory of history: that great men, endowed with great capacity, move history. Much like *A Charlie Brown Christmas,* the plot of *Invictus* does not altogether reject this form, but it does consistently replace it. Ostensibly the story of South Africa's victory in the 1995 Rugby World Cup, the plot makes explicit that the championship itself is not nearly as important as what it achieved: the opportunity for a young and divided nation to see itself come together in unity—if only for a game. While it places Mandela as the "Great Man" who recognizes the potential for the game to serve in that capacity, the plot quickly sets out to deindividualize the achievement, and the vision.

The first way in which the plot deinvidualizes its "Great Man" form is through the figure of Francois Pienaar, the captain of the South African national rugby team. When the story begins, Francois is simply the captain of a poorly performing rugby squad—all of whom find themselves in the middle of a South Africa undergoing radical social transformation. As the story progresses, however, Francois undergoes a transformation. Inspired by the example of Mandela, Francois begins to translate selflessness and commitment to a higher purpose, to the team, its performance, and its goal: victory. The level of Francois's transformation is signified when he stages a field trip to the former penal colony Robben Island as a means to inspire his team—to play for a future South Africa, not the past.

The other means by which the plot restructures the Great Man form is by emphasizing the discourses and mandates that guide Mandela. Reconciliation instead of retribution, unity instead of power, greatness and destiny over more mundane material achievements, are credos that Mandela articulates throughout the film: they are an explicit mandate by which, Mandela makes clear, they will all fail or achieve. This consistent voicing of principles points beyond Mandela himself and towards a more transcendent force that shape and transform society positively. Within the film, Mandela is guided by the principles, is made to possess wisdom for understanding them, but is not made the progenitor of them: his passion for the William Ernest Henley poem *Invictus* makes clear that he has come to inherit wisdom, not invent it.

In de-emphasizing Mandela, and highlighting instead the principles that lead to unity through victory, the plot insists that more is at work than just a Great Man: selflessness, reconciliation, and unity, became the means through which destiny was achieved. Structuring these mandates as transcendent principles, the plot draws on Christianity as a foundational discourse. The irreducibility of core principles of Christianity—selflessness, forgiveness, community—rupture the simple coordinates of social and political retribution and power. The history of Christian nonviolence—not just Gandhi and King, but the vision of Isaiah, the work of Francis of Assisi, the Quakers and Mennonites—provide the plot with a material reality that forms the bedrock of certainty guiding Mandela: the transcendent truths that are, for the plot, the real movers of history.

Transdisciplinarity thus brings to theology a set of powerful analytical tools that provide the means to analyze the complexity of culture and cultural signifying practices. At the same time, it provides media and cultural studies with a hermeneutic for social transformation: to see more readily how Christianity operates as a foundational liberationist discourse. That Christianity per se does not always do so has more to do with the operations of institutionalization and a history of power sharing than its fundamental theology—as the next chapter demonstrates. At its core, however, Christianity is a dialectical and dialogical discourse striving to reorder the social existence of the planet—a liberationist impulse that cannot be contained by the church, secular humanism, or its own fundamentalism. This book demonstrates that rather than critique it, shudder from it, or ignore it, cultural studies should engage with it—and get on with the business of changing the world.

2

Hollywood's Hoary History of Biblical Representation

No aesthetic analysis of media and culture would be complete without some attention to the role of Hollywood style and conventions, and their relationship to culture. The consensus among contemporary art and film historians is that dominant styles and conventions develop and maintain themselves in a dialectical relationship between the evolution of the art of the medium—an artist's historical relationship to the art itself and its evolving styles and technologies—and the cultural and social dynamics that art and the artist operate through. In the past, individual scholars may have emphasized one or the other, but few contemporary critics would argue for one influence at the exclusion of the other. Rather, the point is to see how each is subject to external forces that lead to change. Elsewhere I have argued, for example, that many past film historians overemphasized the look, or the style of Italian Neorealist film as the direct result of post-war Italian filmmakers having difficulty obtaining film stock and film equipment—the social conditions brought on by war and occupation.[35] These social conditions are no doubt important, but the style of Italian Neorealism was also a response to the dominance of Hollywood film in the Italian marketplace and its influence on Italian filmmaking—the artists' historical relationship to the art itself. Many of the Neorealist directors worked within the fascist film industry. They experienced firsthand trying to compete against Hollywood by adopting its style. Lastly, having lived through the consequences of Fascism plunging the country into war unnecessarily, Italian Neorealist filmmakers sought to create a style that would make cinema a more active participant in the social dialogue of how to rebuild Italian society. Italian Neorealism clearly worked in and through very specific cultural and social dynamics, but it also operated through the evolving styles of global cinema.

Hollywood's dominant style for biblical representation operates through this same dialectical relationship between the internal history of film style and the social and cultural dynamics through which films address their audiences. In this respect, the pedantic—or dogmatic—style usually found in Hollywood biblical representation is a natural outcome of the cinema's early adoption of melodramatic modes of acting. In fact, it varies little from the acting tradition found in the work of D. W. Griffith, America's first prominent director. A practitioner of the standard two-reeler, Griffith's first long-length feature film was *Judith of Bethulia* (1914), an hour-long epic based on the biblical story of Judith. His style in general became a boilerplate for biblical representation: pedantic narration, melodramatic acting, epic scope, lavish costuming.

Cecil B. DeMille, a contemporary of Griffith's who would have a much longer career, adopted these conventions as well. DeMille made a Joan of Arc film in 1914, *The Ten Commandments* in 1923 (before his 1956 version), and the story of Jesus in *King of Kings* (1927). These films helped cement a dominant style that DeMille would carry from the silent cinema to sound (along with his penchant for using ancient history as stylistic motivation for flaunting titillating costuming and action). In *Sign of the Cross* (1932) and *Samson and Delilah* (1949) these conventions can be seen with little variation, further contributing to their use as a dominant style that would be adopted by other films like MGM's *Quo Vadis* (1951), Twentieth Century Fox's *The Robe* (1953), and DeMille's own *The Ten Commandments* (1956).

It would be a mistake, however, to attribute this style solely to Hollywood's early adoption of melodramatic modes of representation, and the directors who worked through them. The box office success of 1950s religious epics named above demonstrate that, in some way, these films hit their mark: that audiences appreciated biblical discourse articulated in this fashion. More than just Hollywood cultivating a particular style and set of expectations in a vacuum, these conventions engendered a certain aesthetic of Christianity that resonated with American audiences. Tellingly, the style hit its zenith in the culturally conservative 1950s, and began losing its appeal in the socially turbulent 1960s, as George Steven's film *The Greatest Story Ever Told* (1965) testifies.

Steven's epic retelling demonstrates what film scholars David Bordwell, Kristin Thompson, and Janet Staiger have argued is the ability to create variations within a dominant style.[36] *The Greatest Story Ever Told* lacks the pageantry and excess of DeMille's *Ten Commandments,* but remains epic in scope, pedantic in its narrational style, and melodramatic in its acting. Compare, for example, Max Von Sydow's mode of delivery in *The Greatest Story Ever Told* to his performance in *Pelle the Conquerer* (1987). In the former, Von Sydow speaks in a manner that can only be described as "quotationally," conveying to the audience that every word is of grave theological significance. In *Pelle*, however, Von Sydow speaks with a gritty and gruff realism that conveys the everyday quality of an elderly working-class man struggling through a difficult life. The comparison draws into stark relief that the style of speech assigned to each character is a calculated aesthetic choice designed to communicate a specific discourse. Von Sydow's quotational style, no matter how soft-spoken at times, is consistently imperial and authoritative—a significant choice given Jesus of Nazareth's humble origins and his position as an outsider to the power structure of his day.

The discourse of authority that the style engenders, however, draws from the aesthetic used throughout the American church from its origins until well into the 1960s: an aesthetic of authority, obedience, and just as importantly, individualism. The pedantic narrational style and quotational diction all work to invest Jesus with an individual authority that audiences are encouraged to heed—especially through the authority of their respective churches. Moreover, the quotational style favored by Hollywood intersects an important aspect of American Protestantism—which places special emphasis on "the word" or the text of the Bible. The quotational style and the discourse of authority it engenders becomes a self-fulfilling discourse around the authority of the word of God.

The style falters, however, in the 1960s, when Americans begin to question authority, the result of the Vietnam War and social upheaval. It reaches even further heights in the 1970s, when Richard Nixon resigns the presidency, having lost all credibility with the American people. In addition to those secular developments, the Roman Catholic Church's Vatican II Council begins to redefine the concept of church—away from clericalism and authority and towards a concept of the church as the people of God. Mainline Protestant churches, along with other Christian denominations like the Church of England, responded to the theological developments that Vatican II put into motion—especially the reinvigoration of the role of the congregation, as well as retreating from their heretofore open hostility towards modernity.

Though the Hollywood biblical style of representation starts losing its appeal in the 1960s, its decades-long legacy nonetheless established it as the standard convention of representation—a standard equated with realism despite the obvious lack of a historical record by which to judge. While 1970s films such as *Jesus Christ Superstar* (1973) could eschew the conventions based on genre—it's status as a modern "rock opera"—the legacy of Hollywood biblical style and its emphasis on the authority of the word found ways to endure, as a comparison of Mel Gibson's *The Passion of the Christ* (2004) with Martin Scorsese's *The Last Temptation of Christ* (1988) demonstrates. The box office success of *The Passion of the Christ*, and the prior "failure" of *The Last Temptation of Christ* demonstrate the important relationship between stylistic conventions and what Stuart Hall has described as the decoding stage of the communications process: how audiences interact with the structure and message of the text.

The Passion of the Christ, with its heightened realism, is a return to Hollywood's biblical style of representation—though pumped up through the spectacle of torture. From the beginning, the film establishes the epic scope that is standard to the style. The plot starts with the garden of Gethsemane, where Jesus agonizes over his fate. In what could otherwise be a very intimate and personal struggle over faith, the film instead renders the scene as far larger in scope: opening with a shot of the moon, and then descending from the heavens down to the earth, where it finally comes upon Jesus in the garden. From there, the plot cuts to Judas's betrayal. Here too, the film emphasizes an epic scope, showing Judas with the high priest, the priestly court, and the temple guard—all richly adorned in ceremonial costuming. The discourse of the opening is clear: the events here are of enormous magnitude.

Even more significant than the film's use of epic scope is its added emphasis on "the word." The film uses Aramaic as the language of expression, then subtitles what the actors speak. This gesture to historical realism—Aramaic is the language Jesus would have spoken—functions to make the spoken word more authentic. In this manner, *The Passion of the Christ* makes clear its intention to strive for historical and biblical accuracy, for fidelity to the original text (even though there are actually four canonical texts). This discourse of authenticity operates within the long-standing convention of Hollywood biblical representation: the authority of the word. To the surprise of critics, this return to the conventional style resulted in box office success. *The Passion of the Christ* generated over $370 million in sales for a run that lasted over two months. Audiences responded to the authenticity effect that the film created: from the use of the Aramaic language, to costuming (which is largely Hollywood convention), to the makeup which emphasized the injuries to Jesus. No detail seemed too small for the film's narrative to encompass.

This authenticity appealed to two large demographics in America: fundamentalist Christians, for whom the authenticity of the word is paramount, and conservative Catholics, who welcomed Pope John Paul II's return to orthodoxy. For each group the authenticity and traditional emphasis on Jesus' divinity and suffering was seen as a welcome backlash against the modern neglect of Christianity, the church, and "traditional values." *The Passion of the Christ* was seen by these groups as a triumphant return to orthodoxy and the restoration of traditional Christianity. Moreover, the opening intertitle framed "The Passion" in terms these two groups strongly identify with. The film opens with a quote from Isaiah 53: "He was wounded for our transgressions, crushed for our iniquities; by His wounds are we healed." By using this quote, the plot frames the story of *The Passion of the Christ* in a specific context: that the suffering and sacrifice of Jesus revolves around individual salvation. In this manner, the film specifically addresses those for whom Christianity is more about individual faith, piety, and obedience to God's word rather than the call for a collective transformation of society.

The Last Temptation of Christ, conversely, was unsuccessful at the box office, due mostly to pressure from conservative Christian groups, who denounced the film for its departure from Gospel texts—even though for most of the film the plot actually deviates little from the canonical texts. *The Last Temptation of Christ* is an adaptation of the Nikos Kazantzakis novel of the same name—itself a theological reflection operating through the original text. Indeed, what becomes "the last temptation" of Christ is theological conjecture in the tradition of Jewish midrash—filling in the gaps of biblical narrative with creative theological postulation. Filling in gaps of biblical narration is both common and fairly necessary, given the wide amount of information gaps in the canonical texts. *The Passion of the Christ*, for all its desire for fidelity, engages frequently in filling gaps—first seen when Jesus leaves Peter, James, and John in the garden of Gethsemane and the trio begin questioning what is going on.

The Last Temptation of Christ, however, provoked fundamentalists and conservatives alike long before it departed from the canonical texts of the Bible for theological reflection. The first provocation is the film's abandonment of the Hollywood biblical style. From the beginning, the plot rejects (though not necessarily by choice) epic scope. Scorsese's film was notoriously underfunded, so that even in the larger scenes—like the storming of the temple—the filmmaker was forced to recycle extras through the frame so that the scene was populated with more actors than he actually had. The opening scenes of the film, however, announce this abandonment as part of a pronounced aesthetic. After a confrontation with Judas, Jesus steps out of his house to participate in a crucifixion. Historical accuracy demands that crucifixions be carried out by Romans, and the film complies, but the Roman centurions of standard Hollywood biblical representation—with their gleaming burnished leather, red plumes on polished metal helmets, and glinting steel swords—are decidedly absent, replaced by soldiers whose armament is mostly rags and worn leather, and looking as if they have crawled out of the dust. Costume is one of the key elements of biblical representation that *The Last Temptation of Christ* rejects.

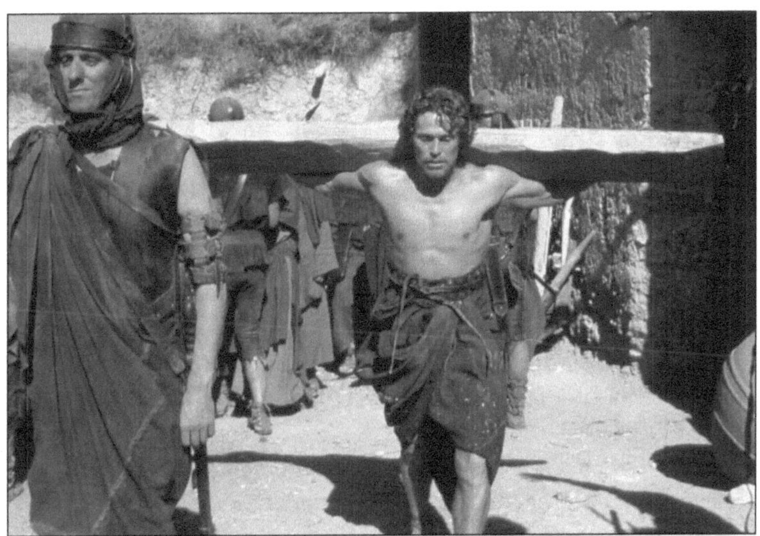

The costume of the Roman soldier is a far cry from the brilliant plumage and shiny leather Hollywood relies on.

Moreover, the scale of this crucifixion is incredibly small—this is not Jerusalem on a high feast day, but a backwater village populated by a couple score of its residents.

The opening of the film prepares the audience for its abandonment of epic scale by showing that its focus is instead on intimate investigation. Primarily, the film investigates the dual nature of Jesus of Nazareth as both fully human and fully divine. The film opens with a quote from the novel on "the dual substance of 'Christ.'" It then continues with shots of Jesus, lying on the ground, as the voice-over describes his internal struggles. As the plot continues, it confirms that the interior struggle of Jesus is the primary element organizing plot. Jesus must struggle to understand his dual nature: his visions and revelations, his mission, and how to accomplish his mandate. In stressing this struggle and the limitations his humanity imposes, the film presents an image of Jesus that very much contradicts the more fundamentalist and conservative view of him as God—as fully divine.

The humanity of Jesus is further emphasized by the rejection of another stylistic convention of Hollywood Biblical representation: quotational mode of address. *The Last Temptation of Christ* decidedly replaces the quotational style of address for a more conversational tone. Both the abandonment of epic scope and the adoption of an intimate investigation help motivate this shift to everyday speech. Willem Dafoe's Jesus speaks intensely, spiritedly, and at times intimately, but never imperiously—even when addressing groups. Rather, because he possesses a dual nature, the Jesus who inhabits *The Last Temptation of Christ* is confused and afraid—constantly searching for the right path to the mission. As Judas, played by Harvey Keitel, angrily puts it (barely hiding a Brooklyn accent), "Every day you have a different plan. First it's love, then it's the axe, and now you have to die?!" Dafoe's delivery conveys his uncertainty, virtually eliminating the imperious tone of Hollywood convention. Gone is Hollywood's Jesus who, because he is God, knows everything. In his place, the film presents an agonized and confused Jesus who looks over his shoulder and admits he is afraid. The all-powerful Messiah is replaced by a cowering servant. Fundamentalist and conservative Christians rejected this interpretation of Christ, preferring the omniscient—and entirely divine—Jesus in his stead.

The most vociferous objections, however, were leveled at the crucial moment of the plot, where, the narrative speculates, Jesus underwent his last temptation. Motivated by the plot's focus on Jesus' dual nature, the narrative reflects that Jesus must have been tempted to end his suffering on the cross—a very human temptation. It then speculates on what the temptation would have been: to leave behind his suffering and impending death for the sake of living a normal life with a wife—Mary Magdalene—and children. The narrative then depicts that life, including consummating the relationship with Mary, before having to move on to unions with other women. What the plot makes clear, however, is that, in the end, the vision Jesus has of the alternative was, in fact, Satan's last temptation for him.

The intense reactions of conservative Christian groups demonstrate a stout unwillingness to engage—or to use Hall's term, decode—a creative theological exploration. To further employ the concepts of semiotics, fundamentalists adamantly refused to move beyond denotation—the literal meaning of the sign. The fervent attachment that fundamentalists of all religions maintain towards literal belief in sacred texts manifests what Lacan describes as the passion of the signifier. Fundamentalism depends on the word, as such, to produce stasis and stability: to drive the relationality of meaning away, and produce instead the finite and the whole. It matters not that the sign itself is dependent on translation, nor that denotation is also determined by codes, social context, and periodization—in short, the operations of ideology. Rather, fundamentalism responds to this relationality of meaning by reinvesting desire in the status of the signifier.

In Lacanian theory, desire is the response to a fundamental lack in being, a lack that is "beyond anything which can represent it." Desire results from this inability to represent lack: substituting the signifier—which names and becomes the object of desire in the place of lack. At its core, religious fundamentalism remains transfixed on the unrepresentability of lack, and the anxiety that ensues. The inaccessibility of an unknown, infinite God that cannot be represented—much like the lack in being that characterizes the individual—is contained through a belief in the materiality of the word, not just as a sign of God, but as a remnant.

The Last Temptation of Christ demonstrates a profound ambivalence around the word, if not an outright rejection of its denotative status. For the majority of the plot, the spirit of the word, or the signified, is favored over the word itself. Many scenes recontextualize the discourse of Jesus, and change the exact discourse as a result, as with the stoning of the adulterous woman, or the wedding at Cana, both of which replace the central female character with Mary Magdalene. In the former scene, the contextual difference is enormous. In John's gospel, Jesus is teaching in the temple when a group brings in an adulterous woman. The text makes clear that the purpose is to test Jesus and see if he will denounce the law of Moses. Jesus calmly passes the test by intoning, "Let the one among you who is without sin be the first to throw a stone at her."[37] In the film, however, Jesus comes upon a crowd taking action, on the verge of executing his close friend Mary Magdalene. Jesus jumps in, shields Magdalene with his body, and halts the action. He then confronts the crowd by asking, "Who has never sinned? Who?" He then pushes his point, holding two large rocks while he re-asks his question, "Which one of you people has never sinned?" He then gives a dramatic pause before saying, "Whoever that is, *come up here*, and *throw these*!" Rather than the magisterial Jesus pronouncing judgment based on his authority as the son of God, the Jesus of *The Last Temptation of Christ* is personally involved and outraged. He passionately places his own body on the line, then confronts a hostile group with his anger and his wits.

The modifications to the actual biblical text are slight, but the change in the context is dramatic. The plot's aim is directed at the word's connotation, more than its denotation. It favors an exploration of connotations as a means of reinvigorating the meaning that the signifier is designed to point at. In the climactic scene, the plot draws attention to the relationship between context, connotation, and meaning. In this scene, as the Romans carry out their destruction of Jerusalem, Jesus lays dying, having led a full life after being rescued from the cross by God. First, Peter and Nathaniel, then Judas, come to visit their dying master. Peter, caught in the gravity of the situation, and bound by social convention, comes to honor Jesus and sympathize at his passing. Judas, however, confronts Jesus over his cowardice. In the confrontation, Jesus comes to see that God did not save him from the cross, but rather, Satan. He understands that the desire to not die on the cross came from the fully human part of his nature: the desire to be saved from that agony and demise was his last temptation.

Judas makes it clear to Jesus when he states: "If you die this way, you die like a man. You turn against God, your father. There's no sacrifice, there's no salvation." Responding to Judas's provocation, Jesus then slowly crawls from his deathbed to the outside, where, in the background Jerusalem is being destroyed. As he scrapes his way across the floor, Satan tells him to "die like a man." In the context of Hollywood film, and American culture in general, the expression "die like a man" always means to die courageously and selflessly—to face death unafraid. Through its narrative, however, *The Last Temptation of Christ* creates the opposite meaning for the phrase. In the context of Jesus and his choice to live out his temptation, it now means to die like a coward and a lesser being. In this manner, the plot drives towards a resolution over the mystery of Jesus' dual nature—fully human and fully divine. The humanity of Jesus is corporeal and dependent. It weighs down on his being through pain, pleasure, desire, and temptation. Jesus' return to the cross and his crucifixion is accomplished through the power of God, but the plot determines that the return comes only because the humanity of Jesus begs for crucifixion—finds the courage to overcome. In this manner, it resists a simple dichotomy of fully human/fully divine as: human = weak/ divine = powerful. Rather, the ability for Jesus to overcome temptation and weakness is found within his humanity—maintaining the duality as a complex mystery.

The last words of Jesus, "It is accomplished," maintains that mystery by generating a dual meaning. Within the operations of the plot, the phrase is a play on words from John 19:30, which is usually translated, "It is finished." The slight change in wording operates to fulfill the meaning of John 19:30 while at the same time closing off the narrative. Satan had tried to trick Jesus into believing that because he had chosen temptation, the outcome could not be changed. God, however, restored Jesus to the cross, allowing the sacrifice to be made, and the Messiah to fulfill his mission. The phrase "It is accomplished" thus functions to declare that God did change the outcome, that the Messiah's work was fulfilled, while at the same time, generating the same meaning of the original text.

This joining together of two different spheres of meaning allows the plot to make clear that its exploration of meaning is a vehicle of theological reflection, not critique. Freed from the conventions of the Hollywood biblical style, *The Last Temptation of Christ*, attempts to go beyond the signifier and glimpse the spirit of the signified.

The reception of the film, however, demonstrates that the exploration of connotations requires a decoding process that engenders both critical and creative reflection on the meaning of the word: its relationality, its dependence on context and structure—all antithetical to a belief in the word as remnant. The plot's focus on exploring a core mystery of Christianity—what it means to be fully human and fully divine—is on a collision course with the decoding preferences of a specific audience segment. Warner Brothers' mistake in marketing the film, and letting it collapse a the box office, was letting that audience segment speak for all of Christianity. Warner Brothers also broke a fundamental rule of entertainment—controversy sells—and paid the price for it.

The Passion of the Christ and *The Last Temptation of Christ* both show, though in opposite ways, the proclivity of audiences to engage in and respond affirmatively to messages that confirm their own ideological beliefs. Messages which challenge those beliefs, or in the case of *The Last Temptation of Christ,* stray from delivering those beliefs in straightforward and aesthetically familiar ways, risk alienating their audience. As Hall argues, "there exists a pattern of 'preferred readings'; and these both have the institutional/political/ideological order imprinted in them and have themselves become institutionalized."[38] *The Passion of the Christ* met with such popular success and was supported so enthusiastically by institutional Christianity because it represented the "preferred" reading on the Gospel narrative. This preferred method of decoding is not solely determined by Hollywood via the codes of biblical representation, but also by institutional Christianity and its aesthetic preference for discourses of authority, obedience, and power. *The Last Temptation of Christ* works against that aesthetic as a means of articulating a different discourse: one that drives towards reestablishing mystery in favor of authority, that seeks the spirit behind meaning, rather than cementing meaning.

The price that *The Last Temptation of Christ* would pay for working against the Hollywood biblical style would be high. Hollywood turned cold to biblical drama until Mel Gibson used his power of celebrity to push through *The Passion of the Christ*. It would remain open to comedic approaches, as chapter 5 discusses, but would continue to shy away from big-budget drama as too risky. As a result, biblical drama remained marginalized in Hollywood, locked between two aesthetic approaches, neither of which seemed viable. Working against the Hollywood biblical style, as *The Last Temptation of Christ* did, was deemed too risky. Faithful adoption of the style, like *The Passion of the Christ,* was likewise seen as too risky: as offering too little room for variation, and inviting too much comparison.

NOAH AND THE DEMAND FOR RECYCLED CONTENT

By 2014, Hollywood had been so negatively impacted by digital media that it was in a recycling frenzy, desperately chasing bankable success by pursuing the promise of proven source material. Producers and writers had long since begun combing through old television hits looking for material (*Charlie's Angels* in 2000 and 2003, *The Simpsons* in 2007, *Sex and the City, The X-Files,* and *Get Smart,* all in 2008, *Star Trek,* recycled for a second time starting in 2009, and *21 Jump Street* in 2012, to name a few). It was also resurrecting several comic book heroes (*Iron Man* in 2008, *Captain America, The Green Hornet,* and *Thor,* all in 2011, on top of the continuation of the Batman franchise). The push for recycled content meant that no stone should be left unturned where a potential audience could be found. Moreover, as a business that recognizes and markets to audience segments and tastes, Hollywood did not just simply recycle content for the original audience as much as it reinterpreted it for a new audience: creating new contexts and plot conflicts rooted in contemporary ideological conflicts. Fresh off his success with *Black Swan* (2010) Darren Aronofsky was keenly positioned to recycle biblical drama.

The challenge that Aronofsky and co-writer Ari Handel faced was that unlike other recycled content, their source material—the Bible—was already overly familiar to audiences and came with too much baggage in terms of stylistic expectations—as *The Last Temptation of Christ* and *The Passion of the Christ* both discovered. From the outset then, their script works to defamiliarize the story and inscribe a conflict that invokes the source material, seemingly arises from it, but is nonetheless grounded in contemporary ideological conflict. To achieve this defamiliarization without risking alienating the audience and their stylistic expectations, Aronofsky and Handel resituated the story through another successful Hollywood genre: the action-adventure film. Their large-scale rendition of a Bible story carefully foregrounds the generic conventions of the action-adventure genre as a means of retaining key elements of the Biblical style but displacing them onto genre (an external displacement) or plot dynamics (an internal displacement). The film's opening introduces these modes of displacement. Within the first three minutes of the story, the plot conveniently introduces a small group of marauders into the tranquility of Noah's life. Their insertion into the plot leads to dramatic confrontation and physical action: Noah must quickly polish off three bad guys (who look as if they stepped out of a Mad Max film), despite radiating a Franciscan-like presence only moments before. This introduction quickly assures its audience that far from being a plodding account of the man who listened to God and built an ark, *Noah* is going to be an action-packed thriller. In this manner, the introduction makes clear that the generic expectations of action-adventure are primary, allowing elements of plot to be attributed to the genre.

More than just spicing up the plot with compelling fight scenes, the action-adventure genre provides the film with several key conventions of the Hollywood style: epic scope, lavish costumes, and a melodramatic mode that promotes a Manichean world view with clear distinctions between good and evil, an effective vehicle for delivering pedantic or didactic discourse. By displacing these elements onto genre, the film gets to have its cake and eat it too: employing stale conventions that audiences are familiar with, but disguising them through external devices. Casting Russell Crowe as Noah is a prime example. The protagonist in several action-adventure films like *Gladiator* (2000), *Master and Commander: The Far Side of the World* (2001), *Robin Hood* (2010), and *The Man with the Iron Fists* (2012), Crowe is widely recognized by audiences as a man-of-action figure. His guile and ability to fend off marauders in the opening scene works to assure audiences that despite Noah's reverence and deep spirituality, he can be counted on to kick a little butt along the way.

Even more significantly, Crowe's acting style includes a measured and breathy vocal delivery. The film makes use of it to deliver the quotational style associated with biblical representation, but displacing it onto the known mannerisms of Crowe. Immediately after disposing of the marauders, for example, Noah explains to his own sons why the descendants of Cain eat meat, intoning, "They forget; strength comes from the creator." Crowe's delivery here is both pronounced and didactic, replicating the quotational style of Hollywood biblical conventions. Audiences can readily assign the style, however, as fairly typical Russell Crowe mannerisms more than conventional biblical style.

In addition to Crowe's specific acting style, the action-adventure genre's proclivity for melodramatic modes of address provide the means for the villain, Tubal-cain, to likewise speak in a manner very close to, if not replicating, a quotational style. The same can be said of both Noah's wife Naameh and his daughter-in-law Ila. A key difference, however, is that Tubal-cain nearly always speaks melodramatically. Naameh and Ila, however, have different delivery styles within the film. In some scenes they are conversational; in others, like the aftermath of Noah's revelation, or Ila's reconciliation, they are more pronounced, didactic, and/or melodramatic. The plot, however, motivates these different modes of delivery through its ongoing dynamics. These characters speak more conversationally when actions demand it, and more melodramatically when contemplating the ongoing events or upcoming action.

Drawing on the epic scope of the action-adventure drama, the plot also defamiliarizes the story through setting, which constructs a historical/temporal disparity through what can only be described as contradictory iconography. Noah and his family are in a time period so ancient that the doglike animal that Noah comes upon in the opening scene is pseudo-reptilian, sporting scales like an armadillo. The clothing and domicile of Noah and his family, however, are too advanced in their weaving technology to comfortably fit in such a time period. This subtle disparity might be overlooked were it not for the way in which it becomes even more pronounced on the journey to Methuselah, where Noah and his family come upon a mining operation that is so technologically advanced that it uses large-scale finished steel-drilling equipment. More than just simple defamiliarizing, these historical contradictions work to create a discourse within the plot of evolutionary discordance: that humanity, and the earth, evolved in a specific trajectory that was then destroyed by the flood, replaced with a different evolutionary trajectory descending from Noah's family.

This evolutionary discordance functions to defamiliarize, but also works to create a complex story world with intricate plot dynamics that internally displace or subordinate the biblical style. The plot's construction of an ancient and alternative world provides the means to populate the story with fantastical beings like the Watchers who are celestial in origin. Such fantastical characters help build out the epic scope of the film, bringing not only the history of all humanity into the story, but celestial creation as well. At the same time, the invention of the Watchers brings into the story a biblical exposition usually ignored in the Noah story: Genesis 6:1–4. A short exposition sandwiched between the genealogy of Noah (Genesis 5) and God's revelation to Noah (Genesis 6: 5–13), Genesis 6: 1–4 works in part to justify God's destruction by asserting that in the age of Noah, celestial beings inhabited the earth and brought great sin. Working under this discourse, the film creates the Watchers as a means of asserting this biblical discourse, but displacing it onto the epic scope and genre of the film.

Plot dynamics operate in a similar manner, as the journey to Methuselah demonstrates. A significant scene for the manner in which it introduces several different plot strands, the journey is not in the source material, but is instead extra-biblical. Methuselah is described in the genealogy as Noah's grandfather, but plays no other role in the story. The film brings Methuselah into the story, however, as a means of creating complex plot dynamics: actions and their consequences, conflicts, alliances, and betrayals. The journey starts off simply enough as Noah seeking guidance for his revelations. As the journey unfolds, however, the plot will become increasing complex, introducing several strands that will both compel action and elevate biblical discourse.

The first of these is Noah's mistake. In both the introduction and the subsequent progression of events, Noah is shown to be able-bodied, wise, and devoted—both to his family and to the Creator. When the family comes across the deserted mining operation, however, Noah makes a crucial mistake. Naameh asks if they should go around—skirt the mining site, and its potential for danger. Noah, however, makes the decision to go through, despite evidence that there has been recent human activity at the site. As a result, Noah and his family are detected by a very large band of marauders, who chase them down into the no-man's-land of the Watchers.

Though not conveyed as a significant decision or character flaw at the time, Noah's mistake is both uncharacteristic and important to the narrative conflict and resolution. The decision is uncharacteristic for two reasons. First, as a wise and able-bodied patriarch, Noah should not make such a tactical blunder when the all the evidence points to high risk and danger. Second, and just as significantly, Noah is both called and guided by the Creator, which should ensure the safety and success of his journey. Instead, Noah makes an uncharacteristically rash and foolish decision that nearly gets the family killed.

The events that result from Noah's decision, however, take on enormous narrative significance and complexity, allowing the film to insert its biblical discourse within the ongoing action. The first consequence of going straight through the mining site is the family discovering and saving Ila, who will become Shem's wife and bring the new line of humans to the restored world. In addition, fleeing from the marauders drives the family into the Watchers, the fantastical beings with celestial origins who at first imprison the family, but end up helping build the ark and protecting the family from the army of the descendants of Cain.

These positive outcomes not only move the narrative away from Noah's blunder, they begin to articulate a significant theological discourse on divine intervention that will ultimately resolve the plot's central conflict. The addition of Ila and the Watchers indicate that Noah was being guided—not as a puppet on a string, but as one independent agent whose decisions and actions unfold in a plan of enormous scope and magnitude, intersecting other independent agents, all of whom think and act based on their individual histories and relationship to the Creator. Noah was, in fact, guided and protected, moving through a dynamic web of relationships more than a set path prescribed before hand. The complexity of plot, and the rising and falling of action, however, displaces that discourse into the margins and out of a more didactic and dominant position.

In addition to displacing discourse, complex plot dynamics also serves the broader purpose of defamiliarizing what is otherwise a too familiar story, the primary reason for bringing the action-adventure drama on board to begin with. Chief among the plot's techniques for defamiliarizing is reversing generic expectations. Halfway through the film, the plot shifts the scope from epic battle to internal struggle, as the story moves from the land surrounding Methuselah's mountain, recently populated by the army of Tubal-cain, to the far smaller space of the ark itself. Inside the ark, Noah is relieved from having to fight off an army, but must now struggle against his family to complete what he believes is the task assigned by the Creator.

The shift from epic to intimate, from action to ideas, signals a shift in the film's external and internal dynamics. From this point on, the film's theological discourse plays a primary role, while the action and plot twists continue to both dramatize and displace the discourse onto genre. Internally, the plot continues to displace the discourse through the continuing process of defamiliarization. The voyage itself, barely commented upon in the source text, becomes the new site of the central conflict. Even more significantly, Noah's obedience, a central theme of the Bible story, no longer functions as a virtue but a danger. The hero of the all-too-familiar Bible story now functions in the film as the antihero, as the one working against the story line that the audience already knows. If Noah has his way, the story, and humanity itself, will cease to exist. In this manner, the film turns over-familiarity with story from a liability into an asset by aligning audience sympathy and identification with maintaining the original story line.

In a similar way, the plot is able to transform Noah's obedience from a virtue into vice by constructing it around a familiar theological problem: the inaccessibility of the Divine. Noah believes that acting faithfully will lead to revelation, which then allows one to continue acting faithfully, the circularity of which creates an intimate relationship with the Divine. Noah is opposed in this belief by Tubal-cain, who believes that the fact that the Creator no longer speaks directly is evidence that the Creator has turned his back on creation, or no longer cares. As a result, man must use the gifts of intellect and will to seize what he can from creation. In creating this opposition, however, the plot avoids making a simple conflict between two positions and aligning the audience with one over the other. Rather, the plot aligns the audience elsewhere: with characters who are trying to protect the source text, but whose actual position remains unclear—they are neither with Noah nor with Tubal-cain.

The plot's construction of a conflict that has no position for the audience to align with not only runs against generic expectations, but operates to inscribe contemporary ideological conflict into the narrative. In creating Tubal-cain as the opposing belief to Noah, the plot avoids making a simple opposition between belief and unbelief. Tubal-cain is not an atheist, but rather, believes in the ability of man as a result of the Creator. He believes, as he states to Ham, that humans are at the pinnacle of creation, and designed to subdue it. The rationalism that Tubal-cain exercises to justify his actions and beliefs works to define his character as a secular humanist. Having compartmentalized the Divine into the unheard and unverifiable, he comes to believe instead in power as the force which shapes and determines humanity.

Rather than a binary conflict between belief and unbelief, atheism vs. theism, the plot instead constructs a rift between secular humanism and its most vociferous opponent in contemporary American culture: Christian fundamentalism. The plot disguises this conflict by delaying it within the story. At first Noah believes in a complex concept of revelation: that the Divine does communicate, and is involved in the ongoing story of humanity, but the meaning of revelation must be discerned and interpreted. He seeks out his grandfather Methuselah to aid in such interpretation. The shift in Noah's character, however, is a shift from discernment and interpretation to a belief in the self-evident meaning of signs. The shift begins with Noah's certainty that his interpretation of the Creator's will is self-evident. The plot facilitates this certainty be making it appear reasonable, if not tragic. Huddled with his family in the ark, Noah recounts the story of creation to his family. He describes how man brought evil into the world, and reaches the conclusion that the Creator wiped out mankind with the flood as a means to create a new Eden without man. The family, Noah concludes, is not saved because of their righteousness, but rather, to carry out a mission: to help restore creation after the flood, and then die out as a race.

Noah's tragic conclusion, however, turns into a rigid belief that creates a shift in both his character and the plot dynamics. His obedience is turned into obstinance over his belief in the denotative status of the sign—as well as what constitutes a sign from the Divine. For Noah, the only signs that count are the signs that function as remnant, signs which have some kind of direct link to the Divine: the wildflower from the rain, the Watchers, the arrival of the animals, and the flood. Each of these can only be accounted for by some kind of direct link. Moreover, their meaning is seemingly self-evident and denotative: the plan is real, the Creator is sending a flood.

The shift in this denotative status comes as Noah gazes through the ark's hatch at the raging waters and the continued deluge. He states to Naameh, "Everything out there must be dead. It had to be what he wanted: a world without man." What Noah fails to see in his conclusion is that he has taken an interpretive leap, no longer reading the signs as evidence that the revelation is real, but rather, as proof of what is in the mind of the Creator. The raging water and continuing deluge are all remnants of the Creator's intervention, but Noah refuses to recognize that their meaning is no longer self-evident. He stares into the storm helplessly, waiting for their meaning to be made known. When nothing is forthcoming, Noah forces his own interpretations onto the status of denotation.

Noah's desperation for an inherent—or fundamental—meaning to these signs redefines his character from obedient to fundamentalist: a character convinced that the meaning of the signs is self-evident and not subject to interpretation. He first looks to Naameh to accept the self-evident status of the signs by asking "You see that now, don't you?" Naameh, however, demurs, stating "What I see is how hard this was for you to do. As a man who respects life, who loves his children. You've been strong, but it's done. It's done now. And you can put that burden down." For Naameh, fundamental meaning ends with the plan for the flood. Interpreting how the plan unfolds in the future is a burden that is no longer asked of them.

The fundamentalist conviction to Noah's character is further emphasized by his inability to accept information that contradicts his interpretation. Ila's miraculous conception (aided by the healing power of Methuselah) is a sign of the possibility for an alternative divine plan. Noah, however, refuses to accept it, clinging instead to one set of signs as self-evident, and dismissing anything else as proof of disobedience to the Creator's will. This refusal to abandon his belief in the denotative status of the sign, elevates the central conflict of the plot, as Naameh aligns herself with the rest of the family in opposing Noah's interpretation and plans.

Despite elevating the conflict, however, the plot rejects both sides of it. Tubal-cain is ultimately killed, though significantly, not by Noah. After his death, no character carries forward his secular humanist ideology, despite Shem aligning himself with it earlier. Likewise, the plot continues to reject Noah's fundamentalism by demonstrating his continuing inability to integrate contradictory information. As Noah emerges from the battle with Tubal-cain, and moves forward to kill Ila's daughters, he justifies himself to Ham by pointing to their unexpected landing as a sign from the Divine. He states, "The Creator has not forgotten us" and starts walking away to murder. Ham, however, confronts Noah's blindness to mistakes by reminding him about the girl he could have rescued, but abandoned because of his certainty of The Creator's plan. "Her name was Na'el," states Ham. "She was innocent. She was good." For his part, Noah cannot come up with a response. He cannot integrate Ham's information into his convictions that the Creator is now calling him to kill.

The plot's rejection of fundamentalism as an answer for the inaccessibility of the Divine can be seen in the disparity between Noah's convictions and the information that challenges his conclusion. Rather than siding with innocence, goodness, and beauty—all remnants of the Divine—Noah aligns himself with murder and death, the very rejection of the Divine. Emphasizing this contradiction, the plot resists a simple resolution to a conflict between secular humanism and fundamentalism, rejecting both instead. Noah does not succeed in his mission because Ila chooses an alternative—another answer to the problem of inaccessibility: she acts in faith without certainty, which leads her to love, solidarity, and peace. Ila refuses to abandon her babies to Noah but insists on holding them while he kills them—an act of solidarity. Likewise, she refuses to let him kill the children while they are crying, pleading instead that she be allowed to quiet them. Ila not only creates solidarity between herself and her children, but also appeals to the solidarity between Noah and herself when she sings the children the lullaby that Noah used so many years ago to calm Ila.

The significance of Ila's actions is their irreducible uncertainty. Her actions are neither a calculated plan for persuasion nor a prescription for future action. Instead, she acts in faith that her love, solidarity, and peace will, in some incalculable way, invoke the Divine in some manner for her children, even if it will not save them. At the very least, they will die in peace—in the peace that the Creator endowed to the world—rather than in distress.

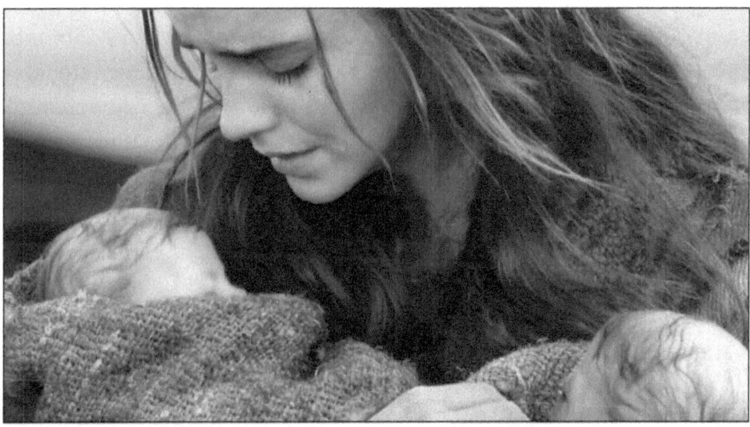

Ila resists Noah by insisting that her babies die in peace, not anguish.

Noah then finds himself unable to act—unable to bring forth murder in the name of the Divine while the presence of the Divine is being invoked. Like Abraham, Noah finds that his hand is stayed, and he abandons his will to kill the children.

The plot emphasizes Ila's alternative to the simple binary conflict by having Noah fail to understand his inaction. When the waters subside, Noah abandons his family in shame, disgusted with himself for failing to be obedient. Noah can only come to this position, however, by holding on to his fundamental conviction that the Creator's plan was a world without humanity. Ila seeks him out, however, and challenges Noah's conclusion that he failed. "Did you?" she asks when Noah states that he failed. "He chose you for a reason, Noah," she insists. "He showed you the wickedness of men, and knew you would not look away. But then you saw goodness too," she reminds him, concluding, "The choice was put in your hands because he put it there. He asked you to decide if we were worth saving. And you chose mercy. You chose love." In counseling Noah, Ila articulates a new understanding to the problem of divine inaccessibility—one that rejects the certainty of fundamentalism and accepts instead the radical contingencies that come with free will. Ila has come to understand that faith is not certainty in the word as remnant as much as it "the assurance of things hoped for, a conviction of things not seen."[39]

The didacticism of Ila's counsel is displaced both internally and externally. Internally, her pronouncement is less the quotational mode of biblical style because it comes during the narrative denouement—that stage of plot where the climax and its actions/outcomes are explained. In addition, the scene also draws upon a sophisticated plot device that goes beyond the contained story of the film itself—an extra-textual, or to use the terminology of film studies, an intertextual reference. In casting Emma Watson as Ila, the film places an actress well known for another role into its story: Hermione Granger in the Harry Potter series. This allows the plot to draw into its operations the characterizations, gestures, and actions of the prior character. Ila's counsel of Noah creates just such similarities to the sage understanding that Hermione frequently offers Harry. The scene is reminiscent of both the bridge scene with Harry and Hermione in *Harry Potter and the Goblet of Fire* (2005), where Hermione tries to persuade Harry of the difficulty of the tournament, and the tower scene at the end of *Harry Potter and the Half Blood Prince* (2009), where Hermione counsels Harry on his need for Ron and herself in his quest for Horcruxes.[40]

Hermione's similarities to Ila are more than passing. Each character is required to love two males simultaneously: one like a sibling, the other romantically. Both characters must draw on inner courage to help other characters in need—Hermione with Harry's quests, Ila with retrieving Ham, and later standing steadfast against Noah. By drawing on the Hermione character through the casting of Emma Watson, the plot brings into the scene the preestablished love, courage, and wisdom that Hermione brought into her relationship with Harry. These elements from Hermione's character not only invest and enhance Ila's character with the authority of those qualities, it helps displace the didacticism of her discourse.

Ila is not the only character the plot uses to create intertextual references. In casting Jennifer Connelly as Naameh, the film makes Russell Crowe her husband for the second time in her career. Earlier, Connelly played the wife of Russell Crowe in *A Beautiful Mind* (2001), the story of John Nash Jr., the brilliant mathematician who struggles against schizophrenia. Playing Alicia Larde Nash, Connelly begins as a student, but becomes his wife as the two fall in love. As Nash's illness progresses, Alicia finds that her role must change: from lover of the great mind to caretaker for the diminished man. She must assume a position of authority never envisioned when their relationship first blossomed. The plot of *Noah* draws that authoritative role into its operations as Noah shifts from obedience to obstinance. Here, the film's complex range of knowledge is significant. There is a wide disparity between the audience and Noah with respect to knowing events within the story. The audience, for example, knows that Tubal-cain is hiding in the ark, while Noah does not. In film narratology, that difference is described as unrestricted narration. In addition, the audience has access to information from outside the film—extra-textual knowledge of events from knowing the biblical story. As a result, the audience knows that Noah is wrong—that his interpretation is incorrect. Based on the biblical story, the audience knows that the line of men must continue with Noah's family.

The film's narration itself, however, restricts audience knowledge of the outcome of events. The audience is completely unsure what action is going to intercede and prevent Noah from carrying through on his misinterpretation. In a manner similar to Ila's character, Naameh is invested with the authority of bringing in Jennifer Connelly's character Alicia Larde Nash. The plot integrates this authority into its operations by having Naameh attempt three different times to sway Noah: first with her subtle rejection of Noah's interpretation, then with her threat of leaving him, and finally with her tearful attempt at the ladder after Noah hears the babies' cries from atop the ark. The audience, anticipating a plot development that will succeed in stopping Noah, bring into their anticipation the potential for Naameh to intercede—based not only on her position as Noah's wife, but on the intertextual authority her character brings in from Alicia's authority.

The scope of plot complexity—from intertextuality, to varying range of narration, multiple plot strands that create dynamic alliances and betrayals—demonstrate the degree to which the film attempts to elevate theological discourse while at the same time displacing it from a prominent position within the narrative. The significance of *Noah* lies not so much in either critical or box office success per se, but rather, its hesitancy to embrace the traditional Hollywood biblical style. The intricate and complex maneuvers it employs are symptomatic of the industry's confidence that the style is exhausted in its ability to reach audiences in compelling ways. Even a film whose story is explicitly religious has a tendency to have theological meaning operate off to the side of a linear narrative—work in the margins of the story.

This reworking of the biblical style, coupled with a marginalizing of theology, is not always a recipe for success, as ABC's ill-conceived miniseries *Of Kings and Prophets* (2016) demonstrates. Starting with the biblical character of Saul, Israel's first king, the miniseries is similar to *Noah* in the way that it reestablishes but reworks epic scope, while at the same time drawing on—and expanding—the aesthetic of squalor used by *The Last Temptation of Christ* to construct a hyperrealist discourse. Costumes are much simpler in the miniseries, much like *The Last Temptation of Christ*, where the clothing looks like it was constructed with first century technology rather than with the finesse of Hollywood designers and drapers. And just like *The Last Temptation of Christ,* Saul's soldiers wear ill-fitting leather armor and helmets that are crudely constructed. Going one step further, *Of Kings and Prophets* makes a point of casting dark-eyed, olive-skinned, black-haired, Semitic-looking actors into principal roles. Maisie Richardson-Sellars, Haaz Sleiman, and Simone Kessell are a far cry from the Hollywood and British cinema norm of using Europeans posing as ancient Semites (the casting of Ray Winstone as Saul is a noticeable departure from this tendency; Olly Rix, also British, cast as David, is less so). To add further to its realism, *Of Prophets and Kings* highlights violence and sexuality, underscoring its presence in the biblical text.

For all its work at creating a realist discourse, however, the failed miniseries never quite figured out the purpose of its realism: theology is displaced to the margins of the plot. The David that emerges from the opening episodes is a happy-go-lucky, bored, but brave shepherd who has to be reminded by Saul's daughter that he did not kill a lion single-handedly, but was aided in his efforts by Elohim (God). More significantly, the plot renders the difficulties of a theology of revelation as an ideological conflict: an ongoing struggle for power between the self-assured prophet Samuel (who, because he communes with God, can turn into a ninja-like warrior as needed) convinced he could never be wrong in his interpretations, and Saul, who single-mindedly obeys until he is asked to act immorally in the name of God.

Rather than making theology relevant, the ideological conflict remains displaced and unimportant: a kind of quaint mind-set of the ancients that fails to draw a meaningful connection to contemporary hegemonic struggles. *Of Kings and Prophets* struggles at what Stuart Hall describes as the encoding process: at the intersection of what he defines as the "professional codes" of the production process and the dominant social codes of culture.[41] In Hall's model, the professional codes of the production process are the "organization and combinations of practices within media"[42] and include "historically defined technical skills, professional ideologies, institutional knowledge, definitions and assumptions, assumptions about the audience" and they work to "frame the constitution of the program."[43] What Hall's model brings into focus is the manner in which those professional codes must conjoin in their operations the dominant social hegemonic meanings that audiences are engaged in making. *Of Kings and Prophets* attempts to experiment with the professional codes—with the stylistic norms of Biblical representation, as well as with redefining the audience for biblical representation by highlighting sex and violence—without transposing that experiment into the realm of meaningful ideological and hegemonic struggle.

Of Kings and Prophets depended on aesthetics alone to find and engage an audience. There was too much confidence that aesthetically reworking the biblical style through more contemporary Hollywood realism and form could itself create compelling discourse about theology, effectively shunting theology to the margins. *Of Kings and Prophets*—which was canceled after two episodes—is but another example of Hollywood's inability to effectively represent Biblical discourse directly. The long line of critical and box office failures in the genre of Biblical representation evidences a little noticed but significant limitation to the Hollywood aesthetic and its dominant style: somehow it is able to see the promised land, but it cannot enter.

The focus of this book, however, pursues an irony in that limitation. While Hollywood is ineffectual in directly representing biblical narrative, its style, form, and aesthetic can nonetheless compellingly articulate the discourses of Christianity from the margins of its narratives—and far more compellingly than the institutional church can. The role of critical analysis in this book is to investigate those margins and delineate where and how a new aesthetic of Christianity is evolving.

The popular racehorse film *Seabiscuit* (2003) is a striking example of that process. A remake that remained closer to the actual history of the horse, *Seabiscuit* conforms to the basic narrative conventions of a racehorse film: horse and owner overcome obstacles to win. As with many classic narratives, the plot of *Seabiscuit* must work to overcome predictability of the story type. In the case of *Seabiscuit,* the plot weaves an intricate pattern that brings together several people—all unknown to each other, but all sharing experiences of great loss and isolation.

The first character in the pattern is Charles Howard, the car-dealer tycoon who lost his son in a tragic accident and subsequently his wife, who leaves because she could not overcome her grief. The next character is the jockey, Red Pollard, who lost his family as a result of poverty (his father sells him as a jockey to a small-time horse breeder). The last character brought into the life of the horse is Tom Smith, a loner and expert horse trainer who has lost his place in history. Tom belongs to an earlier time of men and horses, and clearly no longer belongs to the modern era—evidenced by his sleeping out on the range in Mexico near the horse track. So dominant is the plot's pattern of bringing together the lost and the injured that the character who actually brings everyone together, Marcela Howard, is relegated to secondary status (what Vladimir Propp would classify as a "helper" character).

Marcela is a healing presence: she brings Charles out of his loss, and her desire to become a race-horse owner with Charles is what ultimately brings all the characters together around the main character, Seabiscuit, who is also lost and injured. An undersized, knobby-kneed racehorse, Seabiscuit came from a strong bloodline, but was rejected by his legendary trainer in favor of another horse, but not before he was whipped frequently around the track, used as a training horse where he was forced to lose, and then over-raced in small-time claiming races. By the time Tom Smith saw him, the narration states, the horse had a limp and was wheezing. Soon after Smith acquires Seasbiscuit for the Howards, the plot indicates the role the horse will play. Tom is walking away from the horse after a jockey refuses to ride the violent horse. As Tom walks away, he hears a solitary voice taunting for a fight and finds Red Pollard facing off against four other stable workers. The plot stages the action around Tom's gaze: Red Pollard is in front of him, fighting off a group of young men, and Seabiscuit is behind him, fighting against stable hands trying to contain him. Smith pauses, looks behind him at Seabiscuit, and then back at Pollard, who we see in an over-the-shoulder shot of Smith. When Smith turns back around again to look at Seabiscuit, the camera rack focuses, putting Pollard out of focus and concentrating on Smith. In doing so, the plot signifies that Smith is coming up with an inspired idea: to combine the uncontrollable Seabiscuit with the antagonistic Pollard. The combination is an inspired success.

What the plot implies is that, left to themselves, both Pollard and Seabiscuit would have been individual disasters: each consumed by their own anger and frustration. By bonding, however, the two brought out the winning potential of the other, harnessing and focusing their competitive spirit where it belonged: on the track. As the plot continues to intertwine the lives of all these broken characters, the narrative moves forward in classic style, with successes and setbacks, all leading to a climactic moment. The climax itself is noteworthy for two reasons. First, it summarizes the narrative for the audience—a rare and risky move for any film as explicit summaries frequently come across as stylistic heavy-handedness. More importantly for this analysis, the climax demonstrates how Hollywood is capable of reimagining Christianity more powerfully than the church—even when it is not conscious of doing so.

The climactic scene in *Seabiscuit* is the return to the Santa Anita Handicap after the horse has injured his leg. The significance of the race for the narrative is that Seabiscuit had never won the Santa Anita, despite many entries. As the plot heads for its climactic ending, with Seabiscuit making another come-from-behind victory, the music begins to swell. With the horses heading into the final stretch, the film goes into slow motion, emphasizing, as slow motion often does, the drama of the moment. With *Seabiscuit*, however, slow motion does more: it emphasizes the beauty of motion—of the horse and its gait, but also just the speed of moving down the track, which it shows in a tracking shot. As the race unfolds in slow motion, Red begins explaining, in a voice-over narration, the significance of the race, and the story, stating: "You know, everybody thinks we found this broken down horse and fixed him. But we didn't . . . . He fixed us. Every one of us. And I guess, in a way, we kind of fixed each other too." As the voice-over moves through this discourse, the plot cuts to each of the principal characters: Tom, Howard, and back to Red mounted on Seabiscuit—all in slow motion.

Were it not for the visual style of the plot, the climax to *Seabiscuit* would remain predominantly a discourse about healing and redemption: all of the characters made to feel whole again and redeemed through victory—a victory achieved by each healing one another. The narration makes this healing theme explicit just prior to the climax, when the injured Red is passed over to ride in the big race out of concern for his health. Howard tells him, "You can't do it. You could be crippled for the rest of your life." Red responds however, "I *was* crippled for the rest of my life. He made me better. Hell, you made me better." Red's statement lays the foundation for the climax, but also confirms the theme that the narrative has been interweaving from the start: that the interaction of the broken characters is what heals them all.

Healing and redemption are central to *Seabiscuit's* narrative. The plot's use of slow motion in the climax, however, creates a separate discourse even more theologically complex than redemption. As the presence of the voice-over narration attests, part of what slow motion does in this scene is take the action out of time: out of the time of the action and on to a higher plane, where the audience can reflect on and contemplate the significance of this culminating action. In addition, by taking it out of real time, the slow motion allows the audience to see the beauty of the horse's motion: the musculature and the coordinated movement that hurls him down the track. The slow motion focuses on the figure of the horse—the main character—but tellingly, also directs its gaze elsewhere: at the "audience," the cheering crowds in the stands, and finally at the image of Red Pollard realizing the final victory of horse and rider.

The climactic scene conveys both adulation and jubilation, but all of it centered around the figure of the horse, a figure enhanced and displayed through slow motion—elevated to another plane beyond the immediate reality. These visual elements combine to structure the climax as a discourse of transfiguration. Even more, however, the climax allows the audience to see—and thus comprehend—what it means to be transfigured: the heightened sense of being achieved on another plane of existence. Red's jubilation testifies to the overwhelming joy and fulfillment that exists in this other—or higher—plane of existence, while the crowd's adulation simultaneously bears witness to it, and propels it forward. In this respect, the crowd's role is to confirm the transformative aspect to transfiguration: that the point of realizing a higher plane of existence is to move humanity forward. The narrative makes clear, in this respect, that the crowd is not there to just see a horse race. Rather, they showed up in record numbers to see Seabiscuit make his comeback and achieve a victory he had never won. The crowd came, in other words, to see Seabiscuit reach fulfillment and the culmination of his illustrious career. What the plot also makes clear, in several places, is that what the crowd sees in Seasbiscuit is their own struggle being overcome through heart and determination. The crowd is moved, therefore, because they identify with Seabiscuit, enjoin themselves to him, as a means of vicariously experiencing another plane of existence.

Far from arguing that *Seabiscuit* is borrowing biblical concepts or symbols, I am arguing the opposite—that independent of the church and for the most part Christian theology, *Seabiscuit* introduces the sacred into the margins of the text. Much like *A Charlie Brown Christmas,* the story itself uses elements of comedy, tragedy, and melodrama without fitting comfortably into either. Rather, a hybridizing form emerges that puts redemption and transfiguration at the core of resolution. Neither *A Charlie Brown*

Christmas nor *Seabiscuit* look to restore past forms, but rather, step forward to creating a new aesthetic. Inscribing the discourse of the sacred within the plot, *Seabiscuit* expounds on, or dramatizes, a theological concept in an aesthetic far beyond the ability of the institutional church: in a manner that moves audiences. Compare the climactic scene of *Seabiscuit* with the scene of transfiguration from the first account written in what is now the Gospel canon—the book of Mark:

> After six days Jesus took Peter, James, and John and led them up a high mountain apart by themselves. And he was transfigured before them, and his clothes became dazzling white, such as no fuller on earth could bleach them. Then Elijah appeared to them along with Moses, and they were conversing with Jesus. Then Peter said to Jesus in reply, "Rabbi, it is good that we are here! Let us make three tents: one for you, one for Moses, and one for Elijah." He hardly knew what to say, they were so terrified. Then a cloud came, casting a shadow over them; then from the cloud came a voice, "This is my beloved Son. Listen to him." Suddenly, looking around, they no longer saw anyone but Jesus alone with them.[44]

Two things are immediately striking about the role of the transfiguration in the gospel narrative: its motivation and its meaning. Biblical scholars concur that there are numerous gaps in the Gospel narratives, but the lack of motivation for the transfiguration is striking. Why it occurs at this moment in the story and not earlier or later is pretty much unexplained. Moreover, the meaning of the transfiguration is also fairly unexplained, as is demonstrated by Peter's response and the narrative clarification that the followers actually did not know what to say. Jesus appears with the heavyweights of Judaism, and then is endorsed by God himself to a select few of Jesus' followers, but the reason for doing so remains largely enigmatic. It was obviously done for the benefit of witnesses—the point of taking three of his closest followers—but for what purpose remains unclear: to prove he was God? to make sure they "listened"? The text, as is frequently the case, is not forthcoming.

The result of these gaps is that the scene is fairly lacking in drama—despite a host of dramatic elements: Jesus' figure changing form, the appearance of two historical figures, the voice of God coming from a cloud. The speed with which the events unfold, however, and Peter's confused response, all take away from the drama of the scene. From a narrational standpoint, the drama must be placed into the event via the knowledge of the reader—who knows the significance of Moses and Elijah, and knows what a big deal it is for God to make himself present to humans. The text itself does little to engender the majesty and drama of the event. Not surprisingly, then, the transfiguration of Jesus fails to become the central iconic event of the Christian narrative—or even one of the central iconic events. Theologically, there is no reason why transfiguration is so inherently secondary in Christianity: it can easily be configured as the culminating point that gives meaning to crucifixion and resurrection. Instead, transfiguration is dwarfed by crucifixion, resurrection, and ascension—not to mention healing of the sick, multiplication of loaves and fishes, and rebellion in the temple precincts.

What *Seabiscuit* visualizes through its editing and its inclusion of a tracking shot of the crowd is that the point of transfiguration is the collective, not the individual. The sequence demonstrates that transfiguration testifies to a higher existence for humanity—that heart, determination, and above all, the caring community can elevate all, not just the one. Most significantly for this study, *Seabiscuit* conveys this message intimately: with a visual style that encourages proximity between the viewer and the fictional event. In many ways, as the next chapter will explore more fully, the aesthetic principles of *Seabiscuit* are the opposite of the institutional church: which too frequently uses a distancing hierarchical authority to communicate its message.

Aesthetic analysis of media, however, enables the church to learn a different set of aesthetic principles and transfer them to the discourse of Christianity. The institutional church may not be able to communicate solely through visual style, but it can restructure its aesthetic as a means of realizing the full potential of its theology. Analyzing the margins of popular media, the following chapters will attempt to identify aesthetic principles that can more readily communicate that potential.

3

Mary Poppins and the Dialogic Imagination of Christianity

In 2013, Walt Disney Pictures released the film *Saving Mr. Banks* (2013), a biography that tells the story of the making of the classic Disney film *Mary Poppins* (1964). Ostensibly the story of Walt Disney's collaboration with P. L. Travers to convert the author's beloved children's book into a movie, the film is nonetheless a major film studio's history of itself: a multimillion-dollar investment to tell its own history. The seriousness of this endeavor is demonstrated by the top talent that the studio cast for the film. Tom Hanks, one of the biggest male stars in Hollywood, portrays Walt Disney, while Emma Thompson, one of the quintessential British actresses of her time, performs the role of P. L. Travers. The star power does not end with the lead roles. Colin Farrel, one of Ireland's most famous actor, plays Travers's father Travers Goff, while Bradley Whitford of *The West Wing* and the well-known Paul Giamatti each play supporting roles.

In telling a story about itself, Walt Disney Pictures chose, not surprisingly, to structure a narrative that would lionize the founder and former head of the studio. The history the film tells is of two creative geniuses—Walt Disney and P. L. Travers—struggling to collaborate. The difference in their mediums (film vs. literature), their cultural differences (American vs. British—though as the Disney staffers come to discover, Travers is actually Australian), and their different lifestyles (family man vs. single woman) all become obstacles preventing Travers's approval for an adaptation of her book. The struggle between the two characters then motivates the film's investigation of another historical discourse: the creation of the book itself.

Through flashback scenes, the film recounts Travers's life as a little girl, positing, along the way, that the people and events of her childhood were inspiration for her creation of *Mary Poppins.*

Each of these historical discourses calls upon what historiographers describe as the "Great Man" (or in this case, woman) theory of history: that great individuals, acting upon their social context, move history. In England and the United States, which feature social hierarchies and varying degrees of social mobility, Great Man theories of history are popular for their ability to naturalize the social order: they implicitly suggest that the people on top of a social hierarchy are there for a reason. Ken Burns's ground-breaking documentary *The Civil War,* and David McCullough's biographies *Truman* and *John Adams* are all examples of Great Man theories of history. The fundamental limitation of a Great Man theory of history, is, no matter how meticulous the research, and how wide the scope of its investigation, the tendency of the narrative is to plaster over the complexity of social dynamics.

By reducing the history of *Mary Poppins* to a struggle between two artists to collaborate, *Saving Mr. Banks* pushes out of the story complex economic and social forces that, together, brought discourses of Christianity into the narrative—this despite the fact that the two principal authorial agents, Disney and Travers, had little to no compelling motivation to weave significant Christian mandates into a children's film. Even though the Great Man history of *Saving Mr. Banks* can arrive at the important finding that *Mary Poppins* is ultimately about the father's redemption, its focus on authorial inspiration and creativity ultimately masks over how the film operates as a complex cultural discourse negotiating the conflicts and tensions of secular culture.

This chapter examines the film as a cultural artifact, as a significant site of cultural production where different—and powerful—social tensions, cultural conflicts, and ideological mandates manifest themselves as discourses: as messages whose goal is to shape and define culture. As a film production, *Mary Poppins* took over three years to complete, from 1961–1964. As a cultural production, it continues to manifest several social currents of the period. More specifically, the film's plot and its style evidence and respond to specific aesthetic crises, each arising from growing and particular cultural tensions within modernism: the passing of the classical Hollywood Studio system and its style, the closing of the post-war Eisenhower era and its strained social stability (and with it, the growing turbulence of the 1960s), and the ongoing struggles of institutional Christianity to adequately respond to the triumph of secular humanism. In particular, the film's response to Hollywood's aesthetic crisis—itself a vivid example of how cultural mandates and social tensions manifest themselves within a film's style—serves to illuminate the aesthetic crisis of institutional Christianity, and offers solutions to resolve the crisis.

Disney Studios obtained the rights to *Mary Poppins* in 1961, however, negotiations with P. L. Travers began in the 1940s. Among other reasons why Travers was reluctant to sell the rights to Disney was that, at the time, the studio had never produced a live-action film. By the time they did obtain the rights, Disney Studios had produced several live action films and TV shows. Indeed, through the 1950s, Disney Studios developed into a large, well-established studio producing educational films, animated features of classic fairy tales, animated shorts, patriotic biographies from American history, and children's and family television.

When work began on *Mary Poppins* in 1961, however, Disney Studios found itself in a very different era of Hollywood. Both the studio system and the classical Hollywood style were exhausting themselves, in no small part due to the impact of television. The system itself, as Janet Staiger demonstrates, shifted from an industrial model—where the studios employed large numbers of specialized laborers to mass produce films—to a postindustrial model, where the studios shed their labor and turned to a system of financing and distributing independently produced films. Moreover, Staiger demonstrates that the economic tensions creating the dramatic shift in modes of production exerted stylistic pressures as well, forcing the film industry to concentrate on creating highly differentiated products, normally on the basis of "innovations, story, and stars."[45]

Several stylistic elements of *Mary Poppins* give voice to these economic tensions—the first of which directly addresses the demand for innovation. Disney Studios employed every technological advancement they had in *Mary Poppins*, including animatronics, glass matte paintings (with pin holes to display candlelight in real time) and traveling matte technology—the latter to mix live action with animation. These advancements were all employed within one film not solely for aesthetic reasons, but also economic: the studio was seeking to market itself through technological and stylistic innovation. Indeed, innovation was becoming the brand identity for Disney Studios, which had redefined the relationship between film studios and television in the 1950s (with ABC), and then later created niche programming by producing solely for color television (with NBC). *Mary Poppins* is not the first film to mix live action with animation; Disney Studios had attempted it before with *Song of the South* (1946). Rather, *Mary Poppins* used a new technology for combining live action with animation, and then further combined it with other technologies and stylistic extravagance as a means of creating a "highly differentiated product" as well as showcasing and defining itself as an industry innovator.

In marketing itself as a stylistic innovator, Disney Studios responded to the crisis of the classical Hollywood style that was already in decline. In particular, *Mary Poppins* breaks out of classical unity by its lack of generic conformity. This break manifests itself through an inmixing of several genres and their license to stylize. Among these genres are the musical, comedy, the children's film, fantasy, and the animated film (itself defined stylistically by Disney). Here too, *Mary Poppins* is not so much a historic first—several musicals are also comedies—as much as it is a new strategy for an industry in transition. Immixing several genres allows *Mary Poppins* to display a stylistic excess that will in turn define a brand and a market strategy for Disney.

These industrial dynamics become the means by which broader cultural tensions enter into the signifying practice of the film. No longer secure that humorous stories or patriotic film delivered in a monolithic style would provide market share and profitability, Disney Studios used *Mary Poppins* as a vehicle to open up plot to broader cultural discourses and social tensions of its era. The film's setting in particular is a site for such cultural discourse: operating allegorically to announce the closing of the Eisenhower postwar era and its strained social stability.[46] Although the book version of *Mary Poppins* sets its story in Depression-era England, the film's adaptation shifts the setting to Edwardian England. The significance of this shift lies in its ability to create a parallel between the film's setting and its own contemporary social context. The film draws attention to its setting in its ironic introduction of George, the children's father, who revels in song about Edwardian England as "the age of men!" The era about which he waxes eloquent—the age of modern industrial men and their empires—is headed for a disastrous collapse in only four short years as Europe's empires, spurred on by their industrial strength, destroy themselves in World War I. This irony points to a parallel between the film's setting and its own historical context. England and Europe, blinded by the ideology of power politics, plunged into World War I unaware that they were headed into modern, mechanized warfare: the scale and consequence of which they could not yet fathom. George thus stands at the dawning of the end of an era: Europe about to be undone. In a parallel way, the film's historical context stands at the dawning of the end of an era that will see its society come undone: the Eisenhower postwar era. By the time *Mary Poppins* is adapted into a screenplay, the US has extricated itself from one Cold War military engagement—Korea—only to get involved in another. Blinded by the ideology of Cold War politics, America was immersing itself into the Vietnam War unaware that it was not engaging in conventional warfare. *Mary Poppins* establishes a self-conscious parallel between Edwardian England and Eisenhower America as a means of questioning power: a growing cultural mandate of the 1960s.

Just as Disney Studios was struggling with the aesthetic crises of the Hollywood cinema, institutional Christianity was struggling with its own aesthetic crisis. Both Disney Studios and institutional Christianity were seeking to cultivate audiences within a newly emerging secularized society. The manner and style in which Christianity should be signified within this secular society was becoming increasingly difficult. The Roman Catholic Church, under the leadership of Pope John XXIII, opened its Second Vatican Council as an acknowledgment that its resistance to modernism was not working—that the medieval aesthetic of the church could no longer successfully confront and contest this society. For its part, Disney Studios could no longer be confident that the form of pedantic religious sentimentalism it had used before could still be effective in such a transitional era. *Mary Poppins* actually responds to Christianity's aesthetic crisis by offering a profound and compelling narrative about the transformative power of Christianity. Unlike its other cultural critiques, *Mary Poppins* does not use the guise of the children's film and the plot's stylistic excesses to contain the ideological challenges of its Christian discourses, but rather, to create them. The work of the film's style provides images of Christian mandates freed from its medieval aesthetics and the "two-realm" ideology that dominates institutional Christianity: the ideology that produces good—and as Michel Foucault would say docile—Christian citizens for the nation-states. Rather, from the margins of its narrative discourse, *Mary Poppins* attempts to create a new Christian aesthetic structured around liberation and social transformation.

The genius of *Mary Poppins*, however, is also its problem. Because Mary Poppins presents itself as a children's film—and subsequently revels in its stylistic extravagances—the social tensions, cultural conflicts, and ideological mandates that the film responds to are easily missed. At best it seems that the film's challenges, criticisms, and alternatives operate within the margins of the narrative, one level below the main focus of the audience. Mikhail Bakhtin's work, however, insists that social and cultural discourses are more than just hidden within a narrative: they are the very basis of narrative. Bakhtin's work demonstrates the necessity of seeing past narrative coherence and delineating instead the relationship between social discourses that produces such coherence. Indeed, Bakhtin is one of the first theorists to see language not as an inert system of signs, but rather as a principle site for the struggle over power in any given society—where each inflection and use is a site of competition to assert one point of view over another. This cauldron of competition, this glot, as it were, of differing (and hence hetero) perspectives struggling against each other, is called "heteroglossia" by Bakhtin, and he argues that it leaves its traces on any cultural production, on every symbolic exchange within culture.[47]

Mary Poppins is a vivid example of heteroglossia, where the fantasy genre and the plot's stylistic excess provide a loose coherence for an array of distinct cultural discourses. The plot thus manifests a response to both Hollywood's aesthetic crisis as well as the aesthetic crisis of Christianity: the inability to signify in compelling ways core dimensions of Christianity—grace, witness, redemption, transformation—as they relate to lived experience. As Stanley Hauerwas, John Howard Yoder, Dietrich Bonhoeffer, and Karl Barth all argue—and *Mary Poppins* demonstrates—Christianity conflicts with both modernism and modern culture. Hauerwas, for example, argues, "The reason Christian convictions have lost their power for many Christians and non-Christians alike is that many Christians have failed to challenge the cultural accommodation of the church to the world."[48] *Mary Poppins,* however, provides images of contestation, rejecting accomodationism, and advocating instead transformation.

The principal means by which the film attempts to move beyond standard representation and overcome this crisis of representation is to incorporate liberationist discourses located outside institutional Christianity. Specifically, at the site of Mary Poppins's character are the discourses of Mary the mother of Jesus (herein referred to as Miryam of Nazareth), Therese of Lisieux, and Francis of Assisi. Operating under the guise of genre, these discourses are interconnected and fundamental to the plot's trajectory, yet they escape from being read as overtly dogmatic or pious. The value of Bakhtin's concept of heteroglossia here is that it allows us to see these specific discourses as constructing dynamic relations with each other—as performing particular textual and ideological functions. Thus, rather than the more static concept of Mary as a passive "symbol" of some aspect of Christianity, she is, instead, the site through which different discourses are organized and articulated with a specific ideological goal.

The first such discourse is articulated in the film's opening, in which Mary is sitting on the clouds. While overtly functioning to construct Mary's character as otherworldly, the iconography nonetheless falls in line with classical representations of Miryam of Nazareth as being assumed into heaven. It would be fairly easy to dismiss this iconography as coincidence (especially given the plot's sight gag that mimics Disney Studios' earlier film *Dumbo* [1941]), but the film's insistence on Mary's relationship with the supernatural makes the iconography more than a passive reference. Instead, it is part of a Marian discourse that is articulated elsewhere in the plot. The most significant articulation is the Immaculate Conception.

In her initial scene with the children, Mary takes out a tape measure to see how the children "measure up." The tape, however, does not give a numerical measure, but rather a pronouncement of character. In the case of Mary, it reads, "Mary Poppins, practically perfect in every way." The logic of the statement succinctly summarizes the complex theological issues surrounding the doctrine of the Immaculate Conception. This doctrine maintains that Miryam of Nazareth, the mother of Jesus, is elevated in her humanity, but is herself not God (not a member, for example, of the Holy Trinity). Because she is not God, however, Miryam of Nazareth is not considered perfect. She is, however, worshipped as being *elevated* in her humanity because she is born without original sin. Without this fallenness weighing down on her humanity, she is, effectively, "practically perfect."

Significant to the film's ideological functioning, these Marian discourses function not to create an ideal mother figure to replace the mother lost through social activism, but rather, as part of a broader Christian discourse about liberation and transformation. Like Miryam of Nazareth, Mary's role is to usher in a new age of liberation. The nannies that queue outside 17 Cherry Tree Lane inspire no hope from Jane and Michael that their life without an adult who actually cares for them will change. Mary not only enters from above, but, as with Miryam of Nazareth, her ability to bring forth a new time of liberation is preceded by the intervention of the Spirit: the nannies applying for the job are blown away from the house by the force of wind intimately connected to Mary. Thus, even though Mary's introduction in the film is firmly rooted in traditional iconography of Miryam of Nazareth—seated in the heavens—the film quickly reverses this mode of representation (Mary descends) to inaugurate a different Marian discourse: a discourse centered around liberation.

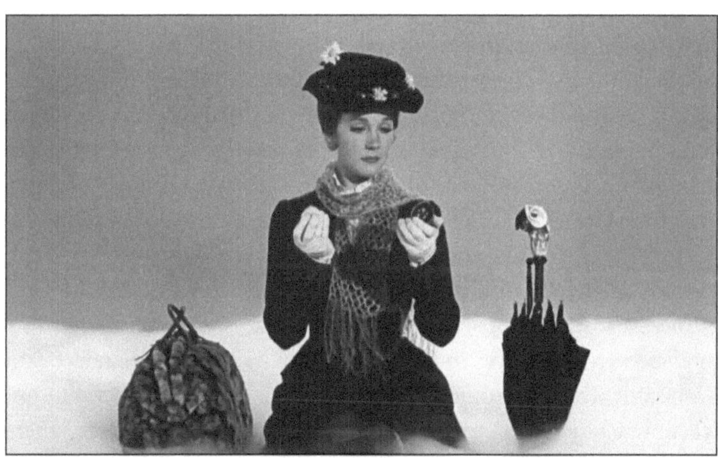

Mary is introduced in the narrative sitting in the clouds.

The complexity of that liberation can be seen in the other voice articulated in Mary's character, Therese of Lisieux. A Carmelite nun who was declared a Doctor of the Church in 1997, Therese would, at first sight, seem very much defined by the institutional church. The "Spoonful of Sugar" scene, however, makes clear that the discourse of Therese is rooted outside the institutional—and especially, medieval—church, and instead, promotes a radical vision of transformation. "A Spoonful of Sugar" makes clear to both the children and the spectator that Mary's liberating effect is not a mandate for anarchy. Rather, it teaches the role of individual responsibility (and discipline) in the process of social transformation. Through the presence of Mary and her song, the nursery is transformed into a magical place where inanimate objects come to life. As Mary makes clear in her introduction to the musical number, however, the purpose is a didactic one: Mary is trying to teach the children to look at things in a particular way. She thus begins by teaching the children that in every job an element of fun that makes the task enjoyable can be located. She then employs the song and the manipulation of reality to prove her point and in the process, engage the children in picking up the nursery—a task for which they have utter disdain.

The scene illustrates vividly Bakhtin's concept of dialogic meaning. The lesson Mary ties to impart serves two purposes—two different logics—that are opposed to each other. On the one hand, the object of Mary's lesson is to instill discipline in the children: to get them to adopt a routine—a discipline—of keeping the nursery tidy. Mary attempts nothing less than imposing order and control on the anarchy of the children's play by getting them to adopt certain behaviors. In this respect, Mary is already molding the children into taking their place as disciplined citizens in an ordered society. Bakhtin's theory of language, however, demonstrates that the goal of a discourse is never directly achieved. Bakhtin argues that when language attempts to convey meaning—strives to represent a particular thing—it cannot help but also convey the other meanings attached to it by different social groups and their particular points of view. For Bakhtin, the object of a discourse is already "entangled, shot through with shared thoughts, points of view, alien value judgments and accents, weaves in and out of complex interrelationships . . . ."[49] These complex interrelationships are found in the lesson that Mary is trying to impart to the children—a lesson based on the philosophy of Therese of Lisieux, what she described as her "Little Way."

Therese's "way" is a particular outlook that stresses an individual's ability to empower themselves in any situation by examining it dialectically. A modern saint, Therese promoted a spirituality intended for everyone and in direct confrontation to a medieval, heirarchalized religion. Indeed, Therese's spirituality moved away from the medieval fear of a judgmental God and proposed instead that people enter into a personal relationship with a loving God—to be children of God. As with Mary's lesson, freedom for Therese was not a hyper-individualized ability to do anything, but rather the ability to enter into unseen relationships. As Mary Frohlich argues, Therese believed that "In mundane acts of love, here and now, the nothingness of the here-and-now may be transformed into fire, and thus reveal God."[50] Therese advocated committing oneself wholly to the task at hand—and as her autobiography demonstrates, to the people who come into a person's everyday life. Mary imparts to the children this commitment to the tasks in their everyday lives—and just as importantly for the plot, to the people that they will meet.

Further, the scene insists that Mary's vision is not an inward retreat into fantasy, but the opposite: a means by which to interact with transcendence in the outer world. As Ann Belford Ulanov demonstrates, Therese's spirituality is designed to uncover "an energy of tremendous intensity in daily life."[51] The film visualizes this energy through the supernatural animation of the objects in the room, which leap to the places where they belong. Significantly, they do not take on a life of their own, but conform to the task at hand—a daily chore. This conformity to daily chores is itself the dialogism in Therese's spirituality. With its emphasis on tasks and work routines, Therese's teaching seems like the worst form of accommodationism: of accepting working conditions no matter how exploitive or alienating.[52] Therese, however, stressed resistance to dehumanization by insisting that the utopian impulse could be found and carried out in the performance of the most mundane tasks, chores, or routines. Thus, rather than be disciplined to accommodating the social conditions of labor, to accept the frustrations of alienated and exploitive work, Therese showed a way to transform the relationship between the individual and their work as a means of transforming the social network itself.

This transformative effect is evidenced in the plot by the children, who are so enthralled with Mary's animation of their chores that Michael prefers staying rather than going to his preferred activity: playing in the park. Moreover, by having Michael and Jane's excitement spill over to the other characters—who sing refrains from the song in their chores—the transformation of the nursery is not directed at the objects that became animated, but at the community surrounding Jane and Michael, who now carry a different vision. Far from learning to be good little citizens, Jane and Michael begin to carry around a different social vision—one that will come in direct conflict later in the plot with the British imperialism the children are supposed to be adopting. In this respect, the film constructs the scene around the social imperatives that Therese put in motion: a childlike awe and amazement at the interrelatedness of being, joy, and love.

In addition to the discourse of Therese of Lisieux, the scene also constructs itself around the discourses and aesthetics of Francis of Assisi. Here too, the plot appropriates a series of discourses that coalesced around creating a new aesthetic of Christianity—and particularly in the case of Francis, one that fundamentally rejects medieval authoritarianism and hierarchy. As Jacques Le Goff argues, in Francis's vision, "lay people had to be associated in the life of the Church instead of being subject to the domination of the clergy . . . ."[53] Unlike Therese, Francis did not join a religious order, but ended by founding one. Creating a religious order, however, was subordinate to Francis's first priority: reforming Christianity—not just from the outside, but from the margins. The son of a rich merchant, Francis not only came to renounce wealth, but all materialism, subsequently living on the margins of society and begging for food. For Francis, material life impedes humanity: continually obscuring the profound harmony—and beauty—of creation. In this respect, Lawrence Cunningham argues that "Poverty was the hermeneutical lens through which he read the gospel."[54] Francis thus worked to bring a new vision, a new meaning of Christianity as a way of life. Cunningham details this vision when he argues:

> There is in the early legends a joy that Francis expresses in his love for music, his eye for beauty, his reaction to the wonders of creation, his tenderness to dumb animals, his concern for the poor . . . . It is almost as if by dispossessing himself of his worldly goods he took on a new eye for the beauties of the world and those who inhabit it.[55]

Franciscan spirituality is thus constructed around a new aesthetic: of creating a new form of lived experience as a means of perceiving the beauty of existence. Moreover, the very trajectory of *Mary Poppins* is constructed around a "new eye for the beauties of the world" and just as significantly "those who inhabit it." This "new eye" of the Franciscan aesthetic is introduced in the "Spoonful of Sugar" scene. Structured around the wonders that Mary creates, the scene also incorporates classic Franciscan iconography.

In the midst of the number, Mary, hearing the birds singing outside the window, reaches out in order to have a robin fly over and perch on her finger. She then brings the bird into the room, to the amazement and wonder of the children. As she does, the bird begins harmonizing with Mary's singing. This ability to commune and interact with nature, specifically the singing birds, is modeled upon the most popular of Franciscan iconography: the gentle saint with the birds.

Just as with the appropriation of Therese, however, the incorporation of a Franciscan iconography is not a passive reference, but rather the articulation of a specific discourse that activates a very particular social vision. Emphasized through the special effects of animatronics, this part of the scene functions as what Bakhtin describes as a discourse event—as a moment in the text intended to highlight a particular discourse in all its aspects.[56] This dramatizing of Franciscan discourse occurs first through special effects, then through the trajectory of plot. Franciscan iconography is introduced in "A Spoonful of Sugar," so that its social dimensions can be dramatically articulated later in "Feed the Birds."

Consistent with the way in which the voices of Christianity speak from the margins of the film, "Feed the Birds" is introduced as a narrative detour. It functions as a break from the plot's rising conflict, which is created by Mary's liberatory presence. As the scene unfolds, however, it starts to make clear that, far from a detour, "Feed the Birds" functions pivotally within the narrative: the site of political critique cloaked by aesthetic tour-de-force. Within the musical number, a Franciscan spirituality is unleashed as a means of establishing an antagonism between imperial capitalism (characterized in the film by its "practicality" and "frugalism") and Christianity—an antagonism that will be the culminating point of the plot.

The plot first introduces Franciscan spirituality in the scene through the character of the Bird Woman. Through her affinity with the birds, she evokes a Franciscan-like kinship and appreciation for "the least of these" that Mary first introduced in "A Spoonful of Sugar." In addition to Franciscan references—and closely allied with Franciscan spirituality—The Bird Woman also functions to represent the marginalized within Edwardian England. She is clearly of little means, if not destitute, and lives on the fringes of society: the steps of the cathedral, a traditional site for society's marginalized. This discourse of marginalization is also made intertextually—by referencing the discourses of other film texts. The casting of Jane Darwell as the Bird Woman draws into the scene the discourses of marginalization and poverty from *The Grapes of Wrath* (1940), where Darwell played the role of Ma Joad. Disney not only coaxed Darwell out of retirement to take the part, but modeled her costuming on the character of the earlier film. In this manner, the film constructs a complex discourse about marginalization.

The complexity of this discourse is also demonstrated through the status of the character. What the plot indicates through Mary's introduction is that the Bird Woman's marginalization is not a matter of inequity and victimization, but rather it is also about alternative understanding and transcendence. The Bird Woman functions as a site of Francis's fundamental rejection of a social order based on materialism and inequity. Cunningham thus argues,

> Francis had a radical vision of the equality of all persons who, after all, were icons of Christ and, as such, had an inherent dignity which demand that they be treated with justice and out of a sense of love. There is in any radical adoption of this deep Christological truth a certain way in which class and social distinctions are deconstructed and relativized.[57]

Marie Dennis further describes the social vision of Franciscan spirituality as a paradox that is difficult to accept because it contradicts both materialism and individualism. She argues, "Poverty is ugly and dehumanizing; it is an evil that must be eliminated. Yet, in encountering the poor, we often discover beauty and graced humanity."[58] The construction of the Bird Woman's character—Darwell's performance, the special effects, and the lyrics of the song—all work to evoke a sense of the graced humanity of a marginalized person. This is further underscored through juxtaposition with Andrew's virtuoso performance—a powerful but angelic voice that animates the sense of profound grace that the scene attempts to evoke.

Lastly, the lyrics of the song itself are an explicit endorsement of the Bird Woman's social outlook. The last verse, in fact, states:

> All around the cathedral, the saints and apostles
> Look down as she sells her wares.
> Although you can't see it,
> You know they are smiling,
> Each time someone shows that he cares.

At first glance, the lyrics seem like classic religious sentimentalism: invisible saints smiling at specific individuals for acting nice. In this respect, they seem cast within the confines of a "personal" religion—a religion that is focused solely on an individual and their relationship to an invisible God. In their dialogism, however, the lyrics go beyond this function. The actions that the lyrics authorize—that the saints smile upon—are more than just acting nice: they are an alternative social action. And while "feeding the birds" specifically seems fairly insignificant, it nonetheless operates within a specific social vision and political economy—the biblical mandate of "stewardship." As opposed to capitalism, which sees nature as a commodity—as raw material endlessly subject to transformation into finished products to fulfill the human demands for profit—stewardship imposes a responsibility on humanity to care for nature. The Bird Woman carves out a space for stewardship even within a modern urban setting, and the lyrics of the song strongly endorse it.

Thus, rather than an ideologically harmless "gentle saint" the discourses within "Feed the Birds" communicate a message with powerful political resonance. The image track attempts to clarify this goal by creating a dissolve between Mary's uplifted, radiant face, and the cathedral of St. Paul. The effect is otherworldly, placing the scene in another plane of existence beyond the here and now. It is a brief glimpse of the kind of alternative reality frequently associated with Mary.

The structure of the plot, however, also ensures that, while positioned in the margins, these discourses will not be marginalized and contained. Rather, they will become foundational to the narrative and the discourses it endorses. Indeed, the plot expands the social dimensions and political resonance of Franciscan spirituality by transforming the scene from a detour into a pivotal scene. This transformation is signaled by a shift in the narrative trajectory. After "Feed the Birds," the narrative is no longer constructed around Jane and Michael and their emancipation, but opens out to include—if not elevate—George and his redemption, a redemption achieved through emancipation.

The scene immediately following "Feed the Birds" establishes this shift by having George take the children to the bank (the result of being tricked into doing so by Mary). En route to the bank, the children see the Bird Woman and, inspired by Mary's teaching, ask to give her tuppence. Despite George's refusal, Michael holds onto the desire to give to the Bird Woman, subsequently refusing to deposit his money with Dawes Sr., the bank director. Michael's vocal refusal creates a commotion that is overheard by the bank's depositors, who fear that it is a sign of a run on the bank. Their ensuing panic creates an actual run on the bank, and the bank is forced to close its doors. The narrative events are here quite pointed. Jane and Michael's childlike—that is, unencumbered—grasp of the Franciscan mandate is stronger than the fragile symbolic contingencies necessary for the operation of capitalism. Indeed, the narrative will twice emphasize that capitalism cannot stand face to face with Christianity's transformative power.

Jane and Michael escape the increasing chaos, and the narrative temporarily abandons George. When it does return to George, it is to register the effects of Jane and Michael's actions: George is summoned, and subsequently fired from the bank. The turning point of the narrative, however, is that George, upon being subjected to humiliation (comically rendered) at his sacking, comes fully into the consciousness that he has opposed all along. George leaves the bank a very different man than when he entered it: embracing the alternative consciousness Mary Poppins has shown, and returning to his family to take his place as a loving father.

Such a condensed summary of the plot betrays the intricate (and pervasive) infusion of the Franciscan and Christian discourses that dominate the last half of the film. Moreover, without closer analysis, the narrative's shift in focus from the children to George seems very much to function as the restoration of patriarchy that is at the core of the children's genre. The film's dialogism—specifically its mobilization of Christian discourses—prevents such a simplistic ideological function to the narrative. Rather, the film's inscription of Christian mandates freed from institutionalization operates to critique not only patriarchy, but capitalism and imperialism as well. Two narrative elements in particular—the tuppence and the story's ending—demonstrate that the liberationist mandates operating through the Marian, Theresean, and Franciscan discourses, take as their object nothing less than social transformation and the creation of the egalitarian community.

The tuppence are a recurring motif within the narrative, manifesting four different times, and changing their meaning each time. The first time the tuppence appears in the narrative is the above mentioned outing to the bank. Here, the tuppence works to reference a Franciscan discourse of caring after the least of these: both the Bird Woman herself, and the birds she attends to. In this respect, the tuppence come to represent alms. Their power is not defined by what they can purchase, but what they can do, both for the giver and the receiver.

The next time the tuppence make an appearance within the narrative is at the bank. In this scene, the bank directors' complete inability to hear out Michael's desire for almsgiving is motivated by their own perceptions of the tuppence. As their musical number elaborates, tuppence—though small—is the foundation upon which the world of capitalism and imperialism function. In a caricature of the Franciscan view of tuppence, the song elaborates that its value is not in its worth, but what it represents: railroads in Africa, dams across the Nile, plantations of ripening tea. Significantly, the film's turning point is constructed around a struggle over the meaning of the tuppence. Dawes Sr. can only conceive of tuppence in capitalist utilitarian terms: "Fiddlesticks boy! Feed the birds and what have you got? Fat birds!" Assigning Michael's Franciscan desire to childishness, Dawes snatches the tuppence, and starts in motion the run on the bank. The commotion itself, however, is generated by Michael's steadfast refusal to give up the Franciscan mandate the tuppence represents for him.

The next time the tuppence appears in the narrative their meaning transforms into one of redemption and devotion. The tuppence comes back into the plot when the children come into the parlor to apologize to George for their role in the catastrophic events. As the scene plays out, however, the actions become less about forgiveness than about redemption. The children give back the tuppence in the hope that it will resolve the problems that they have caused George—it is a clear attempt to restore him. George, knowing how much the tuppence means to the children, is visibly moved by their generosity.

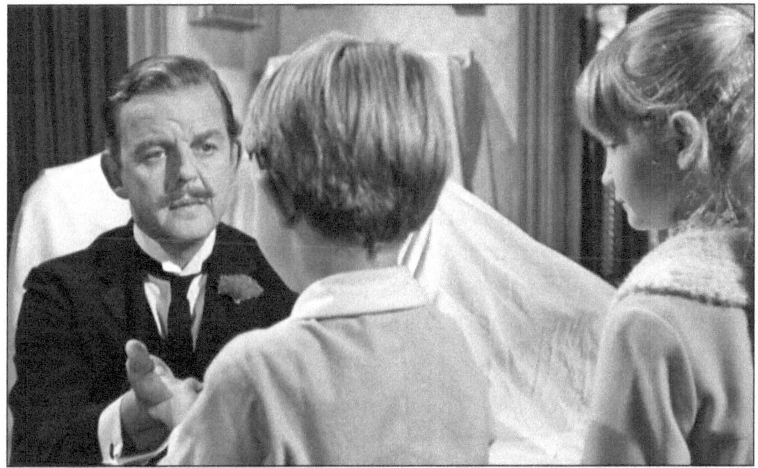

The children attempt to redeem George by giving him the tuppence.

As a result, the scene confirms that the plot's use of tuppence is a veiled reference to a Gospel parable: the widow's mite. In this parable, a poor widow gives two coins to the temple—giving from her own need, as opposed to the rich, who give from their surplus. In this scene, George is on the receiving end of that kind of generosity—a generosity based on devotion. The children's devotion lifts George from his despair and allows him to finally discover their profound love for him. The power of that love then fortifies George to go and face his dismissal from the bank.

Not coincidentally then, the tuppence appears again in the dismissal scene. Here, the film underscores its rejection of capitalism for a redeemed society by first retracing the journey that George took with the children. This repetition articulates the now-growing conflict between Christianity and capitalism, as his route takes him first to the steps of the cathedral, then to the steps of the bank. As George encounters the cathedral, however, the refrain from "Feed the Birds" swells on the soundtrack, suggesting that the real journey that George is making is a journey of consciousness. The plot's comparison of the two buildings—each modeled upon classical Romanesque temples—functions dialogically. It casts the two in opposition—as two opposing ends to a journey—yet also articulates their similarities: each conveying a sense of power, and each functioning as a temple. This latter function results not only from their comparative placements, but from the Roman architecture chosen for the bank. This classical style, with its large pillars, pediment, and steps up to the main entrance, finds its roots in the Temple of Saturn, which was used by Romans not only as a place of worship, but to store their money. The plot's comparison of the two buildings thus functions dialogically: it suggests a line of continuity between Roman and British imperialism, and at the same time underscores the ideological conflict between the two temples.

In the dismissal scene, the meaning of the tuppence becomes the culminating point of the narrative: where the plot will resolve the conflict between capitalist imperialism and the mandates of Christianity. Strikingly, the plot's resolution is achieved by reinterpreting what Ched Myers describes as "one of the most abused texts in the gospels," the mandate to render unto Caesar what is Caesar's (Mark 12:13–17).[59] Myers criticizes conventional understanding of this gospel mandate because, as he argues:

> Jesus' pronouncement in 12:17 . . . taken out of context as an abstract principle, is easy prey for manipulation. Its radical antithesis is presumed to be neat parallelism, and then exploited by those already committed to a Reformation "two realms" theory. This invariably occasions a homily on "church and state" or the responsibilities of the "Christian citizen."[60]

For Myers, then, the mandate to render unto Caesar, far from a vision of church-state assimilation, is a call to act according to "allegiances, stated clearly as opposites."[61] In the dismissal scene *Mary Poppins* structures a response to Christianity's aesthetic crisis by returning the mandate back to the concept of allegiance, and rejecting the earthly realm of capitalist imperialism for an alternative realm: the kingdom on earth.

The principal means by which the scene references this gospel mandate is in the close-up of the tuppence, heretofore never scene in close-up. In the dismissal scene however, a close-up of the coins is motivated by plot when George is called to account for himself by Dawes Sr. Humiliated and at a loss for words, Georges fumbles through his pockets and comes across the coins. He then retrieves the coins, and gazes at them, neatly modeling how the interlocutors of Jesus were first told to look at the coins, only to find the image of an earthly ruler. In like fashion, the tuppence, shown in close-up, reveals both the image of Britain's earthly ruler, and the figure of a Greek/Romanesque figure on the other side of the coin—once again suggesting a line of continuity between ancient empire and the British Empire. In gazing at the coin, however, George comes into consciousness: he begins to understand the alternative consciousness that Mary has been imparting on the children represents an alternative existence based on love, devotion, redemption, and caring for the least of these.

George thus comes to reject his prior consciousness, constructed around the mandates of capitalist imperialism, in favor of Mary Poppins's alternative existence. This rejection is demonstrated by George forcing the tuppence into the hand of the crusty and incomprehending bank chairman, Dawes Sr. The film thus creates an image of the liberationist meaning of Mark 12:17. George renders unto Caesar what is Caesar's. He leaves what the plot describes as "cold heartless money" with the cold and heartless, Dawes (who dreams of foreclosures). George abandons his desire for conquest and acquisition in order to give himself over to the spirit that he has discovered through Mary Poppins and his children.

Mary Poppins thus responds to Christianity's aesthetic crisis by rejecting the "two realm" theory, providing instead images built around the kinds of social—and personal—transformation that Christianity's liberationist mandates strive for. Under the guise of the children's film, the plot has a wide latitude to offer such cloaked ideological critique, but can only go so far before it conflicts with the film's economic mandates: to cultivate middle-class sensibilities. *Mary Poppins*'s rejection of imperialist capitalism is so clear, and so radically antithetical to institutional Christianity's comfortable acceptance of the "two realm" theory, that the film's economic mandates thus require the plot to exercise containment. The plot resolves its conflicting mandates by constructing an ending which resists closure. It thus provides an ending that offers classical containment, but in the process, resists the ideological containment the closure seeks to impose.

The film's ending revolves around George's reuniting with the family. Having mended Jane and Michael's kite, George leads the children into going out and flying a kite with the musical number "Let's Go Fly a Kite." Caught up in the family's enthusiasm, Winnifred offers one of her suffragette banners as the tail for the kite—signifying her return to the family from the absence her activism created. In this respect, the film seems to successfully contain all the ideological volatility that it has conjured up through the trajectory of the narrative: the fall of capitalism in the face of Christianity has been lost to the family's integration and happiness, and the political threat of women's liberation has been contained with Winnifred giving up the cause for the sake of her family. The weight of the film's conclusion is thus clearly centered around a happy ending that ties up all the potential threats and challenges to family—and social stability. As with the rest of the film, however, the ending functions dialogically: working to resist the very stability that it established.

Rather than end with the image of the reunited Banks family, the plot shifts to Mary and her departure. This shift functions fundamentally as a turning away from the ending at hand: the image of the happily reconciled Banks family restored to their upper-class comfort and security. The turn to Mary, who comments on the scene along with her talking umbrella, abstracts the closing, while at the same time preventing it from actually concluding. In what amounts to complex character exposition, the plot reiterates the issue of Mary's love for the children that first introduced the scene. When asked by her talking parrot-head umbrella if she cares that the children have left without saying goodbye, Mary replies, "Practically perfect people never permit sentiment to muddle their thinking." By raising the question, the plot revisits the question of Mary's love, making clear that Mary does indeed love the children, even if she evades the issue. By avoiding an explicit statement, however, the plot refrains from reducing Mary's love for the children to a simple statement—and hence a simple, or simplistic, concept. The stable image of family love and tranquility is disrupted by the inability to properly place Mary in relationship to that love and tranquility.

Precisely what the text implies is that Mary's love exceeds that image—cannot be contained within the boundaries of human relationships. Mary's role in the narrative far exceeds redeeming George, just as it involves far more than being a simple replacement for the maternal love that is absent for Jane and Michael. It is inconceivable, for example, that Mary could adopt the kind of traditional role that Winnifred so easily assumes within the scene. So excessive is the concept of Mary's love that neither the scene nor the narrative can contain it. Rather, Mary's love forces the narrative away from closure and towards an open ending.

The inability of the narrative to adequately symbolize the complexity of Mary's love points to a reality beyond the compendium of Christian discourses that converge around Mary's character. Rather, the scene suggests that the excess of Mary's transformational love constructs her as the feminine spirit of God: the location where all those discourses are one. Mary's gliding out into the sky to close the narrative is then confirmation of this construction. She neither ascends into the heavens, nor is she assumed into them—which would model either a Marian or Christological discourse. Instead, Mary's actions—her flying over the scene—emulates spirit gliding above the earth, viewing the newly transformed world.

In this way, the film finalizes its construction of Mary's character as the feminine spirit of God, or, more accurately, what Rosemary Radford Reuther describes as God/ess. As Reuther describes the concept: "images of God/ess must be transformative, pointing us back to our authentic potential and forward to new redeemed possibilities."[62] The film's ending resists closure by fulfilling this mandate. It provides an image of characters (George, the children, and even, to a degree, the bank directors) experiencing their authentic potential. Further, Burt's farewell to Mary—"Don't stay away too long"—opens out the narrative to look forward to new redeemed possibilities.

The plot's resistance to closure thus insists on the kind of social transformation that other elements work to contain. In constructing an image of a realized transformation of social hierarchies—especially capitalist imperialism—*Mary Poppins* rejects the accommodationism of institutional Christianity, and begins to construct instead a new aesthetic. *Mary Poppins*, then, is an important model for developing a new aesthetic, and for articulating liberationist discourses from the margins which resist containment. Indeed, the mandate for liberation and social transformation articulated in *Mary Poppins* continued as a dominant social mandate throughout the 1960s and would remain so until the American economic crises of the mid and late 1970s. As the hope for social progress of the Kennedy era exploded into the social volatility of the 1960s, however, Disney Studios' marketing strategy would shift away from the bold experimentation of *Mary Poppins*, and move instead towards a retreat into pedantic wholesomeness delivered in a classical style: where middle-class families, shuddering from cultural volatility, could find respite. The experimentation with an emerging aesthetic so predominant in *Mary Poppins* would be abandoned.

THE AESTHETICS OF DIALOGISM

Unabashed advocacy of social transformation is rare in film. Likewise is the attempt to disengage Christianity from its aesthetic of authority and bring forward instead its liberationist discourses. That being the case, the job of theory is now twofold: to find other locations where the aesthetic continues to try and form itself, and to venture beyond analysis and help it come more fully into being. The contemporary Culture Machine has been very effective in recirculating discourses of materialism and consumption, the necessity and glorification of violence, and hedonistic sexuality (itself modeled as a form of consumption). Christianity, on the other hand, has failed to match that success: it has failed to successfully recirculate its discourses or effectively contest the discourses just mentioned. The significance of *Mary Poppins* is that it became at least one site in secular popular culture where the dominant discourses of materialism, violence, and hedonistic sexuality were *not* reproduced—indeed, they were replaced by Christian discourses of the mystical and the social power of transformational love. That the film and its discourses end up being a drop in the bucket compared to the overwhelming recirculation of dominant secular ideologies is less a measure of the film's ineffectualness than it is a testimony to the challenge that faces Christianity when it tries to compete in the cultural marketplace.

In this respect, the purpose of analysis here—of delineating the Christian discourses as articulated in *Mary Poppins*—is to discern how *Mary Poppins* can be used as a model: to begin to understand the principles by which an emerging Christian aesthetic can more effectively address and engage its audience. *Mary Poppins*'s bricolage approach to genres and cultural forms demonstrate a modernist aesthetic that can best be illuminated by the work of critical theorist Walter Benjamin. As S. Brent Plate ably demonstrates, Benjamin eschewed the traditional concept of aesthetics as centered around the analysis of beauty, and theorized instead about the "dispersing, disrupting forces that perpetually take totalities apart."[63] Rather than an end in themselves, however, dispersion and disruption are valued by Benjamin as creative forces.

As his essay "The Work of Art in the Age of Mechanical Reproduction" makes clear, Benjamin's main concern is the way in which art is controlled by and used to reinforce power and hierarchy. Benjamin's prime concern with aesthetics, then, is theorizing how the work of art in the modern age can enable mass audiences to see through the ideological illusions that define the boundaries and parameters that regulate their social existence. Dispersion and disruption tear away at the structures of authority and the "aura" of art and its ability to create a complete (or totalizing) world view—a view that, in turn, confirms the social hierarchies and structures of power that endow art to begin with. Far from being just destructive forces, dispersion and disruption are creative forces as well—constructing new combinations and juxtapositions of elements outside the boundaries of established meanings and perspectives.

Like Bakhtin, Benjamin was interested in the profane, not for its own sake, but for its relationship to power and authority and their designation of the sacred. In particular, Benjamin investigates the liminal spaces between the sacred and the profane, the margins, that fall outside the gaze of authority. As Plate argues, "The possibilities for change are located in the movement between the sacred and profane, that is, in the activities of consecration and deconsecration. Power and meaning are not found in the thing itself, but at its margins, in the passages between art and reality, object and subject."[64] As the previous discussions of the film demonstrate, *Mary Poppins* is actively engaged in these marginal spaces, especially in terms of reconsecrating the transcendent.

The modernist aesthetic of *Mary Poppins* is a significant model both for its disruption and its dialogism. Under the guise of the children's genre, fantasy, and comedy, the disruption is successful at tearing away structures of authority—particularly patriarchy—without alienating its audience, a principle that will be explored more fully in other chapters. Interrelated to the disruptive aspect of the film, is the dialogism of *Mary Poppins*. The dialogical mode by which the film speaks of the transcendent underscores that one of the fundamental aesthetic problems with Christianity is that a dialogic theology has been rendered monologic through the operations of institutionalization, hegemonic appropriation (what Hauerwas and others describe as "Constantinianism"), and fundamentalism. Those operations engendered their own aesthetics to contain both the ideological audaciousness of Christianity, and the fundamental dynamism engendered in its dialogical discourse. This dialogism is evident in the actions and discourses of the founder, Jesus of Nazareth, who deconstructed and reinterpreted both Hebrew Scripture and the concept of the Divine to his contemporaries.

Nor does Christianity represent the discourses and actions of its founder in a monologic way. The life of Jesus of Nazareth comes represented through four different narrative perspectives, each writing with particular goals for specific communities. These narrative accounts are then accompanied by a collection of letters reflecting on the life and teachings of Jesus that were written by numerous authors (many of whom cannot be ascertained) addressing different coummunites at distinct times in their formation. The Hebrew Scriptures that these writers draw upon to make their case for the divinity of Jesus are likewise dialogical, combining history with many other literary genres. Even the history provided in Hebrew Scriptures is anything but monological—as the allegory and mixing of different stories in Genesis heavily attests.

Returning to its dialogical origins is both a fundamental and complicated challenge for the institutional church, which has depended on an aesthetic of authority for far too long. The dialogism that *Mary Poppins* employs, and its aesthetic strategy of speaking from the margins, born of necessity, is an important model that stands in stark opposition to the aesthetic of authority the institutional church still leans on. In the aesthetic of authority, the discourses of Christianity speak from the position of power: either the power of the medieval and/or Renaissance Church, or the power of the state. Frescoes that adorn the ceilings and alcoves of medieval churches articulate this power: they speak from above to an audience down below. They glorify the power of God, either through representations of his son, through his saints, through the mother of Jesus, or in the case of the Sistine Chapel, through a representation of God himself. Furthermore, the aesthetic of authority uses evolving codes of realism to underscore the reality of this power. A Christianity that combined earthly power with spiritual power projects its discourses from the position of power. As a result, its texts consistently strive for a homology between the representation of power and the position of its discourse: its texts speak of and from power.

Mary Poppins, conversely, articulates its Christian discourse from the margins. This positioning is not coincidental. *Mary Poppins* is a Hollywood film that conforms to dominant conventions—even as it challenges generic conventions. As a result, it speaks with the displaced authority that is characteristic of Hollywood films. The discourse emanates from an abstract and omniscient narration that functions as the position of the discourse—a discursive function that places at a remove the hegemonic power located within the Hollywood entertainment industry that is the actual source of the discourse.

Within that stylistic convention, omniscient narration and story hold a privileged place, and all other stylistic conventions must conform to the demands of each—servicing the aesthetic requirements of both story and its omniscient narration. In conforming to that style, *Mary Poppins* avoids the aesthetic failures of overtly Christian or religious films like *The Robe* (1953) or *The Ten Commandments* (1956), which locate the source of omniscient narration within the authority of religion. In these films, a particular form of piety functions as the source of omniscient narration, overwhelming and sapping the aesthetic strength of story and style.

Mary Poppins, conversely, eschews piety and locates its Christian discourses within the margins. Although a strategy adopted of necessity, it is nonetheless particularly consonant as an aesthetic of Christianity—especially contemporary Christianity. Speaking from the margins is not only the origins of Christian discourses but—much to the dismay and disappointment of Nietzsche—its enduring legacy and its ultimate transformational goal. Christianity sets itself to contest earthly power, to challenge principalities. Precisely what Francis of Assisi discovers, as Marie Dennis has argued, is the "graced humanity" residing in the margins. Indeed, the New Testament's discourses on the birth of Jesus of Nazareth in a stable, his habit of consorting with outcasts, and the scandal of the cross, all articulate Christianity's inversion of power. That Christianity assumed earthly power—became a principality—for nearly 1,500 years functioned to displace the position of its voice—and as a result, compromised its discourse. What *Mary Poppins* demonstrates is that relocating the position of discourse back to the margins might be an essential element in moving from a medieval aesthetic to a contemporary one.

As a cinematic text, however, *Mary Poppins* models several other aesthetic principles for a contemporary Christian aesthetic. Among these are:

harmony, proximity, homology, and sublimity. The first of these concepts—harmony—draws directly from the film's cinematic properties: film's propensity for being a polyvocal text. Certain films and specific cinematic styles approach cinema's polyvocality and simultaneity of signifying elements in various ways—sometimes minimally, other times hierarchically—but *Mary Poppins* approaches it complexly and, as further discussion demonstrates, homologistically. The film weaves its Christian discourses through simultaneous combinations of actions, language, settings, gestures, and music, creating a complex mix of clever wordplay, character interactions, and musical accompaniment, all working simultaneously to produce density and depth to its discourse.

The significance of harmony for a Christian aesthetic is not, however, in privileging complexity over simplicity: indeed, simplicity is another significant aesthetic principle for Christianity. Rather, harmony can represent and articulate the dialectal structure that is fundamental to Christianity. Despite fundamentalist tendencies to reduce Christianity to a static set of beliefs and practices, Christianity—like the Judaism from which it evolved—is a mystical religion that stubbornly resists guaranteeing that formulaic methods or practices will obtain spiritual goals, or closeness to God. James Martin, for example, collected essays from luminaries and writers that answer the question, "How can I find God?" The essays are nearly always enlightening, some fascinating, but none can deliver iron-clad "success."[65] Elsewhere, Martin documents how Mother Teresa of Calcutta, who spent a lifetime of service to the poor, suffered from spiritual darkness for most of her adult life.[66] Rather than feeling closer to God by working for the poor, Mother Teresa felt abandoned.

Despite what televangelists might claim, Christianity does not offer a formula for success, let alone, as Mother Teresa's life demonstrates, a guaranteed closeness to God.[67] Instead, Christianity asks for a never-ending struggle to give oneself over to a variety of mandates: the needs of others, the need for prayer, the necessity of nonviolence, or care for creation, to name but a few. The impossibility of fulfilling any of these mandates, let alone combining them, leads the individual not only toward the necessity of going beyond the self, but also to the need for community. Harmony calls on creative ways to combine mandates, enabling specific elements to contribute in ways that they cannot individually. Harmony privileges the collective over the individual elements without diminishing the value of the latter—inscribing precisely the logic of Christianity.

Interdependent but distinct from harmony is the concept of homology. Simply put, homology is an analogical relationship between signifying elements—their form—and the message that they articulate. Homology has been an elusive, if not erratic, and risky aesthetic strategy in film style.

The Soviet filmmaker Sergei Eisenstein, for example, once theorized—in a stunning and complex essay—about the correspondence between music, movement, and the actual visual composition of the shot.[68] What Eisenstein was working toward (and failed at), *Mary Poppins* achieves: an organic unity between the sign and its message. The earlier discussion of "Feed The Birds" points to this unity. Julie Andrews's vocal performance functions as an analogue to the very spiritual domain about which she sings—her singing serves as the voice of an angel.

Making such an aesthetic claim, however, confronts one of the most significant contributions and objectives of both modernism and postmodernism: the dissolution of such organic relationships. Not only Saussure and semiotics, and Freud with psychoanalysis, but also Nietzsche and Heidegger and, later, Derrida, Foucault, and Delueze, successfully demonstrate what has come to be called the decentering of meaning: eradicating truth claims based on some sort of "objectivity"—the basis of which is, in some way, an inherent relationship between the sign and its referent. As David Bentley Hart argues, postmodernism is a philosophical awakening (which began under modernism) to the "ultimate foundationlessness of 'truth.'"[69] For aesthetic inquiry to wander back into the search for organic unity between sign and message is at worst an outright rejection of contemporary theory, at best a turn into the thorniest area for the postmodern: the transcendent.

Andrews's virtuoso performance in "Feed the Birds," layered as it is with equally inspired music from the Sherman Brothers and the stunning special effects supervised by Peter Ellenshaw, transcends the more pedestrian goals of "entertainment" and, as its lyrics indicate, clearly strives to reach beyond—to give a sense or even a brief glimpse—of the transcendent.

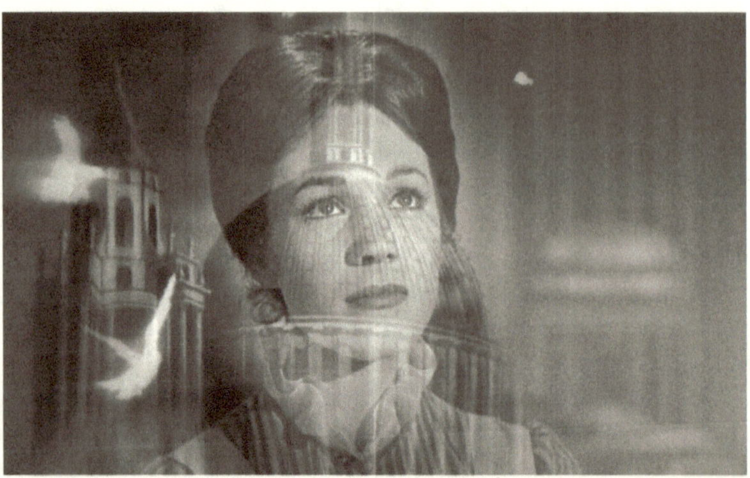

The dissolve between Mary and the cathedral is one of the ways the scene strives for the transcendent.

In this respect, theology has a distinct advantage over postmodern intellectual thought, insofar as it has no mandate either to rationalize that which is beyond representation—that which resists symbolization entirely. As Hart argues, the difference between Christianity and postmodern secular philosophy with respect to the transcendent is that Christianity can philosophically conceptualize the transcendent as part of the infinite and inescapable reality of God. Further, Hart argues that "the Christian infinite belongs to an ontology of original and ultimate peace, and as a consequence, allows a construal of beauty and of peace inconceivable in . . . the thought of Nietzsche and his heirs."[70] Christian aesthetics do not have to reject all of postmodern theory—indeed, the postmodern emphasis and critique of power and its complex relations is of great value—but neither does it need to abandon its own insights on the transcendent and the role of signifying practice to aspire to it.

This discussion of homology and the transcendent leads to the next concept, sublimity—or, to side with Hart, beauty. This discussion keeps returning to "Feed the Birds," because, as the previous discussion of homology indicates, the scene achieves a sense of beauty rarely accomplished—indeed, it evokes an indefinable response that can be described only as the effect of the beautiful. This indefinable aspect, itself an indication of the transcendent, is both a fundamental problem and principle of beauty. The sheer volume of images of beauty that the contemporary Culture Machine churns out so effortlessly has reduced the concept of beauty to just another commodity. This leads Hart to argue that there is a modern disenchantment with beauty, to the point at which it is almost meaningless: "neither exactly a quality, nor a property, nor a function, not even really a subjective reaction to an object or occurrence."[71] In this respect, it is the transcendent that restores beauty to a meaningful, if not complex, concept.

Hart argues that the transcendent returns to the concept of beauty the property of being "essentially indescribable" and allows us to see how beauty can appear both "on the vastest of scales and on the most minute, at once familiar and strange, near and remote."[72] These properties and experiences of the beautiful accompany "Feed the Birds." The messages in the "comments" section of YouTube, where a clip of "Feed The Birds" is posted, are dominated by people talking about being moved, indescribably, to tears by the scene. Poster TINIG, for example, writes, "i can't help crying ev'rytime i hear it," a response that is led, in part, by poster LOVEHOWARDBANNISTER's message that "This song still remains by [sic] favorite Disney song ever. It always gives me goosebumps. The end always makes me cry . . . I can understand why this was Walt Disney's favorite song, it's so beautiful." Indeed, of the fourteen comments posted on YouTube, eight reference crying as their reaction.[73]

Disney's own attraction to the song, alluded to by the previous message, is discussed by the Sherman Brothers in the thirtieth anniversary edition's bonus footage documentary on the making of *Mary Poppins*. The brothers describe how Walt would regularly call them into his office and ask them to play the song as he gazed out the window, misty-eyed.

These examples are not even remotely a scientific sampling—rather, they point to a shared experience, beyond the individual analysis here, of the power of the scene to evoke the kind of indescribable response that is one of the properties of beauty. Moreover, that this particular scene, striving as it does to reach the transcendent—to figure, as it were, the sublime reality of the spiritual world—ends up achieving beauty is hardly coincidental. The combined talents that were brought to bear on the scene were specifically directed to the source of beauty—and this is what a contemporary Christian aesthetic cannot lose sight of. A contemporary Christian aesthetic is surrounded by the elegant, lush, and evocative play of image craft that secular postmodernism can almost effortlessly create—and with high volume. For all its technical mastery, and even evocative capacities, however, secular postmodern image craft is fundamentally plastic. It delights in the play of images—of clever reference, homage, and quotation—as a means of papering over the horror that modernist and postmodernist theory uncovered: the abyss of nonmeaning that the decentering of the sign has exposed.

For contemporary Christian aesthetics, the abyss of nonmeaning is neither a horror to hide from, nor is the play of images a necessary escape. For Christianity, the abyss is the separation from God—the chasm, or even original sin, that makes unity with God impossible in humankind's present condition. The transcendent, the sublime, beauty—all point to the beyond of the abyss: they provide a glimpse, however momentary, and however limited, of the Divine. In this respect, beauty must be a goal of a contemporary Christian aesthetic, because, as Hart argues, "Worldly beauty shows creation to be the real theater of divine glory—good, gracious, lovely, desirable, participating in God's splendor . . . ."[74] Thus, simply put, a contemporary Christian aesthetic must strive for beauty—must take beauty as its goal—because beauty is both the source and the aim of its striving. The Culture Machine clearly demonstrates that an enormous amount (especially in terms of commercial success and power) can be achieved without such striving. A Christian aesthetic can ill afford to follow that path. Neither, as further chapters and *Mary Poppins* both demonstrate, does a Christian aesthetic need to outright reject the impulse to address audiences at the level of their interests and desires as constituted by secular humanism—one of the fundamental formulas that spurs commercial success.

Beauty is certainly nothing new to a Christian aesthetic, as Byzantine mosaics and icon paintings, Gregorian chants, Mozart's Requiem Mass, and the previously mentioned frescoes in medieval and Renaissance churches all indicate. The last principle identified here—proximity—articulates *how* beauty should be communicated. Film theory, from a variety of approaches, has long since delineated the means by which film—unlike the theater—encompasses the spectator into the sphere of the action. Codes of editing and camera positioning do more than just give the spectator the "best seat in the house" or a "close look" at the action. Rather, what the cinema provides is an intimate view of the narrative. Cinematic language works to make the spectator a silent but ever-present *participant* in the world of the story.

Proximity thus indicates an intimacy between the voice that issues the discourse, and the spectator that it addresses. As the previous discussion indicates, the cultural context for Christian discourse to "speak from on high" has long since passed—and with it, the efficacy of speaking from such a position. Proximity speaks instead to specific, contemporary cultural imperatives that Christianity fundamentally addresses. Chief among these is community. The fundamental problem with speaking from on high is the way that it alienates and individualizes the spectator. There is a distinct divide between the elevated authority from which the voice speaks and the lower position of the individual audience member. Further, the sense of awe that it seeks to instill further individualizes the audience members: they are meant to experience their own limitations as much as revel in the glory of God. What the cinema demonstrates with its propensity for proximity is the potential to engender community within the articulation of discourse. Within the cinematic text, the spectator is encouraged to become part of a story world, part of a community—however much cinematic spectatorship also encourages separation from the other individuals present at a viewing. The challenge for a Christian aesthetic is to replicate the proximity of cinematic discourse without overprivileging virtual community for actual community. What Christian aesthetics can learn from the cinematic text, then, is the power of intimate address—a power that comes from engendering community in discourse. Such an aesthetic principle is particularly relevant in a contemporary society that is experiencing the breakdown of community on almost every level imaginable.

What *Mary Poppins* demonstrates, precisely, is how effective and enduring a combination of layering, homology, beauty, and proximity can be in articulating the discourse of Christianity. That it did so only from the margins is not, as previously discussed, a sign of ineffectualness. To begin with, *Mary Poppins* provides a powerful model for how to speak from the margins when hegemonic power necessitates such a position. As further chapters will demonstrate, however, the efficacy of *Mary Poppins* can be measured in another way: as artistically preparing the way for more explicit articulations of Christianity, like *Sister Act* (1992), *Bruce Almighty* (2003), and *Evan Almighty* (2007).

4

The West Wing and the Aesthetics of Hegemony

The West Wing (1999–2006) first aired on September 22, 1999 and quickly became a popular and critical success. In its first year, the show ranked twenty-fifth in the Nielsen ratings, and climbed to number thirteen by its second season.[75] In its first outing at the Emmy awards, the show took nine awards, including Outstanding Drama Series, Outstanding Writing, Directing, Cinematography, and Art Direction, respectively. It would continue to win Outstanding Drama for another three years in a row, tying for most wins in the category with *Hill Street Blues* (1981–87), *L.A. Law* (1986–1994), and *Mad Men* (2007–2015). Tellingly, these shows share several generic characteristics: they all have ensemble casts, they focus on social issues through the life and work of their characters, and the drama is placed more on issues than dramatic action per se. In addition to sharing generic characteristics, all these shows—*The West Wing* included—are perceived by their audiences as "quality television"—a slippery yet illuminating term used to demarcate certain television shows through a number of stylistic conventions, modes of address, and audience demographics.

As Jane Feur, Christina Lane, and several other critics note, *The West Wing* firmly positions itself as quality television.[76] While *Hill Street Blues* may have inaugurated the ensemble cast drama, and what has become known as quality television, *The West Wing* more closely resembles *L.A. Law*, a show which inspired a whole generation of lawyers to enter the legal profession. Like *L.A. Law*, the drama in *The West Wing* revolves around what characters say about a social issue, the stand they take, and how they fight for the right and moral cause. As Lane argues, "*The West Wing* dramatizes the moral ambiguity and complex layered relationships between the private and public spheres . . . [It] launches a number of contradictory positions while maintaining . . . a moral center."[77] With its emphasis on morality and relationships, *The West Wing*, like *L.A. Law* before it, structures its narrative so that what characters say carries the weight of the drama. In fact, it is not too far a stretch to say that both shows put discourse on display. They both turned talking into action: restoring discourse to its preeminent place in shaping society. But where *L.A. Law* focused on the legal system and the law, *The West Wing* set its drama around the world of politics. By focusing in on the operations of politics, *The West Wing* allowed social issues to become inherently political—as part of the political process itself.

Even more than *L.A. Law*, the design of *The West Wing* is literally to give voice to the specific ideas, issues, and perspectives within American society that struggle for political power. This struggle for power and influence is at the core of what Antonio Gramsci defined as hegemony. Too often understood statically as "the balance of power," Gramsci's concept is a far more fluid examination of how social control is maintained through a complex process involving different modes persuasion, enactment, and consent rather than, for example, the sheer force of the military or police. Like Mikhail Bakhtin, Gramsci saw the social field as a cauldron of competing influences and ideas pushing for power and control. He argued that schools, churches, labor unions, and other social institutions were political, functioning as important sites where the struggle for power is conducted through discourse and its ability produce knowledge—knowledge that, as the work of Foucault demonstrates, operates to regulate social practices.

Stuart Hall notes that the importance of Gramsci's concept of hegemony is the manner in which it forsakes the top-down model of power—especially class power—and promotes instead a more fluid and dynamic concept of struggle and competition in a social system. Christine Gledhill concurs when she argues:

> [P]ower in a bourgeois democracy is as much a matter of persuasion and consent as of force, it is never secured once and for all. . . . Unlike the fixed grip over society implied by "domination," "hegemony" is won in the to-and-fro of negotiation between competing social, political and ideological forces through which power is contested, shifted or reformed.[78]

Gledhill's summary is significant for the manner in which it underlines the concept of power as a dynamic process: how it shifts, is contested, and reforms.

In addition, Gledhill emphasizes the fluidity of social groups: how they are constituted, how they conduct themselves, the allegiances they require, but also, how much they overlap. Here, the media is an important example. Entertainment media produce and circulate content that employs the talent and abilities of various artists, but they nonetheless operate as large corporations. The profit motive which drives their decision-making disciplines media professionals at every level—producers, directors, writers, production assistants, and set decorators—leads them to work within established practices and aesthetic principles that both produce efficiencies and procure audience satisfaction and pleasure.

This disciplining not only stifles innovation, but commands a high degree of allegiance from artists. Women and African Americans, for example, not only had to play degrading roles in entertainment media, but write stereotypical characters, or use camera angles that objectify or denigrate. The price for working in the industry was and always is conforming to aesthetic principles and practices that the individual might otherwise object to. Gramsci's model of hegemony, however, disallows an analysis to treat this process as absolute and static. While the demand for efficiency and proven formulas have a tendency to stifle innovation, the profit demand also pushes in the opposite direction: encouraging product differentiation that can facilitate aesthetic change. Likewise, several African American and female media professionals have found ways to push back against aesthetic cliches and stereotypes—Spike Lee, Julie Dash, and Madonna are just a few examples.

In Gramsci's theory, aesthetic pushback comes under the category of counter-hegemonic activity: as participating in the struggle to contest or shift power in the realm of cultural signifying practices. The risk of counter-hegemonic artistic practice is alienating the audience from the aesthetic forms or symbolic meanings they have come to be attached to, as the earlier discussion of Hall's concept of encoding demonstrates. Elsewhere I have written, for example, about the tendency of white film critics and journalists to misinterpret Spike Lee's confrontational film *Do the Right Thing* (1988).[79] Because Lee's film was so confrontational in both its style and its unrelenting examination of racial dynamics, several critics misinterpreted it, opining that Lee's film advocated violence (a conclusion that overlooks how Lee's character in the film is an antihero whose actions the narration criticizes).[80]

The West Wing, conversely, demonstrates a keen awareness of the risks incurred in operating counter-hegemonically. Rather than reject or subvert dominant stylistic norms, *The West Wing* appropriates them for its own persuasive—and counter-hegemonic—purposes. Indeed, the show embraces what could only be described as virtuoso style, deftly shifting from Hollywood big-budget scenes with intricate camerawork, complex choreography, and music montages, to small and intimate scenes using long camera takes and slow pacing. This bold display of style became the brand identity of the show, along with the detailed display of the political process behind the scenes. The flaunting of both style and the political process from a progressive point of view allowed the show to structure its narrative to explicitly and implicitly validate counter-hegemonic positions, attempting, through its discourse, to not only contest the power of dominant ideological formations, but to shift power towards alternative ideologies.

The primary site of *The West Wing's* counter-hegemonic practice is its validation of progressive politics and the progressive Left. The show not only consistently invests the progressive Left with intellectual authority, but moral authority as well. The main plot line in the pilot episode revolves around whether deputy chief of staff Josh Lyman will lose his position after making an over-the-top criticism to a member of the Christian Right during a TV face-off. More than just contesting their position, the plot decidedly abandons the overwhelming respect that mainstream news media affords the Christian Right. Rather, the plot portrays the majority of characters representing the Christian Right as decidedly unchristian: as cold-hearted, calculating, anti-Semitic, and all too willing to embrace the grossly inappropriate tactics of their radical fringe. To reinforce how unchristian they are, the plot goes so far as to have one of the members misquote Scripture, undermining the popular image of Christian fundamentalists being able to quote chapter and verse. Rather, it is the Jewish Toby Ziegler, White House director of communications, and the Catholic Josiah Bartlet, president of the United States, who are able to quote chapter and verse accurately. This decidedly partisan alternative to how Christianity is represented operates to contest the respectability and power of the Christian Right, and begin a process of substituting an alternative image and concept of Christianity.

Eboo Patel, for example, describes a particular dynamic between the media and the Christian right at the time, arguing,

> Jerry Falwell, Pat Robertson and Franklin Graham make inflammatory statements . . . precisely so they can get on television talk shows to further elaborate on their hateful views. And dutifully, talk shows invite them on . . . . [T]he mainstream media is happily providing a microphone and a spotlight for religious extremists . . . . Extremists will continue doing inflammatory things to get on television, cameras will continue to show up, and people will continue to watch.[81]

Even though the mainstream news media might think they are "examining" the Christian Right in their coverage, they fail to see the legitimizing process that takes place with the repetition of their coverage. This process is so common that it caused FaithfulAmerica.org to organize a campaign in 2012 urging the progressive-market–oriented MSNBC to stop inviting Tony Perkins (of the right-wing Family Research Council) on the air.[82] This process of privileging and legitimizing the Christian right is described by Michael Livingston, president of the National Council of Churches, as "the preponderance of mainstream media reporting on a minority of U.S. Christians."[83]

In addition to—or rather, as—a major part of *The West Wing's* counter-hegemonic discourse, the series pushes back against both the overvaluation of the Christian Right and media definitions of Christianity itself, deploying the full range of its stylistic practice to accomplish this goal. Chief among the techniques it uses is realism. The series' "high realist" style provides the discourse of authority to the process of validating the progressive positions the plot articulates, including (in the first season alone) gun control ("Five Votes Down" S1, E4), opposing strip-mining on Federal lands ("Enemies" S1, E8), capital punishment ("Take this Sabbath Day" S1, E14), and flag-burning amendments ("20 Hours in L. A." S1, E16). The president opposes missile-shield defense ("The Drop In" S2, E12), and he and his staff work for campaign finance reform, trying to reduce the role of money in politics, while at the same time opposing the US Military's "Don't Ask, Don't Tell" policy ("Let Bartlet be Bartlet" S1, E19). The work that the fictional White House performs is not just marginalized leftist fantasies, but rather, under the authority of realist narrative, an image of actual progressive politics realizing its goals (however idealized).

In this process of validating progressive politics through the discourse of realism, *The West Wing* makes a point to consistently lend the authority of realist style to the realm of spirituality and the discourse of Christianity. Unlike *Mary Poppins*, the spirituality and the discourses of Christianity are not assigned to the margins, but rather, are frequently—and strategically—placed front and center as the driving force behind the characters' commitments to progressive idealism. The main character, President Bartlet, is not just a Catholic, but a Catholic intellectual who graduated from Notre Dame and sends his daughter Zoey to Georgetown. As several scenes demonstrate, Bartlet is not a casual Catholic, but rather, a super Catholic: his Catholicism defines his outlook and actions; it is at the core of his character. The pilot introduces this dimension of his character, and "Take This Sabbath Day" (S1, E13) then expands upon it. The central conflict in this episode is that the devoutly Catholic President Bartlet is faced with a decision to commute a death sentence for a convicted murderer who has exhausted all his appeals. Bartlet, who opposes capital punishment, is torn between his beliefs and realpolitik, his desire to be an effective, and hopefully reelected, president. The conflict for Bartlet, then, becomes a conflict of allegiance, over whom he will ultimately serve: the God he believes in so fervently, or the demands of realpolitik that he govern from the center.

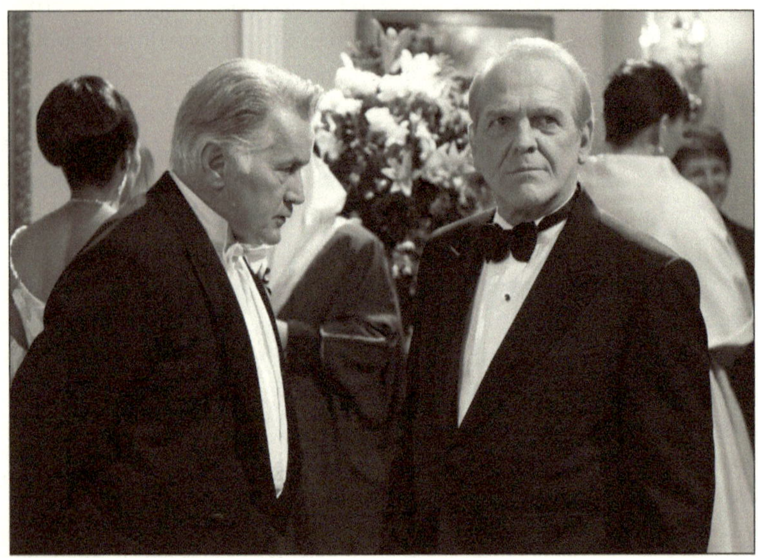

Leo (the chief of staff) and the president represent the choice of allegiance between realpolitik and biblical imperatives.

To underscore the conflict, two characters will come to represent the positions that Bartlet must choose from. The chief of staff, Leo, embodies the realpolitik, and he does throughout the series. Leo is sympathetic to both opposing capital punishment and to Bartlet's moral struggle, but he believes wholly in realpolitik. The other side of the conflict, governing from moral principle, is represented through Toby's character. Using Toby's character is a strategic way for the episode to confront the conservative Christian advocacy for the death penalty based on the Old Testament injunction of "an eye for an eye." By using Toby, the devoutly Jewish character, the episode makes clear that Judaism, from which the "eye for an eye" injunction originates, opposes capital punishment, removing the religious foundation that authorizes it.

The episode not only makes this clear—not only gives voice to the Jewish theological opposition to the death penalty—but does so through the aesthetic of spirituality. The argument against capital punishment is first articulated by Toby's rabbi during temple services, locating the space of the argument within sacred space—the temple—and within sacred time—the feast of Passover. Appropriating this Jewish holy day serves two functions. First, it gives spiritual authority to opposing capital punishment, undermining those who would stand upon "an eye for an eye" as a Biblical mandate. Second, locating the argument within Passover creates an ironic commentary: Passover was the time in which Jesus of Nazareth became a victim of capital punishment. The irony is part of a broader process to create continuity between Judaism and Christianity in opposing capital punishment—a continuity that builds through the episode.

Within the temple sermon, the rabbi tells his congregation that they will "be reminded by the Haggadah the simple truth: Violence begets violence. Vengeance is not Jewish." The episode goes on to reinforce this discourse by having the rabbi further state, "No matter how deep our desire to witness the suffering of our enemies, we are commanded to relocate our humanity. Vengeance is not Jewish." The setting, and the articulation of these discourses from a rabbi, make clear that the theological basis for retaliatory justice is without foundation. There is thus no tradition to appeal to—either theological or cultural—for maintaining or justifying capital punishment. The scene's rhetorical function is to make explicit that support for capital punishment is based instead on a desire for vengeance, not a biblical mandate.

In keeping with its counter-hegemonic aspirations and style, the plot does not just put the theological discourse against capital punishment on display, it puts it into conflict with other discourses, reinforcing the position and allowing it to prevail. The story line repeatedly returns to the spiritual foundations of Jewish and Christian theology as the basis for prohibiting capital punishment. The first instance is when Toby returns to the synagogue to discuss the clemency issue facing the White House. Just before Toby arrives, the cantor for the synagogue takes to the pulpit to rehearse, singing throughout the ensuing discussion between Toby and Rabbi Glassman. This setting allows Jewish spirituality to define the scene. Not only has the plot returned to sacred space, but it brings liturgical music—a symbol of spirituality—into the foreground, then keeps it constantly in the background of the entire scene. Moreover, the song itself, *Hashkiveinu*, serves to make theological commentary on the issue at hand. Toby and the rabbi's conversation about the death penalty is interspersed with the lyrics of *Haskiveinu* sung in the background—lyrics which convey a soul preparing to die asking for peace, comfort, and mercy. Indeed, the lyrics to *Haskiveinu*, though in Hebrew, function pointedly in the scene, beseeching God to "spread over us the shelter of Your peace," and to "Set us aright with good counsel . . . ." Even if English-speaking audiences do not understand the lyrics, the power of the music and their lyrics affect the characters.

For his part, Toby is opposed to the death penalty, but believes the White House will suffer irreparable political damage if it grants clemency to a double murderer. At the time of his conversation with the rabbi, Toby is on the side of realpolitik. Rabbi Glassman, however, argues beyond politics, and insists instead on consistent moral values guided by religious principles. In doing so, Glassman stresses the continuity between Jewish and Christian theological opposition to capital punishment by referencing Catholicism's unambiguous opposition, stating: "Say what you will about the Catholic Church, but their position on life is unimpeachable: no abortion, no death penalty."

More than just stressing continuity between Jewish and Christian theological opposition, the scene dismantles biblical justification of capital punishment even more explicitly than the prior scene in the temple. When Toby says to the rabbi that the Torah does not prohibit capital punishment, Glassman replies, "You know what is also says? It says a rebellious child can be brought to the city gates and stoned to death. It says homosexuality is an abomination and punishable by death. It says men can be polygamous, and slavery is acceptable." Glassman then continues, "For all I know, that thinking represented the best wisdom of its time. But it's just plain wrong by any modern standard." From this theological argument about sacred texts, Glassman then moves the discussion back to the relationship between theology and society, providing theological judgment of how society can properly conduct itself. He argues to Toby, "Society has a right to protect itself, but it doesn't have a right to be vengeful. It has a right to punish, but it doesn't have a right to kill."

Glassman's denunciation of the literalist position and its obvious, but well disguised, selectivity not only decimates the idea of a biblical injunction for capital punishment, it reestablishes biblical morality over the historicism of the texts that are used to try to convey it. Further, in his clarification of what a society can and cannot do, Glassman articulates the Roman Catholic Church's position on capital punishment, further establishing the continuity of the two religious traditions and their opposition.

Glassman's emphasis on "modern standards" serves another counter-hegemonic function. It helps define Glassman within a liberal tradition, and further, establishes him as a model for discerning the relationship between church and state in a secular society. A rabbi who is not afraid to weigh in on social issues from a religious foundation, Glassman advocates that government actions—especially those actions directly involving the individual—be tempered, if not regulated, by the moral foundations of religious traditions. Glassman's Jewishness is key to this model. Rather than the conservative Protestant model which looks to government to impose Christianity in the public square—prayer in public schools, displays of religious art in courthouses and other government offices—Glassman pushes for a humane and just government that draws its principles from the justice imperatives of religious traditions. Rather than being imposed on individuals, the morality of religious traditions can save individuals from an overly political government.

Despite Rabbi Glassman's effective rhetoric, the scene ultimately privileges spirituality as the foundation for the theological and rhetorical imperatives of the discourse. This privileging is acknowledged by Toby's response to Glassman and his discourse. Acknowledging that he has been swayed, Toby replies to Glassman with a question, "Do you know what I think? I think you knew I was coming back here. And I think you put her there on purpose." Toby's response brings to the foreground the fact that the cantor's song underscored all of Glassman's discourse—literally, the backdrop, and figuratively, the foundation from which he speaks. Glassman confirms this role when he replies back to Toby, "She's *our* communications director." The humor that Glassman injects into the conversation performs a standard function of humor: making light of serious or even threatening situations.

The seriousness, or even threat, in this situation is the manner in which reason and rationalism fall to a higher power. Toby has been persuaded out of his secular political realism and into acting on his beliefs. The absurdity of such a possibility is articulated earlier in the scene, when Toby says to Glassman, "You want me to go into the Oval Office and say vengeance is not Jewish?" to which Glassman responds, "Why not?" Toby replies, "Well, for one thing, neither is the president!" The humor that points out the absurdity of overcoming reason with the moral imperatives of spirituality is then used at the end of the scene to contain that very ideological threat.

Conforming to the ideological constraints of mainstream television, the episode does, in the end, allow realpolitik to win over the moral imperatives that both Bartlet and Toby share. Toby does go to the president and, for all intents and purposes, does say vengeance is not Jewish. Indeed, in a move that would assuredly cost him credibility, Toby prefaces his comments by telling Bartlet that he had spoken to his rabbi. When Bartlet tries to eliminate biblical opposition to the death penalty, Toby responds, "Even two thousand years ago, the rabbis of the Talmud couldn't . . . stomach it. I mean, they weren't about to rewrite the Torah, but they came up with another way. They came up with legal restrictions that make our criminal justice system look . . . . They made it impossible for the state to punish someone by killing him." Toby's position, however, does not prevail. He is easily dismissed through discourse when Leo, the ultimate pragmatist and advocate of realpolitik, enters the room and Bartlet tells him, "Toby's been to shul." The look on Toby's face confirms that the discourse was meant to belittle his position—religion can not stand in the place of realpolitik—and Toby retreats.

What is significant for the episode's counter-hegemonic strategy, however, is the manner in which it restores Toby's position to a place of privilege in the text. The episode conforms to the dictates of realism by allowing realpolitik to win the day. In this respect, it rejects the temptation to create an idealist ending, siding instead with the political realism of the day. The evaluative system of the text, however, makes clear that while realpolitik won the day, the fact that it did so is a tragedy: a measure of how immoral American society has become, of how out of step it is with the Judeo-Christian values that it lays claim to. This position is explicitly stated by the character of Fr. Thomas Cavanaugh, who President Bartlet invites to the White House as he struggles with the issue. Cavanaugh holds President Bartlet to the biblical standard, telling him, "'Vengeance is mine, sayeth the Lord.' Do you know what that means? God is the only one that gets to kill people." Like Rabbi Glassman before him, Cavanaugh then turns to the sociopolitical when he tells Bartlet, "That was your way out."

The episode drives home the point that capital punishment is immoral in the scene's closing. As Bartlet struggles over his own morality in the execution, he looks at his watch right as the second hand ticks closer to midnight—the appointed hour of the execution. As he does so, the first notes of the *Haskiveinu* begin playing quietly in the background. The music continues as Cavanaugh counsels Bartlet that wisdom on this issue did indeed come to him, he just ignored it. When Bartlet receives notification that the execution was conducted, the music comes to the foreground. To emphasize the moral gravity of the situation, and assert its fundamental role, the scene goes silent: Bartlet reading the message about the execution, and walking over to his desk to register its impact on him. Gesture in particular is significant here. As Bartlet approaches his desk, he stops at the front, grabbing the top, and then bowing his head in resignation. The gesture, seen from the reverse in a long shot, makes clear that despite his towering intellect (he is a Nobel Prize winner in Economics) and devout Catholicism, Bartlet allowed the powers of the office to overwhelm his personal morality.

Bartlet returns from the desk after Cavanaugh asks the president if he would like the priest to hear his confession. The significance of Cavanaugh's question is that it affirms that Bartlet is morally culpable for allowing the execution to go through. This is emphasized by the manner in which Cavanaugh phrases his question. At the beginning of the scene, Cavanaugh asks

President Bartlet how he should be addressed. Bartlet makes clear that it is best while in the Oval Office to address him as Mr. President. Throughout the scene, Cavanaugh complies with this request—until the closing, where he asks, "Jed, do you want me to hear your confession?" In shifting to the familiar, Cavanaugh gently makes clear that Bartlet cannot hide behind the office of the presidency, but is instead individually responsible for failing to act when he had the power to.

The scene then closes with a crane shot of Bartlet receiving confession, kneeling on the carpet as he does so. The crane shot, combined with the same music of the *Haskiveinu* from the synagogue, brings emphasis to Bartlet's confession. In addition, it makes clear that the spectator is not to identify with Bartlet, but rather, to judge him. The crane shot not only moves away from Bartlet, but diminishes him by looking at him from above. It is from this position that the spectator is to look down on Bartlet for his moral failure.

The closing shot functions beyond the discursive function of the scene: asserting the morality of opposing capital punishment over the power of realpolitik. The shot also serves to create the kind of idealized image that it resisted previously when allowing realpolitik to win the day. The image created by the crane shot allows the spectator to see President Bartlet kneeling on the Seal of the President, which is embroidered in the carpet of the Oval Office. This image functions as an ideal image—to set an ideal for moral leadership guided by the social justice imperatives of biblical teaching, and humbled by the inability to live up to them. In this way, the episode makes clear that, while the realpolitik of secular culture has political—and by extension, social—power, its power does not compare to the moral power that is the potential of a society. It cannot compare to a society where each individual is responsible for striving to create the just society.

The plot's construction of asserting morality over power—of suggesting that morality actually has more power than the political—aligns the plot with the form of melodrama. *The West Wing*, however, goes beyond melodrama by affirming the sacred: by insisting that the source of morality is located firmly, and unequivocally, in the Divine, and in this particular case, divine mandates. Bartlet's struggle is ultimately a struggle over allegiance, and the scene finds him wanting in the strength it takes to maintain his primary allegiance.

The episode thus functions counter-hegemonically by criticizing the current social configuration and encouraging its audience instead to desire something different—something beyond what consent has comfortably settled for. Indeed, the episode engages in the most of radical of hegemonic activities: reawakening and redirecting the desire of the audience out of complacency and towards more utopian possibilities. Here, the realism of the show works against the traditional containment function of realism. The realism of the show insists that the moral imperatives confronting Toby and President Bartlet are real—as is their source, a God who speaks through history and through an infinite number of other ways: sacred texts, music, and the individuals who cross our paths, to name but a few.

In his discussion of realism, John Fiske argues against understanding realism as the result of art having an affinity with reality. There are no stylistic techniques, like the handheld camera, long-take editing, or a crane shot, that can endow a text with a privileged, and/or closer, relationship with reality. Rather, stylistic techniques work together discursively—to create the effect, or more accurately, the discourse of realism. Fiske argues—drawing on the work of Stuart Hall—that this realism effect, the perception that a text is "realistic" as a result of its discursive strategies—is the result of producers and audiences sharing both the same ideology and the same experience of stylistic conventions to deliver that shared ideology.[84]

The significance of *The West Wing* for Christian aesthetics is the way in which it capitalizes on both of these principles. *The West Wing* reacquaints viewers with the disruptive discourses of Christianity, demonstrating their social implications in a contemporary secular world. Within the ongoing drama of the show, Christianity is never an issue of private faith, but rather, a moral and spiritual imperative that compels characters to transform the social, no matter how small. In addition, it elevates its Christian discourses through its realist—and virtuoso—style. Another episode that foregrounds the president's Catholicism, "7A WF 83429" (S5, E1), demonstrates this point.

Tasked with maintaining the suspense and excitement from the concluding episode of the fourth season, when the president's daughter Zoey is kidnapped, the premiere episode for season five employs one of its signature dramatic conventions—the music montage—for its conclusion. Unbound by the conventions of strict narrative structure and expectations, the scene draws heavily on style: investing objects and the relationships between images with heightened symbolic significance through the play and contrast between sound and images. The progression of the scene evolves around a series of contrasts and connections.

The most pronounced of these contrasts comes from the difference between spaces that stand in solidarity, hope, and remembrance of Zoey, and spaces which seek to retaliate against the suspected terrorist organization that took her. A series of contrasts results from the comparison of these spaces: pacifism vs. militarism, humanization vs. dehumanization, and finally church vs. state. The episode validates, and empowers, the Christian discourses in these contrasts, through a variety of narrational and stylistic operations. Primarily, the scene gives a larger voice to the discourse of Christianity than it does secularism, creating three distinct spaces for comparison, and assigning two of them to the transcendent power of Christianity.

The first space the scene creates is the space of a Catholic church that the Bartlet family attends to pray for Zoey. The narrative goes to great lengths to motivate and naturalize the intimacy of this space. The church is small and unpopulated by a congregation, and the interior lighting is warm and low key. The space, its lighting, and its iconography is decidedly different from the church in *Sister Act*, for example, whose cavernous, turn-of-the-century architecture conveys the sense of a now crumbling era. The second space the scene constructs is the sidewalk outside of the White House, where people have set up an impromptu memorial to Zoey. Both these spaces come to signify spaces for the transcendent: where hope, love, and solidarity are the operative modes. The third space, occupied by White House chief of staff Leo McGarry, is the White House Situation Room—the space of the state, of power, technology, and coercive force. The scene links and compares these spaces, through similarity, relationships, and actions. As the montage plays out, the spaces of faith and hope—the church and the sidewalk—are spaces of soft, warm light: hues of yellow, orange and red. The space of the State, by contrast, is one of cold blues and greens—the light cast by high technology display screens.

These stylistic contrasts are established with the introduction to the scene itself. The music comes up over the image of a motorcade approaching a church. As the scene plays out, the Bartlet family will exit the motorcade and enter the church. The six-shot sequence is notable both for its intricate choreography/big-budget attention to elaborate detail, but also for its introduction of a color scheme. The sequence is dark, punctuated by the bright white light of headlights, blue light from police cruisers, or green light from street lamps. The church itself, in the background, while bathed in bright white light, nonetheless reflects a warm, brown color. The sequence ends, however, with President Bartlet and his daughter Ellie walking from the motorcade, the church offscreen, the president and his daughter surrounded by darkness and bright lights. In this manner, the sequence establishes the color coding for the entire scene: cold light for the state, warm light and tones for the church.

The connection between these two domains is introduced with a dissolve from the motorcade into a bright blue LCD display panel showing a fictionalized map of the Mideast. A dark shot, it replicates in tone the previous shot of a dark exterior illuminated by the bright glare of headlights and punctuated by the cold blue of a strobing police lights. Here, the blue light from the screen casts the figure of Leo McGarry in a dark silhouette, while the right side of the screen shows symbols of the combat aircraft and naval craft that are being employed. The sequence further connects the two spaces by dissolving between a shot of Leo sitting down at the table and the president sitting in the church. As the shot dissolves from one to the other, the Seal of the President, hanging on the wall of the situation room, hovers between the two men.

From the church, the sequence soon pivots from interior space to the exterior space of the sidewalk and the public shrine to Zoey. Even though the sequence has alternated from interior to exterior, the two spaces are linked visually through light and color hues. The shots of the shrine are illuminated with the warm glow of candlelight, and earth tones dominate the space, punctuated by street lamps whose white light complements the lights of the many candles—unlike the earlier shot outside the church where the street lamps glowed green.

The meaning of these color schemes becomes clear as the sequence plays out and returns to Leo and the situation room. The LCD panel shows computer code tracking the bombing mission to the fictional state of Qumar, and symbols for two combat aircraft: the F/A 18c Super Hornet and the aircraft for the 101 Airborne Division A-10 Squadron. As the shot comes to the fore, it pans left, showing yellow dashed lines advancing across a map. To the left of the dashed lines, computer data scrolls past, designating the tracking information of the mission being represented on the screen. The symbols in the cold light of the situation room are representations of the state carrying out acts of violence. As arbitrary symbols, they are detached from the destruction and violence they represent—their function to dehumanize the death that is being unleashed in the actual place they represent.

The display screen dissolves into another shot of the sidewalk vigil, a close-up of a hand-painted sign that says, "We Love You Zoey," but as that shot comes to the fore, the computer data from the previous shot lingers in the left side of the frame. The warm photograph then dissolves back again to the cold display screen, tracking the approach of the bombing mission. The visual contrast between the two spaces works to underscore their fundamental difference. Although both spaces represent people, they do so in vastly different ways. The space of the vigil represents a person through her name and image, and with other people joining in solidarity to profess their hope for her. The display screen, conversely, dehumanizes the people it is representing—the attackers and their targets—by reducing them to data. In the warm space of the church and sidewalk vigil is hope, love, and humanity; in the cold displays of the situation room is dehumanization, vengeance (the mission is purely retaliatory), and violence.

The scene's culmination, of the guilt-ridden President Bartlet receiving communion while the soundtrack reaches its crescendo, is a finalizing indication that the narration sides with nonviolence over violence—indeed, it seeks to empower nonviolence through its aesthetic virtuosity. The scene diminishes the political and hegemonic power of war and violence by stripping away its moral foundations. Within the scene, the state only possesses power: military power, technological power, and the political power to bring those to bear. The state, however, is shown to be bereft of the moral authority to make such exercises of power meaningful—as just, for example.

The realist style of the scene is significant for this counter-hegemonic process. By employing a melodramatic form and coupling it with a realist style, the scene does more than just contrast Christianity with the state and endorse the former over the latter. Rather, the scene employs its melodramatic form to insist that the moral imperatives of Christianity are more real than the pragmatic politics of the state. By using dissolves to transition between shots, the scene creates unity between the spaces, even as it contrasts them. Compare this transitional technique with cutting between the shots, which divides and separates spaces. The use of the dissolves in this scene, instead, works to tie the spaces together, creating relationships between these different spaces. The first of these relationships is constructed around Leo and Bartlet, who occupy the two different spaces, but are both tied to the ongoing mission.

The differences between Leo and Bartlet, however, points to a fundamental relationship between the two spaces. Leo stays in the situation room to see the mission through. He is keenly aware, and concerned, that the retaliatory mission may well mean the death of Zoey, but knows that politics must—and did—rule the day on the decision to green-light the mission. Bartlet, on the other hand, is in the church, guilt-ridden and troubled that his actions and decisions—his participation in the cycle of violence—caused Zoey's kidnapping to begin with. The focus on Bartlet's inner turmoil is then extended to the rest of the family. The scene's comparative structure revolves around returning to each member of the Bartlet family as they receive communion.

Combined with the emotion-laden soundtrack, and the dissolves between shots, the scene establishes the interiority of the space in the church over the exterior actions and the artificiality of representation in the space of the state. In this manner, the scene mobilizes a realist style in the service of its melodramatic form as a means of pointing to, then insisting upon, the reality of Christian morality. The rhetoric of the scene, in fact, is that the morality that stems from the Divine is more real than the empty exercise of power currently enacted by the White House. The scene thus reinvests

Christianity with an alternative and greater power: the morality and aesthetics that form the basis of, and produce consent to begin with.

The relationship between the film's realist style and the music on the soundtrack is also a significant site for the aesthetics of Christianity. The soundtrack uses Lisa Gerrard's "Sanvean," an emotionally charged song that uses vocal tones without words. Lacking any language, the vocal tones, as such, are left to convey emotion—they heighten the melodramatic tone of the scene, and underscore the sense of tangibility to the transcendent. In "Sanvean," the tone, inflections, and variations of Gerrards's voice enters into and combines with the music as its own instrument. As the emotion of the "lyrics" outstrips the language that carries it, the song itself conveys a striving beyond: to move its audience past the realm of the literal that language creates and into the transcendent. The emotional force of the song and its striving for the transcendent reinforces the scene's discourse that the state is limited—if not locked into—literal reality. The scene emphasizes, instead, that only Christianity can strive beyond for a more powerful existence.

In addition to appropriating realism, *The West Wing* incorporates a number of other counter-hegemonic strategies, contradicting Colin MacCabe's position that the conventionality of realist narrative will always contain—or diffuse—the ideological challenges that it sometimes raises. The concept of ideological containment is one of the most controversial theories in media studies, involving detailed analyses of how style and structure operate, and how audiences respond to those operations. As a theorist who argues for the concept of ideological containment, MacCabe draws attention to how certain structures of realist narrative, like omniscient narration, are so familiar that they create their own discourse that actually undermines or defuses any ideological challenge that the plot brings up. MacCabe creates a hierarchical model of how meaning operates through the text, with the "metadiscourses" of narrative effectively vanquishing any radical or challenging discourse that the story puts forward.

MacCabe, following in the footsteps of several Marxist critics, leans heavily towards a concept that textual operations rather flawlessly achieve their objective of maintaining dominant ideology, regardless of the specific, and often times isolated ideological challenge that a particular story will appropriate. For MacCabe and theorists like him, the utter consistency of metadiscourses containing or marginalizing the ideological challenges that appear in a story overwhelms the possibility and potential for popular media to function counter-hegemonically.

On the other side of the spectrum are theorists like John Fiske, who point out the variety of ways in which audiences frequently make and take their own meaning from a media text. Starting with research that shows black audiences of early television frequently criticized the shows they watched, and moving on to women's reactions to 1970s shows about women, Fiske contends that despite the stylistic and ideological sophistication that can be brought to bear, the textual containment of ideological challenges is never wholly accomplished. Using *Charlie's Angels* and *Cagney and Lacy* as examples, Fiske argues that the "portrayal of the liberated, active, strong woman" was rooted in "material social existence" and could not be completely contained by the textual strategies employed to defuse the ideological challenges that are raised.[85]

As Fiske demonstrates, the problem with cultural containment theories like MacCabe's is the absolute dismissiveness of any kind of textual strategy other than a radical assault on conventional style. Likewise, the limitations of theorists who follow Fiske, as Judith Williams points out, is a tendency to overemphasize audience resistance and to overvalue what she describes as "strands" of subversive elements "in every piece of pop culture from Street Style to Soap Opera."[86] Even Fiske, who offers the most sustained, and balanced, critique of containment theory, cedes the high ground, in the form of the role of metadiscourse, to MacCabe. Drawing on some of the theoretical foundations as MacCabe—especially semiotics and psychoanalysis—Fiske argues diligently that the television text is too polysemous to achieve the kind of rigid ideological control that MacCabe postulates: that textual operations like irony, contradiction, jokes, and excess all function to open the text out into multiple readings and interpretations that resist containment. Likewise, Hall asserts that the preferred or "dominant" mode of decoding a text is not the only mode available for audiences. Rather, Hall demonstrates that there are both "negotiated" and "oppositional" modes for decoding the meaning of the text.[87]

Hall's work is particularly important here for his recognition of the manner in which "professional codes" of television production reproduce "hegemonic codes"—that television forms and styles are not ideologically neutral. Hall introduces into that discussion of "encoding" what he asserts for the process of "decoding": that nothing is completely ideologically determined. Hall argues instead that "conflicts, contradictions and even misunderstandings regularly arise between the dominant and the professional significations and their signifying agencies."[88] What Hall's discussion opens up is the possibility that television can contest ideology on the level of metadiscourse itself. The significance of *The West Wing* lies precisely in that realm: in the way it uses its structure as a serialized television drama to operate counter-hegemonically through the metadiscourses of omniscience, causality, individualism, and closure. As with realism, *The West Wing* does not construct a radical assault on these forms, but rather, appropriates them for its own counter-hegemonic purpose, undermining their generic discourse, and replacing them with its own.

Omniscience is the most significant metadiscourse for MacCabe. Drawing from narratology's concept of omniscient narration—the fact that the narration "knows all" about the story, even if it withholds information—MacCabe defines the metadiscourse of omniscience as the effect of transferring that sense to the audience. For MacCabe, and other containment theorists, omniscient narration creates a frame of mind for the audience that they know all, or know all they need to know, with respect to the story world and the meanings assigned to it. As a result, argue containment theorists, audiences do not feel compelled to question or interrogate the meanings of the text, and most importantly, the social constructions those meanings draw upon or assign.

The West Wing does not so much dismantle the sense of "all knowingness"—far from it. The narration does "know all," from the moral failings of President Bartlet, to the unspoken love between Donna and Josh, to Leo's impending heart attack and eventual return to the White House. Rather, *The West Wing* appropriates omniscience for progressive politics. What the narration of *The West Wing* "knows" ultimately, is that progressive politics is "right," is the fate and future of society. In the world of *The West Wing*, conservative goals like smaller government may have merit, and individual conservatives like Cliff Calley or Glenallen Walken may be admirable, but progressive politics, its drive for equality and protection for all, is on the side of evolution, and is de facto "right."

A scene from "Institutional Memory" (S7, E21) highlights both the progressivism of the omniscient narration, and its distinct limitations, or boundaries, that prevent it from being radical. In this scene, C. J. Cregg, recently promoted to chief of staff but now nearing the end of her White House career, interviews for a job with Franklin Hollis—a fictional character modeled upon Microsoft founder and billionaire Bill Gates. Hollis wants C. J. to help ensure that his foundation can fix some major problem—of her choosing. When Hollis tosses out the idea of AIDS in Africa, C. J. counters with "roads," informing Hollis that the major obstacle to relief work is the lack of infrastructure. She then goes on to tell him that the next step would be plumbing. The progressivism here is clear and distinct. There is no toying with Africa's problems for some sort of political gain, or tying aid to Africa to more investment opportunity for American companies. Rather, C. J.'s proposal is classic liberalism: spending on large-scale social projects that will be accessible to all and help the most people.

The narration aligns itself and endorses C. J.'s ideas. It draws on C. J.'s authority as chief of staff (she clearly knows world problems more in depth than most), and her keen analytical insight (a world-renowned figure like Hollis is instantly impressed). In aligning itself with C. J., the narration discreetly lends its own authority to C. J.'s proposal. Indeed, by placing the proposal within the now familiar formula of White House staff coming up with brilliant ideas, the narration combines familiarity with its own authority to validate the idea as a wise solution to solve the problems of Africa, and help it achieve progress.

In MacCabe's theory, the combining of familiarity with the authority of narration seals off the issue from needing further investigation, which is what happens here. Aligning omniscience with C. J.'s progressive plan certifies modernization/development as the *de facto* answer to the problems of Africa—one of the few remaining places where hunter-gatherer societies still exist. There is no acknowledgment of the manner in which modernization—especially in the form of European colonization—has contributed to the problems of Africa to begin with. More to the point, the scene is progressive and not radical because it leaves no possibility that Africa requires a unique solution that can save its natural resources from the demands for consumption imposed by capitalism, and can chart a different future for tribal cultures other than eventual integration into modernization. C. J.'s plan, delivered with such certitude, will not rest until all of Africa is developed—with, of course, the requisite delineation of some space as game and natural reserves, turning nature into a tourist business and forcing tribal cultures to either modernize or turn themselves into historical models like Williamsburg, Virginia. Within the mechanics of textual operations, however, there is no opening for questioning, no imperative to continue to think about options. Even more significantly, however, is the manner in which the scene constructs no space or opportunity to examine why the fate of Africa should be decided in a room by two powerful Americans rather than by Africans themselves.

Constrained in this manner, the scene articulates the limits of its progressivism. It is firmly entrenched within the boundaries of liberalism, with reforming and regulating both market economics and modernity, but unwilling to go any further. C. J.'s plan for Africa demonstrates the complete willingness to build up the marketplace and modernity, and the absolute inability to think of dismantling it and replacing it with something different.

Where the omniscient narration does approach a more radical position is in its assertion of, and alignment with, the Divine, which, as stated earlier, employs realism to insist on the reality of the Divine. Even more than appropriating realism, omniscient narration's alignment with the Divine manifests itself in several ways: articulating the materiality of the Divine, rejecting simplistic concepts of the Divine, siding with Christian imperatives, and rejecting secular humanism and its concomitant belief in power—seeing both as inferior. Combined, these omniscient discourses about the Divine invest both spirituality and the nature of the Divine with the decided authority of the narration.

The narration's assertion of the materiality of the Divine is articulated in several episodes, but a scene in "Somebody's Going to Emergency, Somebody's Going to Jail" (S2, E16) articulates a common theme for the show: that the materiality of the Divine often manifests itself through the agency of others. In this episode, deputy communications director Sam Seaborn is struggling with the discovery of his father's long-term infidelity when he is asked by Donna's friend Stephanie to help her grandfather receive a posthumous presidential pardon for his controversial conviction of espionage during the early years of the Cold War. Sam enthusiastically takes up the case, only to be shown top-secret files by the NSA director that not only prove the grandfather was a Soviet spy, but that he arranged for the murder of a translator who was going to reveal his identity to the government. Later, Donna discovers Sam mulling things over in the dining room, where he confronts her for telling Stephanie to use flattery to get him to take up the case. When Donna admits to it, Sam's mood deepens, despite her sincere apology: it is the third betrayal of the day.

Acting on his woundedness, Sam leaves the dining room to meet with Stephanie and reveal that her grandfather was indeed a spy who committed treason. Donna pleads with Sam to refrain, not just for her friend's sake, but for Sam's. She understands that he is reacting emotionally to the things going on in his life, and is just looking to hurt someone as he has been hurt. She counsels Sam, "Listen to me. You're in a bad place right now, and you shouldn't make this decision. If you don't tell her tonight, you can tell her tomorrow. If you tell her tonight, that's it." Sam, however, rejects her advice, and walks on to his office to confront Stephanie. What the narration withholds is that Donna is slowly following. As Sam enters his office, Stephanie greets him by rising and stating, "Tell me there's good news." Rather than tell her good news, however, Sam begins to lay out the groundwork for confronting her with the truth by asking, "Have you ever heard of a woman named Shaba Demski?" Stephanie answers no, and when Sam starts hesitating, she becomes wary and prompts him, asking, "Sam?" Just as he is about to clarify, however, Sam glances to his right, and sees Donna standing in the doorway. Donna's presence causes Sam to reconsider, and instead of revealing the truth, he covers up the story.

Though quick, and subtly portrayed, Donna's presence is the turning point in Sam's decision and behavior. Donna's presence reminds him that he is only acting out of his own pain: his desire is not for the truth, but to inflict pain on others. By her actions, Donna bears witness to Sam: calling him to act beyond himself and act with compassion. The act of bearing witness, however, operates dynamically, or as semiotics would describe it, polyvocally. It is not only an implicit plea to act nobly, but also a clear message that if Sam is going to act selfishly and hurt Stephanie just because he has been hurt, then he is going to have to do it in the presence of someone else. This will no longer be a private affair, but will live on as a public act that Donna can and will carry forward—it will affect the small community that Sam and Donna are a part of. In this manner, Donna's presence brings a materiality to Sam's actions: they have consequences beyond Stephanie.

Donna's place in these events is nothing less than the witness to truth. On her own, Stephanie would not have known the actual motivations for Sam's confrontation, it would have been interpreted by her as just the revelation of truth. Donna, however, stands in the place of truth. She knows the truth of why Sam is upset, as well as the grandfather's guilt. Donna's gaze, and the subsequent return of her gaze by Sam, makes clear that the truth stands present between them. Donna makes manifest to Sam that the truth is present and watching, calling him to rise above himself. Through the act of bearing witness, Donna brings the materiality of the Divine in the form of truth and compassion that Sam responds to.

In addition to the materiality of the Divine, the omniscient narration consistently rejects simplistic concepts of the Divine, working against the kind of sealing off from social interrogation that MacCabe describes. The most humorous example of this rejection comes in "Jefferson Lives" (S5, E3). In this scene, Abbey Bartlet speaks with Deborah Fiderer, the president's executive secretary. Zoey has just been recently rescued from her kidnapping and Deborah states: "Mrs. Bartlet, I can't tell you how hard I prayed for you," to which Abbey replies, "I appreciate that." Deborah then dolefully responds, "Well, you shouldn't. I'm not very religious, so there's the risk that my praying could be taken as insincere, or even an affront, which, if it's a vengeful God, could have made matters worse." Nonplussed, Abbey answers back, "Well, it didn't. So, maybe there's a clue."

More than just a cagey response, Abbey's reply is simultaneously certain and conditional, given to an agnostic who is struggling with the concept of the Divine. What Abbey's discourse confronts is that the concepts Deborah brings to bear are overly simplistic: a vengeful God who cannot know sincerity and concern and could be so easily affronted or offended, would not, by definition, be the infinite, all loving Divine. Instead, Abbey seeks to replace the simplistic and contained concepts of the Divine with mystery and openness. With utmost certainty, she delivers an enigma whose purpose is to reject simple concepts and begin a search for the unknown instead.

Long before this humorous confrontation with simplistic concepts of the Divine, the president dramatically rejects reducing faith in the Divine to following the letter of the law. In "The Mid-Terms" (S2, E3), Bartlet confronts radio talk show host Jenna Jacobs (a fictional stand in for conservative talk show personality Dr. Laura) for calling homosexuality "an abomination." When Jacobs justifies herself by using the Bible, Leviticus 18:22, the president responds by going through a laundry list of biblical injunctions that everyone rejects: selling children into slavery (Exod 21:7), killing people who work on the Sabbath (Exod 35:2), planting different crops side by side, or wearing garments made of two different threads. Bartlet's unveiled criticism does more than just underscore the relativism fundamentalism employs when it chooses injunctions against homosexuality and abandons other Divine commands, it exposes a core contradiction of fundamentalism—that merely abiding by the letter of the law reduces the complexity of faith in the Divine.

This theme is articulated again in the last season, when presidential candidate Matt Santos wades into the debate on teaching intelligent design in public schools. In "Mr. Frost" (S7, E3) Santos deftly defends the separation of church and state—but from the position of faith, not in defense of secular humanism. In making his case, the candidate emphasizes that the job of theology is to answer complex questions and the issues that they raise, not to consign beliefs into a box or a set of compact answers. The narration here is aligned with Santos's position, providing a platform for asserting the importance of a faith that struggles with complex issues and strives for the Divine, rather than be contented with simple rule following.

The concept of faith as a struggle, and a clear rejection of simplistic concepts of the Divine are the explicit focus in scenes from "Two Cathedrals," the dramatic ending episode of Season 2. In this episode, President Bartlet is struggling with his faith as a result of losing his lifelong friend and executive secretary Dolores Landingham, who dies tragically in an automobile accident. After the funeral, Bartlet confronts God in the National Cathedral, stating, "You're a son of a bitch, you know that? She bought her first new car and you hit her with a drunk driver. What? Was that supposed to be funny?" Soon after Bartlet rhetorically asks "What did I ever do to . . . [your son] but praise his glory and praise his name?" He closes his diatribe against God by stating in Latin, "*haec credam a deo pio, a deo justo, a deo scito? cruciatus in crucem! tuus in terra servus, nuntius fui; officium perfeci. cruciatus in crucem! eas in crucem*," which I translate to "Am I to believe this came from a loving God, a just God, a wise God? Put your punishments on a cross! I was your servant on earth, your messenger, I did my duty. Put your punishments on a cross, and put yourself on the cross."

Bartlet's Latin rant serves multiple purposes here. First, it reemphasizes Bartlet's Catholicism, not to mention his Latin-speaking intellect. In addition, however, it references an older concept of God: of a heavenly, kingly God who meddles in mysterious ways on earth, and strikes people down out of vengeance for sin, and wants nothing more than for people to praise his glory and his name. This is the God that Bartlet tries to barter with, listing his accomplishments and asking, "That's not enough to buy me out of the dog house?"

The narration, however, stays detached from the character during the scene. Tellingly, it appropriates a visual style that normally lends authority to a character—low camera position shooting up, tracking on movement—but these techniques keep the narration unaligned and distanced. Bartlet remains an object of examination here, not a subject to be admired. The closing shots of the scene emphasize this position. Finished venting his rage, Bartlet turns to leave, lighting a cigarette first. The shot which shows this action positions the camera extremely high and looking down, the normal way of belittling a character. After the president angrily stamps out his cigarette the camera tilts up from him, exiting to the rosetta window in the cathedral. The shot not only articulates that the scene has been looking down on him throughout, it also ends with an image of an art form complex in its composition, and dynamic in its play of light—a more appropriate metaphor for the Divine than the one the president is currently employing.

The narration then explicitly criticizes him for resorting to such a shallow concept of God in a later scene. An interiorized Dolores rebukes Bartlet by stating, "God doesn't make cars crash, and you know it. Stop using me as an excuse." Dolores's criticism ultimately realigns Bartlet with the omniscient narration. Both the president and the omniscient narration know that the Divine cannot be contained by simple concepts, a position that Bartlet sneered at in his anger and grief. Rather than the heavenly emperor, the omniscient narration, and Bartlet himself, understand that an infinite, all-loving God cannot be fully comprehended.

Throughout the series the omniscient narration of *The West Wing* rejects the apolitical, "praise his name," simplistic concepts that dominates media discourse about Christianity. Instead, the omniscient narration aligns itself with a far more radical concept of an infinite God: of a God who cannot be explained away, put in a box, or bent to partisan political purposes. The narration knows instead that the Divine is omnipresent, manifests in a variety of ways, and works through an infinite and dynamic interrelationship between individuals. The "all-knowing" narration consistently resists defining the nature of the Divine. It takes the far more radical position of knowing that it cannot know: that the Divine can be experienced, made manifest through grace, but is always unknowable.

This unwillingness to tie down a definition of the Divine is interrelated to *The West Wing's* consistent work against another metadiscourse: closure. The function of narrative closure is, precisely, to seal off the narrative from moving forward (temporally or otherwise), to suspend it in a timeless resolution built around stabilization. In this respect, narrative closure works to finalize the meanings the narrative has constructed and assigned. As a TV series, *The West Wing* is subject to less rigid forces of closure. Serialization allows television narrative to extend and suspend plot lines, introduce new obstacles or dilemmas, and bring in new characters and trajectories. While the plot in TV narrative itself does not seem to close off, individual episodes nonetheless strive to create ideological closure at the end of each episode. Almost every episode of *NCIS*, for example, closes out with the assertion of honor, duty, and some suggestion of the NRA mantra that the only solution to a bad guy with a gun is a good guy with a gun. Even while the plot might be extended, the narrative still operates to close off the kind of social interrogation that McCabe describes.

The West Wing, conversely, frequently resists that kind of ideological closure and promotes instead social interrogation. In "The U.S. Poet Laureate" (S3, E17) the character Tabitha Fortis raises the issue of the US government's refusal to sign on to a treaty banning land mines. In the back-and-forth she has with Toby, Tabitha raises issues and facts that compellingly ask the audience to side with the ban. The plot attempts to contain Tabitha's ideological threat by ultimately personalizing the issue: Tabitha is traumatized by the experience of seeing a young boy blown up by a land mine he snagged while fishing. The plot resolves her conflict with Toby and the White House by having Tabitha back down, but takes great care not to marginalize her, her trauma, or her position. Rather than a left-leaning ideologue, Tabitha is shown as principled, introspective, and humble, able to integrate Toby's arguments into her own decisions. As a result, her challenges remain valid, and remain as yet another arena for progressive ideals to carry on the fight.

In "The Indians in the Lobby" (S3, E8), C. J. is assigned to handle two Native Americans who are quietly staging a protest in the White House lobby on the day before Thanksgiving. C. J.'s first impulse as press secretary is to protect the administration from a messy situation. As the plot line unfolds, however, C. J. is drawn into sympathizing and agreeing with the Native Americans. Just as importantly, the development of the trajectory gives occasion to present the historical facts of how the US government has betrayed and mistreated Native American tribes and culture: the Dawes Act that dispossessed Native Americans of land, the Indian Reorganization Act of 1934, and the promotion of alcohol as a means of assimilation, ending with the speculation that some Native cultures will be "wiped out" in two generations. Here, the show's structure as an ensemble cast drama series plays a significant role. Because the plot follows several character trajectories, the narrative essentially reinforces the Native American issue through repetition. C. J. uncovers facts, the plot abandons her, then returns again for another encounter where more facts are produced. The repetition and return of the grievances not only emphasizes the issue, but conveys the sense of depth and scope to the issue. Rather than close off and contain the issue, C. J.'s resolution—to set up a meeting with the appropriate people on Monday—is an invitation to join in and explore the history of genocide, betrayal, and maltreatment of Native Americans and their culture.

The actual ending to the series shows this same kind of resistance to closure. The series closes out with former President Bartlet and his wife Abbey flying home to New Hampshire. Bartlet has just unwrapped a gift of enormous sentimental value: a napkin that Leo had framed and upon which he had first lured Jed to run for president by writing "Barlet for America." When he discovers it is the napkin, Bartlet is visibly moved, and walks over to Abbey, who has been sitting by herself this whole time. Bartlet then hands the framed napkin to Abbey, whose facial expression registers that she understands the meaning of the gift. He then sits down next to Abbey and stares out the window. When Abbey asks, "What are you thinking about?" Bartlet continues to stare out the window, but responds, "Tomorrow."

Bartlet's response is a clear method for the narrative to resist closure. Instead of finalizing things, it opens the narrative out for speculation—not so much about Bartlet, but about the social possibilities that he is clearly dreaming of. Moreover, the image that follows his response, of the 747 banking left over the Atlantic Ocean as the sun gleams across its surface, finalizes the core role that Christianity exercises within the narrative. Jed's reflecting on the future motivated by a symbol of the love between him and Leo, leads to an image of where that love is supposed to lead: the kingdom. The image of the 747 floating above the earth is particularly significant here. The breathtaking view of the earth from above allows Jed—and by extension, the viewer—to witness the beauty of the world as creation. Flying to New Hampshire, as it is, the view from the plane could have been any number of natural views of mountains, forests, or farmland. Instead, this image is crafted from the three first elements of creation in Genesis: water, light, and sky. The world that Bartlet views is a world without sign of the devastation frequently wreaked by humankind. Rather, it is a pristine world that speaks the beauty of creation, an image of the beauty that a redeemed world would resemble. Reminded of his love for Leo, and the role that it played in their collective struggle, Bartlet dreams of such a redeemed world as the narrative ends. The viewer, by extension, is left dreaming for it too.

The West Wing's resistance to closure is intimately tied to the final site of counter-hegemonic operation at the level of metadiscourse: individualism. Just as ensemble cast TV drama is less rigid with the metadiscourse of closure, it is also more porous with respect to the individualized structure of narrative. With ensemble cast drama, the story is less controlled and centered around a single main character. Similarly, supporting characters are less defined as merely helpers to the main characters. The ensemble structure allows the plot to focus on any character at any point in time, to elevate them to the principle concern of the narrative. The fluidity of plot trajectories and character focus, however, has limits. Within the ensemble cast genre there are still minor characters who never receive plot lines, Bonnie and Ginger, Larry and Ed, and even Leo's executive secretary Margaret never achieve the focus of plot trajectory.

Even with a system of character hierarchy, *The West Wing* demonstrates that the ensemble cast drama can place more emphasis on the mission, journey, or purpose of the collective, rather than main character itself. *Hill Street Blues* (1981–87) can continue with or without Captain Frank Furillo, and even *Grey's Anatomy* (2005–) can operate without title character Meredith Grey (the introduction of Meredith's stepsister, Lexie Grey, all but prepared for that possibility). For all its emphasis on hedonistic sexuality and romantic sexuality (and there is a lot of emphasis on sex in the series), not to mention material comfort and economic security, *Grey's Anatomy* still places the collective mission at the top of its narrative hierarchy: striving for better care in health care. In the narrative world of *Grey's Anatomy,* individual surgeons must be innovative and talented, but the plot makes clear over and again that above all, they must care. To the degree that *Grey's Anatomy* operates counter-hegemonically (and that's a hard case to make), it is the unceasing insistence that faced with an overwhelming health care system driven by profit—and at times outright corporate greed—the individual surgeon must be the site of resistance through their care, not just for their patients, but their colleagues as well.

The West Wing does more than simply adopt the structure of ensemble cast drama and its de-emphasis on the individual, it operates counter-hegemonically through the specific collective mission that moves the plot forward. The interrelationships between Bartlet and his staff—Leo, Josh, Donna, C. J., Toby, and Sam (and then by extension, Charley and later Will)—function under a collective mission to advance the cause of progressivism. As the narrative makes clear in the end, however, the actual mission of the collective was nothing short of what Christianity describes as "kingdom building."

Certainly, the narrative successfully conforms to the ensemble convention of creating endearing characters. The group is lead by the president, a commanding personality who is rooted in a profound intellect and deep moral center, and Leo, the craggy but caring pragmatist. All the other supporting characters likewise bring endearing qualities to the collective: Josh is driven but vulnerable, Donna the voice and honesty of the "Average Joe" (as well as unrequited love for Josh), C. J. the consummate professional who holds her own in a man's world while maintaining her femininity (but with careful attention to avoid projecting a sensuous sexuality), Toby, who brings moral depth and commitment to being irascible, and Sam for being the strikingly able but unassuming second fiddle to whoever needs him. Despite the attention to detail spent on the individual characters (and the details are so well crafted that this group of actors received no less than fifteen Emmy awards) the emphasis is not on the characters themselves, but on their role in the process: where and how they succeed and fail in advancing the ideals and agenda of progressivism. Within the process, however, the emphasis on the group's interrelationships functions to stress another process, the group's journey towards creating the loving community and the struggle to build the kingdom.

Even the subordination of the core group of senior staffers to the idealized Bartlet operates within this journey. Rather than creating the ideal collective coming into consciousness, or even more, the ideal collective achieving its goals of social transformation, the show presents a particular stage of the collective as it struggles to realize itself as a particular kind of collective: the loving community. With only one staff member defined as practicing a formal religion, the staffers are instead more defined by their professions and achievements—as are most people in American society. Moreover, as a group, they are defined by the particular skills and abilities they bring to the operation—as is demonstrated when both Toby and Josh, on separate occasions, attempt to perform C. J.'s job at press conferences and fail miserably.

Through serializing the narrative, however, the show demonstrates how much these core structures of the collective function as obstacles to the group forming the loving community they are one stage away from realizing. The cohesiveness and personal closeness of the group, asserted and sometimes problematized in almost every episode, signifies more than just "good friends." Rather, through the trajectory of the series, the narrative grows the collective, moving them from just partners in the noble struggle, to the loving community engaged in the struggle—willing to risk it all for each other.

Significantly, it is Toby who both introduces and closes this trajectory. In the pilot episode, Toby goes against his best professional instincts and sticks his neck out for Josh, telling him, "I'm going to make a suggestion, but I don't want this gesture to be mistaken as an indication that I like you." For the two Jewish characters, it is a line evoking typical Jewish wry humor (as opposed to Jewish rye bread). The line also works to define Toby as the curmudgeon of the group. Lastly, however, the line also works as a classical joke, which, as Freud demonstrates, belies the truth of the statement that the humor attempts to cover over. Toby does like Josh, and at some level, desires Josh to know that he likes him.

Just as significantly as the verbal discourse here is the discourse of gesture. Richard Schiff, who plays Toby, masterfully changes his facial expression as he informs Josh that "It's my job to tell the president that from a PR standpoint, the best thing he can do is to show you the door." Right as the line shifts to "to show you the door," Schiff changes his expression from hard intensity—conveying his professionalism—to a softer, intense, ambivalence—chiefly conveyed by switching from a direct stare (signifying in this exchange confrontation and one-upmanship) to scanning across Josh's face (signifying a searching, a questioning). At the same time, music comes up from the soundtrack, underlining the dynamic that has just transpired—the movement from the professional to the personal as key to the collective.

That this collective coming into consciousness is defined through Christianity—is something like the body of Christ—is outlined by the concluding scene of the first episode. Here, the staff gathers in the Oval Office, reveling in their victory over a group of Christian right-wingers. Their self-congratulatory glee is quickly brought to a close by the president, who calls them into account for letting their focus drift to the personal at the expense of the professional (which, he will make clear, is the site of the struggle). The president's bringing them back to earth is fundamental for defining the dialectical structure of what a realized Christian collective would be like. On the one hand, the ambitions (and pride) of work must be subordinated to the individual relationships at stake in the collective. Conversely, the actual mission of the collective—the goal of realizing the kingdom of God here on earth—and the kinds of personal sacrifices they require, are precisely what prevents a realized Christian collective from being a 1970s style, "I'm-OK-you're-OK," feel-good-about-yourself commune.

That kingdom building is the enterprise here, the realized Christian collective the goal, is articulated in the scene in two distinct ways. The first is the president's introductory remarks to the staff—his transitional device for "get back to work!" He chooses a story about his granddaughter Annie and a press clipping she found of a little girl in Chile who had sliced opened a tomato and discovered that the flesh inside had formed a perfect rosary. For the president, the point of the story is that theologians remarked on what a very impressive girl this was, while for Annie, it was the tomato that was impressive. The president then tosses the story aside, commenting, "Don't know what made me think of that." He then goes on to describe for the staff how Naval intelligence reports that approximately 1,200 people left Cuba in the morning, with approximately 700 turning back due to severe weather, another 350 missing and presumed dead, and 137 arriving in Miami. He then observes, "With the clothes on their back they came through a storm, and the ones that didn't die want a better life, and they want it here." He then informs the staff that their break is over.

Although at first glance the Annie story seems unrelated to what follows, it nonetheless functions as a framing device. The president's observations about the Cubans seeking freedom in the US defines the parameters of the struggle for the collective: the struggle is not about politics, but rather, a life-and-death struggle for building the kingdom. Within the confines of the Oval Office it would be easy to define the discourse as more predominantly about America as the "beacon of freedom" or other secular characterization. The problem with such a conception is that first, it elides the manner in which those constructs draw on the imagery and aesthetics of Christianity to begin with. Secondly, the unrelated Annie story, coming as it does right before, injects theology back into defining the struggle, to make clear that the struggle is more than noble, but reaches beyond: towards the transcendent that endows "noble" to begin with.

This dialectical relationship between the individual and the struggle is at the core of the culmination of the collective—when the staff comes to terms with meaningfully disintegrating as a group. The climactic point of meaningfully disintegrating occurs in a scene between C. J. and Toby in "Institutional Memory," the second-to-last episode of the series (S7, E21). In this scene, C. J. is now the outgoing White House chief of staff, who has been asked to stay on as a special advisor to the incoming President Santos. Toby has gone from White House communications director to losing his job by leaking classified information to the press. When C. J. comes to visit him, he is awaiting sentencing. C. J.'s visit follows a similar visit by Josh in episode eight of the same season, "The Undecideds." Josh's visit is such a confrontational disaster, that he returns the next day in a failed attempt to repair the relationship. Their conversation ends with a subtle détente over why Toby does not support Josh's candidate Matt Santos.

C. J.'s visit to Toby is likewise predicated on professional matters, but unlike Josh's visit, a member of the collective has already passed on. Leo McGarry has died, and while Toby attended the funeral, he did so by himself. With Toby having removed himself from the close-knit group, and Leo dead, the collective is slowly and painfully coming apart.

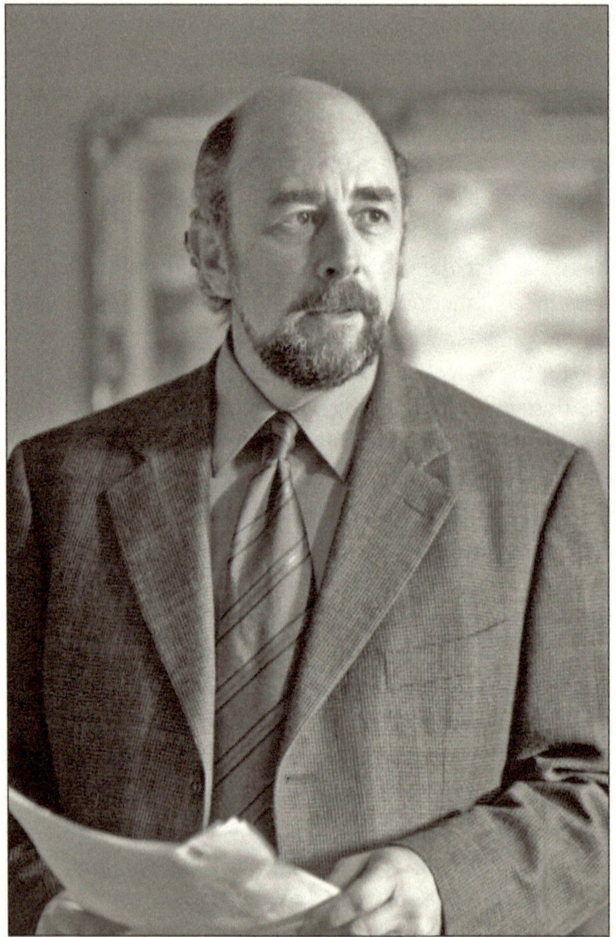

Toby's departure from the staff represents the unraveling of the community.

Facing the inevitable dissolution, C. J. visits Toby—now a political pariah—after his former wife pleads his case for a presidential pardon. As the scene unfolds, however, it becomes clear through character interaction that the presidential pardon was a pretext. The occasion has more to do with their relationship, and the disintegrating collective they once comprised. The scene is conducted in signature *West Wing* style: outstanding and nuanced performances, deft camerawork, and razor-sharp dialogue that shifts directions with the delicate turn of a phrase. The trajectory of the interaction thus goes from polite pleasantries to confrontation, to cooling off, to personal healing, and finally, healing the relationship.

The confrontation between the two characters occurs when Toby puts an end to pleasantries and moves the conversation explicitly into their friendship, telling C. J. "for a moment I actually thought you came here because you gave a crap, and wanted to see how I was doing," to which C.J. responds, "I gave a crap enough to inquire if you wanted a pardon, despite the fact that you walked out on me, and walked out on the president while we still had a job to do." In her response, C. J. moves the discussion from their friendship to their mission as a collective. Her anger at Toby is not so much the betrayal, nor the national security upheaval that he caused, but rather, his forsaking the group's collective struggle, knowing the price would be severing relationships and leaving everyone else to carry on with the work.

Just as significant as the personal confrontation, however, is the resolution between Toby and C. J. Unlike Josh, C. J. has a stronger sense of purpose in visiting Toby. Where Josh is ostensibly visiting to maintain the relationship, his motivation also lies in the future political struggle. C. J.'s motivations, conversely, are more about the group and how it evolves in the future. As a result, she is able to let the confrontation run its course and wait out a resolution. When they do come to reflect on their situation, C. J. remarks, "We had it good there for a while," to which Toby responds, "Yeah, we did." The dialogue here inserts the collective, and the collective struggle back into the scene—emphasizing that the core of the personal relationship was the mission of the collective.

The scene's closing further operates to define the status of the collective, even as it launches a new trajectory. As C. J. prepares to depart, Toby thanks her for bringing up the option of a pardon. C. J. demurs, but Toby insists that she own the healing gesture. The two then engage in a long embrace before C. J. exits. Though a simple enough gesture signifying the closeness of the relationship, the embrace conveys much more. First, it signifies the healing that has taken place in the relationship: the betrayal, the self-imposed silences, the distance and detachment have now all been dispensed and the relationship restored. In addition, and obvious to the scene but not explicit to the series, the long and affectionate embrace underscores the love that the characters hold for each other. Coming, as it does, on the eve of the collective's dissolution, the embrace belies the core purpose of the group: not just to strive to make the world a better place, but to be themselves the loving community that is foundational to building such a place to begin with.

The fate of the loving community in the face of its dissolution becomes a major theme as the series concludes in the episode "Tomorrow" (S7, E22). The episode is structured around a comparison of the two groups on inauguration day: the incoming Santos administration, and the outgoing Bartlet administration. As Bartlet prepares to leave, however, the issue of giving Toby a presidential pardon looms over the president. What the plot makes clear, however, is that the context for considering the pardon is not the political arena, but rather, the responsibility of the individual to the collective. Bartlet's interactions with Abbey, his wife, and C. J., his chief of staff, articulate this discourse.

In two scenes with C. J., the issue of Toby's pardon is explicitly addressed. In the first, C. J. hesitates to hand over the pardon and clemency warrants that need the president's signature, knowing that Toby's pardon is one of them. The president, however, informs her, "I haven't decided to do it." When he asks if C. J. has an opinion, however, C. J. refrains from giving either political assessment or advocating on Toby's behalf. Instead, she offers her faith in the President by stating, "I'm sure you'll do whatever you think is best." In the next scene, it is Debby, the executive secretary, who is pushing the president to sign the warrant when C. J. walks into the office. C. J. enters to give the president a gift from Leo's daughter Mallory, who, unbeknownst to everyone, has sent on the "Bartlet for America" napkin. C. J. admits to the president that she was going to ask Debbie to send it on the plane, and then leaves the rest of her explanation hanging. She has sought one last audience with the president—one last moment to acknowledge their journey together in the presence of Toby's pardon. C. J. implicitly draws attention to that when she stares down at the desk and acknowledges only one of the two documents on the president's desk: the letter to incoming President Santos. Toby's pardon remains in the unspoken realm of the president doing what is best. For his part, the president acknowledges their journey by stating, "It's been a pleasure Claudia Jean," to which C. J. replies, "The pleasure has been mine, sir."

The exchange is at once formal and highly personal. The sentences themselves are at best cordial, professional, farewell lines, but the delivery from each character expresses a warmth and devotion that transcend the literal. As a result, the interaction between the characters attempts to sum up the journey of a collective that has struggled together, yet left only two remaining. The significance of that toll rests on Bartlet as soon as C. J. leaves and he resigns himself to contemplating Toby's fate. Sitting in his chair behind the desk with Toby's pardon, a beleaguered Bartlet gazes upward, the weight of his decision bearing down on him. C. J.'s prompting—her faith in the president to do what he knows is right, and her subtle but powerful injection of Leo's memory and legacy into the moment—helps point Bartlet away from politics and towards the interpersonal relationships of the collective. Bartlet's gesture upward thus conveys a sense of looking for strength to forgive the individual far more than it does contemplating fallout for a political decision. Guided by both his morality and his faith, Bartlet makes the decision to forgive Toby.

Although Bartlet's decision is brief, the significance of the scene to the series and its counter-hegemonic discourse is significant. Bartlet's decision demonstrates the interrelatedness of the plot's focus on the collective with its resistance to closure. In making Toby's pardon, Bartlet performs his last official executive action as president, closing out two different trajectories: the Bartlet presidency and the fate of the collective. Each of those trajectories, however, resists closure. As the plot makes clear, the president has no more capacity to take executive actions, but he still has to function in an official capacity by attending the inauguration. Moreover, as the plot also makes clear, he will need to consider his role as a former president.

Likewise, with the pardon, Toby will not go to jail, but that is the only certainty. What lies ahead for Toby and his relationship with the president is still a continuing matter. A framing device that opens the final season gives some indication, but leaves enough gaps to make the ending less final that it would seem. In a future opening of the Josiah Bartlet Presidential Library, the president greets what is now a small group of former staffers, including Toby. The president thanks him for coming by, stating, "Glad you could make it." Toby replies by thanking Bartlet for the invitation, and the ensuing two-sentence conversation implies that Toby is now at Columbia University, but withholds any other information. Their conversation and demeanor implies that this is their first encounter after the pardon, but the plot refrains from being conclusive.

As a framing device for the entire season—and series—the scene is purposefully enigmatic, but it nonetheless brims with story information. The president greets and briefly converses with each guest, the conversations indicating what each individual is doing now. It is clear that the group has now parted ways, and it is equally clear that each is living a more or less contented and successful life. The summary nature of each conversation, it polite casualness and brevity, however, indicates the narration's detachment from the scene. No character or his or her current professional life is denigrated, but neither is it validated. There is an emptiness to the scene—a tangible chemistry that is no longer there: the bond of the collective in their continuing journey to realize themselves as the loving community struggling to build the kingdom. Sentimentality and affection have replaced interdependency and love.

The role of the kingdom as the underlying goal of the collective is underlined in the introduction to the last episode. The plot begins by surveying a number of characters and how they are starting a momentous day: The inauguration of a new president. The survey stops at President Bartlet as he gazes out the window of the White House residence. Abbey enters the room and begins bantering with Jed, but he is too pensive and detached, so she finally assures him, "You did a lot of good, Jed." She gets no verbal response from him, so she repeats, "A lot of good" before reaching her hand out to him. Later, on the limo ride back from the inauguration, Jed shows the same kind of detachment, staring out the window as Abbey makes small talk. Then she tries to reel him in by stating, "Jed, you made it." When Jed looks at her with no response, she continues, "You're still here."

There is a striking difference in the interpersonal dynamics between Abbey's scenes with the president, and C. J.'s, who is still holding faith for a pardon. With C. J., the president is warm, engaged, and emotional, whereas with his wife he is detached, pensive, and inaccessible. The difference in Bartlet's demeanor articulates a discourse about the collective, their interrelationships, and their journey. Jed is detached from Abbey's conversations because Abbey mistakenly believes that Jed is thinking about the end of his time as president and all the work he has performed. His responses indicate that his thoughts are elsewhere. As his interactions with C. J. start to indicate, and the final shot of the show confirms, Bartlet's thoughts are not on politics and the presidency, but rather, on kingdom building and the collective. In this manner, the narrative insists that its story—as such—was never about the individual, nor constructed around Bartlet as a great individual, a lesson in leadership. Rather, the story was always about the individuals as they join in the fate of the collective, and the obstacles to the collective realizing itself as the loving community and all it entails.

Far from being a radical text, *The West Wing* operates seamlessly, comfortably, and masterfully within the reigning aesthetics of television narrative. Rather than simply—and unconsciously—adopting the dominant ideologies that work through those aesthetics, however, the show makes a conscious effort to work against it. Significantly, it demonstrates that, indeed, a popular culture text can operate against the metadiscourses conveyed through style and structure. As the previous discussions of individualism and closure demonstrate, *The West Wing* is never comfortable with the world of secular politics—even its promise to work for a better world. Instead, the show consistently yearns for more: for a beyond to the promise of a secular version of equality, justice, and a better life. Episode after episode points to the transcendent, strives to glimpse at it, to bring it into view with all the aesthetic force it carries. The series insists that there is something more to strive for—not electoral success, or even power itself, but rather, the kingdom and the loving community it requires to help build it.

CHRISTIANITY AND TELEVISUAL AESTHETICS

The critical and popular success of *The West Wing* make it an object lesson for many different endeavors, not the least of which would be entertainment television itself. In rethinking the aesthetics of Christianity, however, *The West Wing* has three specific aesthetic principles that merit analysis: metadiscourse, didactics, and organicity. All of these principles are part of televisual style, and have been used successfully in other shows, but *The West Wing* was particularly successful in deploying them to advance its own counter-hegemonic agenda.

The previous discussion of metadiscourse is significant because it draws attention to the manner in which both style and structure function as a discourse—even outside of narrative. A clear example is found in the papacy of German academic and Cardinal, Joseph Ratzinger, who became Pope Benedict XVI. In choosing to wear magisterial ermine and red pointed shoes, Pope Benedict sought to restore grandeur to the papacy, hoping to create an image of a pristine church whose orthodoxy would inspire people to return. In choosing magisterial style, however, the Pope drew upon the style, iconography, and discourse of the imperial and medieval church: a church of the haves and have-nots, of power and authority, empire and exclusion. A religious faith that offers a steadfast critique of earthly power, and a constant concern for the poor and marginalized was now choosing to return and reemphasize a past that was nearly completely incongruent with its core beliefs.

Likewise, the harsh criticism and subsequent investigation of the Leadership Conference of Women Religious that began under Benedict's papacy showed a callous, if not careless, lack of regard over structure. The investigation, initiated in 2008 by Vatican officials Cardinal Franc Rode and Cardinal William Levada, sought to bring women religious orders into doctrinal orthodoxy on issues of homosexuality, ordination, and feminist theology in general. Rode, for example, accused American women's religious orders of "a certain secular mentality that has spread in these religious families and, perhaps, also a certain 'feminist' spirit."[90] As the media reported, Pope Benedict believed that American nuns did not speak out enough in terms of condemning abortion, homosexuality, and women's ordination.[91] In praising their work in the arena of social justice before offering its criticism, the

Vatican could not help but offer a discourse that American nuns spent too much time with the poor and not enough time protesting abortion and homosexuality.

In terms of structure functioning as a discourse, however, the Vatican was particularly tone-deaf to the discourse created by empowered and personally enriched men criticizing and exercising power over women religious, who take a vow of poverty and function as the face of the church for the poor, the sick, and the marginalized. The accusations of "feminism" by an elite group of powerful men reinforced the image of the Vatican as hopelessly, and recklessly, patriarchal (at the time, the disgraced Cardinal Law, guilty of ignoring clergy sexual abuse, and a key player in initiating the proceedings, was nonetheless earning $10,000 a month heading up Santa Maria Maggiore in Rome). Likewise, the emphasis on more doctrinal congruity, with increased vocal opposition to homosexuality and abortion, and less emphasis on working with the marginalized, conveyed a discourse of a church that seems irredeemably concerned more with orthodoxy and church bureaucracy than serving the needs of the marginalized, the clearest mandate in all the Gospel accounts of the life of Jesus. The discourse that the entire process created was so antithetical to Christianity that Cardinal Sean O'Malley emphatically described it as a "disaster."[92]

A new aesthetic of Christianity needs to take into account the discourses that both style and structure convey. The response of the Leadership Conference of Women Religious is just such an example. Faced with an elite hierarchy trying to impose orthodoxy from above, the sisters took their case on the road to the people. Spearheaded by Network, a Catholic, progressive, Washington-based lobbying organization that promotes social justice, American nuns organized "Nuns on the Bus," a nine-state bus tour highlighting the social justice work that nuns perform. The tour stopped at homeless shelters, food pantries, schools, and health care facilities run by religious orders. In organizing the tour, Network showed all the communications savvy of a lobbying organization. Where the powerful Vatican speaks through a hierarchical bureaucracy, Nuns on the Bus spoke "on the ground." Unlike powerful Vatican officials who travel by plane, the nuns traveled by bus—the least expensive mode of public transportation. More than just swaying public opinion, Nuns on the Bus moved towards engendering the values of Christianity into the structure of its discourse.

In addition to showing how aesthetics function through metadiscourse, *The West Wing* is a veritable primer on the concept of didactics. The earlier discussion of the narration's discourse against the death penalty delineates an intricate rhetorical assault against the death penalty that is masterful in undermining opposing arguments, creating consensus, and most importantly, providing a road map to victory. What is particularly significant, however, is the manner in which the narration accomplishes this without being "preachy." The narration has a clear opposition to the death penalty, but that position is relayed through delicately orchestrated plot interactions between character dynamics, setting, music, and camerawork. *The West Wing* clearly learned from Hollywood how to sell its ideology through a soft sell approach: letting style do the work to create implicit, but nonetheless understood, discourse.

The West Wing became so good at didactics that it soon turned to teaching the Democratic party how to win at electoral politics. In "Gone Quiet" (S3, E7) the fictional character Bruno Gianelli offers a corrective to the actual Democratic failure to stand up and punch back against Gingrich-era Republican criticisms that made "liberal" a bad word whose function was equating Democrats with being soft on crime, Communism, and defense. By seasons six and seven, the show was even more didactic: offering a blueprint for how Democrats could take back the White House. In creating the character Matt Santos (portrayed by Jimmy Smits), *The West Wing* showed what kind of progressive coalitions could win presidential political campaigns by offering a Democratic presidential candidate who was young, ethnic, eloquent, and religious. The Democratic party followed that formula by nominating Barack Obama, and found the victory that the show predicted would come. Here too, however, the lesson is conducted implicitly, through the dynamics of character and plot.

For decades now, a good deal of film and media studies scholarship has positioned itself to work against Hollywood's inculcation, its clear goal defined as attempting to raise the consciousness of audiences to the kind of manipulative, implicit messaging conveyed through narratives. Comparing the finesse of Hollywood with the hopelessly heavy-handed messaging of institutional Christianity, however, allows us to see that messaging occurs on a spectrum between manipulation on one end, and heavy-handedness on the other, not a strict moral borderline. In other words, it is possible to adopt the aesthetic principles of Hollywood messaging without resorting to cold ideological manipulation. *The Spitfire Grill* (1996) is a clear example of just such an approach, though, ironically, Caryn James of the *New York Times* accused it precisely of just that. Fellow *Times* reviewer Gustav Niebuhr saw a well-made film asserting the values of reconciliation and redemption, that "barely mentions God."[93] James, however, recoiled at the idea that an order of Catholic priests financed a film where it could assert its values, commenting that the film is:

> An effective button pusher . . . [and]resembles an "Afterschool Special" about forgiveness. But watching it with the Sacred Heart League in mind makes all the Biblical imagery seem slightly sinister. When Marcia Gay Harden takes the heroine to meditate in a deserted church, it's hard to forget where the movie's money came from.[94]

James's agenda, however, belies the success of the aesthetic model that *The Spitfire Grill* put forward and *The West Wing* replicated—although there is actually little biblical imagery in the former, and little hesitation to use it in the latter.

The irony of James's criticism lies in her outrage that a religious order is the authority behind a film message. Ignoring the concept of hegemony, James seems incensed that Christianity would engage in the same practice that corporate conglomerates undertake. More to the point of Christian aesthetics, the Hollywood style hides the authority behind its messaging, and several scholars have commented as such, but, in some ways, that is an oversimplification. The Hollywood style engages in the play and interaction of symbols, and that, in itself, is not *de facto* immoral. Indeed, in his role as the head of the Roman Catholic Church, Pope Francis consistently attempts to diffuse his authority in and through his messaging, rather than disguising it, like a Hollywood narrative, or flaunting it, much like his predecessors.

Institutional Christianity is so unpracticed at a more symbolic, less heavy-handed didactics because its two main forms of communication—sermonizing in liturgy and issuing statements from its top officials, both structure authority into the message. For the most part, institutional Christianity lacks communications infrastructure. To be more precise, the communications infrastructure of institutional Christianity is so dispersed and independent as to be atomized and alienated, underdeveloped and ineffectual. The advantage of this independence is that no one person or elite cabal can determine message content and style. There is no Stalin to suddenly announce that montage is dead and from now on, only Socialist realism is acceptable. The downside, however, is that tiny, underfunded fiefdoms are in competition with each other and there is little to no way to cultivate the aggregate creative and intellectual potential and be more productive. In the final chapter I talk about the kinds of structural changes necessary for institutional Christianity to create more coherent, more productive communications infrastructure, but here the point is that a more skillful didactics is crucial for vitalizing the aesthetics of Christianity.

Finally, drawing as it does on televisual style, *The West Wing* demonstrates the effectiveness of organicity: of using the style of signifying elements to insist on a fundamental, organic, relationship between signifiers. The extended analysis of the music montage that closes "7A WF 83429" illustrates this point. Through the use of dissolves, the scene makes clear the interconnectedness between the president and Leo, their past actions, and Zoey's fate, but also, the crowd that gathers in vigil, the shrine they construct, Donna and Josh who witness it, the family gathered at mass, and the priest and his altar attendants. More than just the signifying elements working in harmony, here, the signifying elements insist on the organic unity of all things: that an underlying connectedness that cannot be defined or delimited is nonetheless always present.

While enhanced by the cinematic/televisual technique of the dissolve, organicity certainly does not depend upon it, as the conclusion of "Posse Comitatus" (S3, E23) demonstrates. In this scene, the president has just given the order for the assassination of the fictional Qumari Defense Minister, who secretly engages in terrorism. The president both makes the decision and waits for the results while viewing a performance of the fictional musical "Wars of the Roses." The scene uses irony and cutting between four spaces to underline the interconnectedness of all the characters and their actions. The plot embeds irony by making the specific performance a benefit for Catholic Charities. The Catholic Bartlet wrestles with his Catholic moral teachings, and loses, at the same time that he is supporting a benefit for Catholic Charities. In addition, the play itself contributes to the irony: it is a morality play that mirrors Bartlet's own moral struggle—in which he will come up short.

The irony unfolds, however, by cutting between the spaces. As the play ends with the chorus singing of peace and duty, we see the assassins unpack their weapons in anticipation of killing their target, the NSA staff waiting in the Situation Room, and Bartlet witnessing the play. As the chorus sings the refrain, "And victorious in war, shall be made glorious in peace," Bartlet is shown receiving the news that the assassination was successful. As the musical number climaxes with the chorus repeating the refrain, Bartlet is subsequently shown first in shadow, then in a profile silhouette through the curtain to his box seat. The contrast between the stage and the now obscure president is pointed: the Catholic Barlet is failing in his moral leadership.

All of these stylistic elements work to draw the connections between the signifiers. Bartlet's decision has led to the assassins doing their work, the musical amplifies the morality at stake here, and the lighting makes clear that the president has failed in his personal morality. In this manner, the scene insists on a web of interconnectedness that binds the people and their actions in all four spaces, even if they are physically separated. As with much of the series, the scene constructs a melodramatic rhetoric that shifts and connects spaces to convey the sense that there is an underlying morality that links these spaces. The scene effectively emphasizes that morality—the morality that defines the president through his Catholicism—connects them to part of a greater whole that no one character can see. Rather than a modernist assertion of "the dissolution of an organic and hierarchically cohesive society"[95] that Brooks defines as the underlying epistemology of melodrama, *The West Wing* consistently asserts the reality of a moral universe anchored by the Divine—employing what John Champagne argues is a Catholic melodramatic form. Unlike Brooks, who sees melodrama as a dramatic form "for uncovering, demonstrating, and making operative the essential moral universe in a post-sacred era,"[96] Champagne argues that "melodrama is an extended problematization of the sacred, a problematization that, in different historical moments, is connected to religious belief in different ways."[97] The organicity *The West Wing* employs as an aesthetic can be understood precisely as a response to a historical moment—the crisis of postmodernism and its relegation of the spiritual to the realm of the irrational.

As discussed in the earlier chapter on *Mary Poppins,* Christianity can ill afford to cede its organic view of a connected world that is ultimately rooted and anchored in meaning, even if the totality of that meaning is inaccessible, and our ability to comprehend it limited. Nonetheless, the abyss of non-meaning that plagues modernism and modernity, which spurs postmodernism into a defense-like retreat into the play of forms and images, is neither the fate nor the limit of Christianity: which knows that there is a beyond that reconciles the terror of the abyss. Christianity, and Christians, may suffer the abyss, but that suffering has a meaning beyond—that transcends and reconciles, even if it is not wholly accessible. In this respect, organicity represents the striving of Christianity and its promise of a world made whole in and through the body of Christ.

5

Sister Act, Bruce, and *Evan Almighty*

Christianity Goes to the Movies (and Finds Freud)

Hollywood's inconsistent success with religious drama is offset by its track record with religious comedy, which has been far more dependable—or "bankable," in the industry parlance. In fact, since the 1960s every decade has seen successful religious comedies. In the 1960s, Columbia scored big with *The Trouble with Angels* (1966), featuring former Disney star Haley Mills. The film did so well it motivated a sequel, *Where Angels Go Trouble Follows* (1968). In the 1970s, Warner Brothers saw enormous box-office revenue from *Oh, God!* (1977), a Carl Reiner film that was based off an Avery Corman book and written for the screen by Larry Gelbart. The success of the film, which featured John Denver playing the straight man to George Burns, generated two sequels—all of them using George Burns as God, and all of them using comedy as a vehicle to explore the role of faith and religion in American society. In 1980, Columbia released *Wholly Moses* (1980), an Old Testament satire following the formula of Monty Python's *Life of Brian* (1979). At the end of the decade, Paramount released *We're No Angels* (1989) starring Robert DeNiro, Sean Penn, and Demi Moore in an extensive reworking of the Humphrey Bogart 1955 film of the same title.

(Except for a plot line of escaped convicts, the two films have very little in common.)

In the 1990s, comedies revolving around Christianity saw an even larger resurgence, based on the success of Twentieth Century Fox's *Nuns on the Run* (1990), produced by the British independent studio Handmade Films. The film, featuring Monty Python's Eric Idle and comedian Robbie Coltrane, added a twist to the plot of *We're No Angels*, by having the two male characters hide in a convent impersonating nuns. Much like *We're No Angels*, and the earlier *The Trouble with Angels* and *Where Angels Go Trouble Follows*, *Nuns on the Run* followed a formula where Catholicism and the culture of religious life became the backdrop and subject matter for generating comedy. Each of the films then find spaces within the narrative to bring the background into the foreground and probe theological questions about faith, grace, or religious calling/vocation.

The modest box office and critical success of *Nuns on the Run* was followed by Miramax coproducing *The Pope Must Diet* (1991) and Paramount Pictures releasing *Leap of Faith* (1992) with Steve Martin, while Touchstone Pictures produced a Whoopi Goldberg vehicle, *Sister Act* (1992). All of these films experimented with the aforementioned model of religion as comedic backdrop. Arguably, however, the biggest box-office success of the group, *Sister Act*, goes beyond the model, attempting to create a new formula. Goldberg's character, Deloris Van Cartier, is a an unsuccessful lounge singer in Reno, Nevada, who accidentally witnesses a mob hit ordered by her boss and lover. Placed in a witness protection program, Deloris hides out in a convent in a run-down neighborhood of San Francisco and must pretend to become a nun—much against her will. Frequently clashing with the traditionalist mother superior, played by Maggie Smith, Deloris finds her niche by taking over the convent's hapless choir. This causes even further conflict with the mother superior when Deloris begins infusing pop music into traditional hymns.

As further analysis demonstrates, the film establishes the conflict between Deloris and the mother superior as a means of modifying the romantic comedy genre: replacing romantic love with sacramental love. In doing so, *Sister Act* disrupts the very genre known for disruption and for representing what can otherwise be difficult or provocative content. As this chapter will show, *Sister Act* deftly structures its comedy around acceptable transgression for a number of different audience constituencies. Freud's theory of comedy, as well as other, more structural models of comedy, are particularly useful here in delineating the mechanisms that render the transgressive nature of comedy acceptable.

Freud's theory is particularly instructive because it examines the relationship between the individual—which ultimately comprises the audience—and the social discourses that govern comedy's operations. The role of the audience in relation to the humor is often overlooked in literary and film analysis, which focus instead on the structure or "the text" of comedy. In their construct, the audience can be reduced mainly to a reflex reaction of the text, or simply beyond the purview of the analysis. In comedy, however, audiences must do the work of interpreting the humor, which, as Andrew Horton argues, requires a concept of audience that is active rather than passive.[98] The activity of the audience in interpreting humor is critical for this study because, as the work of Mikhail Bakhtin demonstrates, humor operates within an ideological realm.[99]

One of the early gags in *Sister Act* demonstrates this point. Shortly after her unwilling relocation to the convent, Deloris complains to the mother superior about the inadequacy of the convent furnishings—and convent life in general—lionizing instead her previous lifestyle. In reply, the mother superior quips, "From what I've heard, your singing career was almost nonexistent, and your married lover wants you dead. If you're fooling anyone, it is only yourself. God has brought you here, take the hint." Following Jerry Palmer's theory, this gag can be analyzed structurally or semiotically, as a reversal caused by a clash of syllogisms that creates a contradictory conclusion.[100] Using this approach, it is possible to see the virtues of material life clashing against the virtues of willed simplicity. In this conflict, the conclusion is that faith in the virtues of material life—celebrity, wealth, sexual freedom—were misplaced. Material life is supposed to supply comfort and pleasure, but it really provides neither for Deloris.

Palmer's structural model points to the audience's stake in the process. The source of the humor is how the implausible becomes plausible. Within the ideology of secular humanism, material comfort is both real and satisfying. Giving up those comforts for simplicity and chastity is a fringe alternative at best. Within the structure of the gag, however, the fringe alternative is positioned as a superior way of life. The sophistication of the gag lies in its ability to appeal to several different audiences simultaneously. To a secular and/or non-Catholic audience, the gag is funny because of the reversal on Deloris: her life is so desperately not working—though she cannot acknowledge it—that anything is a better choice. For Catholics, however, the gag has another level of humor: it slips in the superiority of the ideology of Christianity over secular humanism. Within the gag, the mother superior has access to and holds a position of superior knowledge—a knowledge that this segment of the audience shares: of the emptiness of materialism and the superiority of simplicity.

Two fundamental aspects of this gag merit further exploration for aesthetic analysis: its license for ideological challenge, and its compaction of intricate theory. The positioning of an ideological alternative (Christianity) as superior to dominant ideology (secular humanism) slides by with little risk of alienating its secular audience, in part because of the license granted to comedy to challenge and critique dominant ideology. Here, the work of both Sigmund Freud and Michael Bakhtin offer significant contributions. Bakhtin's work in particular focuses on the politics of humor. Analyzing the cultural convention of the carnivals and festivals of medieval society, Bakhtin argued that these events created a space of freedom where traditional social roles and categories could be both abandoned and critiqued. In this respect, Bakhtin's work points to the material function of laughter. The medieval carnival created the physical space where social conventions can be suspended, lampooned, upended and critiqued, but laughter fills out that space. Laughter provides, simultaneously, both the personal and social release from the repression of social mandates and social roles—a process that the Disney animated film *The Hunchback of Notre Dame* (1996) illustrates in the Festival of Fools scene.

The significance of Bakhtin's work for scholars of film (and television) comedy are the strong parallels that can be drawn from his cultural analysis. Like carnival, film comedy operates within a designated social space for laughter—for humor built around social norms, conventions, and mandates. The cinema creates the designated social space both literally, in terms of the theater itself, and figuratively, in the fictional narrative space of the film. Following in the footsteps of cinema, television no longer required the physical space of the theater, but created its own space within the home, where it could operate in the established space of the comedy genre. The cultural convention of comedy provides license to challenge and critique without the immediate threat of alienating the audience. The "take the hint" gag in *Sister Act* operates through this license, upending the superiority of secular materialism and putting Christianity in its place.

The manner in which the gag avoids alienating the audience is where Bakhtin's social analysis reaches its limitations and must turn to Freud. In Bakhtin's model, the freedom created through cultural convention allows humor to be both critical and even highly political. In contemporary liberal democracies, however, the limits of that freedom are more individual than political: the risk is far more in alienating the audience than incurring the wrath of state censorship. In moving from Bakhtin to Freud and psychoanalysis, we move from a social analysis to a model of the individual that mediates the social. Freud's work on jokes provides a cognitive model that delineates the individual's stake in humor—how individual identity plays a role in the process. What Freud began to recognize in the pleasure and release experienced in laughter is the psychic investment the individual makes in specific words and their meanings—an investment that Lacan would later theorize is nothing short of the operations of identity itself.

For Freud, the underlying operation of the joke is a cognitive process: the transfer of the sign from one arena of meaning to another. Henny Youngman's classic one-liner, "Take my wife, please!" demonstrates how this transfer operates. Here, the phrase "take my wife" signifies a shortened version of a longer sentence—a contracted way of saying, "Take my wife as an example." The transfer occurs, however, when the term shifts meaning from the arena of "example" to an expression of marital unhappiness. In Freud's model, the transfer from one arena to another creates a short circuit of meaning that releases the psychic investment—cathexis—that is placed within maintaining these categories. Freud's model argues that we have a stake in the belief that marriage provides happiness, and that likewise, we also have a psychical investment in a belief that we can follow an explanation or exposition: that we have a regard for our intellectual capacity. Youngman's joke, in only four words, transfers us from one of those arenas to another, and in the process upends our normal attitude about one—revealing instead a frequently unacknowledged reality: that marriage also causes strife and unhappiness. The short circuit this transfer creates temporarily releases the energy used to maintain the investment we have in our beliefs: creating the experience of laughter.

What Freud's theory points to, and what Lacan would later elaborate on, is that the ordering and categorizing of the world is not an innate or simple social operation, but works at the level of individual identity itself: it determines and operates the sense of self. Where Lacan emphasizes the psychic investment an individual places in how they categorize the world and the world of meaning, Freud emphasizes the textuality of the joke: that it functions along a trajectory, and that the operation of the trajectory creates a transfer of meaning whose purpose is release. The implications of Freud's model is that, in its release of pleasure, the joke provides a temporary freedom from the ordering effect of the signifier that Lacan emphasizes. Freud's economic theory of jokes lays the foundation of the cultural convention of the space of freedom for humor, through a model of the individual. The joke offers a measure of freedom from the psychic investments in language and categorizations and how they comprise and regulate identity. The cultural convention of jokes, and their license to transgress, replicates this structure of freedom.

The significance of *Sister Act's* "take the hint" gag is its deployment as a setup for larger plot operations. The gag occurs early in the narrative and works to cue its Catholic and/or Christian audience that, in terms of ideology, the film is on their side: that the narrative sees Christianity as superior to secular humanism. Under the cover of a gag, however, it can do so without risk of alienating its secular audience. The joke allows a secular audience to temporarily disengage from their issues with Christianity (and formal religion) and laugh at Deloris's expense: Deloris's career is so hapless that she should try anything as an option. The gag deftly negotiates two different audience identities in its ability to create humor, and more significantly, lay the foundation for future plot dynamics.

As the story goes forward, the plot utilizes comedy's license to separate more traditional Catholics/Christians from their image of church—the church of obedience, chastity, and clericalism—to a more contemporary idea of church. The plot, in fact, uses comedy to cloak a didactic challenge, via the figure of Deloris, that the institutional church needs to change, arguing both implicitly and explicitly that Christianity needs a new aesthetic. The plot moves this challenge forward in the cultural clash between Deloris and the mother superior. Following a comical fish-out-of-water scene where Deloris enters a biker bar, followed by two other nuns, the mother superior confronts Deloris over her transgression.

The scene is important not for the manner in which it establishes the fundamental conflict between Deloris and the mother superior, but rather, for the manner in which it refrains from demonizing the mother superior—even as she is put in the role of antagonist. In her repartee with Deloris, the mother superior argues that "These walls are the only protection they have. The streets are no longer safe for them . . . . These robes no longer protect our sisters. The walls do!" The mother superior's motivation for maintaining a cloistered community is not a blind love of tradition, but rather a desire to protect her community from a fallen and dangerous world—the convent is located in a run-down and desperate section of San Francisco. This walling off from the neighborhood, however, is the logic and the response of the medieval monastery, which, finding itself in the midst of an abject and fallen society, closed itself off in the attempt to make a better world behind its walls.

What the plot makes abundantly clear, however, is that this version of church is no longer viable. The church that the convent is attached to, St. Katherine's, is in desperate need of repair—and as several explicit lines from characters indicate, the convent itself is financially insolvent. *Sister Act* advances a different vision of church that can assimilate itself into popular culture without changing its core values. By creating a conflict between a Vatican II vision of the church and a medieval understanding of the church, the film draws on the formula of romantic comedy to argue for a contemporary church without alienating traditional Catholics.[101] The film uses the formula, and comedy itself, to get traditionalists to let go of their emotional attachments to the medieval church—however briefly—in order to glimpse the possibilities of a different concept of church.

The degree to which the plot is structured around a conflict between a Vatican II version of church and a medieval aesthetic is demonstrated by the manner in which the crime caper consistently fails to move the plot forward. Rather, it is Deloris's struggles with the mother superior over a different approach to church that advances the plot. Deloris, however unwillingly at first, comes into the convent and begins to breathe new life into it, first by causing conflict, then by taking over the choir. Because she has to operate with a disguised identity, Deloris must bring her knowledge of music—and specifically pop music—into the life of the convent through the language and orientation of Catholic religious culture: she must assimilate the two. In this manner, Deloris becomes the vehicle through which the plot will demonstrate that the (medieval) church needs a new aesthetic: that rather than retreat from modernity, it needs to find ways to assimilate it in order to transform it.

The first number that the choir performs demonstrates the contours of that assimilation. The choir starts by singing a very traditional hymn: "Hail Holy Queen." The choir first sings the hymn *a cappella* and in three-part harmony, demonstrating the degree to which Deloris's skill has transformed the previously inept and out-of-tune choir. Just as significantly, by singing the first verse traditionally, the plot demonstrates that Delores and the choir could perform traditionally, that a move towards pop culture was not the easy route requiring less talent. Rather, Deloris and the choir choose to change the aesthetic of worship music: to make it more celebratory and physical. Musically, the hymn shifts from something more akin to Gregorian chant towards something more like American gospel music, complete with individual riffs.

The plot reinforces the musical shift through visual style. In the beginning, when the choir sings in a traditional style, all camera work is stationary. In typical narrative fashion, the plot cuts between different camera angles—sometimes showing the choir, at other times the reaction of the audience, and at still other times Deloris conducting. Without action to move the scene along, the plot resorts to editing different views of the choir as they sing, examining the choir through different two-shots, then returning to longer shots to take in the full choir. Each angle, however, is from a static camera position. Once the music shifts, however, the visual style of the scene shifts as well, integrating fluid camera movements that emphasize the physicality and upbeat style of the music.

In creating a marked shift between two styles, the choir reinvigorates a celebratory song. "Hail, Holy Queen" is a song based on reverence, but in its traditional aesthetic, the reverence has had the life sucked out of it—reducing it to a cerebral meditation. Deloris's reinterpretation brings ecstasy back into reverence, as the performers involve their bodies as well as, in the case of individual riffs, the limits of their voices. Sister Mary Robert's soprano riff is so high—calling to the celestial figures of seraphim and cherubim—that vocalist Andrea Robinson actually sings and actress Wendy Makkena, who portrays Mary Roberts, lip-syncs to the voice.

To underscore the goal of assimilation, the choir integrates Latin verses from another hymn, "*O Sanctissima*," singing "*Mater amata intemerata*" (pure, beloved Mother) and "*Virgo respice, Mater adspice*" (Virgin regard us, Mother behold us), each punctuated with "*Sanctus, sanctus Dominus*" (Holy, holy Lord) which belongs in neither "Hail, Holy Queen" or "*O Sanctissima*." The syncopation of the music and the beat of the hymn breathe new life in the Latin: the words resound with praise, rather than harken back to a dead, medieval time. Surrounded as they are by a dying church in desperate need of repair, the choir fills the rafters not just with music, but with dance and clapping to the beat.

Significant to the plot's argument for a new aesthetic is the synthesis that Deloris employs: drawing in from several sources to create new energy and to reinvigorate the core of the enterprise. Deloris is not engaged in pastiche, which Fredric Jameson describes as the empty play of signifiers without reference to their history. The incorporation of verses from "*O Sanctissima*," for example, interact complexly to create new meanings. The verse "pure, beloved Mother" (*Mater amata intemerata*) articulates the common belief of the sisters that Mary, one of the leaders of the early church, is the quintessential role model and a source of inspiration for women religious. Even more significant is the double meaning of "Virgin regard us, Mother behold us" (*Virgo respice, Mater adspice*). Literally, or denotatively, the verse is an intercession: the nuns praying through their song for protection and strength. In addition, however, the verse creates a connotative twist that functions even more literally than its denotative meaning. Within the context of the song is a concrete exclamation for Mary to "look at us now!" or "look at our attempt to change the church!"

In creating complex meanings through assimilation, the plot makes the case that Deloris's artistic endeavor did not change or corrupt the message, but rather made it more compelling for the audience. It makes this position clear through two developments. First, the effect of the music is almost immediate: drawing people outside the church into the service to see what is going on. In addition, the plot engineers an immediate confrontation between the mother superior and Deloris that will clarify and authorize Deloris's assimilation. Within the confrontation, the mother superior argues that the church is not a theater or a casino. Deloris responds by arguing "Yeah, but that's the problem, see? People like going to theaters and they like going to casinos, but they don't like coming to church. Why? Because it's a drag, but we could change all that." Deloris, in other words, wants to make the church meaningful by reaching people where they are at and with what interests them. For the mother superior, however, the form and aesthetic of the performance—its worldliness—taints the message, arguing that what Deloris has done is blasphemy and has corrupted the choir.

The charge that Deloris's direction for the choir is a form of corruption is not coincidental. For traditionalists, the influence of Vatican II on the church is nothing short of corruption. The plot, however, neutralizes this charge—and the conflict—through a comic one-upmanship. Chastised by the mother superior and removed from her post as choir leader, Deloris is saved by the monsignor, who enters at the height of the argument—having heard the gist of it from the other side of the door. Praising the mother superior for this change in direction, the monsignor deftly restores Deloris by giving credit to the mother superior's leadership—a delicate play between his authority and her ego. Deloris pivots off of the monsignor's endorsement to help institute another change to the life of the convent: getting the sisters involved in rehabilitating the surrounding community—again meeting with the full approval of the monsignor.

The significance of the scene is twofold. First, it advances the narrative towards a Vatican II vision of the church—overcoming the objections of the medieval church with humor as a means of bringing along traditionalists. The monsignor's cleverness, and Deloris's over-the-top praise, operate to prevent alienating traditionalists by providing laughter instead. In this respect, the monsignor's participation in the scene illustrates another important aspect of Freud's theory of the joke: that it reveals unconscious truth. Here, the truth that the humor both glosses over and reveals is a subtle reminder to traditionalists—for whom authority and obedience to church hierarchy is important—that authority cuts both ways. In this instance, clerical authority helps move away from traditionalism and towards a more Vatican II vision of church. The monsignor does more than just allow the choir to continue—he authorizes the convent to begin living as a Vatican II community: engaged with the surrounding community for the purpose of transforming it. The unconscious truth of the monsignor's discourse and actions is a reminder that, rather than a corruption, Vatican II is the authorized discourse of the church: of a church engaged with a fallen society, not retreating from it.

The figure of the monsignor himself is another site of unconscious truth—of uncomfortable history. An aging priest in the 1990s, he is of the generation of men who entered the priesthood at the time of Vatican II. That he fails to align himself with the mother superior demonstrates that he is not a traditionalist. Rather, he serves a place in the narrative to reference a demographic and historical truth: that there is a large generation of priests inspired by Vatican II but then isolated by the papacy of John Paul II and its emphasis on orthodoxy and obedience. Within the narrative he waits patiently for a return of the Vatican II concept of church—which Deloris provides.

The plot first authorizes a vision of a Vatican II church through humor, then idealizes what it would look like as both transformative and reciprocal. Mobilized by Deloris, the nuns enter into the neighborhood during a music montage: meeting people, providing food, daycare, and cleaning up the church and church yard. Likewise, the outside world begins to transform the convent: the sisters have new purpose and new work. Most tellingly, people have returned to the church and give money for its restoration. The principle sign of the reciprocity, however, is with the choir's music. Where the first musical number was a classic religious hymn revised through the music, the next musical number is a pop tune that is revised by changing one word. The choir performs the Motown hit "My Guy," but changes the last word to "God." With one small change, however, the choir transforms the meaning of the song through context. Whereas the original version is a song of a woman's romantic love for a man, the changed version is a song of vowed women's sacramental love and devotion for their God. Here, the context of the song—that it is being sung by a group of nuns—plays in the foreground, visibly transforming its meaning as a devotional.

Within the logic of the plot, the transformative power of synthesizing Christianity with popular culture is both material—changing both the church and the neighborhood—and expansive: moving beyond the neighborhood into the media—where it moves out far enough to reach the attention of the pope. It is also personally transformative, as Sister Mary Roberts awakens to her talent and her vocation as a result of Deloris's efforts (and indeed, the mother superior will likewise be transformed and find her real talents). Just as significantly, the transformation works on the narrative itself, transforming the comic form. Where the norm for modern comedy is a series of obstacles preventing the obtainment of romantic love, *Sister Act* revolves around a conflict in sacramental love. Deloris and the mother superior are in conflict over a vision of church. Deloris's vision, however, prevails—nowhere more clearly than in the announcement scene, where the monsignor informs the sisters that the pope has requested a special performance. When the mother superior suggests a more traditional program, the sisters resist, and ultimately vote for Deloris's pop culture synthesis.

This communal rejection of the mother superior's vision of church is the turning point in the plot. With the result of the voting, the mother superior recognizes that her vision of the church can no longer endure. Her response, however, is the response of the institutional church of John Paul II and Benedict XVI: to retreat even further into traditionalism. The mother superior makes plans to leave the convent in search of another community that still clings to a dying tradition. Within the logic of the plot however, this is the option that can no longer be exercised—is no longer viable and must be transformed. But where the earlier part of the film used the cover of humor to avoid alienating traditionalists, the latter part of the film plays to those identities by transforming the mother superior, and in the process, demonstrating the value of the traditional church.

As is the norm for comedy, plot crisis leads to the climax, providing motivation for the protagonist to overcome an obstacle and achieve their goal. *Sister Act*, however, changes that formula by having the antagonist overcoming obstacles and achieving the protagonist's goal. Deloris's kidnapping is a culminating act that inspires the mother superior—heretofore the antagonist—to overcome an obstacle: her fear of the fallen world around her. Deloris's kidnapping motivates the mother superior to abandon her fear and take action—abandoning her belief that she is a relic, and embracing instead her abilities as a strong woman leader. Rather than retreat into the traditional church as a means of protection from the outside world, mother superior decides instead to marshal the power of Christianity to confront the evil of the world. Here, the virtues that traditionalist practices are designed to produce become manifest. The discipline that mother superior so cherishes gives her strength of character to act decisively and effectively. More than just realizing her "self," however, which is the norm for romantic comedy, the mother superior realizes that the call of Christianity is the call to action: in this case, to attend to those in need like Deloris.

Mobilizing the sisters, the mother superior springs into action. The humor that gets generated in this scene is built around the passive-aggressiveness that the mother superior has consistently and deftly employed as well as the stereotype of Catholic guilt (itself the offspring of Jewish guilt). When a helicopter pilot refuses to fly the nuns to Reno for free, the nuns overwhelm him with fear and guilt by praying aloud for the pilot: beseeching God to protect him in ways that criticize him at the same time. The passive-aggressiveness that mother superior frequently engages in is finally rendered as productive.

Here too, the joke operates to articulate an unconscious and transgressive truth: in this case the necessity of religious tradition. Consistent with its advocacy of assimilation, the gag points to what society would be like without a culture permeated by the institutional church and its religious orders. The pilot is a nice enough guy who, when asked, offers a deep discount on the price of transporting the sisters. Within a culture of the marketplace, the pilot is acting ethically and, to a degree, generously. Until the sisters intercede, however, he is not willing to act outside of the culture of the marketplace—he is unable to actually give. Through their ritual of intercessional prayer, the sisters are able to transport the pilot out of the marketplace and into the space of spirituality—where concern for the other and generosity are the highest value.

The film underscores the dynamic relationship between these spaces by its shift in location. The next place the pilot and the sisters will find themselves in is Reno, a site where, like Las Vegas, the culture of the marketplace has gone to its logical excess: gambling. The image of Reno that the film shows is a hub of activity all built around the circulation, speculation, and risk of money. The sisters represent an entirely different culture built on poverty—or at least, simplicity—and self-denial. They act as a counterweight to the glamour of the marketplace, testifying (literally) to a higher purpose for existence.

Speeding towards its climactic scene, *Sister Act* demonstrates an enormous amount of acumen in appropriating and modifying comic form to articulate a theology of engagement and assimilation. It consistently structures its humor to appeal to both traditional and progressive Christians, as well as secular audiences who engaged in the film through the celebrity appeal of Whoopi Goldberg. In the climactic scene itself, however, *Sister Act* evidences the limitations of ideological challenge—even through the vehicle of comedy. The norm for a climactic scene in romantic comedy is for the would-be couple to realize their love for one another and join together to work against the villain. In *Sister Act*, however, Deloris and the mother superior come to realize their sacramental love for each other—joining protagonist and antagonist together to work against the reintroduced villain.

Right at the point of that realization—of the sacramental love that the mother superior recognizes in Deloris and in their own relationship—the film backs away from the transformative power of Christianity, and allows secular culture and its dependence on violence to reassert itself as the norm. When Deloris is recaptured by the gangster in the presence of all the sisters, the henchmen refuses to shoot her, fearing to do violence to a nun. Their boss, Vinny, urges them to do the crime by stating, "She's a broad, got it? Just a broad." The mother superior then steps forward, arguing, "I guarantee you she is no broad. She is Sister Mary Clarence of St. Katherine's convent. She is a model of generosity, virtue, and love. You have my word for it gentlemen, she is a nun." More than just an attempt at trying to save Deloris's life, the mother superior's words are her own realization that the virtues she uses to describe Deloris are core aspects of being a nun—that celibacy, poverty, obedience, and even cloistering are only a means to reach that end. The mother superior realizes that Deloris, who has been an antagonistic outsider, is, in fact, a cherished member of the community—she is in fact, by her virtues, a nun.

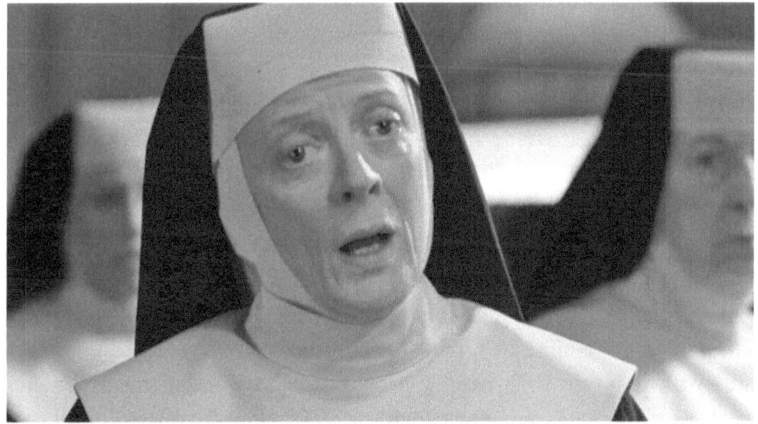

The mother superior, surrounded by the community, is on the verge of putting her life on the line for Delores, but the narrative denies that stand.

The plot, however, does not allow the weight of that conviction to reach its full potential. Just as Vinny is about to execute Deloris, the police lieutenant who has been pursuing them shoots through the glass, breaking into the room and disabling Vinny. The disruption into the plot derails the trajectory of the mother superior's character and her ability to act. Strongly committed to her Christian faith, and realizing her sacramental love for Deloris, the mother superior should be on the verge of leading the others to protecting Deloris with their own bodies—especially given the knowledge that the Catholic Italian-American henchmen are unwilling to hurt them. Rather than assert a powerful image of living out Christian mandates, the plot artificially reasserts the superiority of state-sponsored coercive force that is the cornerstone of secular society.

Just as earlier it cloaked ideological challenges within gags, here the plot covers over its abandonment of the transformative power of

Christianity with more jokes. Deloris rounds on the lieutenant by complaining "I'm glad you're a much better shot than a protector" and then confronts Vinny and says "Bless You" in the form of a "F—k you." Generically, the ideological limitation that the film came to was a tipping point between a romantic comedy and an inspirational film. The plot's insistence on secular violence restores the balance back to romantic comedy. Allowing the film to assert the efficacy of Christian nonviolence would clearly position the film within the inspirational genre, and with it, the high risk of alienating—or eliminating—a secular audience. Prior to the climax, the film is positive about secular culture, demonstrating how its assimilation can reinvigorate the church. The ideological risk to a secular audience is minimal. The climactic scene, however, contained a much higher risk. Asserting the power of Christian nonviolence would have clearly and convincingly asserted the superiority of Christianity over secular society, tipping the generic balance in favor of being inspirational. Such a balance would not only risk alienating secular audiences, it would most likely have kept them out of the theater to begin with.

In keeping with its perceived limits to ideological challenge, *Sister Act* structures its narrative around transforming the institutional church—not society itself. The closing scene of the pope enjoying the special performance from the balcony articulates this position. The scene carefully chooses a John Paul II look-alike to represent the pope—as opposed to a "generic" figure of a pope. In this manner it continues to work within the generic structure of romantic comedy: providing an ideal image of resolution to the prior narrative conflict. Here, the most powerful figure in the institutional church—and the one most opposed to modernism—is seen enjoying the performance of the sisters: a performance built around assimilating modern, secular, music with Christianity. Ironically, the musical number that is performed is the Petula Clark pop tune "I Will Follow Him," a romantic song that the nuns turn into a devotional that tells about the depth of their love and commitment to following Jesus of Nazareth. The contradiction here is that while the nuns are willing to follow, even to the point of death, the narrative itself lacks that conviction: unwilling to allow Christianity's commitment to nonviolence to reach its logical conclusion. Rather, the film chose to assert the necessity of violence in dealing with evil. As a result, the disruption that Deloris causes within the narrative, the challenges that she raises, and the transformation that she ushers in, are all consigned to the church itself: the effect on society is negligible.

In this respect, the plot of *Sister Act* is willing to use comedy to transgress, but in a very contained manner. It is willing to challenge the aesthetics of the church, but not the role of the church in broader society. Even the scenes of the church, as such, transforming the neighborhood fail to mount an ideological challenge to neoliberalist society—which calls on individuals and nonprofit organizations to remedy the inequities and the failures of the economic system. The sisters of the convent clean up the neighborhood in such a contained way that there is never the suggestion that the neighborhood, as such, is the site of government's neglect. The church literally cleans up after the government and the economic system rather than calling it into account. As a result, the ultimate vision of the church that the film articulates is a church that is transformative, but docile.

The credit sequence underscores this point. As the credits roll, the narrative continues via a series of faux magazine covers featuring Deloris and her newfound fame. The secular press reporting on Deloris renders her story as yet another human interest story. Christianity becomes the cute background from which Deloris emerges and finds the celebrity that always escaped her. The closing credit sequence thus creates a hierarchy where contemporary secular society, with its ability to grant celebrity and material comfort, are still the apex, and Christianity is a good and necessary anchor, but one that must remain in its place below. The earlier hints of social transformation that the film put forward are all neatly consigned back into confines of the church.

The plot and trajectory of *Sister Act* are notable for maintaining a delicate ideological balance between Christianity and secular-material culture—especially where audience is concerned. In the earlier part of the film, the plot uses the license of comedy to transgress ideological boundaries and place Christianity above secular culture. In addition to humor, however, the success of that transgression is also due to restoring Christianity to a subordinate position within secular culture—a positioning which kept the film from alienating a secular audience, or being identified as "religious" or "inspirational." Breaking the norm for religious comedy and transforming the genre of romantic comedy, the film created new ground for theology to enter the cinema. Even though its own sequel ended up a dismal failure, *Sister Act* became a model for *Bruce Almighty* (2003), a Jim Carrey vehicle, and its own successful sequel, *Evan Almighty* (2007), which starred Steve Carrell. More than just using religious comedies for star power, *Sister Act* demonstrated how film could use the transgressive nature of comedy to create specific discourses about Christianity—discourses freed from the normal piety and trappings usually imposed on Christianity.

FROM TRANSGRESSION TO TREATISE: *BRUCE ALMIGHTY*

The plot of *Bruce Almighty* draws on two lessons from *Sister Act*: using comedy to transgress, and using gags to pack complex theology into comedic narrative. The story revolves around Bruce Nolan, a self-absorbed television reporter played by Jim Carrey. Bruce is so obsessed with advancing his career that he is blind to the fact that he has a great life: a devoted girlfriend (played by Jennifer Anniston) who is ready to marry him, a job that makes the most of his talents, and a high degree of material comfort. Unlike his girlfriend Grace, however, Bruce has little to no faith in the Divine, and is so neurotic about career advancement and "making it" that he elevates his woes to the level of all the other worldly injustices and blames God. In response, God, played by Morgan Freeman, arranges to meet with Bruce, and hands over all his powers to teach him a lesson. Instead, Bruce uses the powers to achieve his desire—advancing his career—while ignoring all the responsibilities that come with divine power.

Where *Sister Act* used comic gags and plot devices to transgress, but then backed off, *Bruce Almighty* sustains an ongoing critique of secular humanist agnosticism, and in particular, the myth of happiness as defined by secular humanist neoliberal culture. The narrative trajectory makes clear that Bruce is empty inside, and that his object of desire—to become a news anchor—is a hollow goal that will ultimately not fulfill him. Cloaked by its humor, the narrative world is a starkly realistic rendering of contemporary society, where religious faith is hidden in the background of people's private lives, and fails to impact the behavior of most people. Bruce inhabits a world where, like contemporary culture, most people are not spiritual but professional, and sports is the high religion of culture. The primary virtues are success (at all costs) and power (which celebrity provides). Using the transgressive nature of comedy, the film offers implicit but pointed critique at secular society—its sexual hedonism, its lust for power, and its misplaced priorities—and fairly pronounces it as vacuous and empty.

The significance of *Bruce Almighty*, however, is the manner in which it uses humor to both transgress and to offer alternatives: providing sustained theological reflection through humor. The previously discussed "take the hint" gag from *Sister Act* provides an example that *Bruce Almighty* expands upon in its narrative. The unconscious truth that the "take the hint" gag reveals is that, despite appearances, God is involved with the individual's life, and does communicate, only not directly and with difficult messages that must be discerned. The gag, in fact, rejects rationalism's forms of verifiability and asserts instead that the concept of God is more complex than the omnipotent being of the Old Testament who intervenes in history and speaks directly: out of burning bushes, clouds, or the mouths of angels. The theology the gag puts forward is that God is more than an omniscient but detached and inaccessible being always at a remove from the individual. Rather, the unconscious truth the gag reveals is that God is directly involved in the lives of everyone, but the signs for recognizing that involvement are, like all signs, arbitrary: it is the individual's responsibility to discern them.

What the "take the hint" gag emphasizes is a modernist understanding of how the Divine communicates—in a manner where the relationship between signifier and signified are never guaranteed nor clear. As argued previously, Christianity, and specifically, the ministry of Jesus, is the first modernist discourse of Western civilization. The foundation for that modernist discourse is established in Judaism—whose insistence on an abstract, indefinable, deity was the first step towards an arbitrary relationship between humanity and the Divine. Although he adheres to Judaism, Jesus deconstructs Jewish theology from the religious practice of his day. The Gospel accounts show him railing continually at what he saw as strict adherence to the letter of the law in favor of the spirit of the law.

The radical message of Jesus to his contemporaries is nothing less than the fundamental lesson of semiotics: that the signifier—religious ritual—is in fact forever separated from, and has no access to, the signified: the holy. Prior to Jesus, God speaks directly to prophets—privileging those individuals who receive the message. After Jesus, however, the relationship to the Divine is equalized and personalized—everyone, especially the unclean and the sinful, now have access to God. The access and personal relationship, however, come at a cost: communication with the Divine is no longer direct, but subject to the play of the signifier, and completely dependent on interpretation.

Significantly, this will be the foundation of the first religious gag in *Bruce Almighty*. Early on in the film, Bruce is angry and frustrated at being passed over for the anchor position at the local news station. Driving in his car, and desperate for anything that will change his fortunes, he turns to prayer, as his girlfriend Grace suggested earlier in the plot. Bruce prays, saying, "OK God, you want me to talk to you? Then talk back. Tell me what's going on. What should I do? Give me a signal." As he says this, Bruce passes an electronic traffic sign on the side of the road, a sign that displays the message "Caution Ahead." Bruce, oblivious to the coincidence of the sign's message, continues to plead with God, and in response, a big flatbed truck carrying traffic signs cuts in front of him, displaying traffic messages which read: "Stop," "Wrong Way," and "Dead End." The gag here is a striking example of Freud's economic model of jokes. What Bruce sees in front of him are literal signs with specific denotative meaning. The narrative, however, causes those signs—the signifiers—to be transferred from one realm of meaning—road/traffic information—to another realm: theology of divine intervention. The humor that results is the unlikely possibility that signs with such specific denotative meaning can operate and point to another universe of meaning.

Like *Sister Act*, the gag is used to transgress: to suggest that believers in the Divine and the ability of the Divine to communicate are superior in knowledge to secular agnostics and their limited understanding. Comparing the gag to a similar gag from episode one of the fourth season of *Cheers* makes clear the transgressive critique at the heart of the scene. In the *Cheers* episode, Diane is living in a convent in Boston after having canceled her wedding to Frasier. Sam seeks her out and tries to persuade her to go back to working at the bar, but Diane refuses. In discussing the situation with the mother superior, Diane realizes how conflicted she is, and begins to pray as she mops the floor. Like Bruce, Diane prays for a sign to tell her which direction her life should go.

Diane's prayer is a significant departure for the show and its style of comedy. Prior to the episode, Diane has no explicit religion or spirituality. Indeed, her placement in the convent is only a plot device to emphasize how extreme Diane can be. The gags in the convent are constructed, for the most part, around religious life itself. The tenor of the scene shifts dramatically, however, when Diane finds herself wanting to pray. As she does, the camera cuts to a closer shot—the classical Hollywood norm for creating emphasis. Here, however, the emphasis is on a dramatic change in Shelly Long's performance. As she monologues, Long employs a subtlety and vulnerability that previous plot lines never really provide her. There is a depth of character that is rarely called for in her portrayal of a witty but brittle, misplaced intellectual. Underscoring the performance, the camera stays in a long take, also a rarity for TV sitcom, and punctuated even further by a performance that includes dead pauses (even rarer for TV comedy). The conclusion to Diane's prayer creates an even longer pause—suggesting that no sign will be forthcoming, that Diane's prayer will go unanswered.

Just as Diane is about to resign herself to that fact—that God is silent—Sam comes back into the kitchen, asking Diane for directions to the men's room. Diane sends him off in a fit of impatience with the seeming stupidity of a men's room in a cloistered convent. After Sam exits, Diane begins resuming her prayer, but then realizes that she received the sign she had been looking for. The next gag is significant for how the plot manages this departure from its norm and its foray into theology. Long imperceptibly changes her performance at the point of her character's realization: from the subtle vulnerability of the scene to her normal characterizations. She lights up with gratitude and pleasure at having been given a sign, exclaiming, "*Oh*!!!" then shifts to being slightly disappointed, stating, "Well . . . it's not the parting of the Red Sea . . .[but] that's nitpicking" and the episode concludes. The final gag, therefore, is a gag about character: only the nonreligious and secular Diane could pray to God then complain about the results. In this way, the focus is off the actual intervention and on the character instead—allowing the episode to abstain from any cultural critique by limiting the comedy to character excess.

Bruce Almighty avoids this containment through character by sharing the focus between the character and the acts of intervention, and offering a different relationship between viewer and character. In the *Cheers* episode, viewers comfortably adopt a position of superiority towards Diane because she is an extreme character. Ideological differences like believer/nonbeliever, Christian/secularist, are glossed over in favor of Diane's excessive quirkiness. The plot of *Bruce Almighty*, however, offers no safe haven from ideological critique. Bruce's continuing failure to read the signs as the answer to his prayer create a willful ignorance that finds its source less in the extreme traits of character as much as the character's agnosticism: with no faith and knowledge, Bruce does not understand how the Divine communicates indirectly. Locked within both his frustration and his ideology, Bruce is ignorant that his prayer is being answered. In this manner, the plot invites viewers to assume a superior position not just towards Bruce, but towards the ideology he embodies.

To foreground the ideology that is under critique, the plot creates a third "sign" that Bruce misses. Passing the truck, and the signs that are communicating to him, Bruce grabs Grace's prayer beads from the rear view mirror, and says to God, "OK, we'll try it your way." He then tells God that he needs a miracle, asking him to "reach into my life and . . . ." but Bruce never gets the chance to finish the statement. The car dips into a large pothole, causing Bruce to drop the beads. Here too, however, Bruce fails to see that, indeed, God gave him exactly what he was asking for: he reached into Bruce's life with a strong signal—the car hitting the pothole.

The triple deployment of the same gag is a significant plot operation. The repetition is emphasis enough on the act of divine intervention, but the escalation insists on the reality of it—hinting, in fact, that divine intervention is not that indirect. The plot reinforces this insistence of the reality of the Divine through symbolic reference—using a number that is significant to Christian theology: Christ rises on the third day, Peter denies Christ three times, the Christian God is a triune God. In making this reference, the plot signals that its employment of theology is not just cute backdrop for gags, but to use comedy—and narrative—as a means for unraveling complex theological issues. Here, the risk is not so much alienating audiences as much as boring them. Theological treatises are past the borders of popular culture for a reason: they are not engaging, even though the issues they explore might be compelling.

Bruce Almighty recasts theological treatise by placing it within the form of romantic comedy. The comedic form not only makes for more compelling discourse, but allows the ideological critique within theology to transgress—to challenge viewers at the level of identity without provoking alienation. Like *Sister Act,* the plot attempts to cultivate two different sets of viewers: religious and agnostic. For religious viewers, the plot constructs a position of superiority—allowing the viewer to watch Bruce from a place of greater wisdom. For secular agnostics, however, the construction of Bruce's character and the trajectory of plot create a subtle but clear critique that the secular understanding of the Divine is cliche and childlike. Bruce's character is carefully constructed to resemble secular agnostic viewers. Unlike his girlfriend Grace, Bruce is more of a nonbeliever than a believer. A classic agnostic, he neither cares enough nor dares enough to either deny or believe in the Divine. He does not actively disbelieve in a divine entity, but he has no cause or occasion to exercise belief per se. As a result, he has no comprehension of how to commune with God other than the clichés of pop culture: a point the plot will drive home in the narrative's culminating scene where Bruce finally learns what prayer is. What the initial gag makes clear, however, is that Bruce's lack of spirituality, combined with his self absorption, prevent him from being able to discern how God is guiding him.

The trajectory of plot will then insist that Bruce's agnosticism is the source of his self-centeredness. As a main character, Bruce is neither the hero, like Deloris in *Sister Act* nor an antihero—like the character Mookie in *Do The Right Thing* (1989). Rather, the plot creates a character that the two different groups of viewers can sympathize with, but refrain from identifying with. The plot makes it easy for both groups to side with Bruce because bad things happen to him: he is passed over for promotion at the news station, his work is plagiarized by a colleague, and he gets beaten up by a street gang for interceding in a mugging. In the same manner, however, the plot prevents both groups from identifying with Bruce because his ego gets in the way. In this manner, the plot reduces the risk of alienating secular agnostics, by creating a level of detachment from the ideology as it is embodied by the character.

The trajectory of plot, however, insists that failure to believe in the Divine is at the heart of Bruce's self-centeredness. There is an emptiness to Bruce's character that is filled only by an empty signifier: the ambition to be anchor. But while this ambition consumes Bruce, the plot makes clear that it is a hollow ambition that does not fulfill his full talent. The height of Bruce's egotism occurs in the restaurant scene with Grace. The plot shifts spectator knowledge to be aligned with Grace, who is confident that Bruce is going to propose to her. Instead, the buildup is centered solely around Bruce's announcement that he has been promoted. Rather than culminating her hopes, the event makes Grace realize that Bruce is hopelessly narcissistic—that he will never be able to go beyond himself and love her.

Even before Bruce disappoints Grace with the lack of a proposal, he is warned about his self-centeredness. Whisked out of the back alley and onto Mt. Everest, Bruce is confronted by God, who asks, "You've had my powers for a little over a week now. How many people have you helped?" Bruce justifies himself by stating that he righted a few wrongs in his life first, but the rest of the narrative demonstrates his insincerity. He is never interested in helping others, opting instead to grant all prayer requests automatically through email. Bruce is too consumed with using power to achieve his ambitions, demonstrating his inability to step outside himself and show concern for others. He is incapable of *kenosis*—the emptying of the self.

The plot's trajectory, however, makes clear that a relationship with the Divine empowers kenosis as a dialectical relationship: that an openness to the Divine leads away from the self, and allows the individual to be more other-directed. Bruce showed a spark of concern for another person early in the plot, when he interceded on behalf of the sign-holding vagrant, but the trajectory of the plot requires him to genuinely develop that concern: to make it a central part of his life. What the plot makes clear through Bruce's development is that doing good for others is not enough. It is only when Bruce is able to both witness and share Grace's pain that he is able to fully direct himself outward and achieve a measure of self-transformation.

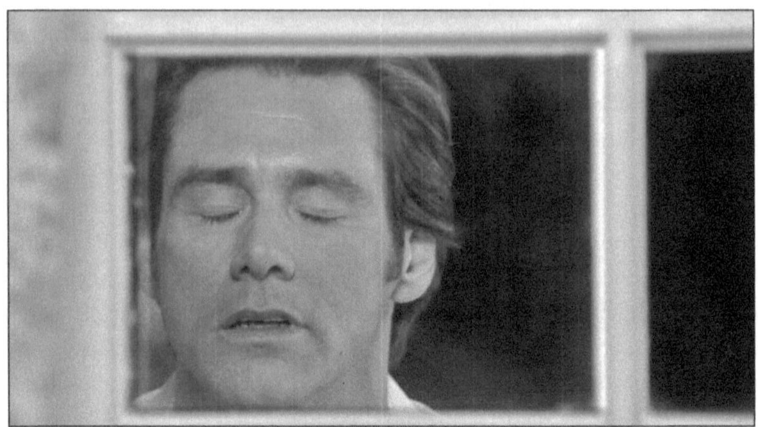

It is not until Bruce actually witnesses Grace's pain that he can begin to see beyond his own self-absorption.

Were it not for the culminating scene's commitment to a sustained theological discourse on prayer, *Bruce Almighty* would fit more comfortably into the genre of romantic comedies that use religion as comic backdrop. Instead, the plot employs several operations to privilege a treatise on the concept of prayer. Following the norms of romantic comedy, the culminating scene is the moment where the last obstacle—Bruce's self-centeredness—is overcome, and the couple can unite. The plot, however, denies the concept of romantic love, and insists on sacramental love as the very foundation by which romantic love can exist. The plot accomplishes this displacement by displacing the form of romantic comedy to begin with. By making Grace's pain the turning point that motivates Bruce's prayer, the plot both privileges prayer within the narrative while making clear that comedy was the vehicle, not the goal, of the narrative itself. Rather, the goal of the narrative is to carve out opportunities within a romantic comedy to provide concrete images for abstract theological concepts and critique—like divine intervention or the less lofty but nonetheless complex concept of prayer.

Part of the way the plot privileges its discourse on prayer is by using only cliched concepts of prayer until the turning point of the narrative. Prior to Grace's prayer, a scene that is stunning in its intimacy and sadness, the plot restricts the form of prayer to just requests and petitions to the higher being to make life better—as formal but one-way communication to what Peter Boullata describes as "the cosmic Santa Claus" in the clouds.[102] There is no alternative to this simplistic concept of prayer. Grace's prayer, however, dramatically shifts that restriction—fulfilling two narrative functions. On the level of plot, it serves as Bruce's motivation to abandon his self-centeredness and begin the search for something else. In addition, however, Grace's prayer is the inauguration of a complex discourse around the concept of prayer. Starting with Grace, the plot introduces a concept of *kenosis*—of prayer as an abstract but intense process of emptying out the self and projecting out into the spirit of the Divine.

Both in shot composition and in the content of Grace's prayer, the plot begins a slow but steady transformation away from common—and even cliched—concepts of prayer as "talking to God" and towards an image of what Thomas Keating describes as prayer as "relationship to God."[103] In terms of setting and composition, Grace is located in her room, positioned on her bed. Locating Grace in the privacy of her bedroom starts the discourse of prayer with the familiar, but also works as a literal image to the figurative concept of the "inner room" as the place for prayer. Keating describes the inner room as the first step in centering prayer. He emphasizes the figurative by stating, "The inner room . . . is not so much a place as an interior disposition of openness and surrender to God."[104] Grace's position on the bed points to this surrender. Grace does not assume a traditional pose of "at prayer" that Diane took on in the scene from *Cheers,* but rather, lies weeping on the bed, propped on the pillows, her knees pulled in, her head resting against the wall and headboard. The plot situates her within the inner room—her bedroom—but her pose and actions signify that she is trying to occupy the inner room of prayer: where she can endure her suffering by abandoning herself and her desires to God.

The camera frames Grace through the mullions of the window that Bruce gazes through. As she prays, Grace beseeches God to help her let go of Bruce—who has hurt her too many times with his self-absorption. Unlike the early scene of Bruce beseeching God to reach into his life, Grace is much more subdued, measurably less histrionic, and her prayer far more intense and intimate. Grace attempts to work through her pain by communing with God: to work through her confusion and anguish. Even as she beseeches God, it is not so much for divine intervention as it is to find what is inside her: the strength to move on. Grace reaches out—projects herself out—as a means for finding the Divine within.

Bruce's witness to the scene is an important addition to the plot's discourse on prayer. As his computer testifies, Grace's outwardly directed prayer is more than an internal process—it manifests into the space of the Divine. The computer functions itself as a silly gag for the fact that prayer has substance and power—matter and energy—that enter into and reside with the spirit of the Divine. The volume of prayer that the plot conveys through various sight gags also signifies the enormous amount of energy that is channeled through prayer. That power, the plot demonstrates, enters into the spirit of the Divine, but then returns to the individual through love: God made manifest. Even though Grace is in emotional pain and suffering, she demonstrates faith that she is not alone and is loved for who she is—even if Bruce cannot provide that love.

Grace's scene provides an alternative image of prayer that introduces an abstract theological discourse on the concept of prayer as real, tangible, and powerful. The plot reinforces this discourse through Bruce's prayer, which first engages in full-blown deconstruction of the pop culture concept of prayer: including placing Bruce in an indeterminate, cloud-filled location talking to a cosmic God. In both the segue to the scene and the development of the scene itself, the plot makes clear that this concept is a cliche that needs to be replaced with something more meaningful and real. The segue introduces the deconstructive approach by highlighting and turning on cliche. Reacting to what he has witnessed in Grace's prayer, Bruce stumbles through the rain until, overcome with anguish, he resorts to prayer. Just as with the earlier scene when he prayed, Bruce resorts to cliched, melodramatic modes. Kneeling in supplication, he calls out loudly to God, "I surrender to your will." The music soundtrack emphasizes the cliche by swelling appropriately, and the mise-en-scene does likewise—engulfing Bruce in a cosmic bright light. The plot, however, quickly turns on itself—exposing the convention by transforming it into a natural part of the plot world: the bright lights are not divine acknowledgment and intervention, but the headlights of a truck that is about to strike Bruce.

This dramatic reversal on the cliche is followed by a sustained deconstruction of prayer. Bruce finds himself dressed in an all white suit, walking through a misty area that is likewise all white. As he walks, however, the film dissolves to a reverse shot of God, whose face replaces Bruce's in the frame. Before a conversation can begin, however, the plot quickly dissolves back to Bruce's face. The use of the dissolve in a shot/reverse-shot sequence is rare in cinema, and its use here works as a special effect: Bruce dissolves into God, and God dissolves into Bruce. The purpose of the special effect is to introduce the discourse of the deconstruction: that God exists within the individual, not in the clouds—a message that the plot will reinforce several times.

The plot then undertakes a deconstruction of the man in the clouds with Bruce's inquiry. Bruce first asks, "Am I . . . ?" but before he can finish the question, God interrupts him, saying, "You can't kneel down in the middle of a highway and live to talk about it, son." Bruce, thinking he has received the answer, then asks, "But why? Why now?" God's answer, however, is once again an evasion. He responds: "Bruce, you have the divine spark. You have the gift of bringing joy and laughter to the world. I know, I created you." The last line, however, is a small joke, a set up for an even larger gag when Bruce responds, "Quit bragging." The functions of these two jokes, however, is to disguise the fact that God avoided an answer to each of Bruce's questions. The first answer appears to be direct and finite, but like all language use, is allowed to slip into other uses and meanings. It is, in fact, a declarative principle more than a direct answer—as the rest of the plot will demonstrate. Bruce, in fact, is not dead, but will not *live to talk* about that experience, either. He will indeed, live, but his will to talk about the experience will not. Rather, it will be directed elsewhere: to unite with Grace, to spread joy and laughter.

The plot's refusal to give direct answers to Bruce's queries is a deconstructive strategy. It avoids fulfilling an image of an afterlife in heaven where the celestial being lives and all will be made known. The gags distract Bruce's attention from the evasion, and instead, provide a segue to the culminating point of the plot: Bruce's prayer. Before it allows the narrative to culminate, however, the plot employs another deconstructive technique against the standard concept of prayer: as one-way call-in requests to the Divine. Asked by God to pray, Bruce is unable to do anything but offer cliches, praying to feed the hungry and bring peace to mankind—a line that is turned into a gag when Bruce asks God, "How's that?" and God replies "Great, if you want to be Miss America." The gag here serves a complex function. Primarily, the gag is a cultural critique: it is a subtle yet pointed criticism of the shallowness of beauty pageants and their predictable recycling of certain expressions. Wrapped within the social critique, however, is a theological critique as well. The gag reveals how readily a simplistic concept of prayer is attached to the sound bite manufactured wholesomeness and utopianness at stake in Miss America pageantry: that the apolitical, asocial, make-no-waves, talking-to-God kind of theology is as artificial as a beauty pageant.

In addition to its primary function, the gag also works both as a classic "relief valve" operation and as a segue. As comic relief, the gag works to cloak over the tension and the anxiety around Bruce's utter inability to let go and open himself up to the Divine. The plot emphasizes this potential anxiety through Bruce's inability to look at God. When Bruce closes his eyes to pray, it's not to look deep inside himself, but rather, as the banality of the prayer suggests, to avoid the gaze of God. The "Miss America" gag lets Bruce know that the attempt has failed, that God sees through him. The gag simultaneously removes the anxiety of the revealing gaze and provides the closure to move on to the actual agenda of the meeting: for Bruce to abandon his facades, ambitions, and inhibitions and get in touch with his genuine self—with the Divine in him.

The theological trajectory that Bruce undertakes here is about abandoning the image of self. Michael Casey describes this trajectory when he argues: "God's saving of us takes place by dragging us beyond our own comfort zone into new territory . . . . It is an act by which we are drawn or even compelled to leave behind the boundaries that our selfhood has imposed on our lives."[105] God's rejection of Bruce's fake prayer, and his request for Bruce to get in touch with what he really cares about represents this movement: for Bruce to leave behind what has defined him and reach beyond himself.

It is only when he is able to abandon himself and take up his concern for Grace that Bruce is able to pray: to commune with the Divine. By having Bruce pray for Grace and her happiness instead of his own, the plot constructs a dynamic image of prayer: it is at once deep down, emanating from the core of one's being, but at the same time is other-centered. Here too, the plot makes use of the gaze to articulate its theology. When Bruce closes his eyes during this prayer, it is not to hide from God's gaze, but to assume it: to move in closer to the core of his being and find the Divine within. Significantly, it is when he has abandoned himself completely and focused solely on the needs of Grace, that Bruce can see and is able to meet the gaze of God.

The plot's dedication to deconstructing cliched concepts of prayer reveals itself here as well, as the play on words around Grace's name is put to use. Within the operations of plot, Bruce receives God's power, but he does not receive grace, or more accurately in the operation of the double entendre, he is not able to recognize grace. It is only when he is able to abandon himself, his desires, and his ambitions that Bruce can finally see Grace (recognize her for who she is) and thus receive grace: the recognition that God has been guiding and accompanying him—that he has been touched by God. The plot emphasizes this double entendre in its final deconstructive gesture. God touches Bruce with both index fingers and instead of filling him with warmth and good feeling, causes him pain. In terms of plot operations, the shock is a plot twist. It temporarily confuses both Bruce and the spectator by its unexpectedness and inappropriateness. The confusion is resolved, however, when the action yanks Bruce from the celestial space back to the reality he left.

As a deconstructive technique, the shock reinforces the message that God does not reside in the distant heavens, but rather, within. The twist in plot ostensibly assigns the space that Bruce has occupied with God to his own mind by returning him to objective reality: where the EMTs are working to save his life. Their parallel action with God suggests that the EMTs are doing "God's work." Also deconstructively, the shock is a theological message about grace: suggesting that grace is not always receiving warm fuzzy feelings, but can be painful.

The scope and range of deconstruction that the plot takes on in the scene in order to critique cliched theological concepts and provide alternative understanding, demonstrates the degree to which theological treatise employs the narrative more than the narrative uses theology as comic backdrop. The plot signals this function of using comic narrative to build out images of theological concepts by the manner in which it closes out the recurring use of Grace's prayer beads. Introduced as a motivated character exchange, the prayer beads later come to signify divine intervention. The plot signals the complex signifying function of the beads by introducing them with a double entendre. Grace first gives the beads to Bruce, saying "You need them more than me," a phrase loaded with multiple meanings. Since the statement comes from Grace, who practices her faith, and is delivered to Bruce, who is agnostic, the meaning is understood by Bruce to mean, "You need prayer beads more than I need prayer beads." Within the context of the plot, however, the statement also serves to accurately assess the level of Bruce's self-absorption: he is so myopic about himself that he needs prayer and communion with the Divine far more than he needs a relationship.

The significance of the beads as an important symbol is then emphasized when a frustrated Bruce tosses them into the river, only to have God fish them out later while his is walking on water with Bruce. Not only does retrieving the item underscore their status as important, but God tells Bruce that he is going to keep them, hinting that they will have a role later on. In the climactic scene, where God teaches Bruce to pray, God places them back in Bruce's hand, confirming their role as a significant symbol to the plot and its resolution. The central place that the beads occupy within the narrative is then explained when Bruce discovers them in his hand again upon returning to objective reality in his hospital bed. The beads confirm to Bruce that his experience with God was more than a dream, more than just an internal, psychological process that happened while he was unconscious. Rather, they are a physical sign—a remnant—that his contact with the Divine was real. Rather than tying faith to such remnants, the film undermines that position by creating a gag. Bruce looks up from his hospital bed, past Grace, and whispers to God, "Now you're just showing off."

By closing out the prop with a gag, the film discourages a concept of faith as depending on proof of the Divine, and asserts instead its position that we need a new image, a new understanding, of how the Divine operates in the world—divine intervention. The prop, and the gag, work to belie a concept of powerful masterstrokes that intervene into objective reality—affirming instead that the Divine works in small ways through others. It is Grace who gave the beads to Bruce, and it is only when they can unite as a couple that the beads truly return to him. In addition, the gag works to reaffirm the role that comedy plays within the narrative. It makes a gag out of the cliched concept of miracle as a supernatural event—a concept that the narrative has been working against all along. It works as a knowing wink that comedy has been the form through which the film engaged complex theological issues and attempted to provide new answers.

UPPING THE ANTE: *EVAN ALMIGHTY* AND THEOLOGICAL TREATISE

Evan Almighty, the sequel to *Bruce Almighty*, takes this subordination of comic form even further, subordinating the narrative itself to theological treatise. Rarely does an actor significantly influence the story line of the script, but when Jim Carrey opted out of the sequel to *Bruce Almighty*, the script was forced to take a different direction with a spin-off character. Freed from the continuity mandates of the original, and benefiting from its status as a sequel, *Evan Almighty* possessed the ability to go further with its predecessor's aesthetic experimentation. Ostensibly, the plot of *Evan Almighty* centers around newsman-turned-newly-elected-congressman Evan Baxter. In *Bruce Almighty*, Evan was a shameless self-promoter who brazenly plagiarized from Bruce to advance his own career. In *Evan Almighty*, however, Evan begins as a more genuine and sincere—if not a little vain—news anchor who runs for Congress out of a desire to change the world. As Evan, his two sons, and his wife Joan (played by Lauren Graham) begin their new life in the Washington DC suburbs, Joan tells Evan that she has prayed that this experience will bring them closer as a family. Later that night Evan prays (not altogether comfortably) to help change the world. The comedy that ensues comes from both Joan and Evan getting what they prayed for—only not in the form that they imagine. As the plot moves forward, Evan struggles to face the challenges brought about by God calling him to build an ark.

Within the operation of plot, however, the film subordinates the dynamics of plot—the goal driven, character-centered, linear causality of the narrative—to the narrative's theological and didactic goals. The plot signals this subordination by the way in which it privileges two didactic scenes of the narrative: Joan's encounter with God, and Evan's last conversation with God. These scenes are distinct from other scenes in the plot in the way that the characters—first Joan, and later Evan in the closing—are subtly isolated within their surroundings. Joan's scene starts out in a restaurant, where she has fled with her children, convinced that Evan has lost his sanity with his insistence on building an ark. As she eats with the children, a television plays above the bar featuring Jon Stewart poking fun at her husband, and Jo Dee Messina's cover of Bob Marley's "One Love" can be heard in the background. As the scene continues, Joan begins talking to God, who is posing as restaurant staff. As the conversation deepens, and God sits down next to her, the scene slowly isolates Joan from the setting. Visually, the single shots of Joan are now at a closer framing, which blurs the background even further. Even more, though, is what happens to the audio track when God begins to give wisdom to Joan. The music in the restaurant imperceptibly fades out, and non-diegetic theme music fades in.

These isolating techniques work to convey an intimacy to the scene—an intimacy that is equaled only in Evan's closing scene.[106]

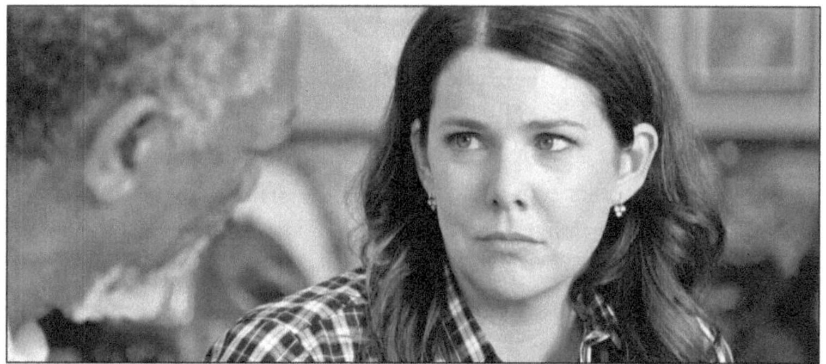

The camera isolates Joan with God as a means of amplifying the discourse.

Together, the two scenes stand out and stand apart because they are privileged moments in the film—they are the didactic moments that the rest of the narrative works to deliver. The means by which each scene escapes from the outlandishness that characterizes most of the other scenes signals both the privileging of the two scenes and the plot's principal means of hiding its subordination of narrative through the cover of elaborate plot operations like the massing of animals in the Capitol Building, or the flood itself engulfing downtown Washington DC.

Film narratologist David Bordwell, borrowing from Russian formalism, describes film narrative as a highly organized system of information gaps that is held together by the logic of causality, spatial relationships, and temporal continuity.[107] In Bordwell's model, the function of plot is to distribute story information efficiently and effectively. With the former, the plot eliminates unnecessary information—information that does not effect or inform the ongoing action. When the main character rides the subway, for example, it is not particularly necessary for the plot to show the action of leaving the train and then departing the station. It is enough to show the character arriving at his destination. Plot efficiency usually, but not always, operates around eliminating extraneous information. Plot effectiveness, on the other hand, operates around withholding information until it is needed in order to achieve the most dramatic effect. The return of Han Solo at the climactic moment in *Star Wars (1978)* is a classic example. The plot withholds the information that Han changed his mind, turned his ship around, and entered into the battle. That information is not revealed until Luke is about to lose his ship and his life. As a result, the action comes as a surprise and achieves dramatic effect.

The plot's designs to surprise—or its opposite, build suspense—points to another important aspect of narrative for Bordwell: the viewer's role. In Bordwell's model, plot distributes the information and the viewer assembles it into a story: a coherent whole. For Bordwell, the plot cues spectators to perform a range of cognitive activities (forming expectations, building hypotheses, evaluating actions and characters) that will enable them to build out the story.[108] This activity is key to *Evan Almighty's* ability to subordinate the narrative to its two privileged scenes. Principally, *Evan Almighty* conforms to the tight, character-driven, linear causality that is the norm for Hollywood narrative. The two privileged scenes are themselves integrated into the narrative through character motivation and action. In order to cloak the subordination of its narrative to its didactic scenes, however, the plot fills out the narrative with intertextual references to movies and TV (*Driving Miss Daisy, The Forty-Year-Old Virgin, Gomer Pyle, The Daily Show, Finding Nemo, The Ten Commandments*), cultural references (Marlboro man, the Bee-Gees, Loggins and Messina) cultural critiques (ecology as non-masculine, tropes of the news media), biblical references, extra-biblical references (the Yiddish proverb "man plans and God laughs"), puns (Joan of Ark, ark as acronym for Acts of Random Kindness), running gags (doing "the dance") and music montages ("Just Like Noah's Ark," "Revolution," "Waiting on the World to Change," and "Are You Ready for a Miracle" during ark building scenes, and "Sharp Dressed Man" for Evan's resistance scene). It addition to all these plot techniques, the film pursues its comic form past the breaking point of plausibility.

Each of these plot techniques draws on both the viewer's activity and knowledge base. Viewers must reach into their own cultural data bank to integrate the references into the ongoing story. As with most intertextual references, especially in comedy, there is a reward system at stake within the plot. Viewers who recognizes the reference, usually in the form of a gag, are not only rewarded with humor, but with the knowledge that they are clever. Intertextual references in comedies establish a self-congratulating system where viewers recognize both the cleverness of plot in creating the reference, and their own cleverness for making the connection. The result of this self-congratulatory process is the sense of intimacy between viewer and text—an intimacy generated by the sense of a virtual club of insiders who are both bound to the text and "in the know."

In a similar manner, the plot keeps the viewer busy with plausibility issues from the time God asks Evan to build the ark to the climactic scene. Palmer's theory that comedy works to render the implausible plausible gets pushed to the breaking point in *Evan Almighty*. The animals following Evan is implausible, but is rendered plausible by the implausible premise of the plot that Evan has been called by God. The plausibility dynamic is on full display in the meeting with Congressman Long scene, where the fish in the aquarium arranged themselves around Evan's head. Despite his many attempts to disperse them, the fish gather as near to him as they can. There is a self-consciousness to the gag in that unlike the other animals that have followed Evan, the fish—being underwater creatures—are not called to the ark. Here, however, the plot pulls the implausibility back into the narrative by having Congressman Long recognize how the fish are attracted to Evan.

With the voyage of the ark scene, however, the film allows plausibility to break down, and implausibility overtakes the narrative. The ark rides the crest of a flood from the suburbs into downtown Washington DC, finally resting at the balcony of the capitol building. When the dam that causes the flood breaks, the CGI effects employed by the plot render a high degree of verisimilitude, as the water from the high reservoir comes crashing into the valley. As the flood continues into downtown DC, however, dramatic effect and plot fulfillment trump the reality effect. Water continues to flood through the main boulevard, but the side streets that intersect it hardly fill—and only do so slowly. The logic of the plot, and the demands of the story, require that the events of the ark be fulfilled, but the plot itself is no longer concerned with codes of realism or plausibility. From the moment the ark traverses a waterfall—the boundary between the suburbs and downtown DC—the plot abandons the plausibility of events in favor of deconstruction and didactics. Plot and story, like the characters on the ark, are just along for the ride.

The plot creates another didactic moment at the height of the scene's action, the Memorial Bridge blocking the path of the ark. Here, the plot deconstructs Hollywood biblical imagery. As the ark hurtles toward the bridge, Evan ascends to the bow stem, with music from the soundtrack rising. With the staff that God has given him in one hand, Evan raises his arms, as if to command the water. When nothing happens, Evan intones,

"I command thee, stop. Halt! Whoa!" Still achieving nothing, Evan changes tack, and pleads, "How about a little help here?!?" at which point, the sky darkens, and a new wave of water hits the boat and pushes it up and over the dam.

Evan's inability to command the water as a Moses figure is a plot maneuver to impart a lesson: God does not act in the way Hollywood biblical cliches portray. The scene goes to great lengths to create the look and feel of a Hollywood biblical moment—and the music swells accordingly with a heavenly-like choir. The plot, however, undermines that imagery and concept of divine intervention. Ultimately, Evan fails in his attempt, because he is mistaking his role and his relationship to the Divine. Evan was called—not empowered. He was asked, at great personal cost, to follow God's plan. In following God's instructions, Evan was not empowered as much as fulfilled. Within the plot, God did not give Evan "power" to command the animals, let alone the flood waters. Rather, the scene points out, God responds to Evan's plea for help—as he did from the beginning when Evan prayed for help to change the world.

That the plot would highlight its message through deconstruction at the climax demonstrates the degree to which plot subordinates the narrative to its didactics. Even though plot action has reached its height, the plausibility of action and events has reached the bottom, with the plot invested instead in theological exposition. Story events play themselves out, conflicts and character interactions are resolved, but the plot itself is more invested in reaching its privileged scene in the denouement, where it can deliver its most powerful lesson. As the film enters its final scene, Evan and his family are hiking in the foothills—fulfilling at last the promised "hike." Reaching a crest, Evan requests that the family take a break, and they begin to take out sandwiches from backpacks. As they do, Evan sees God off in the distance, standing under a tree.

Evan's approach to God marks the scene off much as Joan's earlier scene with God. Though motivated by character and actions, the scene nonetheless isolates a main character from their surroundings as they interact with God. The reverse shot from God's point of view emphasizes this isolation. Although God was in Evan's sight line when he was standing with his family, the family cannot be seen from the opposite angle once Evan approaches God. The sound of their voices is also no longer audible. Rather, Evan and God share a space within the space of the narrative, demarcated by the soft focus of the background. Here, as with the earlier scene with Joan, God imparts his wisdom to the person who has called on him.

The plot uses the privileged place of the ending to elevate the theological discourses that have structured the narrative. The dialogue between

Evan and God revolves around the concepts of omniscience, God's will, and divine intervention. Evan starts the discussion by asking a question in the form of a statement. "You knew all along, didn't you? You knew the dam was unstable. If it hadn't been for the ark: my family, my neighbors . . . ." Significantly, Evan's discourse then changes topics, from God's omniscience to Evan's own response to being called. Evan states, "I fought you every step of the way." The rhetorical shift here is significant for articulating the relationship between God's omniscience and the individual's response to that calling. To underscore its significance, Evan's statement functions within two spheres of meaning: plot operations and theological discourse. In terms of plot, the statement serves as a plot summary: the story of *Evan Almighty* revolves around Evan's step-by-step unwillingness to follow what God has called him to do. Theologically, the statement expresses what the plot has been comically dramatizing all along: the extreme difficulty in following God's will.

The outlandishness of Evan's story is to make clear through exaggeration that following God's will requires abandoning oneself and one's priorities to the wisdom of God—a painstaking and risky undertaking, as Joan's walking out with the kids demonstrates. As a member of the US Congress, Evan has just joined an elite group of power brokers, and will enjoy the prestige and privilege that comes from power. Significantly for the narrative, Evan has not joined this group out of a desire for personal power, but rather, to do good: to change the world. To the degree that there are good reasons to pursue power, Evan is constructed within those parameters. Even so, to follow God, Evan must abandon everything: even his plans for doing good.

God's laughter in the earlier scene, when Evan complains that God's request does not fit in with his plans, is a pointed reference to the Yiddish proverb "man plans and God laughs." Within the scene God has already shown both his power and his wisdom, demonstrated in the natural beauty of the valley as he created it compared to the sprawling suburban development that currently overwhelms it. The self-possessed Evan, who has just been made witness to the grandeur, comes across as comically shortsighted in insisting on his agenda over God's. Through this exchange the plot establishes, and confirms through the trajectory of events, that the individual's inability to follow the will of God is largely due to the confidence invested in our knowledge. Through classic plot disposition *Evan Almighty* slowly reveals what God has known all along: that the dam will break and flood the valley. Evan's knowledge, abilities, and agendas all point somewhere else, and will never allow him to know. Evan's knowledge, as Hans Urs von Balthasar characterizes it, is personal and limited, while God's is absolute.

Evan's struggle underscores the degree to which personal agendas, the desire to control outcomes, and self-image all stand in the way of being able to accept the omniscience of God acting through us. As Balthasar argues, "Faith is the power to transcend one's own personal 'truth,' merely human and of this world, and to attain the absolute truth of the God who unveils and offers himself to us, to let [absolute truth] be decisive in our regard and prevail."[109] Evan's admission that he fought God's request "every step of the way" comes as a realization that his personal "truth"—the image of himself as "successful, powerful, handsome, and happy"—is meaningless compared to the absolute truth that lay within the wisdom of God: saving his family (and neighbors) from destruction is more important.

The scene underscores its discourse of omniscience as absolute truth by demonstrating the incompleteness of Evan's knowledge. Despite his realization of how much he had to let go before God could work within him, Evan's knowledge is still not complete—God must still impart wisdom to him. In response to God's assertion that Evan did good, that, in fact, he changed the world, Evan demurs, "No, no I didn't." God's response then functions as a paradigm shift for Evan—allowing him to see the value of a different agenda when he says, "Well, let's see, spending time with your family, making them very happy. Gave that dog a home." As God goes through the list of accomplishments, the film cuts to Evan's family, playfully romping in the field with the newly adopted dog. It is an image of harmony and grace that Evan overlooks when he replies, "Right. So?" In looking past the value of what God is pointing to, Evan loses touch with the wisdom he has so recently acquired. His response demonstrates instead that Evan's wisdom is still limited, that he is still beholden to the values and criteria of contemporary society.

Using Evan's failure to comprehend, the scene then issues its final discourse on omniscience and divine intervention. Responding to Evan's inability to possess the truth of the moment, God tries to remind Evan of the truth he revealed to him earlier in the plot, asking him, "So how do we change the world?" As Evan recalls that the answer is "One act of random kindness at a time," God begins to trace letters in the dirt at their feet. As he does, the film cuts to a shot of God creating the acronym ARK out of the phrase "Acts of Random Kindness." The significance of the shot lies in its ability to visualize the play of meaning within its theological discourse. There is a simple beauty in the film's ability to create a metaphor out of the story itself in order to emphasize its theological discourse on divine intervention. By privileging "acts of random kindness" as a discourse, the film insists that the Divine operates within the world through the individual acting out on the Divine within them. What the narrative demonstrates is that

God has agency—the gag "sue me" attests to it and downplays it at the same time. Rather than divine intervention as a supernatural event, the film puts forward a concept that people are empowered to bring the Divine into the world through their own actions: by continually acting through kindness without an agenda.

THE AESTHETICS OF RANDOMNESS

A classical analysis of this message from a critical theory or cultural studies perspective would stress its individualistic formula at the expense of collective action.[110] The problem with such a conclusion is that it negates the collective logic that is at the core of the concept. A theology of acts of random kindness insists that action will beget action: that kindness will produce kindness just as violence will produce violence. Even more, kindness has the ability to quell violence, where violence can only produce more violence. Performing acts of random kindness is an aesthetic approach to social transformation: the idea that kindness produces beauty and light that will in turn spawn more. As a model of social transformation, the randomness aspect of the theology is paramount—as demonstrated by Evan's story. Randomness works against the concept of an agenda: an agenda that can be easily co-opted by personal or social truth. Rather, randomness insists on activating and responding with the Divine as circumstances require. In this manner, the individual is called, not driven, and has better opportunity to respond from the Divine rather than from the self.

Randomness lays at the heart of the film's most important running gag: do the dance. The dance, as such, comes into the plot as a character trait of Evan's, but it operates with no background or backstory. As a result, its meaning is not altogether fixed. Evan performs the dance in celebratory moments, but its insistence through the plot and its evolution through the story work to keep any static meaning of the dance at bay. It is celebratory and silly, but it is also unmistakably, and indefinably aesthetic: with simplicity, harmony, and rhythm inscribed within it. In this respect, the dance serves as a metaphor for the film's discourse on random acts of kindness: unpredictably surfacing through the story as a faithful gesture to assert that, simple beauty, just like simple acts, must insist on themselves in the world.

THE AESTHETICS OF HUMOR

The plot's insistence on the dance as a running gag points to the manner in which its theology of random acts of kindness is grounded in aesthetics.

It is a theology of activating and growing beauty: a faith that the beauty that resides within can transform the world in its likeness. *Evan Almighty* is also instructive in terms of its aesthetic principles as well—principles that take on even more significance in their relationship to *Sister Act* and *Bruce Almighty*. Through the operations of its comic form, *Sister Act* demonstrates both the license and the limits of comedy to work within the process of social transformation. Freud's cognitive model of jokes underscores the manner in which individual identity is invested in the very meanings of signifiers: that the manner in which ideology categorizes and classifies reality is introjected—however idiosyncratically, faithfully, or oppositionally—into individual identity. Challenging or critiquing the meaning of the signifier is always more than a social, rational act: the identity of individuals is also at stake in the process.

What *Sister Act* demonstrates is the manner in which humor can provide the ability for the individual to momentarily free identity from its attachment to the signifier. Laughter provides the space in which individuals can detach themselves, however briefly, from the attachment they have to the way in which they order, categorize, and judge social reality. Within that space lies the potential for the individual to recognize and comprehend the utter contingency of the signifier and the ideological formations that endow both its meaning and the way it organizes the world. If the overblown rhetoric of twenty-four cable news stations demonstrates anything, it is the manner in which social discourse, imbued as it is with ideology, is taken in by individuals at the level—and operations—of identity. What psychoanalysis brings to social analysis is the concept that is talked about behind closed doors in the world of politics: that reasoned, factual, counter-discourse is so frequently ineffective in changing minds, altering convictions, or reshaping opinions because the doggedness with which an opinion is held is more likely than not identity itself. Politics and the news media discourse that drives it play towards themes and narratives for a reason: abandoning a conviction brings along the threat of alienation.

Psychoanalysis, then, repositions jokes, comedy, and humor as more than just entertainment. Rather, the comedic form, dependent as it is on jokes, sight gags, and the play of misrecognition, holds within itself a model of social transformation. The liberatory potential of the joke can be used for more than just self-congratulatory social critique—it can be used to cut across the grain as well: to mount a reflexive challenge against the individual's attachments to specific ideological formations. The point for this study, however, is whether humor is an aesthetic principle for Christianity itself. The deepest realms of spirituality, for example, are largely thought of as intense and reflective, not funny and light.

The use of liberatory humor, however, can be found in Scripture itself. Peter Boullata, for example, argues that the book of Jonah is written as parody, and that Jonah functions within it as a proto-fundamentalist. Readers are not meant to identify with Jonah, but rather, judge him critically for his lack of compassion, and narrow-mindedness. The height of the humor, for Boullata, is a reluctant messenger who travels all the way to Nineveh to give God's message, and says only, "Forty days more and Nineveh will be destroyed."[111] The introduction to the Catholic Bible concurs, arguing,

> The book is replete with irony, wherein much of its humor lies. The name "Jonah" means "dove" in Hebrew, but Jonah's character is anything but dove-like . . . . [T]he instant conversion of the Ninevites is greeted by Jonah with anger and sulking (4:1). He reproaches the Lord in words that echo Israel's traditional praise of his mercy (4:2; cf. Ex 34:6–7). Jonah is concerned about the loss of the gourd but not about the possible destruction of 120,000 Ninevites (4:10–11).[112]

Like Boullata, the Catholic Bible commentary points to the humor of a prophet who sulks because God did not destroy people—going so far as to yell at God for being merciful.

The humor of Jonah, its critique in the form of parody, is serious business. Jonah is reflexive humor that calls out exclusiveness and jingoism in the concept of "chosenness"—the belief that the children of Israel are God's chosen people at the exclusion of all others. Readers are called to laugh at Jonah, but in a manner that warns them to not be like him. The parody underscores a threat to the reader's spirituality: that an image of righteousness carries the peril of being judgmental, condescending, and narrow-minded. The humor asks readers to detach briefly from righteousness so that they can see that peril and abandon it. This process of detachment is critical for the comic form's potential to contribute to social transformation. In Lacanian psychoanalysis, identity themes overdetermine every opinion, belief, and commitment. In Lacan's theory, the signifier and social discourses organize and operate individual identity first and foremost, overdetermining how the individual responds to a particular social discourse in the process.

For Lacan, quite simply, people cling ferociously to beliefs and opinions because their identity is anchored in them and operate through them. Jesse DeConto illustrates this psychic dynamic in his autobiography of growing up in the world of fundamentalist Christianity—*This Littler Light.*[113] In DeConto's account, the backbone of fundamentalism in the New Hampshire community he grew up in is comprised of strong women who hold a family together under dire circumstances of one kind or another. Their main support is the community they create from shared beliefs—beliefs that are dominated by male preachers who repeatedly explain that the devil, operating through the world under the guise of liberalism, is the source of all their problems. Raw belief in the word of God is encouraged, and critical reflection is frowned upon. The world created by this community is a Manichean system of good and evil that shuns both complexity and modernity as tools of the devil.

The world that DeConto describes operates around what Slavoj Žižek defines as fantasy. In Žižek's concept, fantasy is not the same as daydream: is not a wish fulfillment narrative projected onto a future. Rather, Žižek argues, based on his reading of Lacanian theory, that fantasy is employed to cover over the failure or the impossibility of the social symbolic system. Žižek argues, "Fantasy conceals the fact that the Other, the symbolic order, is structured around some traumatic impossibility, around something which cannot be symbolized . . . ."[114] The core of fundamentalism is a disavowal of that something that cannot be symbolized—and that something is God. The radical otherness of the Divine, its inability to be contained by a symbol, its refusal to be directly and concretely accessed, called into being, made to fulfill the needs and wishes of its subjects, is a trauma that must be denied, disavowed, or traversed. Fundamentalism is a disavowal of this radical otherness conducted through a collapsing of the signifier—Holy Scripture—with the signified, the Divine. The ardent belief in the authenticity of the word, its connection to the Divine, is an attempt to deny the bar that separates the symbol from what it represents, and indeed, the gulf that separates humanity from the Divine.

The fantasy that arises to conceal the failure to symbolize and in the process "prove" God, is corruption—the degradation of the purity of the signifier. Fundamentalism builds into itself the ability to shut down critical inquiry and interpretation that would open up the meaning of the signifier. It creates a closed circuit by which its meanings are the only meanings and they are guaranteed by their proximate relations to the Divine. Questioning those literal meanings is to reject the purity of the signifier. Within the fantasy scenario of fundamentalism, God would reveal himself and shower the earth with his blessings and riches, if only everyone would strictly adhere to the literal word of Divine Scripture. That everyone does not—when the formula is so assured—is the work of the devil, who sows disbelief, and of liberalism—a tool of the devil—which degrades literal meanings with interpretations and pluralism. The irony for Christian fundamentalism is the manner in which the central figure of their salvation narrative, Jesus of Nazareth, railed against strict adherence to the word, a point driven home by his frequent use of speaking in parables, a practice encouraging followers to look beyond the literal and embrace instead the radical otherness of the spirit of the law, which could not be contained by precepts. The fascinating trajectory of DeConto's story is the manner in which for him, passionate desire to follow the teachings of Jesus inevitably led away from the closed circuit of fundamentalism and towards embracing this radical otherness of the Divine.

The lure of fundamentalism, however, is not restricted to Protestantism, as Catholic priest Fr. Helmut Schuller discovered while leading a discussion on Catholic disobedience. Appearing in a Unitarian Church because he had been banned by Boston's Cardinal Archbishop, Schuller lead a discussion on opening up the priesthood to married men and women. During the question period, an audience member submitted a question that read,

> The last two thousand years of the church have shown, time and again, that priests, radically living out the vows that they made at their ordination to heroic saintly poverty, chastity, and obedience have created the true orthodox reforms of the church. Isn't sainthood of priests, living out radical holiness, the response—not developing false understandings of the priesthood?

Fundamentalism permeates this question in the form of critique, not only in its flight from historical reality—priests have not been ordained in celibacy and poverty for 2,000 years—but in its obsession with the purity of the signifier: "heroic" and "saintly" to designate vows, "true orthodox," and "radical holiness." Here, however, instead of Holy Scripture as signifier, it is the concept of priesthood. Within the fantasy, pure observance of celibacy, poverty, and obedience will bring about the kind of holy priesthood that would pave the way of the kingdom. The vows, the practices they represent, will, in this respect, produce the Divine. Within this fantasy, a failure to conform strictly to orthodoxy, which calls for the pure observance of these vows, is corrupting the church and its ability to bring about the reign of God.

In addition, the critique leveled at Schuller illustrates what Lacan means by his concept of the "Other" with a capital "O." Lacan's reading of Freudian psychoanalysis places at the forefront the effect on the individual psyche of the arbitrariness of the social symbolic system. Starting with the contributions of Semiotic theory, which emphasizes the absolute contingency of meaning and symbols, Lacan formulated the concept of the "Other" to describe how both the individual and the social system, move past the arbitrariness of meaning. In Lacan's theory, the credibility of the social symbolic system is never undermined by its complete contingency. Rather, we pass along a belief that somewhere, in some place, there is an authority "who knows"—who guarantees the authenticity of the social discourses employed and the knowledge (ideology) they impart. The question/critique posed to Schuller hinges on this belief in the Other—that somewhere, some place, there are priests who live in radical holiness by practicing celibacy, poverty, and obedience "purely" and that these priests "guarantee" the sanctity of the church. Just as with fundamentalism's ardent belief in literalism, the Catholic drive for orthodoxy, seemingly guaranteed by an Other—priestly purity, the pope, the magisterium—is an impossibility that has been cloaked through fantasy through centuries, first, according to James Carroll, through anti-Semitism, and then through modernism and liberalism.[115]

Disengaging identity from the social discourses that structure it is the most fundamental of political challenges, and the site where liberal fantasies come into play. If the right wing fantasy is that liberals and liberal excess are the source of all problems, the progressive fantasy is that reason is on their side and will eventually conquer all: if only rigid conservatives would listen to reason, society could be transformed. If the rigidity of conservatives makes them ignorant, the faith in reason of liberals likewise has a tendency to make them condescending and lacking empathy for those who seek the shelter of conservative belief. Lacanian theory insists that no one escapes the overdetermining role of the unconscious operations of identity in their beliefs, convictions, and opinions. The challenge for social transformation then, is to get *each*, not the other, to detach from the operations of the signifier in maintaining identity and forge community. What Freud's theory of the joke provides is a mode of intervening in those operations: a small but effective manner in which the drive to maintain identity through the signifier can be suspended, and a moment of freedom achieved.

The momentary quality of that freedom points to another aesthetic principle that all three comedies share: trajectory. Since the joke or humor is fleeting at best, its potential for meaningful deployment seems minimal. Sustaining humor has the ability to overcome this limitation, but as *Sister Act* and the two *Almighty* films demonstrate, a trajectory for sustaining the humor is a key to efficacy. In all three films, humor starts in one place based on character—with Deloris the clash of cultures, with Bruce self-absorption, and with Evan unwillingness. As the stories unfold, the humor evolves with the character—or in some instances—evolves the characters themselves. The humor and the characters change in a manner that suggests linear development, progress, motion to a specific point—in other words, a trajectory. In this manner, the process of the humor can be sustained, its message reinforced on the way to achieving its goal of transformation.

Reinforcement here is key. Without reinforcing, humor is left to the fleeting moment. Reinforcement is a structure which expands the time of humor and its operations. Without trajectory, however, reinforcing humor can become a simple matter of repetition, which can quickly drain humor of its efficacy. Structuring humor through a trajectory provides the variation and change necessary to avoid repetition while still achieving reinforcement—extending the potential for humor to achieve its ultimate goal: the detachment of the signifier from identity.

AN AESTHETIC OF TRAJECTORY

As an aesthetic principle, trajectory is fundamental for deploying humor effectively, but it is also a principle in its own right. Indeed, trajectory is in the very DNA of Christianity, from the ministerial journey of its central figure, to the early formation of the church, and the spiritual journeys of its followers. Trajectory as an individual principle is paramount for preventing the individual to reach the point where they "possess" God. As Andre Louf argues, "To be on one's guard against idols discerning and acknowledging the true God afresh each day, is an ongoing part of a believer's life. We are always caught up in this turn-about and must over and over again let go of our idols . . . ."[116] For Louf, spiritual life is neither cyclical nor a straight trajectory of achievements from which one never looks back—or falters. Rather, Louf argues that the spiritual life of Christians is a continuing state of conversion: of being constantly open to the true God, and not the God that people create. The trajectory, for Louf, is the striving to go deeper in the conversion process—to be able to abandon oneself even more fully in the experience of grace.

Thomas Groome sees trajectory as a the continuing state of becoming, arguing that "being a person is never a static state or a finished product. The human vocation is a lifelong journey into fullness of life."[117] As a result, Groome emphasizes a concept of trajectory as a guiding vision that inspires people to journey forward. He argues for the centrality of the Christian story and vision as tantamount for Christianity. Story, he argues, inscribes "the continuity and vitality of Christian faith,"[118] engaging people to become participants in a living narrative. Vision, then, is "how the Story challenges Christians to live their faith."[119] For Groome then, a vision of the reign of God serves as "an overarching guideline" that inspires action and helps negotiate Scripture, faith life, and the actions and operations of the church.

Groome's discussion underscores that trajectory can not be limited to a concept of the individual, but inscribes the social dimension of Christianity:

the striving for the kingdom of God on earth. For Stanley Hauerwas, that striving begins with restoring the concept of salvation, which he sees as an "enacted narrative."[120] Far from a concept of the individual, Hauerwas sees salvation as "the defeat of powers that presume to rule outside God's providential care."[121] For Hauerwas, the church as church must realize itself as alternative—and oppositional—to the project of the nation-state. In his formulation, the nation-state is the product of Enlightenment ideals, a project undertaken as a means "to create people incapable of killing other people in the name of God."[122] The modern nation-states have by and large achieved that goal—with the glaring exceptions, of course, of Ireland, Israel, India, Iran, and Iraq—but the achievement is, for Hauerwas, illusory insofar as the nation states mobilize people to kill in just the same manner, but for different reasons. He thus argues, "since the Enlightenment's triumph, people no longer kill one another in the name of God but in the name of the nation-states."[123]

For Hauerwas then, the church must learn to extract itself from the mission of the nation-states, a reeducation process that has no clear path and an even less certain beginning, but inscribes a trajectory nonetheless. Christians must first come to recognize that they are trying to serve two masters, then go about the business of transforming the world instead. The problem for Hauerwas—and Christianity itself—is that the first step is close to insurmountable, and the process to follow daunting and uncharted. Here the work of critical theorist Ernst Bloch makes an invaluable contribution. Bloch identified a utopian impulse in humanity, but unlike others, did not link it to simple egalitarianism. Rather, Bloch theorized a yearning for the Divine to be a primary condition of humanity. He argues, "Throughout all the movements and goals of worldly transformation, [primal religious desire] . . . has been a desire to make room for life, for the attainment of a divine essence, for men to integrate themselves at last, in a millennium, with human kindness, freedom, and the light of the telos."[124]

In Bloch's view, the proper place for economics, the marketplace, politics, the state, and society itself is below the community. Much in keeping with Marxist theory, Bloch saw the necessity of the state withering away, but unlike Marx or mainstream Marxist theory, Bloch argued that the church—and only the church—could bring about the necessary conditions for such social transformation. He argues, ..."Nothing else [but the church] can create the space of community, for a freely self-chosen community *above society* (which merely lifts the burdens), and above a social economy thoroughly organized along . . . [egalitarian] lines, in a classless, and therefore non-violent, order."[125] Bloch's theory inscribes the concept of trajectory not only as an end goal—the utopian community—but also in the means to get there. His hierarchy of social order—community, state, economy—combined with his belief tha[t the state must wither away, implies a path for social transformation.

Drawing on Bloch's interpretation of Marxist theory, the actual presence of the church—the space it occupies—can now be seen to function as a boundary to the state and its totalizing impulse to bring everything within the control of the state or the marketplace. The church literally stands separate from the state, its space outside the control of the state, and its boundaries signify the limits to where the state can go—or conversely, its borders proclaim where the state must stop and a different realm be allowed to exist. Trajectory as a guiding principle for a new Christian aesthetic gives a clear purpose and aim to Hauerwas's salvation project. Christians, and their institutions, must seek to withdraw from the state and expand the domain of Christianity: the space where the state—and the marketplace—cannot go.

In practical terms, Christianity should be interested in shrinking the government, the exact goal of Republican party politics. The difference is that the goals of shrinking government for Republican politics are to free up more capital for markets and to empower economic oligarchies even more by creating less oversight and regulation and more wealth flowing to the top. For Christianity, the goal could not be more opposite: to make the state and the marketplace take their place underneath the egalitarian community. Within Bloch's framework, the specific means by which this is accomplished is by increasing the dominion of the church. In keeping with Hauerwas's vision, this is more than just occupying real estate, it is making God's salvation and the ethos of liberationist Christianity lord of the realm. In the concluding chapter, I discuss the specifics of literally disengaging from the marketplace and from the state, but here it is important to stress Hauerwas's point that first, Christianity has to realize that its eager partnership with the liberal democracy project devours the very heart of Christian theology.

THE AESTHETICS OF RELATIONALITY

As an aesthetic principle, trajectory is both a guiding vision and a practical plan for achieving that vision. It provides specific purpose to what can otherwise be a complex array of religious principles. As the discussions here on *Sister Act*, *Bruce*, and *Evan Almighty* demonstrate, trajectory is very much related to, but distinct from, narrative itself—foundational to the structure of narrative, but not wholly subsumed by it. The distinction is critical for elaborating the last aesthetic principle discussed here: relationality. A simple but deceptively powerful principle, relationality means that within an overall aesthetic, the operating principles and stylistic elements are in a dynamic, non-hierarchical relationship.

David Bordwell and Kristin Thompson introduced the concept of a dynamic relationship between elements to film studies—one of the first academic disciplines to study the polyvocal text. Recognizing that stylistic elements themselves—rapid editing, elaborate crane shots, or a simple shot/reverse shot—function to express meaning, Bordwell and Thompson argue no individual element has its own fixed meaning—that it only takes on meaning in relationship to other elements.[126] The classic example—still taught as standard knowledge in college and university film and video production courses—is that the low camera angle shooting up at the character will endow them with authority and/or power. Looking at *Citizen Kane*, Bordwell and Thompson find many such examples of low-angle shots of Kane that invest him with authority. They also find, however, an example that breaks the convention. The lowest angle in the film operates to make Kane look smaller, and diminished, and it is used in the plot to convey one of the lowest points of Kane's life.[127] An analysis of the shot shows that the scene is done in a wide shot, making the characters on the screen smaller, and the ceiling seem farther. The ceiling itself is made to seem higher by use of a skylight, which opens it up. Moreover, a column in the frame is closer to the camera than the characters—again, diminishing their place within the frame. All of these elements combined—camera angle, camera framing, setting, plot mechanics—operate to diminish Kane and his bearing as a character. Bordwell and Thompson's argument cautions us not to single out one element as itself operating to make meaning, but rather, to look at the intricate relationships off all the elements and how they operate together to convey a message.

In addition to a dynamic relationship between elements—or in this case, aesthetic principles—relationality warns against assigning primacy to any one aesthetic principle. Here, the discussions of *Sister Act* and *Evan Almighty* underscore the point. Given the importance of trajectory—of having an overarching vision to strive towards—it would be easy to grant primacy to that vision or the principle of trajectory itself. I criticize *Sister Act*, in fact, for abandoning its trajectory in favor of the standard Hollywood "violence in the hands of the good will save us" resolution. The narrative of *Sister Act* builds to a very different resolution—where the mother superior would come to recognize that all the spiritual discipline of the pre-Vatican II church had a purpose—to allow Christians to marshal their courage and follow the example of Jesus, even unto death. The narrative trajectory, as discussed, was building to the moment where the mother superior would have made the gangsters shoot her before they could shoot Deloris. Wary that this would cast the film as a religious film with a religious message, the story threw that plot resolution out the window in favor of the police lieutenant crashing into the scene and shooting the bad guy. From an aesthetic perspective, the film lacked the courage to follow its Christian trajectory.

Both *The Way* (2010) and *Evan Almighty*, however, demonstrate that trajectory cannot be given primacy—that, depending on the goal, other aesthetic principles may take precedence. *The Way*, for example, works effectively because it followed what I criticize *Sister Act* for doing: abandoning the trajectory. The plot of *The Way* is constructed around Tom Avery's journey on "el camino de Santiago." A nonreligious Catholic, Tom undertakes the pilgrimage on an impulse—his son Daniel died undertaking the pilgrimage, and Tom had only come to recover the body. Significant to the story is that Daniel was not a religious Catholic either. Rather, Daniel was a free spirit journeying to find himself when he got caught in a freak storm on the camino. As Tom walks along the camino, he spreads Daniel's ashes—giving him a purpose and a means to enact his grief. The more Tom journeys along the camino, however, the more his solitary journey turns otherwise. Fellow pilgrims begin to accompany Tom: first an overweight Dutchman, then a Canadian woman addicted to smoking, and finally, an Irish travel writer experiencing writer's block.

For each of the pilgrims, the journey's end holds the promise of individual healing and transformation. What they each come to find, however, is that the end holds no magic. Rather, the trial of the journey, and the fellowship they create, is where they achieved a measure of healing. The journey and their fellowship is what helps strip away the idols and the ideal images of themselves, and make them confront their authentic self. As a lapsed Catholic, deeply in mourning, struggling through a religious pilgrimage, Tom is positioned to undergo a religious conversion: to find the real meaning of his faith and achieve a measure of grace and h'

ealing from his grief. The film, however, rejects that trajectory as being too easy. Were Tom to experience religious conversion, the film could too readily replace grief and mourning with conversion and grace—and create a story where pain and grief have no place in Christianity. Instead, the film stays with Tom's grieving process, allowing him to achieve a measure of resolution, and of understanding, but not outside the boundary of grief. The plot provides the possibility that Tom's experiences—his trials, his experience of fellowship, his understanding and resolution, and the grace that he received—will provide the foundation for conversion in the future. At the film's end, Tom continues to journey, walking paths that Daniel desired to walk. He is liberated, and his liberation may lead him back to his faith, but the plot only leaves that as a possibility. Instead, the plot remains at the point of resolution in the realm of grief—ending there so as not to dismiss grief, but to insist on its endurance. In the binary structure—and limitation—of narrative, incorporating conversion into the story would run too high a risk of compromising—if not dismissing—that ending.

In a similar manner, *Evan Almighty* refuses to let narrative trajectory take primacy. As discussed earlier, the plot privileges instead its two didactic moments. If the earlier discussion of the didactic scenes stressed their messages, here it is important to discuss their emotional valence. The two scenes—Joan in the restaurant and Evan on the mountaintop—each convey important theological insight, but in addition, work to create the experience of revelation. The scenes mobilize stylistic techniques, and the proximity of cinematic identification, to provide a glimpse of the revelation experience: to put the audience on the side of revelation and the experience of grace. For this effect, the film is willing to subordinate narrative—to build a story that can deliver these two moments.

Trajectory—especially narrative trajectory—can build to a privileged and penultimate moment—as the plot of *Sister Act* was doing with the climactic scene. The danger then, of privileging trajectory itself is the implication that there is one certain approach or path for how best to achieve the goals or the aims of Christianity. If the work of Hauerwas and others insists on anything, it is precisely the opposite. As an aesthetic principle, relationality insists that a Christian aesthetic always be open. That openness—a fundamental unwillingness to privilege one method, one path, is the essence of Christianity, which insists, above all, that pursuit of the Divine, like the Divine itself, is a mystery that cannot be reduced to a simple formula. In this respect, humor is a necessary part of a Christian aesthetic if for no other reason than to contain the terror of knowing that Christianity offers no guarantees.

6

Life is Beautiful, Joyeux Noël, and the Question of Christian Nonviolence

In his book on Christian nonviolence, Robert Brimlow describes an experience that everyone publicly advocating nonviolence nearly always encounters. As Brimlow tells it, "Whenever I would make an argument in favor of pacifism in my philosophy classes, or when addressing an audience, invariably someone would ask me the Hitler question."[128] An exceptionally honest scholar, Brimlow admits that he struggled with both the question and the answer, arguing, "Invariably I would come up with some kind of answer, and invariably I would not be especially happy with it."[129] Brimlow's discomfort comes in part from a nagging sense of hypocrisy: he advocates Christian nonviolence, but admits that "deep down I knew that, if I had the chance, I would probably have killed Hitler using any means possible," which is indeed the path taken by pacifist theologian Dietrich Bonhoeffer.[130] Another reason Brimlow struggled with the question, however, is that he was trying to give an honest answer to a less than honest question. At best the question is rooted in historical speculation, but chiefly, the question is a rhetorical ploy used to silence the ideology of nonviolence, not engage it.

The rhetorical nature of the question is evidenced in the anticipated response—or lack thereof. Drawing on the tragic failure of Chamberlain's appeasement strategy, and the ruthlessness the Nazis employed in both military conquest and genocide, the question is employed as a trump card—as a *fait accompli* that demonstrates the necessity of violence. When deployed, the question bears the expectation that the persons practicing or espousing nonviolence will not have an adequate response—will be forced to admit that they are wrong, tuck their tails between their legs, and walk away. The question, however, is a rhetorical two-step: it employs history while simultaneously repressing it. In order for the *fait accompli* to work, the question cannot allow for the prehistory of Hitler to come into the equation: that the answer to Hitler was Christian nonviolence to begin with. The conditions necessary for Hitler's rise to power depend on World War I and the historical abandonment of nonviolence within Christendom from the start. The question "What about Hitler?" arbitrarily restricts the opportunity for nonviolence before the manifestation of violence, then coyly asks why nonviolence is not effective.

The Hitler question is designed to silence nonviolence because it is an ideological ploy for militarism. Hitler is the signifier par excellence anchoring the truth claims of the necessity of violence—for the belief that there is some evil so powerful that violence is the only answer. Accordingly, the state becomes a necessary bulwark against such evil and violence, by harnessing the power of military force as a deterrent.

The ideology of militarism is rarely challenged in the media. There are notable exceptions, like Richard Attenborough's epic film *Gandhi* (1982), and Stanley Kubrick's *Paths of Glory* (1957). *Gandhi* is a tribute to both the man and his unflinching belief in nonviolence. In the Amritsar massacre scene, and the subsequent trial of General Dyer, the film gives a notable and withering condemnation of militarism, but that critique is both linked to and overwhelmed by the ongoing criticism of colonialism. The film is notable, however, for its unflinching testimony to the superiority of nonviolent resistance. Tellingly, *Paths of Glory* (1957) is one of the few unashamed antiwar films. The film was produced and distributed during the Eisenhower era, and in between the Korean and Vietnam Wars. Though a former general in the US Army, and commander of Allied Forces in World War II, Eisenhower was a fiscal conservative who was averse to military spending and indeed warned his country of a growing economic military-industrial complex.

For a brief period in anti-war American history, then, there was a space for ideological challenge to militarism. Hollywood remained uninterested in exploring that space, however, and resumed its love affair with militarism—a predilection that can still be seen in such films as *The Hunt for Red October* (1990) (and any film based off a Tom Clancy novel), *Independence Day* (1996), *Master and Commander: The Far Side of the World* (2003), and a film designed especially to recruit teens into the ideology of militarism, *Red Dawn* (1984).[131] Hollywood's affection for militarism is replicated by television, with such popular shows as *24* (2001–2010), *NCIS* (2003–), and *JAG* (1995–2005). Television news does not stray from this ideological boundary—falling in line quickly whenever the US government conducts military invasions of foreign countries.

Two films produced outside of Hollywood—and the US for that matter—are significant for opposing the ideology of militarism with Christian nonviolence: Roberto Benigni's *La vita è bella (Life is Beautiful,* 1997) and Christian Carion's *Joyeux Noël* (*Merry Christmas*, 2005). One is a comedy, the other a drama. The first is a cloaked in metaphorical criticism, the other a direct and withering rejection. Each, however, is rooted in Christian nonviolence, and each alters their narrative form to underscore that ideology.

When *La vita è bella* (1997) was released in the United States, no one spoke about it in terms of nonviolence. Rather, discussion and reviews of the film were dominated by another topic: the appropriateness of a comedy whose setting is the Holocaust. This chapter, however, demonstrates that the use of the Holocaust as a setting was not to create an offbeat comedy but rather to appropriate the ultimate signifier of overwhelming power in the service of evil. The film uses comedy to articulate a radical affirmation of nonviolence, and the Holocaust becomes the means to make the assertion at the highest level. Indeed, this analysis will demonstrate that even though the discourses of nonviolence speak from the margins, *La vita è bella* is constructed, precisely, to answer the question, "What about Hitler?" As a means of answering that question the film draws upon the status of Hitler and Nazism as the unquestionable signifier of consummate evil, and the Holocaust as the unquestionable signifier of the inability to resist in the face of overwhelming power—and evil.

The plot itself is organized as a romantic comedy, and typical of the genre, creates a number of transgressions. What is not so typical of the genre is the manner in which the transgressions consistently subvert the very foundations of society itself. The primary means of this subversion is in the narrative foregrounding of what semiotics and psychoanalysis describe as symbolic contingency: the necessity of a pact or agreement within groups or communities to determine meaning. Many of the film's sight gags— the parade in the beginning of the film, the horse that Guido brings into the restaurant, the key from the sky—are based upon what Jaques Lacan has described as the "Answer of the Real." Their comic effect results from the difference between the audience's knowledge, and the characters within the story who witness Guido's shenanigans. The spectator knows that Guido is manipulating events to make them seem real to those around him, while conversely, the characters around Guido do not realize that he is taking advantage of circumstances unseen to them.

The opening of the film itself introduces this process. Guido and his friend Ferrucio find themselves barreling down the road in a car whose brakes have gone out. As they hurtle into a small town, Guido stands in the back of the open car and waves frantically to a crowd gathered along the road to move out of the way. The crowd, which has gathered to greet the king of Italy, mistakes Guido for the king because his arm movements resemble a salute, and the car has become accidentally adorned with branches and leaves from careening through the forest. Three elements anchor the symbolic meaning the crowd think they understand: the timing of the parade, Guido's frantic gesture, and the decorated car. What the scene demonstrates is that all these elements were coincidental—or contingent—but all seem quite "real." As Slavoj Žižek argues, "There is no symbolic communication without some 'piece of the real' to serve as a kind of pawn guaranteeing its consistency."[132] In other words, symbolism always depends on something that appears to be real to guarantee meaning. This leads Žižek to argue that "For things to have meaning, this meaning must be confirmed by some contingent piece of the real that can be read as a 'sign.'"[133] The distinction that Žižek makes here is between the symbol with its arbitrary relationship, and the "sign" which is produced by reality, or is interpreted by the individual as the Real answering back.

The sight gags around Guido's courtship of Dora all revolve around this distinction. Three, in particular, are built on this play between symbol and sign from the real: the key from heaven, the answer from the man, and the dry hat. In the first of these, Guido has earlier witnessed a man call for a key to be dropped down to him where he stands in the street from a woman in the window above named Maria. In the second gag, Guido spots Dr. Lessing, a character from the hotel where Guido works who knows the answer to a riddle they had previously discussed. Finally, the hat has been a running gag from earlier, when Guido steals the hat of Ferruccio's employer. The omniscient narration allows the spectator to know that the key from Maria, the wait for the ice cream, and the dry hat are all produced because of Guido's prior interactions. The humor results from the audience seeing that from Dora's position, these contingencies look like the answer of the real: the key falls from heaven, a man gives an answer, a dry hat is provided. The repetition of these manipulated "signs" expose to the spectator a crucial part of what comprises the misrecognition of the answer of the real. As Žižek argues, "the crucial point here is that the real that serves as support of our symbolic reality must appear to be found and not produced." The distinction that Žižek makes is precisely what separates the spectator's position of knowledge from Dora's. The spectator knows that the answer of the real has been produced by Guido—it does not emanate from reality itself. Dora, conversely, is unaware of the manipulation and believes they are signs from the real—the answer of the real.

The sight gags in Dora's courtship visualize for the audience this contingency of the real and make clear its operations. In this respect, they constitute a subversive unmasking of how the social-symbolic system is not moored to, or anchored by reality, but rather, arbitrarily contingent—and manipulated. Offered through the vehicle of romantic comedy, however, the subversiveness is ideologically harmless: it is set in a quaint, provincial past where fascism is nothing more than a parade of buffoons and poseurs. The plot, however, shifts the film to a more radical, ideologically challenging process by concluding the romantic comedy halfway through the film. Using a transitional device that places the political and ideological dimensions of fascism in the foreground, the plot abandons romantic comedy for tragedy.

The transitional scene that inaugurates this shift is the rescue of Dora, a point in the narrative where fascism, modernism, colonialism, and class structure all intersect to create spectacle. Guido's whisking Dora away from her engagement party on a painted horse goes beyond the standard overcoming of obstacles traditional to the romantic comedy; it operates as a sustained critique of fascism and the class hierarchy and distribution of power that allowed it to operate. Guido's ability to ride the painted horse in the middle of the Grand Hotel is based on the exotic spectacle that the staff of the Grand Hotel is already constructing. Guido rescues Dora by manipulating the circuit of meaning that the spectacle creates, and the "pieces of the real" that the spectacle uses: the enormous Ethiopian cake is carried by "real" black men while the orchestra plays music evocative of North African genres. Guido uses the foreignness of the spectacle to ride in on a horse that has been painted green by anti-Semitic thugs. The horse, like the black men, is thus read by the guests as the ongoing exotica emanating from the real that forms the basis of the spectacle. Here too, the omniscient narration functions such that the spectator, unlike the diegetic audience, knows that rather than the answer of the real, the horse is Guido's manipulation of the circuit of meaning. As if to emphasize this point, the film then closes the scene with the representation of an authentic irruption of the real: the champagne cork pops out of the bottle, strikes an ostrich egg on display, and causes it to fall on the head of Dora's fiancé.

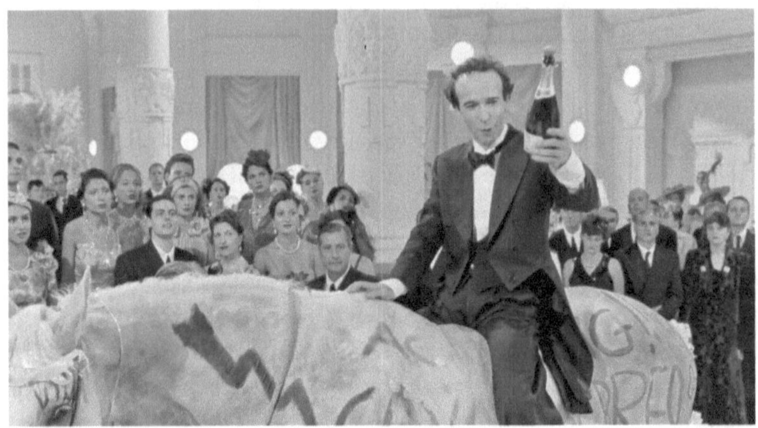

Guido's manipulation of the symbols within the Grand Hotel allow him to rescue Dora.

The significance of the scene, however, is the association the film constructs between politics and Guido's manipulation of the contingency of the real. Within the operations of plot, the scene serves an important transitional function. It is the bridge between the first half of the film as a romantic comedy, and the second half of the film as tragedy. The earlier school house scene vividly illustrates the position of the political within the two halves. In his ongoing attempts to meet Dora, Guido steals the banner of a fascist education official staying in the hotel. He then presents himself to the school as the inspector from Rome. He briefly questions every teacher, before moving down the line to Dora. Instead of asking her a phony question, however, Guido asks what she's doing Sunday night. Disappointed that she is already going to the theater to see Offenbach, Guido prepares to leave, but is pressed into service by the principal to deliver the race manifesto that the inspector was there to deliver.

As the character who has been manipulating the symbolic from the beginning, Guido quickly realizes that under his symbolic mandate as an official, he can say almost anything. Soon, his manifesto on race becomes a critique, delivered through a parody on how handsome he is as a member of the superior race, and he slowly begins to undress in front of the astonished children. Though visibly uncomfortable, the school's principal and teachers must acquiesce to the performance because it comes under the banner of authority.

As Guido begins his address he mentions that he was especially chosen, by "racist" Italian scientists, but the derogatory term goes unnoticed by his audience—overlooked because it is buried within official discourse. Under the protection of the authority of his discourse, Guido pushes his parody to the breaking point. By the time the real inspector enters the school, Guido is dressed only in his underwear and undershirt, and is exposing his belly button to the children, exclaiming, "Take a look at this belly button. What a knot!" He then goes on to say, "But you can't untie it, not even with your teeth. Those racist scientists tried. Not a chance!" When the inspector finally arrives in the room, Guido has gone on to waving his hips and performing a dance. Spotting the inspector, Guido makes an exit through the window, saying to Dora as he goes, "I'll see you in Venice, princess," a veiled reference to her Sunday plans.

The significance of the school house scene is the manner in which it subordinates politics to the humor of the romantic comedy. Guido's political parody and critique are secondary to the humor and his bid to woo Dora. The scene, however, articulates a very complex and controversial political discourse: that the Italians of the fascist era did not really take seriously the racial discourse of the fascist government, that it was a pale imitation of the racial discourse of the Nazis. Only one person in the room—the principal, an agent of the fascist state—is seen to hold stock in the manifesto on race.

That discourse, however, is overshadowed by the outrageousness of Guido's performance, and the plot's emphasis on Dora's fascination with Guido's antics—in other words, with the narrative's focus on the romantic comedy.

With the culmination of the romantic comedy—the rescue of Dora—politics is no longer subordinated to humor. Rather, humor becomes the principle device to contest politics. From the rescue of Dora onwards, Guido's alternative symbolic constructions will be consistently built around a political dimension—will function as rejection of the intolerable social reality imposed upon him and his family. Just as the school house scene prefigures the sight gags of the romantic comedy, so too does the dinner scene at the Grand Hotel prefigure the shift to the political for the upcoming tragic structure the film will employ. In this scene, the principal is discussing education with Dora's fiancé Rodolfo, a town official. In extolling her admiration of the Nazi education system, the principal recites the complexity of a math story problem given to seven-year-olds. The principal states, "A lunatic costs the state four marks a day. A cripple, four and a half marks. An epileptic three and a half marks. Considering that the average is four marks, and there are three-hundred thousand patients, how much would the state save if these individuals were eliminated?" Upon hearing the problem, Dora is incredulous with disgust: she sees the immoral ideology embedded in the problem. Rodolfo, however, ignores the premise and sets to work solving for the equation.

The math problem operates as the turning point in the romantic comedy. From this point on, Dora will seek to escape the path she is walking down—of a luxurious life with a conceited government official—and look toward Guido, who adores her. The turning point, however, places politics in the foreground. More than just a glimpse of Nazi-era and fascist politics, its decided focus on the cost to the state is a not-so-veiled reference to the rise of "New Right" neoliberal economics in the Western democracies, and the neofascism that first brought Berlusconi to power in 1994. The scene draws attention to its shift in political positioning through its visual style: the plot stages the scene in close-ups, de-emphasizing the space of the Grand Hotel, and emphasizing instead the discourse and reactions of the characters.

With this segue into the political, the film will no longer employ the political as a backdrop for comedy. Rather, the plot will use the cover of comedic license to radically contest the power of social formations—and further, to demonstrate that resistance is possible against the power of any social formation. The primary means for this ideological challenge is the repetitive visualization of fantasy as a political weapon. The plot demonstrates how fantasy can be a site for contesting the symbolic mantle imposed by the structure of power within a social formation—much as Guido did with the manifesto on race in the school house. In the second half of the film in particular, Guido's manipulation of the answer of the real makes clear that both the symbolic order and the social-ideological fantasy that preserves it are arbitrary and dependent on the myth of the answer of the real.

Here, Slavoj Žižek's elaboration on Lacan's theory of fantasy is critical. In his discussion of Lacan's theories, Žižek argues that fantasy is not a turning away from "reality" as is commonly understood. Rather, in Lacanian psychoanalysis, fantasy as such is a scenario (or story) that explains away the failures and the utter contingency of a social-symbolic system—that there is no reality backing up the structure of a society, its symbolic system, and most importantly, its distribution of power. Žižek describes fantasy as a scenario that fills out the empty space behind social structures—the space where we expect to find something real that props up or provides the foundation for society. Žižek, Lacan, and most critical theorists, however, argue that there is no real foundation for society to be found in reality—only invisible—and for the most part implicit—consent. For this reason, Žižek refers to fantasy as a screen masking a void"[134] In the second half of the film, the plot shows how fantasy works by highlighting Guido's manipulation of the answer of the real. He creates a screen to protect Joshua from the terror of the camp, and to maintain Joshua's unconscious desire for idyllic childhood. Guido resists both the power and the desire of Nazism to impose its ideological terror on Joshua: to position him as a Jewish victim, both in reality (he hides Joshua) and symbolically: Joshua cannot occupy the position of Jewish victim until he himself completes the circuit of meaning by believing it.

In the face of overwhelming coercive power, Guido finds the means to carve out a space of resistance—denying the ability of the "Other"—the authority with the power to impose symbolic meaning, to achieve its goal. Three scenes in particular—the guard slipping in the showers, the dessert scene, and Lessing's obsession—demonstrate that not only is the "Other" a fantasy, but so is the desire to sustain the "Other" in their place of authority: as the anchor to the social system and its symbolic order. Each of these scenes revolve around the failure of the symbolic, its tenuousness and dependence on desire and ideological fantasy to create a whole, or holistic society—what Žižek describes as "a vision of society . . . which is not split by an antagonistic division."[135]

The first such scene is when the Nazi female guard slips in the dressing room of the gas chambers. As she confidently strides across the room, the guard poses as a figure of authority, and helps maintain the illusion that the men are going to take showers, when, in fact, they are preparing to be gassed to death. Before she successfully makes it across the room, however, the guard stumbles and falls to her knees right in front of Guido's Uncle Eliseo. The older gentleman then stoops and offers to help her up. In this momentary exchange, Uncle Eliseo briefly unnerves the guard by undermining her ability to maintain the ideological fantasy of Jewish people as an abomination of society. The guard must maintain the fantasy of the showers, but even more, she must disavow the manner in which the "dreaded Jew" possesses more humanity than she. If she does not, then her own symbolic identification with Nazism will lose its support, and she will be faced with the terror of the real–the void behind the fantasies that keep Nazism in place: that the Germans are a master race, lead by a quasi-divine leader, Hitler. In that moment, the raw power that Nazism exerts over the lives of the camp's victims is reduced to the tenuous individual desire that support it.

The desire for a pure and master race, free from social antagonism, is also displayed in the dessert scene. Here, Guido once again manipulates social symbols to produce an "Answer of the Real" in order to protect Joshua, who has been surreptitiously placed at the table of German officers' children. When Guido serves Joshua dessert, Joshua responds "Grazie!" revealing that he is an Italian child. The German server working with Guido stalks off to get a superior. By the time he arrives back with the Nazi woman supervising the children, Guido is in the midst of serving all the children and making them say "Grazie." Guido thus successfully shifts "Italianness" and "Jewishness" from the suspected Joshua onto himself: all the children are saying "grazie" because they have been taught by Guido. The rightfully perceived "impurity" within the group of children is masked through Guido's manipulation. In this manner, Guido maintains the desire of the Germans for preserving the purity of their group.

The role of ideological fantasy and its support in individual desire is also articulated through the character of Lessing. The cultured doctor is introduced in the plot as a favorite guest at the hotel who trades riddles with Guido. At the beginning of Dora's rescue scene, however, Lessing is called away on important business to Berlin, presumably exiting the narrative that is now filled with the union of Guido and Dora. Lessing's reintroduction into the narrative as a camp doctor is a dramatic plot twist whose function is to emphasize ideological fantasy. Having met and been acknowledged by Lessing, Guido believes that he has found salvation: that Lessing will find some way to save him and Joshua. To underscore the powerful role that fantasy has in maintaining the symbolic order, the plot makes the reunion with Lessing nothing more than a red herring. To Guido's horror, Lessing is not interested in saving Guido, but rather, in having Guido solve a riddle that Lessing is now obsessed with.

Psychoanalysis demonstrates that the operation of the riddle works by the subject being able to free themselves—to get out from under—the totality of the symbolic network inscribed within the riddle-work. The only way to solve a riddle is for the individuals to extricate themselves from the signifying domain that the riddle constructs, and recognize instead another domain that the signifier also arbitrarily belongs to. Lessing's riddle—the duck—operates allegorically within the plot to dramatically underscore the ideological fantasy surrounding Nazism's obsessive desire for the death camps. Lessing cannot get out from under the literal meaning the riddle creates, because it is an allegorical critique of his desire and ideological fantasy. The riddle states:

> Fat, fat, ugly, ugly, all yellow, in truth. If you ask me, "Where are you?" I respond, "quack, quack, quack." Walking, I make poop. Who am I? Tell me.[136]

As with many riddles, however, there is a play on words—this one particular to Italian. In Italian, the answer to "Where are you?" is "*qua, qua, qua*." The word, however, means both "quack," the sound of the duck, but also, "here." The answer to the riddle then, is not a duck, but rather, the Nazis: who are fat (a stereotype of Germans), ugly (a fairly common moniker for all occupiers and a fairly accurate description of Hitler, Himmler, and Goering) and yellow, or cowards (they travel in armed patrols against unarmed civilian populations). Moreover, having overrun most of Europe, and parts of Asia and Africa, the Germans are here, here, and here. Their walk is a ceremonial goose step, but the riddle also means that as armed conquerers, they are shitting on every place they occupy.

Lessing's manic inability to get out from the literal meaning of the duck is due to his obsessive desire to maintain the ideological fantasy of Nazism. Lessing can not extricate himself from his desire to maintain the position of the Other. Like the female guard earlier, Lessing must maintain the belief in the Other—the power and authority of Nazism—or he would be forced to see the terror created to maintain the Nazi fantasy of the superior Aryan race. Lessing's obsession is thus a manic desire to hide the fact that the credibility and authority of Nazism does not exist—that rather than an organic society, it is only an arbitrary social construction devoid of "truth," "evolution," or any other "real" determinants that create a master race. What Guido discovers is that Lessing was never interested in "saving" Guido from the terror of the camps, because he cannot acknowledge the terror to begin with. The refined, international, and cultured doctor fundamentally cannot recognize that he is nothing more than a low-end accomplice in torture and genocide for an irrational and insane group instituting genocide across Europe.

The trajectory of the film offers pointed illustration that rather than power, there is nothing behind Nazism but a void—and death. Through Lessing, the female guard, and the female supervisor in the officer's quarters, the film uncovers the truth of Nazism: that it is always already dead—maintained only by the manic desire of individuals like Lessing and the other characters. The film points to this "already dead" characteristic through a historical reference. The second half of the film is introduced through the icon of German troops marching through the town, signifying German occupation of Italy. The presence of German troops indicates that the time of the story is now after D-Day and after the Allied landing and occupation of Italy: that period of inevitable German retreat when the Nazis are already finished, already a thing of the past, but, along with the German people, are not willing to admit it.

The scene following the encounter with Lessing, however, demonstrates that Nazism was *always* already dead—that its power and authority was always arbitrary and always based on death. There was never any legitimacy, let alone truth, to Nazi claims of a master race. Nazism was only ever a group of thugs willing to strut, posture, and mouth platitudes that would empower other thugs through sterile and cliched platitudes justifying violence and oppression.

The real effects of Nazism's symbolic constructions and fantasies then erupt into the narrative in almost mythic dimensions. After his failed encounter with Lessing, Guido signals Dora of his continued survival by playing a recording of "*Belle Nuit*"—the music from the theater—on a gramophone. The timing is not coincidental. Having abandoned his own fantasy at rescue, Guido now acts to resist the terror of the camp: to fight back against the horror by filling the camp with beauty, while at the same time sending a message of hope to Dora. Having come out on the other side of his fantasy and engaging in resistance, however, Guido comes face-to-face with the reality of the camps.

As the sound of the music fills the camp, Guido takes Joshua and begins walking back to the barracks. Surrounded by mist, however, Guido loses his way, while Joshua sleeps on his father's shoulder. As Guido makes his way through the mist, the film's setting shifts from its heretofore realism to high stylization. Visually, the scene sets itself off from the rest of the film, and as the music of Offenbach eerily accompanies him, Guido ponders if in fact he and Joshua are in a dream. As he emerges from a thick mist, however, the music disappears, replaced only with the sound of the wind, and Guido stops dead in his tracks, staring dumbfounded ahead. The plot then shifts to Guido's point-of-viewing, revealing an enormous mound of starved, naked corpses, with an even larger mound of similar corpses behind it, and yet another mound behind the second. As the mist climbs over the mountain of corpses, Guido retreats, horrified at what he is seeing. Though right before he discovers the corpses Guido wished that he and Joshua were in a dream, instead, Guido discovers that he is in the presence of the real—that he is face-to-face with the reality of the camps.

The stark reversal of styles from realism to stylization signals and emphasizes the film's ongoing confrontation with the power of Nazism. As the film repeatedly demonstrates, Nazism was not held in place by real power, but rather, fantasies around the symbolic—fantasies that individuals maintained with their own desires. The guns used to maintain that power are kept in place by people like Lessing, the female guard, and the matron at the camp, but more importantly, by people like Rodolfo who acquiesce in the face of it in order to maintain their privilege. The reversal of styles demonstrates that there is nothing real about the uniforms, ranks, manners, and prestige. Rather, they are all part of a fantasy that is founded on violence and death and leaves nothing but violence and death in its wake. What Guido stumbles upon in the mist is the real effects that result from the symbolic mandates—and fantasies—of Nazi society. The mountain of corpses is a profusion of the effects of that society as a terminally insane fantasy to eradicate others in the quest to create a "pure" society.

The trajectory of the narrative, however, insists that there is always the possibility to resist symbolic mandates, no matter how powerfully they are enforced. Guido's repeated manipulations of symbols is a comic pretext for illustrating the potential, the means, and the motivation for resistance—articulating in the process a radical Christian response to the question, "what would you do about Hitler?" The trajectory of the narrative is constructed to show the always present possibilities for resistance that lie at the base of the tenuousness and contingency of every society—a possibility that the Hitler question seeks to deny. As Brimlow's book on Christian nonviolence makes clear, the Hitler question poses so much difficulty and works so effectively because it correctly presupposes that Christians are unwilling to die. As Brimlow argues:

> Our call to follow Jesus and be peacemakers means that we will die. We don't like this message, so we recoil from it and consider it incomprehensible; and we find ways to try and reinterpret the gospel or to understand the "real" meaning of Jesus' message in order to obfuscate and avoid this conclusion.[137]

By constructing a narrative around a father's love for his son, however, *La vita è bella* elevates the circumstances by which someone would be willing to die: out of love, for the sake of their beloved.

Guido's death is the site of a radical alternative to the Hitler question—an alternative based neither on successful resistance nor passive surrender, but on the logic of Christianity, whose response to overwhelming coercive power is what Brimlow and David Toole describe as the way of the cross. As David Toole argues, "the cross is the ultimate trick. For it is at the cross that the Powers lose the one thing left to them—the power to kill in such a way that death is robbed of its meaning."[138] Guido's maneuvers in the climactic scene work to accomplish just such a trick. By sacrificing himself, Guido seals the ruse—takes all possible attention away from Joshua, but at the same time, assures Joshua it is all a game. To the ignorant guard, Guido will be just another meaningless murder of a Jew. Guido, however has determined the meaning of his death—a sacrifice to protect Joshua and Dora. The knowledge that they will live on past his death—and the death of Nazism—allows him to wink at Joshua, and stride off willingly to his execution.

In this manner, the narrative trajectory not only incorporates Christianity's way of the cross, but demonstrates that it has organized itself all along around the structure of sacramental love. The primary indication of this structure is the segue between the film's two halves: the offscreen uniting of the romantic couple. After arriving in the courtyard, Guido takes Dora off the horse and leads her to his uncle's home. Unfortunately for his perfect rescue and getaway, Guido has left the key with his friend Ferrucio. As he struggles to pick the lock with a piece of wire, Dora slowly enters into the flower house located right next to the main house. It is only when he has successfully picked the lock that Guido turns to find that Dora has gone. Tentatively, he enters the flower house himself. As he does, the camera slowly follows him, dollying in, and craning up as he walks up the stairs and into the building.

The camera remains in position on the entrance as Guido exits the frame. Just briefly after Guido exits, however, a small light turns on within the frame, and Dora's voice can be heard calling, "Joshua?" She repeats her call and then is joined by Guido calling. As Dora calls, however, the camera slowly begins pulling back in a reversal of the shot's original camera movement. As it does, a young boy comes bounding into the frame and towards the entrance. Guido and Dora are now outside awaiting their son so that they can start a new day. The camera's pattern here—movement, stasis, and movement—combined with the light switching on, works to create a clever temporal transition: time has clearly passed from the evening that started the scene. In addition, the scene just as clearly indicates that Guido and Dora's romantic union has resulted in a son.

The brevity of the transition, and its clever use of film language, help mask two fundamental discourses articulated by the scene. The first is that the transition signals the end of the romantic comedy: the couple has united. All the barriers to their union, including the locked door, have been overcome—resulting in their union. Just as significantly, the appearance of Joshua articulates the evolution of the couple from romantic love to sacramental love: that their union has gone beyond themselves and created new life. In this manner, the film visualizes the Roman Catholic concept of sacramental marriage and children as "the supreme gift of marriage . . . ."[139] Joshua enters the narrative as such a gift—as evidence of Guido and Dora's love. As the scene unfolds, however, and plunges the narrative deeper into the war, the film confirms that Dora and Guido's love has gone from romantic to sacramental.

The deportation scene dramatically evidences this evolution. Dora has just reconciled with her wealthy and well-connected mother, and they arrive at the house for Joshua's birthday party, only to find the house ransacked and empty. Dora recoils in fear, knowing what has happened: her husband and child have been rounded up. A short time later, Dora arrives at the train station where the Germans have rounded up the Jewish population to deport them to the death camps. Speaking to the German officer in charge, Dora tells him there has been a mistake. The officer consults his ledger—ostensibly confirming that Guido, Uncle Eliseo, and Joshua are Jewish—and replies that no mistake has been made. Dora then responds that she wants to get on the train. Her response is interrupted by a platform worker, looking to dispatch the train. When the German officer turns back to Dora, he intones, "Return to your home, Mrs. Go." Dora then defies him by insisting, "I want to get on the train," causing the officer to pause in his tracks, then stop the train.

Dora's insistence works against the idea that she was acting impulsively. The German officer politely dismisses her—giving her the opportunity to escape the consequences of her noble intentions. Here, the unspoken discourse is just as important as the explicit dialogue. The certainty of the German officer's remark, "there's no mistake," signifies that the Jewish identity of Guido, Joshua, and Uncle Eliseo are known to the state. Subsequently, when he tells Dora to return home, his discourse implies, "You're not Jewish, walk away from this." Rather than impulsive, then, Dora's actions are motivated by the sacramentality of her love for Guido and Joshua—even though odds are she will never see them again. The earlier reconciliation with her mother confirms her motivation. If Dora walks away, she can return to material comfort and to a well-connected Catholic family. She can wait out the war and survive. That she was driven to the train station in an expensive car testifies to that option. Dora has already turned her back on that option, however, when she chose to join her life to Guido. Now, having to choose between living without Guido and Joshua, or risk dying with them, Dora chooses the latter: to be with them even unto death.

This sacrificial position that Dora takes illustrates that the romantic love that motivated Dora to join Guido has now evolved into something more: a sacramental love for Guido and Joshua that is so deep that a voluntary life without them is meaningless. Rather, Dora comes to see that her defiance and insistence denies the power of the Nazis to control and define her love. By choosing sacramental love over survival, Dora eliminates the only hold the Nazis have over her: the fear of death. In this manner, Dora's decision foreshadows Guido's sacrifice at the film's climax by establishing the selflessness their love has achieved by passing from romantic to sacramental love.

The narrative trajectory is built around highlighting this evolution—underscored by the plot's segue that demarcates the two halves to the film. The plot moves from romantic comedy to tragedy, but is not content to stay with the tragic form. Rather, the film's engagement with Christianity determines that the narrative moves beyond tragedy into what David Toole describes as the apocalyptic. Too often misunderstood as cataclysmic end times, apocalypse is more accurately understood theologically, Toole argues, as revelation: as conforming to its Greek root *apokalypsis,* "to reveal," "to disclose," or "to unveil."[140] Toole demonstrates that the apocalyptic revolves around "certain disclosures of divinity, and that the definitive such disclosure occurred at the cross."[141] For Toole, the apocalyptic imagination is far less about a future cataclysm, then it is a paradigm shift in understanding power—a paradigm shift similar to Michel Foucault's analysis of power. Here it is worth quoting Toole at length:

> When I speak of an apocalyptic historiography and an apocalyptic politics, I have in mind a particular style, a particular way of life, that, much like Foucault's aesthetics of existence . . . the otherness of a world that never ceases to be strange. In this world, history continues not because of what kings and Presidents might do, but because ravens keep alive a prophet starving in the desert (First Kings 17) and because even as kings and Presidents count their people and stake their polls and plan the future, the word of God comes into the wilderness (Luke 3).
>
> What the authors of both Kings and Luke knew is that ravens and peasants have more to do with the movement of history than all the best laid plans of kings. To adopt an apocalyptic style is to follow the biblical lead and turn our attention away from the power of kings and toward the power of ravens and peasant prophets in the wilderness.[142]

For both Toole and John Howard Yoder, the fundamental position of Christianity and its apocalyptic imagination is a fundamental refusal to accept the power system of worldly politics as definitive—or more importantly as all encompassing.

The narrative trajectory of *La vita è bella* is constructed around such an apocalyptic imagination. The first such indication is the plot's setting in Arezzo, an outlying, provincial town of little to no political or military strategic importance, but of enormous ideological importance. As D. Medina Lasansky discusses, the fascist government poured resources into Arezzo to "perfect" its medieval and Renaissance architecture and heritage as a means of creating the "new" Italy that fascism tried to create.[143] The story of *La vita è bella*, however, is not an analysis of dictators—Mussolini or Hitler—but rather, their lower minions and the ordinary people they impact: the people who buy into the "new" Italy and its repressive government, the individuals who enact the fantasy of Nazism. The story refuses to elevate the power and authority of the era's leaders, but rather deconstructs and destabilizes that power and authority through Guido's ongoing manipulations of the symbolic order. Moreover, Guido's antics are never a direct assault on the system of power, fascism, or the state apparatus. Rather, Guido is consistently engaged in ideological resistance—refusing to give in to the social reality that fascism and Nazism seek to impose. In this manner, the narrative insists that resistance is always possible, even when revolution is not. The point of the story is not that Nazism could have been stopped, but rather, to demonstrate—and valorize—moral opposition as an option.

In valorizing moral opposition, the narrative chooses the apocalyptic imagination, which eschews the ideology of successful dominion *or* revolution. Plot mechanics, for example, do not speculate that mass moral opposition would have overthrown the Nazis. Instead, the plot elevates moral opposition, and indeed, insists that it will outlive the evil it opposes. The plot's denouement and ending are crucial to this apocalyptic structure. Far from speculating that nonviolent opposition would have overthrown Hitler and the Nazi regime, the narrative confirms the historical record that only more powerful coercive force brought about the end of Nazi power and occupation. The German soldiers are seen burning evidence of the camp and getting rid of prisoners as they prepare for retreat. The empty camp is then liberated by a convoy of Allied troops—led by a Sherman tank and its commander.

The narrative thus refrains from making Guido's resistance a formula for social change: a more clever Gandhi whose tactics can bring down an evil empire. Rather than the pragmatics of overcoming power, the narrative centers itself instead on revelation—on pointing out the fantasy and fallacy that maintains worldly power and insisting instead that real power is elsewhere: in the transcendent love that guides Dora's decision and Guido's sacrifice. The trajectory of plot is built around guiding the audience to the paradigm shift that must occur before they can identify—and identify with—a radically alternative concept of power: the way of the cross. The plot underlines this paradigm shift with the closing shot, where Joshua, reunited with his mother, raises his arms and cries, "We won." The narrative's framing device, however, ensures that Joshua's words are read allegorically.

As soon as Joshua clambers off the tank to reunite with his mother, the voice-over states: "This is my story. This is the sacrifice my father made." The voice-over works to frame Joshua's words within the context of Guido's sacrifice. From Joshua's childhood point of view, the family has won the fictional game that Guido put into place. The adult Joshua who is now narrating, however, places the victory in another context, on a different plane of meaning. Valorizing his father's sacrifice, the adult Joshua engenders the meaning of victory as a triumph over the powers—the Nazis and the fascists, who, indeed, retreated and died away, leaving "the little people" to inherit and thrive in their absence. The victory that Joshua relishes is nothing less than the victory of the cross—which, through Guido, refused to yield to the threat of death, and just as importantly, reversed the meaning of the death imposed by power. Rather, through sacramental love, Guido gladly gave up his life for others, and triumphed over death. Guido's gesture endures, is a story handed down, treasured, and continues to bring light to the darkness. The nameless guard, still clinging to his fantasy of Nazism, is condemned to the ash bin of history, meaninglessness, and death.

In this respect, *La vita è bella* can be understood as appropriating classical cinematic narrative—that system of assigning meaning and value to actions and consequences—as well as the genre of romantic comedy, as a means of privileging the image and vision of the apocalyptic imagination. It confronts the question, "What would you do about Hitler?" with an unlikely answer, "let them kill me so others would live" or "sacrifice my life for others." The plot demonstrates that the answer is not as unlikely as it seems: that sacramental love is already in our midst—in our lives—and that we are just as likely to act upon it as not. What we have to learn to imagine is not so much the sacrifice itself, but rather, the apocalyptic effects: to rob powers of their ability to impose meaning.

JOYEUX NOËL

La vita è bella's appropriation of the classical narrative form to promote the apocalyptic imagination is a daring—and rare—ideological challenge that the film helps render non-threatening by its use of comedy. Christian Carrion's film *Joyeux Noël* is an equally daring challenge that foregoes the use of comedy to cushion its critique against militarism. An historical fiction centered around the outbreak of peace along the trenches of World War I, the film uses the conventions of realism and the historical film genre to insist on the reality of the apocalyptic imagination.

From the beginning, however, *Joyeux Noël* delivers its ideological challenge by subverting classical narrative form. The first such subversion is the plot's rejection of a central, or main, character. The film positions its story away from the powers and principalities and focuses instead on the everyday men who populate the trenches. Rather than the background characters who fill out the narrative for the "Great Men" of history to move through, here, the men in the trenches and their actions, their decisions, their consciousness, create the narrative and its trajectory. Much like *The West Wing,* then, *Joyeux Noël* subverts the classical Hollywood form at the level of metadiscourses, in particular, individualism, causality, and closure.

In choosing to focus on the collective, the film works to undermine not just the concept of individualism, but power as it is defined through the figures of history. This decision to disregard the powers—the people at the top who caused and conducted the war—is a strategic choice to undermine the concept of political power and point instead to a different kind of power. It is, in the terminology of John Howard Yoder, a decision to focus on crosses, not kings, to "dismantle the notion . . . that . . . Caesar is the privileged mover of history."[144] The plot makes this change in focus clear when it chooses the Welsh Chaplain Palmer to serve as the main character for the Scottish soldiers. In a pointed scene early in the story designed to undermine the authority of the military elite, Palmer is dressed down by a major for disobeying orders and attempting to rescue an injured soldier in no-man's-land. The major's public criticism of Palmer insists on "military discipline" and on orders being followed, but also commands him to "drop the St. Bernard act." In the end, the major insists that Palmer return to the back line. While seemingly obeying and accompanying the major, Palmer conducts a coordinated prank by signaling to one of the men. As Palmer leads the major through a line of latrines, a soldier raises his rifle and fires a shot. Reacting to the gunfire, the major dives into the latrine.

The narrative function of Palmer's prank is multifaceted. Primarily, the scene serves to both deconstruct and criticize the authority of the military elite. Having dived into the latrine, the major is now literally full of shit. The uproar of laughter from the rest of the men demonstrates their belief that the major—who has come to insist that the regiment stay on the front lines—is figuratively full of it as well. Just as significantly, the scene demonstrates that the men have developed their own consciousness beyond the ideology that the military elite seeks to impose on them. The signal from Palmer to the other soldier indicates that the prank is well known and well practiced, and no one hesitates to deploy it against the major. Finally, the scene occurs after two other scenes—each of which undermines the competency and morality of the military elite in the other two armies of the narrative: the French Army and the German Army. In the first such scene, a major general sneaks into his son's camp to discuss his plan to transfer the son—Lieutenant Audebert—out of the infantry and into the artillery where he will be safe. During the discussion, however, the major general expresses his dissatisfaction with the last attack on the German trenches. When his son informs him that the Germans had machine guns in the trench and wiped out a third of his men in five minutes, the father ignores him and insists on an alternative interpretation. The plot, however, has already shown the futility—and insanity—of the attack, and sides with Audebert.

Just after the scene, the plot then switches to Germany, where opera diva Anna Sorensen makes a request at German general headquarters to give a recital at the front on Christmas Eve—a recital that will reunite her with her husband, an equally famous opera singer now serving as a foot soldier at the front. When the German commander in charge of logistics turns her down, Anna calmly produces a piece of paper indicating that she has made the request to the crown prince of Germany, who has already granted the request. Anna's scene is significant not only for maintaining the pattern of undermining the authority of the military elite, but for the manner in which it shows the ability of the less powerful to use dominant ideology against itself, against the powers. Anna uses her status as a celebrity and joins it to the belief of the powerful that they support the war effort.

From the beginning then, the film demonstrates that the people who populate the trenches are conscious of the failure and incompetence of those in power, and are willing and able to resist. Moreover, the plot trajectory is then constructed around moving that consciousness to another, deeper consciousness. Unlike the norms of classical Hollywood cinema, the narrative trajectory is not so much advanced around the desire of an individual main character as much as it is centered around the growing consciousness of all the characters. Anna's desire to reunite with her husband may advance the narrative at specific junctures, but their reunion is not the culmination of the narrative. Rather, it is the ability of all the characters to transcend the real limitations imposed on them through the ideology of militarism and find their common humanity. Like any narrative trajectory, narrative movement is advanced and delayed, threatened and redeemed—advancing again to the point of a climax and resolution. Unlike most narrative trajectories, however, movement is constructed around the consciousness of the collective, and how its members come to transcend dominant ideology.

Transcendence lies at the heart of the second metadiscourse the film subverts: causality. Rather than concise motivations spurred by the actions of others and used to overcome clear obstacles, the plot advances around the transcendent as an ill-defined but powerful force that pulls the collective towards consciousness. The first such transcendent power that spurs actions is music. During their Christmas Eve celebration, the Scottish troops sing "I'm Dreaming of Home" to the music of the bagpipes, and the German soldiers are seen listening appreciatively—if not longingly. Then, when there is a break in the Scottish carousing, the German opera-tenor-turned-foot-soldier Sprink sings "Silent Night" to the music of a lone harmonica. The plot shows the effect that the Christmas hymn has on Palmer, the priest who has lead the Scottish bagpipers, and on all the Scottish troops. When the film returns to Sprink and the German trench for the second verse of the hymn, however, the sound of bagpipes can be heard trying to accompany him. Compelled by the gesture, Sprink climbs to the top of the trench, where he can be seen by both sides, and sings to the end of the hymn—at which the Scottish side enthusiastically cheers. As Sprink, and the horrified

German Lieutenant Horstmayer then see, the Scottish have come out to the top of their trench to applaud Sprink.

Sprink's polite bow to his appreciative audience signals both an acknowledgment and the possibility of an end to what could be construed as polite engagement. The priest Palmer, however, sees the opportunity to reach even further—to engage the transcendent at a deeper level. He fills his bagpipes, and begins to play the opening phrase of "*Adeste Fideles*," then stops—waiting to see if Sprink will take up his invitation. Sprink responds by singing the song a capella, then picking up a small Christmas tree that the high command has sent to commemorate Christmas. Continuing to sing, he walks into no-man's-land. As he progresses, the rest of the Scottish pipers begin to accompany him. Palmer's choice of hymns is not coincidental. By choosing a hymn sung in Latin, Palmer attempts to cross linguistic boundaries and venture into the shared space of the two cultures. Sprink recognizes the gesture and not only takes up the music, but physically begins crossing the boundary of the trench into no-man's-land—carrying the Christmas tree as the symbol of their shared beliefs in the transcendent and the point of their commonality. Sprink enters into the space that demarcates the limits of power, the space no power can claim—hence its name. In doing so, Sprink attempts to claim the space for a different kind of power—the transcendent that endows and animates all of them.

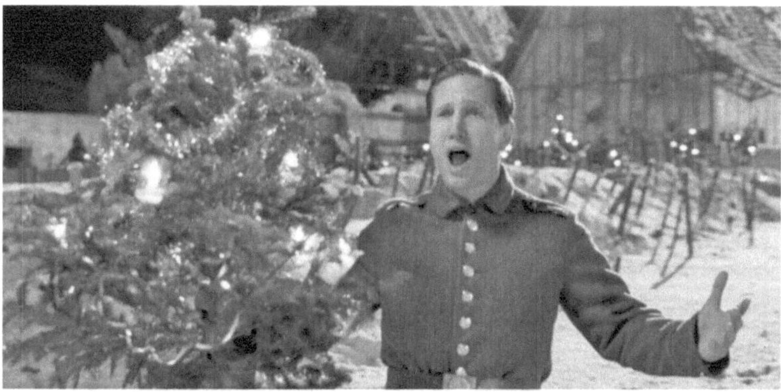

Sprink's gesture of bringing the Christmas tree into no-man's-land moves the troops even further into consciousness of their solidarity.

Sprink's ability to claim the space is the result of both his gesture and its relationship to the lyrics of the song. "*Adeste Fideles*" sings of an invitation to those of faith to come to a small space—Bethlehem—that exists outside the halls of power—Jerusalem—in order to appreciate how the manifestation of God entered into history in the most humble of ways.

Through the song, and his gesture, Sprink appropriates no-man's-land as a metaphor for that place. He gives himself over to the world and symbols of the transcendent—to create, however temporarily, a moment where the light of the transcendent will keep the darkness of the powers at bay. In so doing, Sprink invites the others in all the trenches to be part of the faithful and not the army—again, to the horror of Lt. Horstmayer.

In this manner, the narrative takes up the increasing and irrevocable movement towards fellowship on the part of the characters. The Scottish officer Gordon walks out to no-man's-land to speak with Horstmayer over a formal cease-fire. The French Lieutenant Audebert then joins them, and the cease-fire is arranged. What the officers cannot see at the time is that their actions are another cause that will lead to another effect: an irrepressible fellowship. Their pragmatic and polite responses to accidental gestures of good will undermine strict causality, while at the same time, insisting upon the powerful potential for fellowship to make its claims on the consciousness of men. The point of no return for this process is the nighttime Christmas Eve mass held in no-man's-land, where Anna sings the "*Ave Maria*" to the spellbound troops. From the apocalyptic imagination, it is the culmination of the narrative—from that point forward the sides can no longer perform as strangers, the seed of fellowship having been too firmly implanted. The following day Horstmayer proposes to Gordon and Audebert that they arrange to take care of the dead. A soccer match ensues, drawing the two sides together in an alternative battle, one that only serves to bring them closer together.

The degree to which the apocalyptic imagination—and its politics—has taken hold is then demonstrated in the next development of the narrative trajectory. Horstmayer informs Sprink that he will be arrested for disobeying orders at the front—having left his concert at HQ to join his comrades without permission. Devastated, Sprink asks the Lieutenant, "What's the plan for tomorrow? A little football match and an apertif with those across the way? Or will you shoot them like rabbits having shared champagne? All that is now meaningless. To die tomorrow is even more absurd than yesterday." The scene functions as a microcosm of the apocalyptic structure of the film's narrative. Sprink reaches for the apocalyptic imagination, but it seemingly cannot stand against the powers. Horstmayer appears unswayed, orders Sprink to be quiet, and asks for coffee. Horstmayer, by all appearances, has returned to the role that the powers have assigned for him: overseer of military order and discipline. The following day, however, Horstmayer seeks out Audebert in his trench to warn him that the German artillery will fire on his position in about ten minutes, and suggests that he and the Scots seek shelter in the German trench. As they walk to the

German trenches, Horstmayer states to Audebert, "Had you been relieved, I would not have come to warn your successors."

Horstmayer's statement functions polysemously. On the one hand, it conveys his willingness to return to the safety of military protocol. At the same time, however, it evidences that Sprink's discourse has firmly settled in the lieutenant's consciousness: for the sake of his own humanity he cannot abandon their fellowship. The ideological power of the military to set limits on Horstmayer's behavior and consciousness is kept at bay by the tiny seed of the apocalyptic imagination that Sprink has planted. The plot confirms this apocalyptic mode with the next narrative development. After the German shelling ceases, Gordon proposes the two sides seek shelter in the Allied trenches in anticipation of an almost certain counterattack.

Much like *La vita è bella,* the resolution of *Joyeux Noël* appears at first to have a tragic structure. Anna and Sprink remain behind on the French side and ask to be taken prisoner. The French high command lays hold of all the letters they were carrying for the German soldiers, and reads in great detail about all the fraternization. All the principal characters are punished, and the regiments broken up and reassigned. The brief moment of peace and brotherhood is brutally stamped out by the power of the military, and the war grinds on.

The power of the military, and the nation-state that endows it, is further demonstrated when Palmer's bishop comes to reprimand and relieve him. The one person in authority who could understand Palmer's motivations and actions as being deeply rooted in the Christian ethos is, instead, completely compromised by his allegiance to the state. After implicitly suggesting that Palmer leave the priesthood, the bishop then goes to preach to the regiment sent to replace the group that Palmer "led astray." The bishop begins his sermon by taking a verse from Matthew out of context, extolling, "Think not that I come to bring peace on Earth. I come not to bring peace, but a sword." He then continues to twist the meaning of Christianity by telling the troops that they are involved in "a crusade, a holy war," before urging them to "kill the Germans, good or bad, young or old." This complete subjugation to the interest of the state is then underscored when the bishop ends his sermon by saying, "The Lord be with you." Palmer, attending to the wounded in the other room, removes the cross from around his neck and walks away.

This victory of state ideological power over the impulse of Christianity would signify a tragic structure, but the plot supplants tragedy in favor of an apocalyptic structure by subverting another metadiscourse: closure. The plot undermines the authority and the actions of the bishop through both irony and history. The first such irony occurs when the bishop intones "the

Germans do not act like us, neither do they think like us, for they are not, like us, children of God." The camera, however, has shifted its position from the Bishop to Palmer in the next room. It is a cue to the audience to review what has been seen by Palmer on Christmas Eve and Christmas Day: the Germans acting like and thinking like both the Scots and the French, and attending the night mass as children of God.

The next irony in the bishop's sermon underscores again the difference in historical position—and knowledge—between his character and the audience. In arguing that the Germans are not "like us" the Bishop condemns the Germans by rhetorically asking, "Are those who shell cities populated only by civilians, the children of God?" Yet, in the very next war against the Germans, World War II, the British will engage in just such military action. The bishop's moral position is thus undermined by his very criterion. To underscore the point, the plot incorporates another historical irony when the bishop urges the men to "Kill every one of the them, so that it won't have to be done again." The spectator, however, knows exactly that it will happen again—that young British men will go off again to die against the Germans on a mass scale.

The disparity in knowledge between the bishop and the film audience who observes him is an important part of the narrative's apocalyptic structure. The apocalyptic imagination is, as Toole and Yoder point out, a historical position: a knowledge that God's power moves and works in history in ways not readily seen, not easily understood, and in vastly different ways than earthly power—the power of kings and nation states. The structure of the plot and the narrative trajectory ensures that the audience is in a position to recognize the folly and incompetence of the earthly power portrayed in the film. Not only do the powers blunder into a war—the carnage of which they could not fathom—but they keep insisting on sending unprotected men into machine gun fire in the vain hope that the next charge will end differently than all the others (the very definition of insanity). Moreover, the spectator also knows that the Scottish regiment that replaces the one guilty of fraternization will itself lose most of its men to the war machine.

While the power of the state seemingly crushes the apocalyptic imagination, the audience knows otherwise—knows this is not the end. Unlike the functionaries of the state and the military in the story, the audience knows that the war will lead to the collapse of the empires of Europe, while the apocalyptic imagination of the soldiers will endure. The charge against the men—fraternization—is itself evidence of the weakness of the state to stand against the apocalyptic imagination. The state knows that if brotherhood—especially Christian brotherhood—is established between sides, then war will be impossible. The powers know that a sense of brotherhood will render men incapable of shooting, which is precisely what happens in the Scottish trench. Only the tortured Jonathan, who had to abandon his brother to death in a failed attack, can shoot Germans after brotherhood is established between the troops. In the film's final irony, the German that Jonathan shoots is, in fact, the French soldier Ponchell, who, in cooperation from the German soldiers, disguised himself as one of them so he could visit his mother behind enemy lines.

The narrative trajectory of *Joyeux Noël* is built around the establishment of that brotherhood, and the insistence that it will endure—articulating not only the apocalyptic imagination, but the politics of apocalypse as well. This endurance, and its political implications, can be seen in the closing scene of the film. Horstmayer and his regiment are locked in a rail car when the crown prince of Germany enters. He informs the men that they are being relocated to the Russian front—traveling across Germany, but unable to visit their families. Just before he leaves, the crown prince sees one of the men's harmonicas. He grabs it, and crushes it under his boot: a metaphor for the state's ability to crush the humanitarian impulses that guided the men. As the door closes behind the aristocrat, and he heads for his car, the men begin humming "Dreaming of Home," the song that they heard from the Scottish trench on Christmas Eve.

The narrative draws to a close with the image of the frustrated crown prince, impotent to stop this act of resistance. The song continues to emanate from the railway car as the prince heads to his limousine. In making the closing image that of the railway car pulling away with the song still being hummed by the men, the plot resists not only closure, but tragedy, replacing it with apocalypse—with the assertion that resistance will endure. By choosing "Dreaming of Home," the men articulate their solidarity with the Scots over their identification with the German state. They will fulfill their roles, they will act as they are told to do so, but they make clear that their consciousness will no longer be controlled by the state. Rather, they will dream of a better place, and call that—not the Fatherland—home. Here too, the plot draws upon history to resist closure. The audience knows that the crown prince, heir to a powerful empire, will, in short time, be only an anecdote of history—the empire itself a victim of the war. The brotherhood that now animates the soldiers, however, will persist and endure, indeed, will have to endure yet another world war, but will nonetheless wait patiently for its full realization.

The Aesthetics of Collectivity

Both *La vita è bella* and *Joyeux Noël* appropriate conventional narrative form to affirm a radical apocalyptic discourse, though clearly in different ways. One of the principal differences—aside from the generic difference of comedy vs. drama—is the aesthetic of collectivity. The collective, or the community, is always relegated to the background in *La vita è bella*, much like Hollywood cinema. Subordinating the role of the community to the background performs several significant plot functions for *La vita è bella*. To begin with, it helps emphasize Guido's role as a minority in the first half of the film. Guido is a member of the Italian Jewish community, but isolating him from that community, his minority status is elevated, and his vulnerability is increased.

This vulnerability is important for the plot's didactic goals. As discussed earlier, the plot makes the argument that resistance is always a possibility, and Guido's vulnerability—one man against the occupying Nazi forces—serves to prove the point. Despite the clearly lopsided balance of power, Guido still manages to successfully resist. The plot is also careful, however, that its argument not become prescriptive. As a result, the narrative resists making the suggestion that following Guido would have stopped or brought down the Nazi regime. For this reason, the collective is always subordinated to Guido, always part of the colorful background, whether it be fascists and their sympathizers in the first half of the film, or fellow concentration camp inmates in the second half of the film. The film makes sure that the collective and their consciousness never become a site of potential resistance.

Joyeux Noël, conversely, structures its apocalyptic narrative precisely around the collective coming into consciousness. Each step, each progression, finds the plot exploring the beauty of the collective sharing their fraternal bonds. At the first step, with Sprink singing "Silent Night", accompanied by the bagpipe of Fr. Palmer from the Scottish regiment, the editing cuts between individuals from each side, joining them together through their shared reactions. The reaction of the Scottish regiment to Sprink's brave gesture shifts camera composition to a wider shot that can encompass the group and emphasize the collective response. Tellingly, Palmer's next action is rendered in wide shot as well. Even though it is an individual action, the camera composition emphasizes its role in participating in community building. Sprink takes up the invitation in a single shot, but the Scottish response is then from the group of bagpipers, rendered in wide shot.

As the plot progresses, other important stages of the growing collective consciousness emphasize the collective. The midnight mass employs wide shots that show the men seated in groups that stretch far into the background. When Anna first steps forward to sing, they are the backdrop that she cannot even face, but as she progresses, she turns to include them. The camera then abandons her for an elaborate crane shot that explores the depths of their reaction to the transcendent beauty that fills the space.

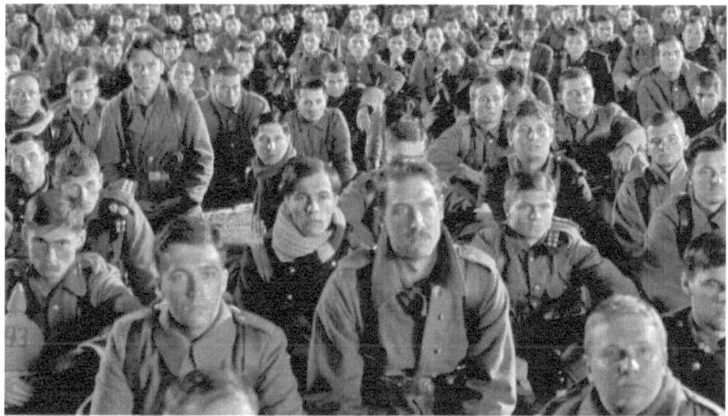

The plot visually emphasizes the collective throughout the film, including this intricate crane shot of all the troops.

Even when the editing returns to Anna, it is in a wide shot that shows the group in the foreground. Later, in the burying of the dead scene, the editing joins together mobile camera shots that render the actions of groups of men attending to the dead, ending with an extreme wide shot that surveys the entire scene of activity, the lonely French farmhouse serving as a dramatic and picturesque backdrop.

As the film progresses to its culmination, several other scenes will likewise come to employ cinematic language to emphasize the collective: the soccer match, the exchange of trenches, the refusal to shoot, and finally, the German soldiers in the box car. In short, the film comes to revel in the beauty of the collective: its growth, its scale, its tension between individual difference and group cohesion. The film elevates the concept of the collective to an aesthetic ideal as a means of articulating that the collective is the central and foundational element of the apocalyptic. In this manner, the plot ensures that the realization of a new collective consciousness is more than just the arc of story or central action, but also a matter of visual style.

The Aesthetics of the Apocalyptic

Significantly, this visual emphasis on collectivity does not come across as even remotely radical—despite the radical, apocalyptic message it imparts.

As the earlier discussion of theorists like Colin MacCabe and John Fiske demonstrate, however, traditional film theory would quickly assert that the radical discourse is somehow compromised, undermined, or contained. This position is reinforced by French critics Jean-Luc Comolli and Jean Paul Narboni, who argued in the late 1960s (in the rhetorical absolutism so characteristic of that era of French theory) that "only films" that attack conventional form and have overtly political content "have any hope of operating against the prevailing ideology."[145] Though rigid in their rhetoric, Comolli and Narboni nevertheless pointed to the way in which film form itself functioned as a discourse.

In many ways, then, Colin MacCabe's work on the metadiscourses of cinematic narration are an extension of this theory. As the discussion of *The West Wing* demonstrates, the limitation of MacCabe's theory of metadiscourse is its inability to account for the possibility that omniscience might be placed on the side of the radical discourse itself—as is the case with both *La vita è bella* and *Joyeux Noël*. In each film, the omniscient narration sides with and encourages the audience to believe in the radical apocalyptic vision. The narration places the audience on the side of history—an analog for omniscience—which knows that Nazism (in *La vita è bella*) and empire (*Joyeux Noël*) are on the verge of collapse. At the same time, the narration insists that the apocalyptic imagination will remain and endure along its own path—in its own time. Moreover, each of the films resist constructing their discourses as models of resistance for contemporary hegemonies of militarism. Rather, each film ends in their own time period in a manner which looks past history going forward, and testifies instead on the endurance of the apocalyptic.

In addition to omniscience, the narratives of both films operate on the metadiscourses of causality and closure. Both *La vita è bella* and *Joyeux Noël* work to undermine causality and appropriate it for the politics of the apocalyptic. As discussed earlier, *La vita è bella*'s comedy frequently revolves around Guido's ability to manipulate the symbolic system and make it seem like it is reality. Whatever the intentions of the dominant order, whatever effects they hope to achieve through their power, are undermined and manipulated through Guido's cleverness and his unwillingness to let authority determine his fate by completing the intended circuit of meaning. Through Guido's shenanigans, the narrative insists on the constant fragility of the social order: fascism and Nazism are always propped up by and emanate from fantasy. The only thing that is real in this narrative is the transcendent: the sacramental love of Guido and Dora. Likewise, in *Joyeux Noël*, causality never seems to work properly for the dominant social order: battle plans always fail, military discipline is shown to be a charade, and Christmas arrangements create the wrong reactions (brotherhood, not nationalism). The only causality that works in the narrative trajectory is the apocalyptic imagination, which starts out as individual love (Anna for her husband, the priest Palmer for Jonathan and his brother) and grows by leaps from one person to another, across national, class, and religious identities until it grows into a brotherhood of the collective.

Just as these narratives appropriate the metadiscourse of causality, they work against the metadiscourse of closure. Closure is the defining moment of cinematic narrative, the point at which plot operations attempt to finalize meanings assigned by narrative operations: the couple finally uniting after all their travails and closing the narrative with a symbol of their lasting affection is one example, the outlaw hero riding off into the sunset—and away from the civilization he rejects, but nonetheless has helped preserve, is another. Each of these examples demonstrates how cinematic narrative attempts to close off its operations by suggesting the permanence of the resolution. The couple will always be in love, and civilization will conquer the West, but the spirit of the cowboy will always live on.

The last example sheds light on the closure strategies of *La vita è bella* and *Joyeux Noël,* not only because it appropriates history in its closure operations—asking the audience to close off the narrative with their knowledge of history—but also because it engenders more continuousness in its closure. The romantic comedy, for example, frequently tries to freeze the moment in time, forever preserving the moment when the couple experience the height of their love—and are free from midnight feedings, changing dirty diapers, and stepping barefoot on little plastic toys designed to cripple adults. The Western, however, closes off the narrative by using the past to explain the present, and beyond: it suggests that civilization as we know it (hierarchical, unequal, and frequently unjust) has evolved this way naturally and inevitably. In this manner, it closes off interrogation and alternative interpretations, and serves the interests of the dominant social order.

La vita è bella and *Joyeux Noël* invoke history for another purpose: working against closure and encouraging instead an alternative consciousness of the role and place of the dominant social order. *La vita è bella* closes with a freeze frame, perhaps the ultimate plot tool for preserving a specific moment in time. The framing device that the plot employs, however, works against this freezing of time. By using the voice-over of the now grown up Joshua to narrate the story, the plot moves the image from the past into the present: it is now the continuing memory of Joshua. Moreover, Joshua's voice-over serves to foreground the act of storytelling. It works to make the audience conscious of a story being told—and to draw their attention to what the narrator identifies as the key aspect of that story: Guido's sacrifice.

Rather than consigning Guido's sacrifice to the past, Joshua's voice-over privileges it as a means of bringing it into the present: to serve as a standard and a mode of action by which to negotiate the present. Fascism and Nazism are consigned by the plot to the past, but the victory of the cross now realized by Dora and Joshua go forward into the present.

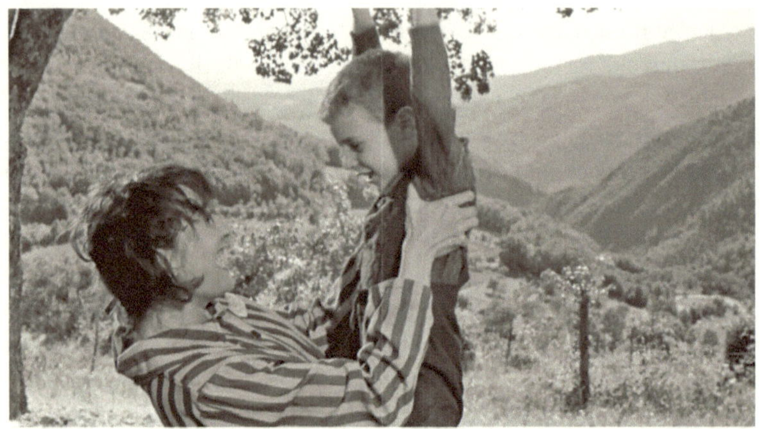

Joshua raises his arms in victory: the victory of the cross.

As it did through most of the plot, *La vita è bella* turns over the conventions of the romantic comedy for the sake of the apocalyptic. Rather than freezing time at the height of romantic love, the plot instead carries forward an image of sacramental love.

Joyeux Noël even more explicitly resists closure and insists on carrying the apocalyptic imagination into the present. Its final image consists of the moving train carrying the soldiers in one part of the frame, and the limousines of the crown prince's entourage in the other part of the frame. The staging of the shot emphasizes the plot's interpretation of the politics of apocalypse. The entourage of the crown prince drives offscreen and into a forgotten place in history—their expensive but open-carriage automobiles, as fragile as their place in history. The train carrying the men, however, moves off into the infinite background of the frame, the humming continuing long after it would be possible to hear. Just before the image begins a slow fade to black, the diegetic humming of the men is overtaken by the non-diegetic voice of a Scotsman, taking up the song while accompanied by a bagpipe. These plot techniques transport the men from the past, to the place of the transcendent. By transferring the song from the diegetic space of the men to the non-diegetic space of the Scotsman, the plot makes clear that the apocalyptic imagination that overcomes nationalism and creates brotherhood will go forward and endure—will be picked up by others and continue on along its own path, its own trajectory.

By employing the metadiscourses of classical cinematic narrative in the service of the apocalyptic, *La vita è bella* and *Joyeux Noël* demonstrate that classical narrative can be appropriated for radical discourses—especially the radical discourse of Christianity—without necessarily, or de facto—being undermined from within. The significance of appropriating conventional narrative as an aesthetic for Christianity is hard overestimate—and equally hard to defend. Narrative is a fundamental mode of comprehending the world, and its persuasive effect has been appropriated by cultural forms for millennia. The caution and skepticism of modernist and postmodernist theory around conventional narrative's ability to serve radical discourses and ideologies is an important caution to the aesthetics of Christianity, but should not be the basis for a rejection of narrative itself. *La vita è bella* and *Joyeux Noël* both demonstrate that narrative is a powerful vehicle for the radical discourses and agendas of Christianity.

In my earlier aesthetic analysis of comedy, I cautioned against overvaluing narrative—the result of narrative's ability to overwhelm and obscure other aesthetic elements. Moreover, narrative is not synonymous with the aesthetic principle discussed there: trajectory. Though the two concepts are interrelated, narrative must be made distinct from trajectory as a result of its highly structured, multivariable operations. The beauty and power of a trajectory is its unidirectional simplicity, the opposite is true of narrative. Narrative has the ability to weave together different spaces and trajectories into complex patterns that elevate discourse. Christian aesthetics must rethink and reconceptualize narrative, if for no other reason than secular humanist culture, via the culture machine, produces it so effectively—especially through the vehicle of simple, implied narratives. The marriage of Prince William to Kate Middleton on April 19, 2011, evidences how implied narratives are disseminated in the cultural marketplace, and most importantly, where the church—and Christianity—failed to assert its own.

The pageantry employed for the wedding was on a scale seen only in Hollywood blockbuster movies, including the traditional open carriage procession featuring the bride and groom in the royal family's 1902 State Landeau. Though built in the early part of the twentieth century, the carriage was designed to convey an implied narrative of timeless chivalry and heraldry associated with Britain's royal family. The timelessness of the tradition helps, in no small measure, prop up the image and status of the cultural—and economic—institution of the British royal family. Chivalry and the age of empire was not the only era on display for the ceremony, however. The Royal Air Force performed a flyover of Buckingham Palace with the Battle of Britain Memorial Flight, a group of airplanes that includes an Avro Lancaster (a bomber), a Hawker Hurricane (a fighter plane). and a Supermarine Spitfire (a fighter plane). After the greeting ceremony on the balcony of Buckingham Palace, the newly married couple left for their residence in an iconic, 1960s Aston Martin DB6 Volante MkII convertible that had been given to Prince Charles by his mother for his twenty-first birthday.

This well orchestrated array of symbols from different periods of British history weaves together a series of implied narratives and ties them to the royal family—the age of chivalry (where Britain evolved into a mighty empire), World War II (and national unity over Nazi Germany), and the 1960s (where British culture from the Beatles, to sports cars, to James Bond enjoyed global success). The function of associating these implied narratives of British cultural history with the royal family is to equate nationhood and British identity with the royal family: an association that is paramount for maintaining an obsolete feudal entity in a postmodern world. The pageantry and the symbolic array that comprises it works to displace attention from the economic privilege of the royal family and onto the concept of national identity. Behind all the symbolism promoting the role of monarchy as essential to British identity is a family that lives in enormous wealth and still holds vast estates. In other words, no matter how obsolete the feudal institution of royalty is, its contractual and legal holdings still hold, providing members of the House of Windsor with enormous wealth and privilege.

For the media covering the event, the most important narrative of the day revolved around Kate Middleton and her status as a commoner. Having met the prince at university, Kate proved that the exclusiveness of nobility was now a thing of the past, and that any girl could now become a princess. With that discourse as a foundation, the media coverage extolled repeatedly that this wedding is "every girl's dream," thus promoting the idea that through Kate, every girl could now legitimately dream of marrying into royalty, wealth, and celebrity. Audiences were encouraged to identify with the dream of a commoner now in possession of everyone's dream: to accede to the highest heights of privilege, wealth, and power signified and legitimated through the title of royalty.

As part of the process and pageantry of bestowing privilege through social hierarchy, of creating celebrity through media, and maintaining power and wealth through politics, the couple was married in the historic Westminster Abbey. There, the Anglican Church literally and formally gave its blessing. The ceremony recreated and reinforced the narrative of medieval church-state relations, where the monarchy ruled, but only with the blessing of the church. In becoming part of the pageantry itself, the Anglican Church elevated its own image, displaying its own grandeur and tradition as an institution. While the splendor and beauty of the Anglican Church—its architecture, music, trappings, and liturgy—are all employed metaphorically to symbolize the greatness of God, the narrative around royalty and power overwhelms and misappropriates the metaphors: associating them instead with the splendor of monarchy and earthly power.

The Anglican Church, in this respect, failed to control the narrative. As a result, its participation in the ceremony constitutes nothing less than a betrayal of the fundamental and radical discourses of Christianity: egalitarianism over social hierarchy, service to others over power, non-materialism over wealth. The Anglican Church allowed pageantry and its implied narratives to repress these core concepts of Christianity. As a result, the media was able to put forward a counter-narrative. The media's insistence that Kate's "dream come true" of becoming a princess counters one of the fundamental narratives of Christianity and the Jewish theology it comes out of. For both Christianity and Judaism, the individual is a unique and special part of an ongoing narrative known as creation. Within this ideology, the individual is no less significant nor less beautiful than the planets and the stars themselves.

The implied—and ongoing—narrative of creation is that the individual is him/herself God's own beloved: cherished, loved, called for, and that indeed, God wants nothing more than an intimate relationship with him/her. That every girl dreams of being a princess is, in this respect, a counter-narrative. In the creation narrative every girl already is a princess—the beloved of the master of the universe, who created her especially for an intimate relationship. Within the Judeo-Christian world view, the fathomless beauty of every individual, unique to all creation, dwarfs the splendor of any king, queen, or princess. Rather than asserting that religious truth, however, Westminster Abbey and the Anglican Church found themselves in a counter-narrative that spoke the exact opposite: that royalty and privilege are the summit of existence—a social and material reality more vital, more resplendent than anything else, and all the more valuable because of its exclusiveness. Against that image, packed as it is with pageantry, wealth, and adoration, the Judeo-Christian ideology of the beauty of the individual seems out of touch and unrealistic. Only the church can argue otherwise—can stand up and assert the validity of its ideology. In this particular event it did not—it was too overwhelmed by the counter-narratives already in place.

Radical and implied Christian narratives are not only possible, but already circulate. In the first year of his papacy, Pope Francis participated in a Holy Week ritual that previous popes have performed with little or no fanfare: washing the feet of twelve people on Holy Thursday in a reenactment of the Gospel story. One of the ideological functions of this ritual is to assert Christianity's concept of servant leadership. In a break with tradition, however, Pope Francis left the Vatican to perform the ritual, and went to a local jail. There, he washed the feet of juvenile prisoners, including individuals who were Muslim, Orthodox, and most shockingly for the ritual, women. Rather than fidelity to the specificity of the text—the apostles were all men—Pope Francis chose instead to emphasize the many dimensions that servant leadership engenders. The pope's actions created an implied narrative that the place of the church is with the marginalized and disenfranchised. Compared to his predecessors, who washed the feet of priests inside the Vatican, Pope Francis's actions rejected exclusion and embraced a radical discourse of inclusion, solidarity, and the mandate for servant leadership.

The appropriation of narrative to advance the radical discourse of Christianity should be a key part of creating a new aesthetic of Christianity. The ability of narrative to serve this function will hardly come as a surprise to theologians—not when the radical discourses of Christianity come, for the most part, from narratives.[146] Issues of translation and of lost historical context have enabled the discourses of Christianity to be misappropriated and its radical social agenda and vision largely—but not completely—silenced. It is now the work of Christian aesthetics to reanimate those discourses, and narrative, as *La vita è bella* and *Joyeux Noël* evidences, can be an important aesthetic tool with which to do so. The last chapter, on the Harry Potter series, demonstrates how conventional narrative can be used to reanimate the discourse of Christianity by reimagining the Christian narrative itself.

7

Harry Potter and the Return of the Repressed Mystical

Of all the praise that was heaped on first-time author J. K. Rowling's enormously successful Harry Potter series, few critics described the books as "original," and with good reason. For all its popularity, there is very little about the story that can be construed as original. Creating a fantasy world of witches and wizards is almost as old as English literature itself, and crafting stories for children with rich symbolic value that lure adult readers is also nothing new. Serialization, an epic battle between good and evil, clever plot twists—all are well-used narrative devices in the pantheon of British literature. In his exploration of the Harry Potter series, John Granger finds the literary influences of Jane Austen, Charles Dickens, William Shakespeare, the Brontë sisters, and Geoffrey Chaucer all operating within the narrative.[147] And yet, for all this stunning lack of originality, the Harry Potter series is arguably the most significant cultural phenomenon of the turn of the century: a work of enormous popularity, incredible misinterpretation, and unequaled economic activity.[148]

As a result of its popularity, Harry Potter was criticized by Christian fundamentalists who feared it was luring children into "witchcraft." It was also criticized by some literary critics and authors, like Harold Bloom and A. S. Byatt, who clearly felt the need to protect high culture from the corrupting influence of the popular. What both the Christian fundamentalists and the defenders of high culture overlook in their criticism, however, is the signifying function of the narrative: the meaning it attempts to impart to its audience through its use of symbols. It's not particularly surprising that

Christian fundamentalists would overlook symbolic meaning—they discipline themselves to focus on the literal. Bloom, however, is a literary scholar trained to analyze literature critically. Even so, he focused on the minutiae: for example, citing Rowling's overuse of the expression "stretch his legs" as evidence that the work lacks merit.[149]

Rather than originality, influences, or craft, my analysis of Harry Potter tries to uncover what makes the story so compelling for its audience. Like John Granger, I draw on narratology to examine a complex and multileveled production of symbols and their meaning, but I also turn to Lacan's theories of identification to delineate what audiences are responding to. In applying these frameworks, I compare differences between the books and their film adaptations. Film adaptation of novels is a complex undertaking, if for no other reason than the profound differences in the mediums. Literature is monovocal—communicating only through language—while film is polyvocal, communicating through language, music, imagery, and a vast array of technical operations like camera work, lighting, and pace of editing, all of which communicate specific meanings within the text. Generically, literature provides for easy access to character consciousness, whereas film has more difficulty with this narrational technique.

Lastly, and most often overlooked, is the vast difference in the length of narration between literature and film. *Harry Potter and the Sorcerer's Stone* is barely over three hundred pages long, a short novel by most standards, but would still take the average reader over 600 minutes to read. The film, however, pares that time down to 152 minutes. At only one-fourth the amount of time, the film obviously compresses a lot of information. This limitation, however, makes film adaptations have a tendency to magnify significant narrative discourses, and eliminate minor ones.[150] The most striking example of these films magnifying a discourse comes in the opening of *Harry Potter and the Deathly Hallows, Part I* (2010). The book opens with an ominous scene inside Malfoy Manor, where the increasingly powerful Voldemort plots his way to power with his inner circle. Many chapters later, on page 96, the book engages in exposition to describe how Hermione and Ron protect their families while they are off fighting Voldemort with Harry. As exposition, the scene in Ron's bedroom is nearly a throwaway scene, and it's emotional weight is offset by a wry comment about Ron giving lessons to Harry in tactfulness.

The film, however, appropriates this undervalued scene and puts it front and center in the opening itself. It replaces the ominous scene of Voldemort with an imposing close-up of the newly appointed Minister of Magic, Rufus Scrimgouer, before moving to an emotionally devastating scene of Hermione eliminating her parents' memories of her. With tears brimming, but remaining stoic, she erases their memories of her as they unknowingly watch television. As Hermione modifies their memories, the camera shows her image slowly dissolving out from of all the family photographs. The film then cuts away to Harry watching the Dursleys leave their home before returning back to Hermione leaving hers. Here, the plot uses the setting to emphasize the emotional weight of the scene even more: showing Hermione leave her house and then starting off across the town square alone, dwarfed by the architecture, heading for the path she has chosen. In this way, the film magnifies a discourse about the enormous personal sacrifice that Harry's friends endure as they try to help him.

The significance of magnified discourses, audience identification, and narratological analysis is the manner in which all these approaches examine how meaning operates dynamically on several different levels. John Granger (no relation to Hermione), for example, draws on Northrop Frye's model of narrative, whereas my analysis turns to Fredric Jameson. Each of these theorists sees narrative as a socially symbolic act, and each posits different levels or planes of meaning. Frye's approach is more structural—examining the relationship between the literary sign and its social reality first (the literal, or surface level), its relationship to other signs in the text (textual context), is second, (the formal, or moral level). Relationship to other literary signs (commonly referred to as intertextuality), constitutes the third (the allegorical level), and finally, its projection of an ideal is last (the anagogical level). Jameson's approach, however, is more suited to the narrative of Harry Potter, because of his insistence that the final level of meaning for narrative is not the idealized individual, but rather, the realization of the collective.

Granger's analysis demonstrates the crucial difference. An astute and thorough analysis, Granger is content to locate Christian motifs as they appear on the allegorical level, where they operate as part of a range of influences, all of which function in a larger project to create a subversive text. As Granger argues, Rowling's narrative is part of a literary tradition that "believe[s] that materialism and reductive thinking are dehumanizing, and thus are arguing against and undermining by parable the modern materialist worldview."[151] Granger's insightful categorization of the work as a subversive text, however, puts the cart before the horse. Rowling's book series is not a subversive work that has elements of Christian symbolism along for the ride. Rather, the discourse of Christianity exercises a primary role in the narrative, operating at all levels, and unleashing the subversive impulse of Christianity in the process.[152] What my ideological analysis of the Harry Potter narrative will show is that more than an assault on the dehumanizing tendency of modern rationalism (which it certainly is), the Harry Potter story is organized around a symbolic reanimating of the Christian narrative:

shaking the dust off a first-century story set in the remote areas of Palestine, whose charged political references have long since lost their valence, silenced by the blanket of time.[153] Harry Potter sets about revitalizing the compelling mystical power Christianity engenders when audiences can enter into the story.

Even here, however, the book is not breaking original ground. Both J. R. R. Tolkien's *Lord of the Rings*, and C. S. Lewis's *Chronicles of Narnia* can likewise be considered as reanimating the Christian narrative. Lewis's work—specifically *The Lion, the Witch, and The Wardrobe*—is an allegory that appropriates motifs and plot lines from the biblical book of Revelation. Tolkien's work is less directly allegorical to a master text, but nonetheless inscribes the discourses and moral ethos of Christianity. Rowling's narrative operates much more along the lines of Tolkien's model, avoiding (for the most part) direct allegory. Main characters like Harry and Albus Dumbledore, for example, do not correspond to biblical characters the way that Narnia's Aslan, the son of the Emperor over the Sea, corresponds to Jesus, the Son of the Most High.

Where Rowling's work makes its most significant departure from both Lewis and Tolkien is at the level of narrative structure. Lewis and Tolkien, writing in the aftermath of two world wars, both reframe the cataclysmic events in tragedies that mourn the loss of a mystical world, while at the same time they breathe a sigh of relief over their victory from the unprecedented forces of evil. In these books, Christianity can be said to operate on what Frye describes as the allegorical level, but less fundamentally on the anagogical. In Lewis's book, the way of the cross is an important subplot that goes so far as to redeem one of the characters—Edmund—but is nonetheless subordinate to a final, cataclysmic battle, and later, the coronation of the children as kings and queens of the magical world of the story. Tolkien's narrative, on the other hand, structures itself around a very long journey filled with hardships and self-sacrifice—appropriating core aspects of the way of the cross. In the end, however, a discourse of the cross is subordinated to a larger tragedy around the dissolution of the mystical, and the ascension of the rational. The Harry Potter series, conversely, structures its core narrative around Christianity's fundamental discourse, the way of the cross, on all three of the subterranean levels: the moral, the allegorical, and the anagogical. As this chapter will show, the narrative makes the way of the cross fundamental not only for narrative trajectory, but for defining and constructing character, establishing the norms and values of the narrative world, and for creating the very ethos of the setting.

Although Granger's analysis finds several different literary influences operating on the moral level of the Harry Potter narrative, the distinguishing role that time plays in the setting is indicative of the determining role Christian discourses exercise on the moral level of the narrative. The fundamental feature of the magical world of Harry Potter is that time has stopped, significantly, at the pre-modern era. There is no electricity (but thankfully, there is indoor plumbing) and people dress in cloaks, brew potions in caldrons, and write with quill pens on parchment. Letters are delivered by owls, testifying to a lack of modern infrastructure, and there is only one engine in this world—the steam engine used to transport students from London to the magical world of Hogwarts. The lack of modern conveniences, however, does not impoverish the magical world. Rather, what the narrative makes clear is that modern conveniences are themselves a response to the inability of normal humans to manipulate physical reality through magic: to produce light or fire, travel through space via apparition (or other magical means), cure afflictions, mend or reassemble what is broken, open what is closed, cook, and animate utensils to do one's bidding.

The premodern emphasis on the setting's magical world displays an organized compendium and progression from medieval, Renaissance, and early industrial age cultures. What the setting demonstrates is that the magical world developed alongside of the non-magic world up to a specific point in history, then stopped. Jameson's model encourages us to analyze this difference ideologically, to see this "coexistence" as "traces or anticipations of modes of production."[154] In this respect, the point at which time stops for the magical world is clearly modernity. This point of departure between the two worlds functions as a significant discourse. Modernity for the narrative is the historical moment where science, ushered in by the age of reason, delivers technologies that transform the productive capacities of humans. Ron's father Arthur Weasley, consistently makes this point, albeit ironically, via his fascination with the machines and devices of the Muggle [non-magical people] world. For example, he comments to Harry in book two that it is "Ingenious, really, how many ways Muggles have found of getting along without magic" (HP II, 43).

In addition to the productive capacities of modernity, science and the age of reason is the moment where humanity turns its back on the mystical realm: dismissing it to the world of the fantastic and the irrational. From this point forward, the world is drained of magic and myth: the mystical is consigned to the place of unreason and fairy tales, while science becomes the reigning ideology empowered to define reality. The narrative emphasizes this point of departure through the language of spells that the wizarding world uses. Many of the spells that are spoken by characters, like "accio" or "cave inimicum" are Latin, or they are crafted to sound like they are Latin (i.e., "expelliarmus"). Other spells in the narrative, like "alohomora" and "avada kedarva" come from the West African Sidiki dialect and ancient Aramaic respectively. The language sources of spells are rooted in organic and mystical societies where the Divine is constantly present and acts in and through nature, can be summoned through ritual, and called upon to intervene in events.

The narrative of Harry Potter uses fantasy to fill in the emptiness of a world that has been eradicated of that mystical presence by science, technology, and the profit motive that fuels them. The gleaming, powerful, medically advanced postmodern society at the turn of the twenty-first century is shown by the narrative to be a bumbling, unobservant, and largely hollow society that depends on technology to make up for its lack: the inability to manipulate the physical world. The series rarely introduces characters who are not wizards or witches, and when it does, they are usually mean-spirited, like the Dursleys, or unable to comprehend the magical world, as with the fictional English prime minister in the opening of book six. The film version replaces the scene of the prime minister by dramatically underscoring the fragility of modernism in its opening. Office workers in an ultramodern office building gaze out the windows as the Dark Mark (Voldemort's sign) hovers above the modern architecture of London. Moments later, Voldemort's Death Eaters attack a modernist walkway over the Thames, emphasizing its susceptibility by showing its cables snapping from the force of magic. Finally, book five raucously pokes fun at modern medicine when Arthur Weasley's wife Molly screams at him for having tried stitches to heal his wounds.

By comparison, the magical world seen through Harry's eyes is full of mystery and wonder, as when he first comes upon Diagon Alley (in both the book and the film), or when he encounters the difference between the outside and the inside of a magical tent in *Harry Potter and the Goblet of Fire* (2005). The film version shows him looking into the tent in amazement before stating, "I love magic." In addition, the world Harry enters into is filled with magical creatures, like Norbert the dragon, and Fluffy the three-headed dog in book one, the giant, venomous serpentlike basilisk in book two, and Buckbeak the hippogriff in book three. Lastly, the magical world is pervaded by powerful forces that transform the very laws of physics, bending them to the will of the individual. In book one, Harry and his friends learn to levitate objects by using a spell, and by book four, Harry is summoning objects using a different spell. In book five Fred and George Weasley have learned to apparate—to leave a place and appear in another—a skill that Harry himself will learn by book six. More than just creating an astounding magical world, the narrative makes clear that the magical world surrounds and pervades the existing world, but modern, non-magical humans—Muggles—are unable to see it.

All of the properties of the magical world—its organic vitality, interconnectedness, the way in which it runs parallel with and preferable to modern reality—operate to create a moral discourse. They construct a magical world that operates as an analogue to the mystical world: where spirit and love operate in tangible ways.[155] Dumbledore's character makes explicit, on several occasions, the moral ethos of this magical/mystical world. He repeatedly insists that love operates as the deepest and most powerful force in this world. He offers proof to Harry in book one when he explains that the protection unwittingly bestowed on Harry by his mother emanates from her self-sacrifice when she tried to save him. Here, as elsewhere in the story world, the power of love is a tangible force—it protects Harry from Voldemort whenever he resides in his aunt's home, for example.

That love can be made manifest—operate as a tangible force—undergirds the mystical power of the universe that Harry Potter comes to inhabit, animating the story with the ethos of Christianity: of the magic of the mystical universe that runs in and through but supersedes reality. The narrative's maintenance of the contemporary world of the reader as parallel to the world of the story is crucial for this moral discourse. Generically, this parallel construction prevents the story from being wholly fantastic—anchoring the magical world to the contemporary world and subjecting it to history and reality.[156] In addition, however, the maintenance of the two parallel worlds allows the magical/mystical world to serve as a critique of the contemporary world and its empty, dehumanizing hubris.[157] In this manner, core discourses of Christianity define the moral vision of the narrative world, and construct the narration's evaluative system—the means by which it judges characters and actions.

The Way of the Cross and the Main Characters

The construction of main characters is another crucial location where a discourse of the way of the cross plays a defining role. Early observations of the successful novel were quick to assert that the success of the story was built around Harry's everyday character. That interpretation not only oversimplifies the concept of identification, but overlooks the more generic "hidden prince" theme to Harry's character, not to mention the outright exceptionalism that makes him anything but an everyday person. Rather than an everyman, Harry is first constructed as a suffering servant, the despised dependent of the Dursley family. Harry is more than just neglected by the Dursleys, he is genuinely unloved and rigorously emotionally abused.

After establishing Harry's character as love-starved and abused, the plot moves on to construct Harry's character through the biblical discourse of "the anointed one." The plot makes this designation first through the scar on Harry's forehead, which operates as the sign of Harry's special status in the narrative as "the boy who lived" (HP I, 17). The scar, acting as sign, sets him apart from everyone in the story world as the only person "ever known" to have survived a killing curse. The next sign of Harry's anointed status also occurs early in the story, when Harry purchases his wand at Ollivander's. After going through many wands that did not suit Harry, Ollivander picks a wand that piques his curiosity, and hands it to Harry. In the novel, Harry swishes the wand around and a stream of red and gold sparks flies out, "throwing dancing spots of light on to the walls" (HP I, 85). This scene's portrayal in the film, however, emphasizes even more that the wand confirms Harry's place as the anointed one. In a classic example of magnifying the discourse, the film version of *Harry Potter and the Sorcerer's Stone* (2001) eschews the red sparks and shows instead an almost divine light shining down on Harry the moment he grasps the wand. A powerful rush of air then raises his hair, while the soundtrack fills with music and a choir. Ollivander's reaction confirms that something extraordinary has happened, and then he proceeds to tell Harry (as he does in the novel) that "we can expect great things from you."

Harry's status as the anointed one is further confirmed in book five, *Harry Potter and the Order of the Phoenix*, when Dumbledore reveals to him that Harry is the subject of a prophecy that designates him as "the chosen one" destined to be the downfall of Voldemort. Throughout the narrative, then, Harry's character comes to possess extraordinary power. He is imbued with such extraordinary talent for flying on a broom that he becomes the first student "in a century" to make his house Quidditch team in his first year. He is able to speak "parseltongue," one of only two contemporary characters who can, and later in the narrative, he is able to produce a "Patronus charm" well before any of his classmates. This exceptionalism culminates in his fellow students turning to him as a teacher in defense against the dark arts in book five.

Harry is defined as a normal character not so much to create broad appeal, but rather, to construct his character with the characteristics of the anointed one. Within biblical discourse, the anointed one is consistently undervalued for his qualities, and looked over because he is not physically endowed or privileged in some manner. Crucial to the discourse of the anointed one is undermining the normal concepts of power and privilege and promoting instead a hidden power that is unseen and undervalued. Like the biblical character David, who Samuel anoints, Harry is distinguished by his heart and soul rather than his physical prowess or imposing stature. Like the discourse of the apocalyptic, the discourse of the anointed one asserts that divine power is not only at odds with earthly power, but appears diminished before it.

Dumbledore articulates Harry's power as the anointed one when he describes a force within Harry " at once more wonderful and more terrible than death, than human intelligence, than forces of nature . . . that you possess in such quantities . . . . That . . . saved you from possession by Voldemort, because he could not bear to reside in a body so full of the force he detests" (HP V, 843). Dumbledore concludes this description of Harry's power by locating this force within Harry's heart—replicating the discourse in 1 Samuel 16:7 and implicitly arguing, as he does through the narrative, that love is the most powerful force in the universe.

The central place that Harry's status as the anointed exercises in the plot is designated by the way the plot constructs the antagonist Voldemort through the direct opposite. Voldemort's character is constructed around discourses of earthly power and his desire for more power. In a dramatic irony, Voldemort's existence is compromised when the narrative begins: he is neither living nor dead. Voldemort exists, in his own words, as "mere shadow and vapor." For the first three books, then, Voldemort exists only as a discourse. The first film clarifies this discourse as unrestrained nihilism, when Voldemort tells Harry, "there is no good and evil, there is only power, and those too weak to seek it."[158] Voldemort's discourse here eradicates the idea of a transcendent morality and asserts instead the modernist/nihilist conception that power defines what is right and wrong, acceptable and unacceptable.

By adding this discourse to Voldemort's character, the film positions Voldemort as a manifestation—the ultimate manifestation—of Nietzsche's superman—unburdened by the repressive forces of guilt, and unashamedly cultivating power. The plot consistently undermines and critiques the contradictions of this nihilist position. To begin with, the narrative consistently undermines the trajectory of Voldemort's desire: there is no substance to or end game for his desire for power. He and his followers ascribe to racial purity—magical vs. non-magical humans—and claim that it is their desire to put Muggles in their proper place of servitude as a primary motivation, but the narrative undermines even this position. Voldemort himself is not a "pureblood" wizard, and neither is Snape, one of his seemingly top lieutenants. On the other side of the conflict, Harry is not a pure-blooded wizard, and his most powerful helper, Hermione, is from non-magical parents: Muggle-born.

What the narrative makes clear in book six, *Harry Potter and the Half-Blood Prince*, is that Voldemort's lust for power is nothing more than a desire to avenge childhood wounds around rejection and shame. The narrative establishes this in book two, when Voldemort refers to his father as a "filthy Muggle" (HP II, 314) and again in book four as a "fool" and a "Muggle" (HP IV, 646). Book four also introduces how Voldemort's Muggle father abandoned both his mother and him by having Voldemort coldly recount the fact to Harry, but it is book six that drives home the depth of this pain. Through Dumbledore's detective work and a magical pensive that displays people's memories, the narrative rebuilds Voldemort's past as Tom Riddle, and how he ended up as an unloved and abandoned child growing up in an orphanage—unable to comprehend the magical powers he possessed. Through this backstory, the narrative endows his character with enormous magical talent and power, while at the same time limiting that power to a never ending pathological desire to heal his wounded ego by taking vengeance on the world.

Voldemort is the nightmare image of what arises in the complete absence of Christian morality—a moral ethos which Nietzsche despised. Moreover, the narrative asserts the Christian ethos by highlighting the contradictions that make Voldemort's extreme nihilism impossible to maintain. The first such contradiction is the status of "pure-blood" as paramount to the ideology of Voldemort and his followers. Voldemort insists on the sanctity of pure-blood, but he is a half-breed himself. He is unworthy to join the very group he has created. Even more important is the antagonism between power and love. Voldemort sees power as distinct and in opposition to love, which he sees as weakness. Taken to its logical endpoint, Voldemort's ideology would force the wizarding world into a world devoid of love and emotion, a Soviet-style fantasy where reproduction is performed solely for the perpetuation of the community.

The narrative emphasizes this contradiction in the betrayal of Voldemort by Narcissa Malfoy. In the final battle and confrontation, Narcissa lies to Voldemort that Harry is dead in hopes that she can reunite with her son Draco. She places her love for her son above her allegiance to Voldemort and his quest for power. Her betrayal underscores the fundamental contradiction between absolute power—power as the thing in itself—and love. Narcissa's actions insist that love has power, and it is stronger than power for its own sake. In the end, Voldemort's undoing results from the actions that unfold from multiple sources where the power of love manifests itself. In this manner, the narrative upends Nietzsche's superman, and exposes his discourse—that power is a thing in itself worth pursuing at all costs—as a myth.

The Way of the Cross in Ron Weasley's Character

Counterposed to Voldemort's lust for power is the antithetical discourse of the way of the cross: first introduced through the character of Ron Weasley. Even before the plot fully explicates Lily Potter's self-sacrifice for her son Harry, Ron is constructed through this alternative discourse of power. The first book reveals this discourse in the rising action towards the climactic scene: in the chess match directed by Ron as the three main characters race to protect the Philosopher's Stone. As Ron maneuvers himself, Harry, and Hermione in the live chess game, he sees the opportunity to win by sacrificing himself. Harry and Hermione protest, but Ron insists, so that the other two can continue the quest.

The film dramatically emphasizes the discourse within Ron's self-sacrifice: his commitment to giving himself over out of love for Harry and for the struggle against evil. In the film, the dialogue around Ron's sacrifice is longer, and it begins with Harry's recognition of Ron's plans. Ron states to Harry, "You understand why, Harry. Once I make my move, the Queen will take me. Then you're free to check the king." Harry protests and Hermione asks what's going on. When Harry informs her, Hermione yells, "No, you can't. There must be another way!" Ron's response is taken from the book, but then expanded upon. He retorts, "Do you want to stop Snape from getting that stone or not? Harry, it's you that has to go on, I know it. Not me, not Hermione, you!" Harry stoically agrees, and Ron moves himself forward, sacrificing himself to the Queen. The self-denial in Ron's sacrifice, his willingness to surrender himself for the greater cause, is the first articulation of the way of the cross.

In his work on a theology of the way of the cross, Douglas Jones demonstrates that self-denial or self-sacrifice is not the only aspect of this discourse. Jones goes on to define the way of the cross as having seven core elements: joyful weakness, renunciation, self-denial, sharing, foolishness, community, and love-overcoming-evil.[159] Ron's character is built around and acts through all of these characteristics. For Jones, joyful weakness refers to the way in which—as the apocalyptic imagination testifies—God works through human weakness and not through the powerful, the privileged, or the wealthy. Ron's character in particular is constructed around this trait because he comes from a family that struggles economically. This dimension of Ron's character is put on display early in the narrative through a contrast with Draco Malfoy, whose family is rich and powerful. Because of his arrogance and lust for power, Draco humiliates Ron in front of the entire first-year class on their very arrival to Hogwarts—publicly making Harry choose between Ron or Draco. Harry's choice not only demonstrates the empathy that runs deep in Harry's character, it also functions as a textual strategy to affirm the way of the cross: weakness over power. Ron does nothing to respond to his humiliation—no quick retorts or attempt at physical retaliation. Rather, he stands quietly, subjected to humiliation, and is able to withstand it.

Jones defines the next characteristic, renunciation, as the rejection of earthly powers such as domination, selfishness, greed, exceptionalism, and greatness. Ron's character consistently displays selflessness over selfishness. Despite his poverty, Ron never really lusts after wealth itself. Book one makes clear that Ron struggles to get out from under the shadow of his brothers, and by book four, Ron is even shown struggling with Harry's fame, but wealth for the sake of wealth is never really one of Ron's temptations. More importantly, the book and the film each emphasize that Ron's character eschews exceptionalism in favor of friendship and loyalty. Here, the comparison to his brothers is significant. Ron's five older brothers are all exceptional. Two of his oldest brothers became "Head Boy" at Hogwarts—demonstrating academic achievement and magical prowess. His other brother, Charlie, was a Quidditch star, a status much more valued by both Ron and Harry. Ron's other two older brothers, the twins Fred and George, are exceptional troublemakers and slackers, but the series makes clear that they have a high degree of talent. The book and the film both make clear that Ron's struggles to distinguish himself from his brothers never overwhelms or controls his character. Rather, his friendship and loyalty to the exceptional Harry always comes to define his character more than the desire to distinguish himself.

As discussed, the film's version of the chess match works around emphasizing the level of Ron's self-denial. Jones, however, expands the concept of self-denial beyond the passive negation of self, to the more active concept of deliverance. For Jones, this aspect of the way of the cross translates into a commitment to mercy, for helping others achieve justice, and for acting with humility. Ron's humility is demonstrated by the degree to which he willingly stands in Harry's shadow, which Hermione points out to Harry in book four. His sense of justice shows through in book one when he encourages Neville to stand up for himself, and further, by his dislike of Snape, who never rewards or punishes fairly. Even his hatred of Malfoy is motivated in large part by his sense of justice. Ron's hatred of Malfoy is not rooted in vengeance or retaliation for his own humiliation, but rather, to see the arrogant abuse of power put in its place: to have a Hogwarts community, and a wizarding world in general, balanced with more humility. Explaining Malfoy's prejudice to Harry and Hermione, he states, "There are some wizards—like Malfoy's family—who think they're better than everyone else because they're what people call pure-blood . . . . It's ridiculous. Most wizards these days are half-blood anyway. If we hadn't married Muggles we'd've died out" (HP II, 116).

Likewise, the fourth aspect Jones identifies in the way of the cross—sharing—is an important part of Ron's character. From the moment he meets Harry on the train, Ron's life is tied to Harry's, first perhaps out of gratefulness for Harry rescuing him from Malfoy's humiliation, but later, the narrative makes clear, out of a sense of love and loyalty to accompany Harry in his struggle against Voldemort. Ron insists—along with Hermione—on going through the trap door in book one, and in accompanying Harry into the Chamber of Secrets in book two. And though all of Ron's best impulses are challenged, and his shortcomings overwhelm him in their quest to destroy Horcruxes in book seven, he returns to Harry and Hermione at the first opportunity.

The quest for Horcruxes, and Ron's temporary failure, is an important site for what Jones calls the way of foolishness, or simply, faith. For Jones, *foolishness* is the more operative term because faith can too readily be simplified into "belief" rather than walking without sight. Jones argues, "the way of the cross recognizes that God works in mysterious, unpredictable, and surprising ways." As a result, Jones contends that "Faith is not just a belief in a super-natural truth, or an easy way into heaven, but a costly way of living contrary to the world."[160] The foolishness of the quest for Horcruxes is nearly always overshadowed for Ron and Hermione, by their faith that justice—and Harry—will prevail. Moreover, the quest is foreshadowed by the race for the stone in book one, where Ron and Hermione go through the trap door with Harry knowing full well that their chance of success is ridiculously small, while the danger—battling against the enchantments of Hogwarts teachers—is exceedingly high. Their loyalty compels them forward in a foolhardy mission.

Ron's attachment to Harry would conform almost solely to Vladimir Propp's definition of the "helper" character were it not for another aspect of the way of the cross that is important to his character: community. Notably for the narrative, Ron initiates the friendship with Harry that will eventually lead to a community forming around Harry. It is Ron who befriends the solitary and anxious Harry, who boards the Hogwarts Express not knowing anyone and not knowing what lies in store for him. Indeed, Harry sticking up for Ron after Malfoy's humiliation is motivated by Ron's initial kindness and empathy. In addition, however, Ron's relationship to Hermione (which starts out as friendship before evolving into romance) operates to define community as a core part of Ron's character and the relationship between the three. The narration emphasizes that their relationship goes beyond friendship right from the beginning. The plot engineers their relationship being forged through fire when Harry and Ron rescue Hermione: who they have unwittingly placed in harm's way. Then, the plot emphasizes the depth of their relationship, the bond of community, in one of the few narrational asides in the whole series, commenting "from that moment on, Hermione Granger became their friend. There are some things you can't share without ending up liking each other, and knocking out a twelve-foot troll is one of them" (HP I, 179). The narrative aside emphasizes the basis upon which the community is formed: not through shared interests, and certainly not through similar personalities, but rather through the shared experience of risking their necks for each other—as Ron will do first in the chess game, and later by diving into the icy water in the Forest of Dean to save Harry from drowning. Throughout the narrative trajectory, the community they build around their bond with each other—its trials and triumphs, betrayals and forgiveness—functions as a core part of Ron's character.

Lastly, Ron's character is defined by his commitment to love-overcoming-evil, as the chess match scene so dramatically illustrates. Ron does not adopt a classic "love your enemies" position of Christianity and the way of the cross. He does, however, place love in the service of conquering evil: giving himself over to violence in the hopes that evil will be vanquished. Ron's well-placed fear of the harm about to befall him, made clear in the film, is overcome by his belief that good can triumph with his sacrifice. What the film magnifies in this scene is the uncertainty of what Ron's sacrifice entails: it is not abundantly clear whether he will survive the chess move he is undertaking.

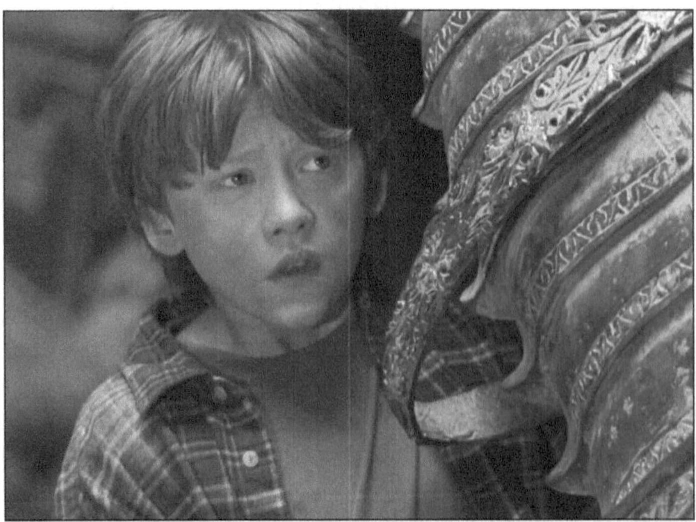

Ron offers to sacrifice himself for the quest to conquer evil, not knowing if he will survive

Nor, having undertaken the sacrifice, is Ron without fear; he recoils as the queen attacks. Nonetheless, he finds courage to make the move in the belief that Harry can succeed through his sacrifice, and as a result, conquer evil.

The Way of the Cross, Hermione, and the *Hagia Sophia*

As the discussion of Ron's character begins to indicate, Hermione's character is also defined through many of the aspects of the way of the cross, but not all. Significantly, Hermione's character is built around exceptionalism. While she does not have the arrogance of Draco Malfoy, her character is decidedly lacking in the level of humility that is at the core of Ron's character. Rather, at several junctures Hermione is eager to show off her encyclopedic knowledge of magic, history, and specialized areas like runes and arithmancy. Hermione's unequaled brain power operates as a fundamental aspect of her character, but only because it leads up to the defining discourse of her character: *hagia sophia*—holy wisdom.

Hermione's unrivaled intelligence is established through the very introduction to her character. Even though she comes from non-magic parents, she knows more about Harry and his fame than Harry does, the result of having read an enormous amount of books. In the book, she has already accomplished spells just by reading. The film has her successfully perform a spell in the train compartment to emphasize this aspect of her character. Even though she is extremely smart and talented, both the book and then the film have Hermione turn to humility at the crucial hour—the quest for the Philosopher's Stone. As Harry is about to set off alone in what seems a hopeless task, Hermione attempts to bolster him by telling Harry that he is a great wizard. Harry's almost instant reply is that Hermione is the better of the two—a response based on the prowess Hermione exercises in the narrative. The plot repeatedly shows Hermione mastering witchcraft at a level that far exceeds the others in her grade.

Hermione's response to Harry, however, is the point at which the narrative first inscribes wisdom to construct her character. She states "Me!?! Books! And cleverness! There are more important things—friendship and bravery and—oh Harry—be *careful*!" (HP I, 287). More than just polite confidence-building, Hermione's discourse is a sincere attempt to get Harry to see the depths of his strength. It also functions, however, to define Hermione's distinctive relationship to the way of the cross. At first, Hermione's discourse clarifies a narrative contradiction—Harry is the hero who must go forward, but throughout the plot, Hermione possesses more magical power than Harry. The plot resolves that contradiction by introducing a paradigm shift in what Gerard Gennette and other narratologists would describe as the evaluative system of the story world. Hermione's self-deprecating comment and encouragement of Harry makes explicit and validates a different paradigm for interpreting power: community, empathy, the thirst for justice—in short, the way of the cross that drives a certain kind of bravery. It is a paradigm shift the other six books will continue to reinforce. At the same time, her pronouncement endows Harry's character to struggle on against enormous odds.

In addition to being a discourse about Harry and articulating the narrative's evaluative system, Hermione's statement draws attention to itself by being self-referential and ironic. In coming to understand the values that really matter—the source of real power—Hermione sees that her own abilities to that point operate within a different realm: books and cleverness. The statement functions ironically, because in order for Hermione to understand these higher principles, she must first come to possess a wisdom that is beyond cleverness—that can recognize and comprehend the paradigm shift of alternative knowledge. At this specific narrative juncture, Hermione comes to let go of *philo sophia*—her love of knowledge for its own sake, and her love of being clever—to embody instead the *hagia sophia*—holy wisdom. As Dick Clifford argues, the biblical concept of wisdom, the *hagia sophia*, "picks agents or witnesses in every age . . ., enters such people, and enables them to understand that the real, abiding world is hidden, yet will be triumphant."[161] Hermione, who works so hard throughout the narrative to be the smartest, here achieves wisdom instead.

As the narrative unfolds, Hermione will consistently act upon that wisdom. In book three she will walk by faith and not by sight, as she takes Harry back in time with the time turner. In book four, she begins to campaign against the prejudice in the wizarding world towards non-human but sentient magical beings. This leads her to inspire Harry in book seven to treat the house-elf Kreacher with empathy, an action that will have important narrative consequences. Finally in book seven, Hermione insists that the group continue to search for Horcruxes and not give in to the temptation to possess Deathly Hallows—objects which would empower them. Dumbledore will even confide in Harry later on, from beyond the grave, that his master plan depended in part on Hermione's wisdom to walk by faith and not by sight—that she would indeed prevail upon Harry to continue with the quest for Horcruxes.

The books are so committed to making *hagia sophia* the central part of Hermione's character, that the stories never create the opportunity for self-sacrifice that Ron makes. The film version, however, works to correct that. In *Harry Potter and the Deathly Hallows Part II* (2011), Harry's journey to surrender to Voldemort is reworked. In the book, Harry sneaks out of the castle to surrender himself to Voldemort. Ron and Hermione are too enmeshed with the family grieving over the loss of Ron's brother George to notice. In the film, however, Ron and Hermione are sitting together on the main staircase—comforting each other, but also anticipating what Harry will do. When Harry reveals his intentions, Ron protests, but Hermione holds him back, and asks Harry instead to reveal what he has come to know.

Hermione's request is more than just curiosity. As the character who has evolved beyond "books and cleverness" and into the kind of holy wisdom that Dumbledore possessed, Hermione has come to understand that Harry is himself the last Horcrux—the last existing crucible for a piece of Voldemort's soul. In what is perhaps the most moving scene in the entire franchise, Harry's response confirms this when he states, "There's a reason I can hear them . . . the Horcruxes. I think I've known for a while." Harry then pauses briefly before confessing, "And I think you have too." Harry reveals to Hermione that he has reached full understanding of the Horcruxes, but significantly, the plot withholds an explicit acknowledgment from Harry as a means of confirming Hermione's wisdom and empathy: the words themselves do not have to be spoken, she knows and understands, having worked out the mystery before Harry.

Harry's confession, however, reduces Hermione to tears, and her response is not to confirm his suspicion, but rather, to state, "I'll go with you." Knowing that Harry is not going off to battle Voldemort, but to surrender himself to death, Hermione's response actually means, "I'll die with you." Her intent is not to help Harry prevail, but rather, to keep Harry from having to die alone.

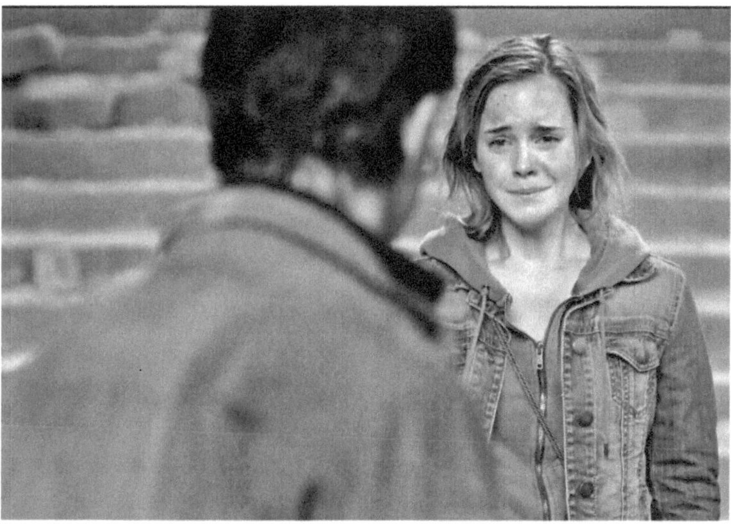

Hermione offers to lay down her life with Harry when she offers to accompany him.

In this manner, the film ensures that Hermione, like both Harry and Ron, is willing and able to walk the final steps of the way of the cross: to lay down her life for someone else and for the greater good—the phrase that the young Grindelwald and Dumbledore had twisted in their youthful dreams of world domination.

Dumbledore, *Hagia Sophia,* and the Way of the Cross

While Hermione's character is built around the biblical concept of wisdom, it is nonetheless Harry's mentor, Hogwarts Headmaster Albus Dumbledore, who is the central figure of wisdom in the book. From the beginning, Dumbledore is the revered character whom all others acknowledge for his wisdom. Crucial to the story's reanimation of the Christian narrative, Dumbledore's character is defined by biblical Wisdom from the very first book. He places Harry in the home of his reluctant aunt rather than have him adopted by a wizard family, saving Harry from having to grow up under the mantle of fame. As he explains to Professor McGonagall, "Famous before he can walk and talk! Famous for something he won't even remember! Can't you see how much better off he'll be, growing up away from all that until he's ready for it?" (HP I, 13). Later, Dumbledore rescues Harry from the enchanting effects of the mirror of Erised (desire) by telling him that the mirror gives neither knowledge nor truth—just an image of what people desire most. He thus warns Harry about the inherent dangers of desire before imparting another lesson in wisdom, telling Harry that "It does not do to dwell on dreams and forget to live" (HP I, 214). While Dumbledore's tutelage here could be interpreted as merely "sage advice," the book's end underscores that Dumbledore possesses biblical Wisdom: the deepest understanding of how love works as a powerful and mystical force in the world. In clarifying Voldemort's limitations to Harry, Dumbledore demonstrates an alternative, and deeper, understanding of mystical power—an understanding that Voldemort lacks because he cannot understand love.

Throughout the series Dumbledore maintains his position as the central site of biblical Wisdom: guiding and preparing Harry, defending the weak and the marginalized (Muggle-born witches and wizards, or "half-bloods," werewolves like Lupin, house-elves like Dobby, and half-giants like Hagrid and Madame Maxime), as well as leading "The Order of the Phoenix"—a group committed to battling Voldemort and his followers. In book seven, however, the narrative makes clear that Dumbledore's wisdom comes from the painful experience of having lusted for power and recognition. His ambitions to rule alongside Grindelwald, another powerful—and eventually dark—wizard lead to catastrophe: a bitter struggle that results in the death of his sister. Dumbledore is chastened, and spends the rest of his life reconciling his youthful foolishness in the belief of power.

The seventh book also retroactively clarifies that Dumbledore's wisdom guides him to the way of the cross: choosing death willingly to advance Harry's quest, and more immediately, to prevent Draco Malfoy from committing murder. Jones's defining characteristics of the way of the cross allow us to see that Dumbledore's actions have been guided by the way of the cross from his introduction in the narrative and right through to the end. A powerful wizard, and the headmaster of Hogwarts, Dumbledore always maintains a detached irony to the received wisdom of the wizarding world. This aspect of his character is most prominently displayed by the way in which he never actually dispenses "magical" knowledge to the students—preferring to make jokes and puns instead, as in the first book when he greets the students by saying, "Welcome to a new year at Hogwarts! Before we begin . . . I would like to say a few words. And they are: Nitwit! Blubber! Oddment Tweak!" (HP I, 123). He frequently addresses adult wizards through verbal one-upmanship, as when he insults Alecto Caldwell by responding to her question, "Think your little jokes'll help you on your deathbed" by replying, "Jokes? No, no, these are manners" (HP VI, 593). In general, Dumbledore rejects exercising power. Hagrid informs Harry in book one that Dumbledore refused the position of Minister of Magic on several occasions, a piece of information that is reconfirmed in book seven. Instead, Dumbledore reveres community and fellowship, as with the Christmas feast in book two, treasures fidelity and loyalty, as when he thanks Harry in book two for his loyalty, and later, in book seven, when he suggests to Harry that the prophecy be revealed to Ron and Hermione. He dedicates himself to opposing power, as his opposition in all the books attest, and his opposition to Cornelius Fudge, the Minister of Magic, attests in books four and five. In fact, his defining characteristic, as book seven makes clear, is the wisdom to know that power corrupts him, and must be rejected.

The Way of the Cross in Narrative Trajectory

The central place of the way of the cross, of *hagia sophia* and its wisdom of where power really lies—in love, loyalty, fidelity, and compassion—demonstrates the defining role that core discourses of Christianity exercises in constructing the main characters. The repetition of self-sacrifice as a mode of action, first with Ron, then retroactively with Lily, then with Dumbledore, and finally with Harry, evidence the centrality of the way of the cross to the narrative trajectory itself. Making a hard-and-fast distinction between narrative trajectory and character is not altogether possible, since characters are defined and constructed through description as well as action. Nonetheless, analyzing the story arc in the series can delineate the central role the way of the cross takes in organizing the narrative. Book seven constructs a very clear parallel, if not metaphor, for the way of the cross by having the main characters journey off together to face a long, lonely trial and temptation. In their hunt for Horcruxes they are lead off into a figurative desert—stripped of their moorings to the world they know and facing instead a trial that requires them to walk by faith and not by sight.

The role of parallel, however, is to make clear that the story arc for the entire series has been constructed from the beginning around the way of the cross and the trial and self-sacrifice that must ensue. Book one, the introduction to the narrative world and its characters, works to establish the community that is central to the way of the cross. As discussed earlier, Harry, Ron, and Hermione must form a deep bond with each other before they are able to walk by faith and not by sight: going through the trap door in an attempt to stop Voldemort's plans. Book two, *Harry Potter and the Chamber of Secrets*, creates another direct confrontation between Harry and Voldemort, but here, the narrative mirrors and bifurcates Ron's self-sacrifice. Harry risks his life to save Ginny, who, he discovers, is unwillingly giving her life to Voldemort so he can take corporeal form again—a mock version of the self-sacrifice that Ron and Harry made in order to save people.

Book three, *Harry Potter and the Prisoner of Azkaban*, is significant for the manner in which it withholds a direct confrontation with Voldemort—a plot device it shares with book six, *Harry Potter and the Half-Blood Prince*. In terms of the narrative trajectory, the lack of direct confrontation functions as a classic delaying function. The respite from Voldemort's actual presence allows the plot of each book to establish character relationships and motivations that will later on drive the narrative trajectory forward to the final, life-and-death confrontation in book seven. The principal means by which book three accomplishes this task is by establishing—and verifying—the ideals of the community, or what Christianity would describe as "glimpses of the kingdom."

Using signature plot twists, the filling out of backstory, and a life-threatening mystery, the plot of book three subtly embeds manifestations of the ideal community as an outgrowth of the community's ideals as they exist now. Two plot trajectories in particular function to underline the ideal community. The first is the Quidditch Cup, which has eluded Harry's Gryffindor team up until this point in the narrative. Even here, the cup seems lost to the Gryffindor team when Harry fails, for the first time in his career, to catch the snitch in their opening game. The team must not only depend on the success of other teams to qualify, but also on each other as a unit to secure ultimate victory: the chasers must score enough to create a lead of sixty points before Harry can end the game with a successful snatch, and the beaters and goal keeper must preserve the lead with staunch defense.

To help ensure his team's success, Oliver Wood, the team captain in his final year, drives the team through vigorous training sessions. When victory comes, it is the result of hard work, endurance, and everyone giving their all for the team. The victory is a culmination for a team that was good enough to win for the previous two years, but always had their opportunity taken away by circumstances outside the games themselves. When the team finally does achieve their goal, and secures the championship, it is a moment of collective achievement and celebration: Harry caught the snitch that ended the game and gave the team the final points to win, but only because the others had done their part to contribute to the victory as well. Significantly, the plot elevates the collective joy over the moment of victory itself. After catching the snitch, Harry soars "above the crowd, an odd ringing in his ears," but the plot fairly refuses to stay on Harry and his moment of achievement, opting instead to focus on the collective in the immediate aftermath:

> Then Wood was speeding toward him, half-blinded by tears; he seized Harry around the neck and sobbed unrestrainedly into his shoulder. Harry felt two large thumps as Fred and George hit them; then Angelina's, Alicia's, and Katie's voices, "*We've won the Cup! We've won the Cup!*" Tangled together in a many-armed hug, the Gryffindor team sank, yelling hoarsely, back to earth (HP III, 312).

The moment of triumph is not so much Harry's accomplishment as much as the realization of a collective dream: to win the championship. Harry's place here, his greatest joy in the narrative, is in the unity of the team sharing their transcendent moment in time.

More than just victory in a game, the experience of transcendence will create a bond among the group that they will never forsake. The team will return to the narrative in book seven to risk their lives for Harry and for a better world in the final battle for Hogwarts against Voldemort's forces. Oliver Wood's role is particularly indicative of how the transcendent experience in book three ends up shaping the team. That Wood would return to do battle in book seven is not particularly out of character—the driven athlete, his desire for even greater battle could be seen as merely consistent with his character. The plot, however, singles out Wood for a different purpose. During a cease-fire in the battle, the plot identifies Wood as tending to the dead:

bringing in the body of little Colin Creavey who died during the fighting. Rather than the bold warrior, Wood instead is depicted as tending to the least of these. Wood's changed role indicates that the Quidditch Championship is more than just an exciting diversion from the narrative trajectory; it is a transcendent and transformative experience for the group that provides a glimpse of an ideal that they will never abandon.

The Gryffindor championship over rival Slytherin in book three runs parallel to and informs a subplot of the ideal community by a process of opposition. The Slytherin team, featuring Harry's hated rival Draco Malfoy, plays dirty, and has a competitive edge over other teams because Draco's father—Lucius Malfoy—has outfitted the team with the fastest brooms money can buy. A hard-and-fast believer in wizarding bloodlines, and a top lieutenant of Voldemort, Lucius uses his money to gain power and influence. When Draco is injured by taunting a hippogriff named Buckbeak, Lucius uses his power to have the hippogriff executed, motivated more by his hate for Hagrid than any real concern about the beast. As Hagrid, Hermione, and later, Ron and Harry, work to secure Buckbeak's acquittal, they are frustrated at every step by Malfoy's ability to influence the Minister of Magic and the committee making the decision.

As the events unfold, the plot of book three makes clear that Harry and his friends were wrong to place their trust in worldly—albeit wizarding—power. The trio mistakenly believes that the political system rests upon truth and justice. What they come to see, however, is how the political system is unconcerned with truth or justice. For all its power to manipulate physical reality and even time itself, the wizarding world still depends on a political system that is shaped and determined by money, power, and the influence it wields. Discovering that the political system is beholden to power is a turning point in the overall narrative. It sends the children to Dumbledore for help in securing justice. Dumbledore, however, neither takes up the battle nor tells Harry and his friends what to do. Instead, Dumbledore sends them on a journey back in time to alter events. In leading Hermione to use her time turner, Dumbledore sends Harry and Hermione to an alternate plane of reality and existence, where they must negotiate a new way to understand time, causality, and outcomes. Without knowing exactly what to do, but trusting in Dumbledore, Harry and Hermione learn to start walking by faith and not by sight. In many respects, it is a replication of the flight through the trap door in book one, but for the overall narrative of the series, it is the first step on their journey of the way of the cross, where they will be motivated by love, trust in wisdom, and the desire to secure justice.

Book four, *Harry Potter and the Goblet of Fire,* resumes the trajectory of the way of the cross, but not without significant delays. The book itself is an exercise in masterly delays. Injecting the Quidditch World Cup into the early stage of the narrative, the plot builds on the excitement of the event to delay Harry and his friends arriving at Hogwarts for 170 pages. When he does arrive at Hogwarts, Harry soon finds that his name has been surreptitiously entered into the Goblet of Fire—signifying his entry into the dangerous Tri-Wizard Tournament. In this respect, *Goblet of Fire* establishes an important principle for the way of the cross: choosing to ignore evil is not a realistic option—it will eventually come for you. To the degree that Harry would like to settle in to a normal life at Hogwarts, books three and four demonstrate that he cannot, that the forces of darkness seek him out.

As a book filled with masterly delays, *Goblet of Fire* is notable for finally placing the antagonist, Voldemort, as a fully formed corporeal character within the narrative—not just a magical but abstract threat. A direct confrontation with Harry in the climax of the book further establishes Harry's courage and sets the course the way of the cross will take when Harry escapes, forcing Voldemort to pursue him for the rest of the series. More than just courageous, however, Harry once again shows his willingness to give his life for others, here risking his own life in order to bring the dead Cedric back to his parents.

Book five, *Harry Potter and the Order of the Phoenix*, creates another direct confrontation between Harry and Voldemort, which seemingly moves the narrative along to its final conclusion. In another well-crafted delaying tactic, though, the plot has Dumbledore battling Voldemort at the climax. Because neither wizard wins the battle, the plot creates the expectation that the two most powerful wizards will battle again later in the series, an expectation that will not be met but nonetheless allows the plot to forestall a confrontation with Harry. The direct confrontation with Voldemort in book five allows the plot to first expand upon a discourse on the way of the cross that was articulated in books three and four: that complacency and the desire to retreat into a normal life are not viable options in the face of evil. By having the Ministry of Magic encroach upon life at Hogwarts, book five reemphasizes that no one is left untouched by the effects of evil. Normal life at Hogwarts is upended and increasingly restricted by the ministry's attempt to take control of the school in a vain political attempt to repress the truth about Voldemort's return.

In addition, the book contributes to the ongoing discourse of power and the way of the cross through the creation of "Dumbledore's Army," the group that forms around Harry to learn defense against the dark arts. Although several students join Harry's group, many of whom possess above-average magical skill, it is the two marginalized characters, the spacey Luna and the bumbling Neville, who come to help Harry in his confrontation with Voldemort. Their loyalty and fellowship are more important than the traditional wizarding concept of power. The series emphasizes this discourse by replicating it in book six: Luna and Neville are the only members of Dumbledore's Army to answer the call to arms when Draco Malfoy leads a band of Voldemort's Death Eaters into Hogwarts.

Like book three, however, book six, *Harry Potter and the Half-blood Prince*, avoids a direct confrontation with Voldemort, making it a calculated device for delaying the outcome of the story. Instead, book six expands on and reemphasizes the discourse of book five concerning the non-viability of ignoring evil. Book six is able to underscore this discourse by seemingly abandoning it for most of the plot. The Hogwarts of book six has been returned to normal with the return of Dumbledore. Gone are the Dementors guarding every entrance to the castle in book three, the foreign guest students competing in the Tri-Wizard tournament in book four, and the ministry of magic officials running the school in book five. Even with Voldemort stalking about in the outside world, the Hogwarts of book six has returned to a normal state of affairs not seen since book one, providing the minor characters of the story world with a false, comforting sense of security, before jarring them into the lesson that Harry and the other main characters have already learned: non-engagement is not an option in the face of rising evil.

The conclusion of book six then leads to the milieu of the concluding book, where the entire wizarding world has been plunged into the inevitable conclusion that evil, left unabated, comes for all. In this manner, the narrative refuses to allow Hogwarts to remain untouched by the encroaching evil that threatens and surrounds it—disallowing, in the process, the conflict between Harry and Voldemort to be personalized. Instead, the comfortable normality or stasis that Harry and everyone else would like to indulge in is denied. The narrative insists that denial and insularity are not an option when the world is dominated by power and exclusion—that evil will inevitably effect all. As a result of this inevitability, Jenny Sawyer criticizes the series in *The Christian Science Monitor* because Harry never faces a real moral struggle.[162] His path, she argues, is predetermined, and there is never any doubt that Harry will go forward with it (the modification to Dumbledore's trustworthiness in book seven notwithstanding).

Sawyer's criterion for criticism, however, is that literature should truly reflect society—that audiences require a main character they can relate to by going through a moral struggle that changes them. She argues, "A passive main character with no authentic moral dilemma is not only hard to relate to, he or she is also no guide in circumstances in which right and wrong are anything less than black and white."[163] Harry Potter, she argues, is a literary symptom of a society "sliding toward moral ambivalence with alarming speed."[164] Ironically, Sawyer is so intent on making the Harry Potter series (and character) a whipping boy for "moral relativism" that she overlooks the narrative's agenda—reanimating the Christian narrative. The social context of the Harry Potter series, however, is a society where the Christian narrative has become moribund and uninspiring. Rather than reflect that, Harry Potter attempts to revitalize the narrative—to reassert its validity and power.

Harry's lack of choice or absence of moral struggle is not so much an inability to reflect reality as it is a rearticulation of a fundamental tenet of the theology of the cross. As Dietrich Bonhoeffer's work demonstrates, there is no alternative to the way of the cross for Christianity: the cross is the only path that can be followed, the only way that leads to life and freedom. For Bonhoeffer, and for many subsequent theologians, the church's accommodation with the state—first with Rome, and later with medieval kingdoms—began a process of marginalizing the way of the cross. As Bonhoeffer argues, the creation of medieval monasticism simultaneously preserved the way of the cross as the core path of Christianity—and Christians—while at the same time, designating this path as the domain of "a restricted group of specialists" and creating a "lower standard" for the rest of the church.[166] The cost of making it easier for Christians to accommodate the world rather than follow the way of the cross is, for Bonhoeffer, a seismic shift away from radical discipleship and towards obedience to the church.[167] The end result, for Bonhoeffer, is "cheap grace," as opposed to realizing the kingdom.

The series refrains from creating a choice for Harry between comfortable accommodation and the path of self-denial as a means of signifying the spiritual reality of the way of the cross over the arbitrary social reality of the world. Sawyer's observation that Harry never really gets to choose is accurate, but the criticism misplaced. Harry is both compelled and forced towards a preordained path because, as Bonhoeffer argues, "every Christian has his own cross waiting for him, a cross destined to and appointed by God."[166] The narrative trajectory asserts the fundamental inability to resolve the way of the cross with worldly comfort and compromise by withholding these choices from Harry's struggle.

The last book in the series, *Harry Potter and the Deathly Hallows*, draws attention to this lack of choice by refusing to let Harry, Ron, and Hermione resume their school days at Hogwarts, denying to its readers the thing they love most about the narrative—the world of Hogwarts—and replacing it instead with a lonely journey filled with trial, tribulations, doubt, and betrayal. The film version magnifies this discourse in the Forest of Dean scene with Hermione and Harry. Having just escaped an encounter with Voldemort through Hermione's prodigious skill, Harry finds himself transported to the middle of a tranquil forest. He comments to Hermione, "You've outdone yourself this time, Hermione." Reflecting on how she knew of the forest from her childhood, Hermione then expresses her weariness in the struggle by saying, "Maybe we should just stay here Harry . . . grow old . . . ." Hermione's suggestion, however, is short-lived. She and Harry both know that it is an impractical choice to remain in a sheltered cage for the rest of their lives in exchange for safety. Just as much as Harry, Hermione understands that their only real option is the path forward: self-denial and sacrifice in order to achieve the goal of conquering evil.

The narrative trajectory further inscribes the discourse of the way of the cross with the transformation of Neville Longbottom—the character designed to parallel Harry. Neville is introduced as a kind but bumbling minor character in the first book. His haplessness draws the empathy of Harry, Ron, and Hermione, who befriend him, but Neville remains a convenient minor character through most of the narrative. The second film emphasizes this role when it adds material to the pixie scene. Where the book has the pixies suspend Neville from a chandelier that comes crashing down in short order, the film leaves him suspended there, where he inquires, almost as a narrative aside, "Why is it always me?" The line draws awareness to the manner in which Neville can operate as a convenient prop to the ongoing needs of the narrative because of his status as a minor character.

Even as late in the series as book four, Neville is still introduced as "a round faced, forgetful boy," signifying his ongoing status as a minor character (HP IV, 167). Later in the story he becomes a substitute date for Ron's sister Ginny so that she can attend the Yule Ball—maintaining his function as a convenient prop that can be used as plot requires. In *The Order of the Phoenix*, however, Neville's character grows in stature in two significant ways. First, Neville joins Dumbledore's Army, the group forming around Harry that resists the new regime at Hogwarts. Coached by Harry and fueled by his desire to fight the forces who tortured his parents into insanity, Neville grows slowly out of his ineptitude, and starts to become a stronger wizard. Even more significantly, Dumbledore reveals at the end of the book that Harry's fate as "The Chosen One" was not set at birth: that the prophecy which ultimately determined his path was the fate of either Harry or Neville.

The parallel that the prophecy establishes between Harry and Neville creates an important trajectory for Neville towards the way of the cross. Neville must learn from Harry more than defensive spells and how to duel Dark Wizards. Rather, he must learn faith and hunger for justice. The events of book five and book seven articulate this transformation. In the *Order of the Phoenix,* the newly trained Neville joins in the battle against Voldemort's Death Eaters. Even with the vast improvement in his skills, however, Neville proves himself hopelessly inept in the battle. In this manner, the plot denies the discourse of revenge, refusing to allow it to transform Neville's character into a powerful wizard.

In *The Deathly Hallows*, however, Neville is animated by other motivations. Having taken over Harry's place at Hogwarts as the leader of Dumbledore's Army, Neville learns to take up the cause for justice. That he is severely and repeatedly punished fails to sway him from that cause. Rather, as he tells Harry, he learned from Harry's own example that continuing to stand up against injustice, even after being punished, inspires other to join the struggle. That inspiration moves Neville to be the first to resist Voldemort after Harry is presumed to be dead. In his defiance, Neville not only continues the quest for justice, but demonstrates his willingness to sacrifice himself in order to inspire others to remain in the struggle.

Within the narrative trajectory, Neville has abandoned revenge and replaced it with self-denial and the desire for justice. As a result, when Voldemort attempts to kill Neville for standing up to him, the magical Sword of Gryffindor presents itself to Neville, recognizing his selfless courage, loyalty, and need. With the sword of Gryffindor now in his possession, Neville springs into action, destroying Nagini, the serpent that Voldemort had made into a Horcrux, and significantly impacting the narrative. Along with Dumbledore, Harry, Ron, and Hermione, Neville has destroyed a Horcrux through his courage and decisive action. By walking the way of the cross, Neville elevates himself from the well-intentioned but inept minor character to a major character who parallels Harry in courage, selflessness, and action.

The plot's largest twist replicates Neville's parallel to Harry in an oppositional way. By having Severus Snape, Harry's most difficult nemesis, revealed to have been protecting Harry all along, the plot structures another character traversing the way of the cross. Snape's motivation for protecting Harry is his undying love for Lily, and his profound remorse at having contributed to her death. He masks this role, and his motivations, behind a shroud of intense dislike of Harry—compromising the aspect of fellowship in Snape's journey. Even in the scene that reveals all of Snape's past, the plot never makes clear Snape's deepest feelings about Harry. Nonetheless, while Snape's fellowship with Harry is questionable at best, his loyalty to Dumbledore is unswerving, his courage in duping Voldemort to further the struggle against evil is without equal, and the selflessness in playing his role is both complex and profound. And although Snape does not knowingly willingly walk to his death like Harry will, he nonetheless puts himself in the position for Voldemort to murder him, and advances the struggle against evil by giving his memories to Harry even as he lies dying—memories that will allow Harry to prevail.

The plot's replication of the way of the cross through all the major characters and at the core of the narrative trajectory itself demonstrates the fundamental role it exercises in the narrative. The last point of emphasis for this discourse comes through a series of twists and formulations surrounding Harry's journey and return from an in-between state of life and death. Tellingly, the plot structures Harry's return as a victory of the cross rather than resurrection itself, a metaphor that would invite Jesus of Nazareth analogies. To make the distinction, the plot places Harry in an idealized re-creation of King's Cross. It then makes clear, through Dumbledore's explanations, that Harry did not die. Instead, Voldemort destroyed the part of his own soul that resided within Harry. Harry could have chosen to go "on"—could have chosen a life after death, but rather, Harry chooses to go back to the struggle over evil. Having achieved the victory of the cross, Harry returns to finally end the struggle over evil, to bring about the long awaited magical world that the restoration of peace to the wizarding world would create.

Significant to the central place of the way of the cross, Harry's self-sacrifice functions within the plot as the culminating action more than the final battle with Voldemort itself. The book, in fact, structures the final battle as an anticlimax. Voldemort dies by his own hand more than he is killed by Harry, and the plot works to de-emphasize both the death and the victory:

> Harry, with the unerring skill of the Seeker, caught the wand in his free hand as Voldemort fell backwards, arms splayed, the slit pupils of the scarlet eyes rolling upwards. Tom Riddle hit the floor with a mundane finality, his body feeble and shrunken, the white hands empty, the snake-like face vacant and unknowing. Voldemort was dead, killed by his own rebounding curse, and Harry stood with two wands in his hand, staring down at his enemy's shell (HP VII, 744).

Key to downplaying Harry's victory is the narration's clarification that Voldemort was killed by "his own rebounding" curse. The plot saves Harry's character from having killed someone, while at the same time reasserting the foolishness of worldly power. Voldemort has so much faith in the common understanding of power in the magical world that it blinds him to the hard evidence of a more powerful force. In the end, he dies having tried to kill Harry in the same manner that mortally wounded him at the very start of the narrative. Voldemort willfully disregards how the self-sacrifice motivated by love works as a shield against a killing curse, and dies as a result.

He dies, as Dumbledore so knowingly asserted earlier, woefully ignorant of the power of love.

Audience Identification with the Way of the Cross

It is one thing for an author to craft a narrative around the theological concept of the way of the cross. It is another thing altogether for audiences to identify with it. To the degree that J. K. Rowling's work is masterful, it is because she achieved just that. Through the years before and after Harry Potter, the term "identification" has come to be used so loosely that it has lost all the theoretical precision that it can offer. I turn to the work of Jacques Lacan here because he offers an intricate understanding to the complex process of identification that can explicate how important Rowling's narrative is for Christian aesthetics.

For both Freud and Lacan, identification is a process where individuals build and maintain their identities. For each, individual identity is not an essence of being, but an accumulation of images, beliefs, values, and experiences that operate as an identity. In their theories, identification is a process whereby individuals seek out images and discourses to keep their identities intact: to confirm their identities. What Lacan stresses in his theory is that identification is above all the psychic ability to abstract—to achieve a level of separation from the here and now of the physical world. Like Freud, Lacan explicates that the process of identification is a simultaneous process: a taking in and a projecting out of identity. Individuals literally place themselves psychically in another place. They likewise bring those exterior places, identities, and effects into their own identities—not as illusion, not even so much as full-fledged fantasy, but as an abstraction.

Lacan's theory is particularly insightful for media analysis because he delineates three distinct modes of identification: identifying with sensory effects (primary identification), identifying with an image (secondary or *image*-inary identification), and identification with social discourse (symbolic, or tertiary identification). Each of these modes is characterized by a different level of abstraction, and hence, a different identificatory alignment.[168]

Lacan's different modes of identification are particularly important for the Harry Potter series because they help demonstrate the manner in which the story's vivid setting encourages readers to identify with the enchanted world just as much as they do with Harry and the other characters. In fact, what makes the Harry Potter series so distinctive is the manner in which imaginary identification is structured just as much around setting as it is around main character. Many science fiction, fantasy, and gothic narratives possess this potential, but by tying romantic trajectory so prominently to the main trajectory, they greatly diminish that potential, directing identification onto the romantic couple instead. Conversely, the Western genre uses the setting of the rugged West to define its characters, add to their travails, and provide a dramatic backdrop, while simultaneously encouraging audience fascination with and desire for the rugged Western environment.

Within the films especially, the narrative works just as much to direct audience identification towards setting as it does towards Harry: to encourage the sense of mastery and control that the wizarding world promises through its ability to manipulate the laws governing reality. Hagrid's famous introduction to the wizarding world, "Welcome, Harry, to Diagon Alley" is one of the more striking examples of how the film structures imaginary identification around the setting itself. After Hagrid delivers his introduction, the film shows Harry entering Diagon Alley through the magic passage. As Harry walks forward the camera performs an elaborate movement to stay with Harry, but take in all the scenery as well. The camera first zooms back as Harry approaches, then turns to follow him as he walks by. As it does, it starts a slow crane movement up, allowing itself to gaze more comprehensively at the scope of things. As Harry becomes smaller, Diagon Alley becomes larger. The camera's position and movement emphasizes the wonder of a whole new world that Harry did not previously know existed. Old world-style shops are crammed together on a cobblestone passageway too thin for cars to pass, and people talk animatedly about all the merchandise that is displayed in the street. More than just wonder, the camerawork underscores the plenitude and enchantment that characterizes the magical world: a world that promises control, mastery, and bountifulness—an alluring picture, in short, of freedom from want. All these properties work to secure the audience's imaginary identification.

Although the narrative abandons Hogwarts as a setting in book seven, it only does so as a means for readers to identify with the loss that Harry, Hermione, and Ron experience by choosing the way of the cross: they must give up the security of Hogwarts in order to walk their long, hard journey of self-sacrifice. In this manner, the plot attaches discourses of community and fellowship onto setting itself, creating continuity between imaginary identification—with the control and mastery that enchantment promises—and symbolic identification with its discourses of fellowship, community, and self-sacrifice. As with most classical narrative, the plot uses imaginary identification as a lure, as the image of wholeness and completeness that can be fulfilled once narrative obstacles have been overcome. Significant for the plot's symbolic identification with the way of the cross, the narrative resists providing that image as a conclusion. In both the book and the film, the conclusion is structured around Harry's renunciation of power, not the restoration of the narrative world. Even the postscript, which glimpses the restored wizarding world nineteen years later, is more concerned with confirmation of character coupling than it is privileging an image of stasis and wholeness: Harry and Ginny have united and had children, as have Ron and Hermione.[169] The sending off of the children to Hogwarts, where they will see Neville, now a professor there, is structured far more around the image of the wizarding world being able to continue on than it is of a penultimate moment of wholeness and resolution.

In this respect, while the narrative uses images and concepts of mastery and wholeness as trajectories of desire, their function is to prevent the trajectory of the way of the cross from being a dour enterprise unable to secure identification. The way of the cross that Harry, Ron, and Hermione traverse is instead imbued with purpose: the restoration of an ideal image of the enchanted world. Using that image to secure imaginary identification, the narrative then sets about ennobling the way of the cross: privileging it with greater purpose and meaning. The plot thus works to secure symbolic identification around what are otherwise difficult values: self-renunciation, foolishness, humility, and trial. In crafting a narrative that secures identification with these values, the Harry Potter series reanimates the Christian narrative by restoring the drama to its core discourse in a manner that inspires people to identify with it. Rather than a distant story from the past, the way of the cross becomes an immediate and enchanting experience for readers. In this manner, the narrative encourages its audience to see through the empty promise of material well-being and aspire instead to the challenges of the way of the cross: the only path, the narrative asserts, to true freedom and wholeness that only self-renunciation, faith, and community can provide.

Harry Potter and the Aesthetics of Identification

In some respects, all the aesthetic analysis of the previous chapters has been building towards answering the most important question aesthetics engages: what is the best way to engage an audience? Lacan's answer, based on Freud, is very simple: identification. Though this answer is simple, the dynamics of identification are anything but—as the media has discovered on countless occasions.[171] Lacan delineates three very distinct modes of identification, but has also compared them to a Gordian knot for their inability to be completely separate. For Lacan, the unconscious operations of identification are complex, dynamic, and intimately tied to the ongoing process of maintaining identity.

One key to the operations of identification is Lacan's argument that the unconscious is structured like a language. Drawing on the Freudian principles of condensation and displacement, Lacan sees the image-bank part of the unconscious as functioning through the operations of metaphor and metonomy. In his view, this part of the unconscious has no temporality and limited spatial relations. It can only operate based on relations of similarity or contiguity of images. For Lacan, the deepest impulses and instincts attach themselves to and express themselves through this imagistic portion of the unconscious. Freud would point to the operation of dreams as being able to illustrate how this part of the unconscious worked, but his dynamic model was misunderstood by even some of his closest followers, who offered more static symbologies of unconscious operations. Lacan's theory insists on the radical contingencies of unconscious images, and how they connect to and work off of other images to give shape and meaning to unconscious impulses.

In addition to the imagistic unconscious, Lacan delineates how identification with abstract discourses regulate and displace unconscious desires through the operations of another register of the unconscious: the symbolic. Significantly, Lacan avoids a simple dualistic structure to identity by insisting on the operations of what he described as the Real: that people are indeed "wired" in hyper-individualistic ways, have specific chemical balances, ebbs, and flows, and are subjected to outside stimuli that intrude, interrupt, and intervene.

The success of Harry Potter, and in particular, the attempts to model its success, begin to illustrate the contours of an aesthetic around this multifaceted and dynamic process of identification. Imitators flocked around the generic elements of Harry Potter—fantasy, magic, adolescent protagonists—but ironically for literature, many ignored the actual discourse of the narrative. In semiotic terms, imitators like Jenny Nimmo's Charlie Bone series appropriated the signifiers or symbols from Harry Potter, but tossed out the signified—the underlying meanings that gave them significance to begin with. Nimmo's inaugural attempt, *Midnight for Charlie Bone,* is a painfully transparent copy where children with special—or magical—gifts like Charlie, who can hear people in photographs talking, go to a special school in a Gothic-style mansion and battle against the nemeses they find there. Operating on thinly disguised features of Harry Potter, Charlie Bone fails to move beyond these surface level signifiers: depending on adolescent empowerment as the signified that will drive identification. As such, it remains a poor imitation.

Two other imitators, however, each engage the discourse of Harry Potter in provocative and differing ways—each with popular success. Terry

Pratchett's Tiffany Aching series, a part of his broader "Discworld" narrative series, is a study of genre opposition on both the level of the signifier and the signified. In Pratchett's narrative, the main character Tiffany Aching comes from humble beginnings, but is quickly defined as an exceptional character in an unexceptional part of the story world. Because of her inborn talent, Tiffany is not the kind of 'everyman' that Harry is first presented as. Also, like Rowling's narrative world, the reality that Tiffany Aching moves through is filled with magic, but with a significant difference: it exists within the reality of all characters, to varying degrees, not hidden away. Most significantly, in training to become a witch, Tiffany learns that spells and incantations—in short, magic—is only used by witches who are not smart enough to think their way out of a problem. Tiffany defeats all her foes with her intelligence, bravery, and cunning, not the magical prowess with which she is endowed. Indeed, what the series makes clear is that Tiffany's intelligence, bravery, cunning, and compassion is the magic that she possesses in such abundance.

Pratchett's narrative is an exercise in generic correction: undermining the appeal of empowerment through magic by pointing out the enormous power of the mind and spirit. It is difficult, in fact, to see the Tiffany Aching series as only coincidentally a subtle critique of Harry Potter. Where Harry Potter is infused with, and attempts to reanimate the ideology of Christianity, Tiffany Aching is a steadfast proponent of secular humanism: insisting that the magic is within. Tiffany draws from a deep well of family and cultural wisdom, her wits, and also her empathy. As a result, she is consistently able to rise above the daunting powers of the mystical world and defeat them, no matter what form they take. In many ways, the mystical world of the Tiffany Aching series is the domain of raw ignorance and destructive force, whose sway and power entraps and imprisons, maims and destroys. Tiffany demonstrates that only the light of reason, sound judgment, and empathy can keep the darkness at bay. On both the level of the signifier and the signified, Tiffany Aching operates in nearly perfect aligned opposition to Harry Potter.

Rick Riordan's Percy Jackson and the Olympians narrative, on the other hand, operates as a reinterpretation of Harry Potter through disguising the discourse of the signified. Riordan's narrative operates in a manner that recognizes the discourse of Christianity within Harry Potter, and crafts a narrative by changing the signifier of the signified—substituting Greek polytheism for Christianity. Much like Harry Potter, the main character Percy Jackson is an everyday guy who only comes to discover that he has exceptional powers: he is a demigod, a son of Poseidon, embued with certain powers. As Percy moves through the narrative series he finds that his powers—especially as they relate to water—are exceptional. Much like Harry, Percy seems to be "the anointed one" because he seems to be the character of "the prophecy." With such strong similarities the plot cloaks the resemblance through narration. Harry Potter is third-person narration, and Percy Jackson is first person. Moreover, Percy models his narrating on J. D. Salinger's popular character Holden Caulfield. Like Caulfield, Percy frequently makes wisecracking narrative asides (but with a quality that is more Disney teen entertainment than the literary subtlety of Salinger).

The imitation of narrative discourse is also maintained in the way of the cross. Like Harry, Ron, and Hermione, Percy and his friends must take up several quests that will likewise require hardship, self-denial, community, and faith. Their task is arduous, and they must venture out alone. In both of these journeys, the life of the community is at stake. Where Harry is in a fateful battle against a Nietzschean superman who will destroy civil society, Percy is in a fateful battle with Kronos, who will destroy civilization. Most significantly, the journey's end will lead to courageous acts of self-sacrifice and nonviolence.

Like Harry Potter, the Percy Jackson series insists that it takes more courage to give oneself over to trust and faith than it does to simply fight and do battle. In the climactic scene to the first series, Percy battles Kronos on Mt. Olympus, which has now moved to the top of the Empire State Building. Percy, who defeated Ares, the god of war, earlier in the series, must now defeat Kronos or the world will be destroyed. Percy battles bravely, but at the crucial moment Percy must choose between trying to kill Kronos himself, or handing his weapon over to Luke, who betrayed Percy earlier in the series, but now hosts Kronos in his body. In the milliseconds during the battle's climax, Percy must make a decision helped along by the clues from the prophecy: he must trust that, despite the earlier betrayal, Luke's love for Annabeth will overcome his allegiance to Kronos. Taking a leap of faith, Percy gives up his weapon and allows Luke to sacrifice himself as a means of killing Kronos.

The significance of Percy Jackson is the repetition and enhancement of the hero's act of nonviolence. Going against the ideology of militarism that pervades contemporary culture, both these books create narratives that ask adolescents to identify with an alternative image of power: the power of nonviolence. Drawing on desires for power and wholeness, the narratives direct identification toward one of the fundamental discourses of Christianity—nonviolence. In both cases, the choice for nonviolence occurs in the midst of violence and battle. For each, the hero chooses nonviolence as a testament to strength, not weakness—their prowess having been repeatedly demonstrated, they choose instead a different path, a different form of power.

Harry Potter and Percy Jackson both give image to fundamental discourses of Christianity through a narrative structure whose goal is identification with alternative images and discourses of power. Contesting the images of strength and fulfillment that secular humanism constructs, these narratives craft signifiers that will lead identification towards radically different images of sacrifice, faithfulness, and nonviolence. Using the form of classical narrative, they adhere image to discourse in a manner that seeks nothing less than to replace the dominant discourses mainstream audiences of contemporary culture identify with. Harry Potter and Percy Jackson take both the material and images of contemporary and classical culture, as well as the form of classical narrative, to create identification with a radical alternative, the sole purpose of which is the radical reshaping of identity: away from the materialism and violence of postmodern secular humanism and towards the distant mystical vision that came out of the Judean desert. They animate that vision with images and symbols that signify empowerment, but point towards a different signified: a transcendent power that lays beyond representation—that has no form, no shape, only presence. They use the license of fantasy, combined with codes of realism, to testify to the reality of the transcendent and its power.

The aesthetic significance of Harry Potter and Percy Jackson is the degree to which they achieve their goal of identification with a radical discourse. Mobilizing the aesthetics of classical narration, in particular authority/omniscience (the audience trusts the narration), proximity (the audience draws close to the narrative), and trajectory (the audience enjoys the prolonged serialization of the narrative), these narratives attempt nothing less than to intercede in the identity of their audience: to redirect them to an alternative discourse that they will take in and project themselves out towards. Rather than a radical assault on representation—on narrative form and structure—they constitute instead an appropriation of form to constitute a subtle redirection towards identification with a radical discourse.

Appropriation is key here for understanding the manner in which these texts procure identification: through continuity. The regulatory function of symbolic identification depends upon an almost seamless relationship between image and discourse: that the one attaches itself to the other so readily that it appears naturally. In her discussion of Lacanian theory, Ellie Ragland-Sullivan describes conscious identity as the point of continuity between image and a regulating discourse—which Lacan defined as the Other(A). Here again, the Charlie Bone series is instructive. By reshaping and reworking the generic symbols of Harry Potter, the Charlie Bone series fails to create continuity between those images and a meaningful discourse—they are worked formulaically instead.

The Harry Potter series, conversely, looks to create continuity between image and a foundational, but now marginalized discourse of Western culture. This continuity is accomplished through the process that Freud describes as condensation: where the symbolic function of the image is invested with several meanings. Rowling's accomplishment as an author lies in her ability to wed ahistorical desires and fantasies of empowerment to a contemporary image of a magical world, and animate it with the discourse of Christianity—disguised, as it is, through her narrative. Audiences do not perceive an author working out a symbolized discourse of Christianity nearly so much as they perceive a richly built fantasy of a magical world. As a result, audience and readers are able to identify with the foundational discourses they find in Harry Potter—however cloaked they are through symbolization.

What the popularity of the Harry Potter series begins to demonstrate is the dualism that constitutes contemporary identity formation. To the degree that many people construct their identities around discourses of Christianity, dominant secular humanist culture effectively persuades them to identify with counter discourses instead: materialism, hedonism, violence. The hegemonic struggle between secular humanist culture and Christianity operates at the level of cultural discourse precisely as a means to shape and determine identity. The drive to marginalize and contain the viability of the discourses of Christianity operates to direct identification away from it—to shape identities that will conform to and operate around the culture of the neoliberal marketplace economy.

The success of the Harry Potter series demonstrates that these discourses of Christianity, however marginalized and contained, are nonetheless a part of identity for many people within contemporary culture. Harry Potter constructs its symbols and images in a manner that achieves continuity with marginalized—and perhaps even repressed—discourses of Christianity. At least part of the reason these discourses are marginalized and contained is because they lack a functional image: they are tied to an ancient narrative, or images and discourses of "impractical," "other-worldly," or "unrealistic." Harry Potter draws on the license of fantasy to reconfigure symbols and attach them to the marginalized discourses of Christianity with the kind of continuity that makes identification possible: to create new valence, new identifications, and new identities. To awaken Christianity at the level of audience identity, to create the new—that's the magic of Harry Potter.

8

Epilogue

Towards an Aesthetic of the Kingdom

In many ways, the guiding principle of this book has been simple: Christianity does not have a theology problem, but a communications problem. Theologians like Stanley Hauerwas might vociferously disagree, arguing that Constantinianism has corrupted the theology of Christianity, imposing such false concepts as the "two-realm" doctrine, which tells Christians to be good and docile citizens while they follow Jesus quietly in their hearts. I do not so much disagree with theologians like Hauerwas, as much as I suggest that even if institutional Christianity were to unshackle itself from Constantinianism, it would not know how to communicate its bold and radical message. Institutional Christianity fundamentally does not know how to speak in compelling ways that engage and inspire people. Hollywood, conversely, knows how to elicit audiences even, as I have tried to show, when the message is challenging or radical. Certainly, every Hollywood product is not successful, but the strict adherence to a certain style demonstrates that Hollywood is successful because it crafted an effective and engaging aesthetic.

I have turned to film, television, and literature, employing the analytical tools of media and cultural studies, to try and discern what Christianity can learn from Hollywood in creating a new aesthetic. In this final chapter, I attempt to draw on the previous analyses to begin theorizing ways for Christianity to be more effective in the cultural marketplace. In this respect, I am trying to follow the earlier criticisms of Fredric Jameson and Meaghan Morris and make the study of media and culture speak beyond the media text itself and theorize about changing actual social conditions. In what follows, I examine some existing social practices and institutions both for how they engender some of the aesthetic principles discussed here, and how they operate as alternative practices. I then theorize from these examples about other alternative practices or institutions that could be next steps towards realizing the potential of Christianity.

The Paulist Center – Boston

The Paulist Center in Boston is a Catholic community located at the top of the Boston Common, a stone's throw from the state capitol building. The Paulist Center was established in 1957, at the request of then Boston Archbishop Richard Cushing, who wanted a site dedicated to the work of evangelization. The Paulist Center serves as the residence of several Paulist priests, and it operates several different ministries, including a food pantry, a weekly meal service for the homeless, formation and catechetical training, and daily masses. The Paulist Center prides itself on being an incubator for social justice projects, the largest of which is *The Walk for Hunger*, which started as a Paulist Center project and now operates through Project Bread, organizing over 2,000 volunteers for an annual fundraising walk with over 40,000 participants.

The Paulist Center is many different things to many different people, but the one thing it is not is a parish. Nonetheless, its Sunday masses in the Holy Spirit chapel have become the spiritual home for many Catholics who embrace the vision of Vatican II, and could not find that shared vision at their local parish. In many respects the Paulist Center is a parish, but a different kind of parish. Rather than being defined geographically—and canonically—the Paulist Center is defined ideologically: it operates as a Catholic church for those Catholics who wish to remain within the institutional church, but want a church that speaks to and acts with mercy and social justice. The shared vision of its members help create both a sustainable community and liturgical practices committed to breathing life and energy into the practice of worship.

Three aesthetic principles in particular are important to this discussion of the Paulist Center: pageantry, proximity, and trajectory. The first of these, pageantry, speaks directly to the liturgical practices of the Paulist Center. As a site that offers Roman Catholic mass, the Paulist Center devotes an enormous amount of its collective talent around elevating the sacramentality of Catholic worship. At baptisms the congregation sings, rather than recites, the renewal of the baptismal vows, and after the water has been poured on the child's head, and the blessing completed, the congregation sings, "You are God's great work of art, fashioned with great love." One of the child's parents will then gather the child up, and hold him or her up to the congregation, who applaud while singing the refrain again. The ceremony highlights that baptism is more than just individual salvation, it is also about welcoming another member into the community—a sign that the community is renewing itself. In a similar manner, wedding rites at the Paulist Center are performed with the couple standing in the sanctuary, their backs to the altar, facing the congregation. Rather than the congregation looking upon the priest administer vows, which is the normal arrangement in a church, the congregation actually witnesses the vows of the couple—emphasizing again the central role of community in spiritual life. Masses in the Paulist Center that incorporate incense are frequently conducted through liturgical dance, and the music at all the masses is both varied and inspired (without being excessively performative).

The purpose of all of these liturgical practices is to magnify the significance of sacramental life and to continually breathe life into them by reaching for the transcendent. In attempting to convey the sublimity of sacramental existence, liturgical practices at the Paulist Center strive to reawaken the sense of the Divine as both transcendent and within individual members: to inspire them to go out and live the Gospel message. In this manner, the Paulist Center remains firmly within the domain of Roman Catholicism, and the institutional church as such, but steadfastly works towards a new concept of church.

Defining a parish ideologically rather than geographically is fraught with peril, not the least of which is the potential for stamping out all kinds of diversity. Creating parish communities based on ideology too closely resembles the kind of selective exposure that dominates media consumption, where only information that will confirm and conform is deemed acceptable and credible. In this respect, the Paulist Center is not a viable model for restructuring the concept of parish. One of the ministries of the Paulist Center, however, points to such an alternative model.

In 2012, a small group at the Paulist Center formed a new ministry: The St. Joseph Society. The group was formed to perform acts of charity through labor: performing small-scale renovation and repair projects for nonprofit organizations who otherwise could not afford them. The St. Joseph Society not only performs the repairs, but raises the funds for the materials, leaving the organizations that they serve with the ability to spread their resources further. In many ways, the St. Joseph Society is a version of Habitat for Humanity: both marshal resources and labor to help the less fortunate. Each are also based on the factory system of production, especially in terms of the concentration and organization of labor.

One of the organizations that the St. Joseph Society has served is Crossroads Family Shelter in East Boston. Like most shelter organizations serving the homeless, Crossroads is also organized around the factory model insofar as the homeless are concentrated at a specific site that can then offer ancillary services as well as shelter. The factory model of treating homelessness is so common that it is not unusual for municipal shelters to house over a hundred clients a night. Crossroads is a little more unique because it houses whole families, but the factory model of treating homelessness is so ingrained in our culture that it is difficult to imagine alternatives. Reconceptualizing a parish of the future, however, might be one such alternative. Rather than organizing a parish based solely on geography or ideology, parishes might be organized around purpose—and one such purpose could be providing housing and ancillary services and support for homeless families, many of whom need only transitional assistance.

Many existing parishes already have the existing space and infrastructure to provide such shelter on a small basis, the result of their construction from an earlier era. The bigger challenge would be organizing parishioners to provide the services and supervision that a family or small group would require. The goal here is to re-create the purpose of a parish by bringing purposefulness to the life of a parish. Attending to the least of these would no longer an ideal, but the lived experience of the parish. Moreover, such a purpose brings the concept of trajectory to the life of a parish, when it can successfully transition homeless families from need to stable lives. The pope took a step towards advancing this concept of parish in September of 2015, when he called on every parish in Europe to take in one refugee family. Combined, there are far more homeless and refugees than can be housed by churches, but the idea here is not an alternative to homelessness and migration much as it is an alternative to the existing concept of church.[172]

The Cleveland Greater University Circle Initiative and the Productive Capabilities of Local Capital

In this section I analyze Christianity's role in the cultural marketplace by looking at how the marketplace might employ Christian mandates to be productive rather than simply profitable. I begin with a comparison. In 2002, Brown-Forman closed the Lenox crystal stemware factory in Mt. Pleasant, Pennsylvania. Lenox had itself bought the factory by acquiring Bryce crystal in the 1960s. Bryce specialized in hand-blown, high-end crystal that was used by US embassies from the 1920s through the 1950s.[171] Nixon used Lenox crystal to toast Chinese Premier Chou En Lai in 1972, and Presidents Reagan through George W. Bush received nine-inch engraved bowls as inaugural gifts from Congress.[173] Lenox was clearly the prestige US crystal manufacturer, but by 2002, the market had changed dramatically. Brown-Forman argued that American culture had become more leisurely, and people no longer bought expensive crystal stemware (nor, for that matter, sterling silverware sets) for fine dining. In addition, Brown-Forman pointed to fierce foreign competition that manufactured crystal by machine and could put out millions of units per year at dramatically lower costs. As a result, the factory was shuttered, the assets were sold off, the union the workers belonged to lost members, and the state of Pennsylvania paid out for both unemployment benefits and retraining programs.

The story of industrial plant closings is nothing new to the city of Cleveland, Ohio. At the height of America's industrial economy, Cleveland was an important and vibrant city whose impact outstripped its actual size. With the decline of American manufacturing, Cleveland, like the rest of the "rust belt," fell into decline: experiencing high unemployment, declining values, and depopulation as factory after factory in the area closed its doors. For years The Cleveland Foundation, a nonprofit philanthropy dedicated to improving the city, spent millions of dollars and saw very little in return. By the early 2000's, the foundation wanted more dramatic results for its philanthropy, so in 2006 they awarded a grant to the Democracy Collaborative to hold a day-and-a-half–long Community Wealth Building Roundtable for a broad range of stakeholders concerned with community and economic development. The key development of the roundtable was "the idea of connecting the needs of anchor institutions" in the university district "to the need for local jobs . . . because of its potential for long-term impact and job creation."[174]

Encouraged by the roundtable, The Cleveland Foundation invited the Democracy Collaborative to conduct a feasibility study. Interviewing stakeholders from across the community, the Democracy Collaborative developed a "three-legged stool" strategy:

1. Leveraging the purchasing needs of anchor institutions;
2. Developing a network of community-based cooperatives owned and run by GUC residents geared towards meeting those procurement needs; and

3. Taking advantage of the strategic opportunities emerging in the green economy space, given the sustainability commitments of the anchor institutions.[175]

Guided by these three principles, the Democracy Collaborative proposed the creation of three different cooperatively owned business entities: Evergreen Cooperative Laundry, which sees to the laundering needs of hospitals and universities, Ohio Cooperative Solar, which generates green energy for anchor institutions by installing and maintaining solar panels across the large roof profiles of the GUC, and finally, Green City Growers Cooperative, which supplies produce for anchor institutions, by growing lettuce and herbs hydroponically in a greenhouse that spans four city acres.

Prior to the GUC Initiative, the city of Cleveland had engaged in the creation of "empowerment zones" the highly vaunted community development program favored by both the political left and right. Cleveland's experience was similar to many communities: businesses came in taking advantage of tax breaks, and then left when the tax breaks expired or the business flourished enough to relocate. The fundamental difference between empowerment zones and the structure of the GUC Initiative is the role of capital. With empowerment zones, capital flows: costs are lowered for businesses, which reduces margins and increases the possibility for profit. That profit is then free to flow to any part of the global economy, which it frequently did. With the GUC Initiative, capital circulates, moving from one part of the community to another, and frequently back again. The difference, in short, is between the profit motive of capitalism, and the productive capacities of capitalism.

The business entities created within the GUC Initiative are more than just "employee owned." They are very much modeled upon the Mondragon Cooperatives founded by Fr. Jose Maria Arizmendiarrieta in the Basque region of Spain. In an effort to deal with the widespread unemployment and economic fallout of World War II as it impacted an ethnic minority in Spain, Fr. Jose created small cooperatives which emphasized the fostering of relationships and community. As the Institute for Sustainable Communities notes, "after 50 years of self-development by a historically marginalized ethnic minority, the current Mondragon Cooperative Corporation now includes 120 industrial, financial, and retail cooperatives with 90,000 employees."[176] More than just an abstract model, Mondragon is a living example that members of the roundtable visited as they drew up their plans.

The lessons of Mondragon, of community building and cooperative ownership, became structural principles for the GUC Initiative. Workers within the cooperatives, for example, must live in one of the six neighborhoods the cooperatives are trying to stabilize, and they must build equity within the company. As stakeholders, they have voice in the operations and decisions of the company, and must grapple with daily issues that confront traditionally hard-to-employ workers: attendance, punctuality, theft, disagreements. Here, the principle of proximity exercises a significant role. Because the workers are the company, not just exploited or alienated labor, the role of management and leadership has an altogether different focus. Rather than profit for private—and removed—stockholders, management works closely with the shareholders—the workers—for productivity and harmony. As Stephen Kiel, CEO of the solar cooperative, states: "Part of the job of the CEO is to get to know the people really, really well. The person running the business has got to know something about the problem set or you can't manage it; and then it's frustrating for both parties."[177] This proximity to workers is so imperative to the model that Evergreen Cooperatives are committed to making the next generation of CEOs come from within the cooperatives.

The anchor institutions approach to making capital circulate within a city rather than taking flight into global markets is having an effect. Both the Ford Foundation and the Casey Foundation are working to create a similar anchor institution model with the medical and education institutions in Camden, Ohio.[178] Not all the interest in this model comes from the Rust Belt or deindustrialized cities, either. Both New Orleans and San Francisco are working with the Democracy Collaborative to explore their potential for economic development using the anchor institutions model, as is Toronto, Canada. Impressed by the idea of making capital circulate within the municipality, the Mowat Centre and the Atkinson Foundation studied the city of Toronto's $1.5 billion-dollar budget and concluded that if only 2 percent of spending were directed towards small local businesses, the city would spend $30 million in the local economy annually.[179]

The logic of proximity that is at work in this anchor institution model is not too far removed from how businesses and municipalities used to operate before the post-World War II economy, with capital circulating locally. Certainly, a global economy has been in place at least since the Roman empire, and global mercantile capitalism is what allowed Western civilization to evolve out of feudalism and into industrial capitalism. What the anchor institution model recognizes, however, is the high cost of profit when capital fails to circulate locally, closely, in proximity to the community.

The anchor institution model could not have saved Lenox crystal, but with all the stakeholders involved—employees, unions, and the state of Pennsylvania—adopting a Mondragon model might have. The combined capital of both the union and the state had potential for drawing an equity investor that could finance buying the company as an employee-owned enterprise. Moreover, as an employee-owned, community-based manufacturer, Lenox could pursue and promote markets that were neither substantial nor accessible before. For example, recognizing that it would save millions in unemployment benefits and job retraining programs, the state of Pennsylvania could itself have become a large purchaser of commemorative crystal for official events, and likewise promoted other governmental agencies, entities, and for-profit corporations to do the same. More than just saving money, the more the state of Pennsylvania could have promoted using Lenox crystal for corporate and governmental commemorations, the more tax dollars would have flowed back to the state. The future of Lenox was not in competing for the low end, nor in trying to bring back certain dining traditions. Rather, the future of Lenox could have been promoting a vision of employee-owned craftsmanship: handmade, high-end, commemorative crystal, made in America.

The lesson of Lenox crystal, of Cleveland and Mondragon should be for unions, states, and other large institutions to recognize themselves as stakeholders and look for alternative models that embrace proximity and the productive capacity of capital. In the following two examples, I examine how these principles could be extended to create new alternatives.

The New Franciscan University

The anchor institution model is an inherently practical and demonstrably effective approach to community wealth creation that reinstantiates the proximity of more organic communities from the premodern era—if not feudalism itself. In this section I examine in the abstract an equally organic and outdated model—the ecclesiastical model—as an economic alternative to the reckless corporate model currently adopted by higher education. That the current model of higher education is unsustainable is readily apparent to everyone except those running higher education institutions. Steve Odland, writing for *Forbes*, notes that: "Since 1985, the overall consumer price index has risen 115% while the college education inflation rate has risen nearly 500%."[180] To put costs into perspective, he then quotes Gordon Wadsworth, author of *The College Trap*, who argues: "if the cost of college tuition was $10,000 in 1986, it would now cost the same student over $21,500 if education had increased as much as the average inflation rate but instead education is $59,800 or over 2 ½ times the inflation rate." These rising costs have convinced many state legislatures that the cost of higher education has become unsustainable. Unfortunately, instead of insisting on reform, they have simply retreated from funding state institutions. The American Council on Education reports that only two states, Wyoming and North Dakota, have maintained the same level of spending since the 1980s—with Wyoming spending 2.3 percent of its budget and North Dakota spending 0.8 percent. All the other states have decreased spending anywhere from 14.8 to 64.9 percent.[181]

The root cause of these dramatic cost increases is the corporatization of higher education. The corporatization of higher education began in the 1980s, increased dramatically in the 1990s, and mushroomed even further in the first two decades of the twenty-first century. Corporatization, which should have brought benefits like rigorous cost-benefit analysis, instead ushered in two enormously detrimental side effects: uncontrolled bureaucracy, over-professionalization, and CEO salaries for college and university presidents. The administering of higher education has grown so dramatically that the *Wall Street Journal* reports that:

> Across U.S. higher education, nonclassroom costs have ballooned, administrative payrolls being a prime example. The number of employees hired by colleges and universities to manage or administer people, programs and regulations increased 50% faster than the number of instructors between 2001 and 2011, the U.S. Department of Education says. It's part of the reason that tuition, according to the Bureau of Labor Statistics, has risen even faster than health-care costs.[182]

In addition to just the sheer numbers of higher education administrators, the cost of administrative salaries is fundamentally out of proportion to the core enterprise of the institution: education. The chief cause of disproportionate compensation is presidential salaries. *The Chronicle of Higher Education* reports that the typical public higher education president earns $428,000 a year, and for eighty percent of those, housing and a car are included as additional compensation.[183] As daunting as presidential compensation is, the larger problem it creates is raising the bar for other administrative salaries. According to *The Chronicle of Higher Education*, the median salary for a provost is $187,000 (with the average research university paying $336,500), while an associate provost earns $130,00. Because neither position directly oversees operations on a daily basis, a chief business officer earns $180,000, and a chief of external affairs officer makes $167,000, while a chief athletics administrator makes $115,000, and a chief development officer earns $161,000. Then, of course, there is the academic side of the institution, where the average arts & sciences dean makes $150,000 ($250,000 at a research institution) followed by associate and assistant deans who make

$111,000 and $95,000 respectively—with more than one person typically working at that level.[184]

Far from bringing efficiency and cost-benefit analysis to higher education, corporatization of higher education has fueled a dramatic increase in pricing that is both unaffordable and unsustainable. Worse still, corporate higher education has disguised the high cost of bureaucracy by steadily decreasing the amount of full-time professors. As Paul Compos notes, "Forty-five years ago 78 percent of college and university professors were full time, today half of postsecondary faculty members are lower-paid part-time employees, meaning that the average salaries of the people who do the teaching in American higher education are actually quite a bit lower than they were in 1970."[185] For all of its bureaucracy, corporatized higher education has actually lowered the quality of education, even while it drove up the price. Higher education has become little more than minor fiefdoms, bestowing wealth on a privileged few while it extorts enormous sums from the masses. As Thomas Frank argues:

> The coming of "academic capitalism" has been anticipated and praised for years; today it is here. Colleges and universities clamor greedily these days for pharmaceutical patents and ownership chunks of high-tech startups; they boast of being "entrepreneurial"; they have rationalized and outsourced countless aspects of their operations in the search for cash; they fight their workers nearly as ferociously as a nineteenth-century railroad baron; and the richest among them have turned their endowments into in-house hedge funds.[186]

Reforming existing institutions from their entrenched corporate structure is all but impossible at this stage. Dismantling bureaucracy never comes easy, and always comes with an enormous amount of upheaval and blood-letting. And on the opposite side of the coin, faculty are too invested in the academic disciplines as protection against educational bureaucracy to respond accordingly if the bureaucracy was miraculously eliminated.

For this reason, I propose creating a new Franciscan university: Franciscan insofar as it would adopt simplicity and dedication to purpose as its model, and abandon all the material and extraneous undertakings that dominate higher education but are secondary at best to learning. A new Franciscan university would retreat from the marketplace by adopting a more ecclesiastical and holistic model—one that could dramatically lower costs while improving the quality of education. Here, proximity and collectivity become key principles that can substitute purpose for profit by adopting the following parameters:

- Creating a campus at minimal cost as part of a broader economic renewal project (for example, converting abandoned factories, former state hospitals, or decommissioned military bases).
- Using the campus rehabilitation process to implement sustainability into every facet of the college: energy consumption and renewable energy sources, waste management, water use and reuse, food procurement, and landscaping.
- Employing a residential faculty and using faculty housing as part of the overall compensation package to reduce salaries.
- Drastically streamlining the administration and the staffing of the college, with a goal of capping these numbers at one-third the size of the faculty and restricting compensation of senior administrators to the same levels as faculty.
- Reducing and reforming academic disciplinarity to deliver critical education developmentally, coherently, and more efficiently.
- Eliminating nonessential services and amenities that are peripheral to the core mission of education: i.e., multimillion-dollar, spa-styled sports facilities, high-rise style and apartment-type housing, and intervarsity athletic teams.
- Creating collaborative relationships with the local municipality as a means of creating economies of scale in day-to-day operations (i.e. library, auditorium, sports facilities).
- Establishing an academic village-style senior housing community of 100–150 units as part of the campus to create a tax base for the local municipality and to create a larger footprint for renewable energy technologies.

By themselves, none of these parameters are original. Tiny Lasell College in Massachusetts has an academic village senior housing community (in fact, it established the landmark case that the institution's tax-exempt status can not be extended to senior housing). Faculty residential colleges are also nothing new, though they are becoming the hot new trend for the large research institutions, which offer them as a perk to students. And as the Evergreen Cooperatives in Cleveland demonstrate, locally sourcing food, even in an urban environment, is not only possible, but allows the institution to be an economic driver in the community.

What a modified ecclesiastical model adds to the equation is a specific purpose for bringing all these parameters together in a unified whole: reducing the cost of education by retreating from the marketplace and replacing corporate structure with community. The residential faculty is the heart of this collective logic. Offering faculty housing as part of the overall compensation can dramatically lower the cost of teaching. The fact is, most professors do not go into careers in higher education for the money, but they do need to support themselves and their families. When they are employed in the current corporate model, as alienated labor, their overall cost is expensive. An institution has to pay each individual enough to cover the cost of living: housing, transportation, food, and insurance to name but a few. This alternative model, however, recognizes that faculty could live quite comfortably if living expenses were already paid for as part of the overall costs of the institution. The individual salaries could then be dramatically lower but still provide a quality lifestyle.

The collective aspect of a faculty residential college also defers the cost of institutional upkeep. As an atomized individual in the marketplace, the normal professor does their own lawn care, cleaning, and maintenance at their private residence—or pays someone else to do it. In this model, however, that labor can be organized collectively: no longer an individual responsibility in a private setting, but a collective endeavor in a community. This same logic can be applied to transportation costs. Individual faculty no longer need to own private vehicles paid out of their personal income, but can share vehicles purchased and insured by the institution. The cost effectiveness of such a plan is dramatic considering how many hours a day a private vehicle is *not* used.

Retreating from, or perhaps reforming, the marketplace is also a core principle of creating the college as part of an economic redevelopment plan. Repurposing infrastructure can bring value to buildings and areas that have been radically depreciated by the market. Again, that principle is nothing new. In the 1970s, New York City artists took advantage of the space afforded by a largely abandoned light-industrial district in Manhattan, repurposing it as combined living/studio space and turning Soho into one of the most desirable neighborhoods in the city. With the deinstitutionalizing process that began under the Carter administration, states are now in the business of repurposing state hospital campuses, many of which, like Medfield in Massachusetts, offer compelling turn-of-the-century or early twentieth-century architecture. Jennifer Pinck, of Pinck Associates, did a site survey of the Medfield campus and estimated that gut-rehabbing it all would cost $100 million. That's hardly a drop in the bucket, but not a bad price tag when you compare it to the $95 million cost of building one new student center at the University of Massachusetts Lowell. For its part, the state should be willing to finance such an undertaking, and turn it over to a private faculty collective as a means of providing affordable higher education to its constituents, and for creating pricing competition for its own public institutions. With the added value of creating an economic engine within a development project, the value to the state exceeds the initial investment considerably.

In addition to defunct state hospitals, there are still moth-balled military bases that need repurposing and development, and many states have abandoned or little-used factory and mill districts. The city of Detroit, for example, has become so depopulated that it has too much space and property on its hands. As the Cleveland Greater University District Initiative demonstrates, creating a new higher education institution provides an anchor for development that, under this model, would include renewable energy installation as a means of lowering overall operating costs. It would also create the need for local food sourcing, which could not only generate local and urban agriculture as in Cleveland, but also create a market for nearby rural growers, dairy, and ranchers looking for direct market opportunities. Retreating from the marketplace in this fashion is not so much a plan to actually shrink economic activity, but rather stimulate it locally: to make an economy productive rather than exploitive.

Another means of stimulating local economy and productivity by withdrawing from the marketplace is with the creation of an academic village-style senior housing community as part of the university. Here too, the goal is not so much to create profit in a specialized segment of the housing market, but to add to the community in productive ways. The margins for such an undertaking do not have to be high and generate loads of income to reduce the price of tuition. Rather, margins could be quite small insofar as the added community of seniors would displace the cost of upkeep, fitness facilities, and libraries that would be shared. A senior community could also provide a larger footprint for renewable energy production like solar and wind, lowering overall operating costs for both. In addition, a senior community adds to the collective identity of the institution, providing an at-home and local audience for the creative productions, intellectual, and cultural events of the institution.

A new Franciscan university does not have to be religious, but in order to fundamentally reform higher education and bring back affordability, it must embrace a more ecclesiastical model: one where collectivity and proximity replace profit and pricing, where the fundamental purpose of teaching and learning is the core focus, and where the concept of a learning community is more than just a marketing term. While online education can provide the individual student with an on-demand approach to learning, offering convenience and the promise of lower prices (which, oddly, it has largely failed to provide), the residential learning environment offers superior learning and development. If the residential college system is to survive in anything other than an elite environment, a new Franciscan university is going to have to be created.

Spiritus.TV: Organizing the Collective Potential in Christian Higher Education

If Christianity has a communications problem, there is no better place for solving it than Christian colleges and universities, which in theory are laboratories for ideas and innovation—and they are, except, by and large, for the issues confronting Christianity. The higher education marketplace creates enormous pressure on Christian colleges and universities. On one side of the marketplace are secular institutions (many of them, like Harvard and Yale, are formerly church affiliated) which offer elite access or quality education (or at least, their marketing says so). Christian colleges and universities operate in a manner that ensures they offer not just the same quality of education as secular competitors, but the same education period. As a result, the concept of their identity is frequently a contentious issue: how and where the religious mission enters into and informs the educational process.[187]

On the other side of the marketplace are fundamentalist Bible colleges, whose primary purpose, as Jesse DeConto relates, is to instill a circularity of reason that will refer all things back to the Bible. Catholic colleges and universities in particular feel the pressure of both the past—where the perception was that they offered a similar, insular, sectarian education—and the present, where they do not want to be associated with Bible colleges. To be sure, many Bible colleges are accredited institutions whose simple mission is to put God before all things. But the marketplace is also filled with Bible colleges that use their own accrediting agencies like the Transnational Association of Christian Colleges and Schools Accreditation Commission (recognized by the US Department of Education).

In addition to these market pressures, Christian colleges and universities face the same market pressures from the "consumer" that every higher education institution experiences: the demand for professional training and marketability (in other words, ensuring that its graduates get jobs) that increases with cost. These market forces combine in such a manner as to compel Christian colleges and universities to provide identical professional training within the disciplines as their secular competition. As a result, the ability for Christian higher education institutions to function as laboratories that can provide innovative solutions to the problems and crises of Christianity is greatly compromised.

The fields of communications, media studies, and production, however, offer bold examples for how these competing interests can be satisfied and yet function as laboratories for creating a new Christian aesthetic. Media production in particular is well positioned because the market demands of this discipline are calling for dramatic changes in the training methods and pedagogy that guides and shapes teaching. For the last several decades, training in film and video production has, for the most part, been structured around learning the skills and normative practices of the broadcast industry: how to achieve the high production values that the industry seems to effortlessly deliver every hour of every day. Students learn that it is anything but effortless—that it requires an enormous amount of skill, practice, and money to replicate those kind of production values.

Different media production programs then compete for students based on how they structure this training. Some programs, like New York University, the University of Southern California, and the University of California at Los Angeles, try to offer students more production courses where they can receive more actual practice through their coursework. Students also receive courses in media history, aesthetics, and sometimes even theory to then round out their education. Programs like NYU, USC, and UCLA also happen to be located in major production hubs, so their students have the opportunity to pursue valuable internship experience working for production companies and studios—though that work is rarely, if ever, doing actual production. Outlying programs like Ithaca College in upstate New York or Emerson College in Boston try to give their students the same advantage of exposure to the industry by building multimillion-dollar Los Angeles campuses.

In the end, all these programmatic features come down to one basic approach: teaching students to imitate the forms, styles, and production values of the broadcast industry. A basic studio television production course will teach students how to put on a news program, and likewise, a single camera or field production course will have a thirty-second commercial or a small documentary (and most likely both) as projects. This basic structure and pedagogy has served the industry and the institutions well for decades (though with the low job placement rate for graduates, it's arguable that it has served students well). The problem is, this approach will no longer serve the needs of the industry, which is experiencing enormous disruption.

The impact of the Internet and the ability to stream digital video across multiple platforms—computers, gaming devices, phones, and tablets—has fundamentally shifted media consumption patterns. Television, per se, is no longer the dominant media form, but has been displaced by the Internet. And as with every transition from one dominant media form to another, it has brought about both changes in culture and changes in media consumption. Video, like the rest of digital culture, has transformed from a time-specific broadcast model to an on-demand webcast model. People do not rush home on the subway to catch their favorite shows; rather, they watch their favorite shows on the subway. The industry, which for decades financed its operations by being able to measure its audience at specific times, is now experiencing the kind of volatile disruption that every medium experiences when it is displaced as the dominant media form. In general, the audience for broadcast television is shrinking, as are cable subscribers. Television consumption is declining in every age group, but none more dramatically than 18-to-24-year-olds, a key demographic, prompting *Business Insider*, for example, to proclaim that "TV viewing in the US is plummeting," backing up this rhetoric with statistics showing the decline of TV viewing in every age group, particularly 18-to-24-year-olds, an important trendsetter demographic.[188]

Being able to binge watch favorite shows is not the only change that the Internet has brought about. As a new distribution network with no barriers to access it has ushered in new forms, formats, and styles from alternative producers. Digital technology and digital standards have made access to production easily affordable, and many independent producers are using YouTube, Vimeo, and other consolidator sites to stream their work to large audiences. These audiences do not challenge broadcast audiences in terms of individual programs, but collectively they constitute a large shift in viewing patterns, and individually the represent a sustainable model. The top YouTube producer of 2015, PewDiePie, for example, has over 38 million subscribers, and over 9 billion total views of their content, with annual earnings estimated at $2.3–18.2 million. That's more viewers and income than the channels for pop stars Rhianna, Katy Perry, Eminem, and Taylor Swift.[189] Another popular YouTube star is Jenna Marbles, whose Socialblade subscribers rank is 22nd, and video view ranking is 192nd, but still has 15 million subscribers and a lifetime view count (ranging back to 2010) of 1.6 billion views.[190] Her annual estimated earnings are $80,000 to $1.3 million a year for making random humor videos.

The list of small content providers streaming videos that range from playing video games with commentaries to unwrapping and playing with toys is well over a hundred. With millions of subscribers and billions of views, the impact of these content providers cannot be ignored, especially considering how much they occupy the 12-to-18-year-old and 18-to-24-year-old markets. These age groups are content with relatively unsophisticated humor like Annoying Orange, Shane TV, Jenna Marbles, or video game commentary, but their consumption rates are enormous, and as their tastes change, a creative and flexible content community will attempt to change with them and provide for their evolving content needs.

The growing popularity and impact of streaming video across the web, or webcasting, also ushers in a new paradigm shift in the entertainment marketplace. In the age of broadcast, and then cable-cast television, the reigning paradigm was the gatekeeper system, where access to production and distribution was controlled by a small amount of powerful people who determined what audiences would see. In the webcasting era, nearly anyone can have access both to production and distribution. The gatekeepers are gone, and in their place is an over-saturated distribution pipeline that resembles a library turned upside down and shaken. The new paradigm is content recognition: getting a mass audience to locate your content in a sea of small videos.

Media production programs in higher education will need to face head-on the paradigmatic challenges that webcasting presents if for no other reason than jobs in the broadcast industry will continue to shrink, while they continue to expand for video content creation on the web. Institutions will need to provide their students with the kind of critical skills that will empower them to create the new forms, formats, genres, and styles that the on-demand environment of webcasting is creating. For all its lackluster style or form, the video game commentary, or "let's play," is a new genre that has no roots in television or cinema. It is, however, a dominant form and genre that rakes in millions of dollars. It requires so little production skills as to allow anyone with a camera to become a content producer. University production programs clearly do not need to train students for this genre, but they do need to train students to anticipate and create the next generation of genres. The 12-to-18-year-old market that dominates consumption is a dynamic, if not volatile, demographic, one whose tastes evolve and mature. When their fascination with video games commentary (finally) comes to an end, they will look for other kinds of content. Current media production programs are not oriented towards teaching students to anticipate and create new forms, but rather, imitate existing ones. They run a high risk of becoming obsolete very quickly.

With this kind of disruption coming to the college and university media production marketplace, Christian institutions of higher education will find themselves in a unique position to reorient their programs and take advantage of their collective potential. Currently independent and atomized, these programs could stop competing with each other for students, and instead work collectively to produce video content for a single, aggregator-type website offering mission-oriented content, that finds ways to promote Christian values and theology. Such an endeavor would be an extraordinary undertaking, and require enormous institutional effort and change (which institutions are profoundly bad at) but, conversely, would require no capital investment from their end. On the opposite side of the equation, however, participation in such a collective endeavor would be a money-making enterprise for each institution.

The website itself could offer three distinct revenue streams for its participants. The first would be ad revenues from the fifteen-second spots that would play before each stream. As the website grows its audience, this revenue will subsequently grow, with strong potential to be a significant source of revenue. The second source of income would come from marketing institutional merchandise on the site—not only the coffee mugs, T-shirts, and sweat shirts with the institution's logo, but merchandise that might arise from the content itself. Where the site itself will take a percentage of the ad revenue, the merchandising revenue would go directly to the individual institution.

The last source of revenue for participants would come from resale or redistribution of successful content. In many ways, the system would operate as a farm system for the broader entertainment market. If a particular program became a big hit, larger media or broadcast companies will be interested in obtaining the rights and producing it on a mass scale. Such practice is already widespread with Internet content. Cartoon Network bought Internet sensation *Annoying Orange*, but not until its animator/creator, Dane Boedigheimer, made a bundle streaming it on YouTube and merchandising his characters. *Wired* magazine writer Ryan Tate summarizes the relationship between YouTube video and traditional media when he writes:

> If you want a glimpse into the future of the television studio, look no further than Disney's acquisition of Maker Studios . . . . [T]he $500 million deal—announced last week—provides Disney with a clear path to the way TV production and distribution will work in the years to come. The acquisition gives the company an established way of reaching people as they shift from watching cable TV to watching online videos. But it also provides direct access to a vast community of video producers who could be the TV artists of tomorrow, and it serves up a vast trove of viewing data that can help Disney fine tune offerings throughout its entertainment empire.[191]

Disney is not alone in making significant investments in this kind of farm system. Hearst, AT&T, Time Warner, and DreamWorks Animation all bought interests in YouTube channels.

For all their large investments, however, the major media corporations are leaving one market segment untouched: the religious oriented. It is not an oversight. There is strong potential for this particular market niche to be enormous, but there is no developmental system to produce content, and as a result, there is little to no compelling or interesting content out there. Christian higher education could change all that by becoming the laboratory or incubators for creating that kind of content, but that would require significant change, and change comes slowly to higher education.

The point, however, is that change and disruption is coming, and reorienting media production programs is already a necessity, so the real issue is whether leadership in these institutions will take advantage of disruption and move in a direction that will bring vitality to their identity, provide superior training for their students, and bring in outside revenue to the institution. Joining together to create content for an aggregator site provides the financial incentive to do so. The fundamental issue then becomes how to reorient programs whose basic pedagogy is imitation.

The answer, as I have argued elsewhere, is with client-based, critically oriented instruction.[192] Typically, for example, single-camera video production courses assign a thirty-second spot as a graded assignment. The assignment is standard because it asks students to bring together all the skills they need in production and post-production, but on a limited scale (only thirty seconds of content). The place where this project falls short, however, is that the focus is on imitating production values, and the real work of the students is channeled into pretend clients. In my single-camera video course, students are assigned to create a thirty-second Public Service Announcement (PSA) for a nonprofit organization that needs one, but cannot afford it. Students do not pretend to create something for the American Cancer Society, which can readily pay for big budget ad campaigns, but rather, must go out into the community and find organizations in need. Modifying the assignment in this way still requires students to mobilize all their production skills, but adds to the task the necessity of thinking critically, of assessing the communications needs of an organization, and coming up with a solution through a visual medium. In addition, because they are working with real clients, the assignment brings focus and added motivation to the students' work, as well as teaching them how to cultivate clients. Frequently, the PSAs are streamed on the client's website—demonstrating that undergraduate student work can have professional production values. Just as importantly, the assignment teaches students the value of raising up the voices of those in the community who are not adequately heard.

Client-based instruction does not always require an actual client. In a studio production course, for example, I have used the university itself as the virtual client. Normal studio television production courses, working out of the imitation model, usually produce a news show as one of the graded projects. Without extraordinary help, their production values will not be as high as the local network affiliate, and their content will either be restricted to campus news, which severely restricts the potential for audience, or will imitate the local news, but without the resources for reporting. In contrast, the first project in studio production courses I taught was a media critique program. The setting and lighting resemble that of a news program (though it does not have to), but the content is focused on critiquing news and entertainment media using theories that students have worked with in their media studies courses. They search for content in print, web, and cable-cast television, import it digitally, and subject it to examination with critical models they have already learned. The project not only reinforces the critical approaches to media so necessary to future endeavors, but creates content that can compete in the marketplace—there is a paucity of media critique in network programming, with the exception of the comic approach to media critique of *The Daily Show*.

This type of first project may lack the kind of polish necessary to grow a large audience, but it lays the foundation for more advanced production courses to build upon. The model here is sequencing: converting advanced courses into a practicum-style course where every week students create a new episode of the same show. In this respect, the lower courses can function as sites for experimenting with forms, formats, and genres, and advanced courses produce the more successful programs on a regular basis. This critically based approach not only teaches students production skills, but gets them attuned to thinking of markets, audiences, and how forms and formats intersect with them.

The only thing left for Christian institutions to add to a client-based critical approach model is Christian values, themes, or theology—a challenge, but not insurmountable. The media critique program discussed here, for example, can add a Christian perspective to critique. The kinds of glorified materialism, violence, and sexual hedonism that secular media criticism largely ignores can be put under the microscope in terms of their conflict with core principles of Christianity—questioning how that conflict consistently gets swept under the rug. That kind of critique should not be confused or equated with the current kind of religious programming one already sees on EWTN or from other religious broadcasters, where a group of theologians sit around a table and discuss faith, catechism, or even the issues of the day. That format is already being done, and is failing to secure an audience. Rather, the point of bringing this model into the media production programs of Christian colleges and universities is to experiment and create formats and genres that do not yet exist. Nor should thinking about new forms and content be limited to media production courses or communications departments themselves. An interdisciplinary approach where faculty and students from English, theology, philosophy, art, psychology, and sociology—to name a few—come together and brainstorm, would not only expand the scope of experimental thought, but have the added advantage of putting the concept of Christian identity, values, and beliefs in the forefront of institutional life.

The feasibility of actually getting a number of institutions to take on a bold initiative requiring large institutional change and work collectively rather than competitively verges almost on fantasy, but for two compelling dynamics. First, the potential market size here is extraordinarily large, so the potential for significant external revenue is high—and universities are eager for external revenue. Second, as a group, the institutions who participate will offer superior training to their undergraduate students, which will give them a decided competitive advantage in the higher education marketplace—and all with no real capital investment. Universities may very well be in the position of looking for new instructors that can teach from different paradigms, and be able to make connections between production and Christianity, but as argued above, changes and disruption are coming about regardless: better to embrace it fully within the mission of the institution than ignore it and be caught falling behind competitively.

The feasibility of such an undertaking is also a question of producing the volume of content necessary to sustain an aggregator site. The map below demarcates a theoretical network of Christian institutions of higher education that already possess active media programs spread across the country, including Southern Methodist University and Baylor University in Texas—affiliated with the Texas Baptist Convention—and Loyola Marymount University in Los Angeles, a Jesuit institution affiliated with the Roman Catholic Church. To the north are more Jesuit institutions, including the University of San Francisco, Seattle and Gonzaga Universities, and Creighton University in Nebraska. Other Jesuit institutions include Boston College in Massachusetts, and Georgetown in Washington DC. In the Midwest and New York there are Catholic institutions that are not Jesuit, such as DePaul in Chicago (Vincentian), the University of Detroit-Mercy (Jesuit and the Sisters of Mercy), the University of Dayton in Ohio (Marianist), and St. John's University in New York City (Vincentian). These institutions represent a rough sampling, not an exhaustive list, and still comprise a network that gives some geographical representation, as well as different kinds of affiliations to Christian identity.

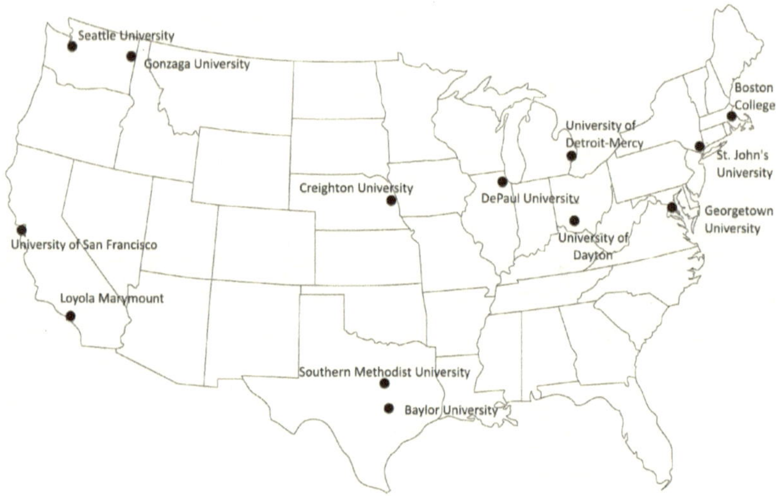

Just as significantly, they all have robust potential in the area of media production.

In terms of potential output, if each institution only produced ten episodes of one program, which could be easily accomplished in one semester, then they could adequately fill the site with content. Providing content for an aggregator site is a fundamentally different enterprise from programming for broadcast. The latter operates in terms of filling time around the clock with content—an enormous undertaking. Webcasting video, conversely, operates on demand. The task is not so much to create enough content to fill out the clock as much as it is to provide enough content when it is demanded. By having related content, but different forms, formats, and genres, the aggregator site can provide the amount of content to meet on-demand needs without taxing the productive capabilities of participating institutions.

Participating in such a collective endeavor allows member institutions to provide superior professional and critical training for its students—creating balance between a critical, liberal arts education with intensive professional training. It also provides the institutions with more purpose to create graduate programs: they could not only increase their productive capacity, but expand on the depth of experimentation. In the end, the fundamental purpose of creating such a collaborative is not the potential for revenue, but rather the experimentation. The massive audience potential in religious programming remains untouched by corporate media for a reason: they do not want to spend the enormous capital outlay required to experiment with successful forms, format, genre, style, and content. Colleges and universities, conversely, have already spent that capital; now, the task is channeling those investment dollars towards productive, mission-oriented experimentation rather than unproductive imitation of the secular broadcast industry.

Certainly, the broadcast industry is not going away, but it is shrinking. The broadcast media will continue to produce the kinds of content that the project proposed here never will. Big budget, multilocation, ensemble-cast dramas like *The West Wing* and *Grey's Anatomy* will continue to be produced by the entertainment industry, and will always be out of the reach of this project. Given the high risk, and relatively low margins of these kinds of productions, the challenge of making them has little to no place in higher education institutions. Creating the new forms, new styles, and new aesthetics that can make Christianity compelling and vital again, that can inspire people to create a "church of the poor" rather than follow a "church of the law," however, is precisely the kind of challenge worth taking.

Conclusion

I close out this discussion of media and aesthetics by theorizing alternative social institutions and practices, as a response to the ubiquitousness of for-profit media and the contemporary culture machine. The pervasiveness of modern media culture was built brick by brick, text by text, with stunning successes and phenomenal failures, but mostly with an enormous amount of collective labor. Christianity can no longer afford to wait for the institutional church to build its own alternative communications infrastructure. Not only can it ill afford to do so, but it has already shown itself as fundamentally incapable. Rather, Christianity needs to build infrastructure collectively, drawing on the hidden potential of its existing institutions and the creativity of its grassroots organizations. Christianity already possesses a compelling vision that contests the materialism, exclusivity, and violence that characterizes so much of contemporary culture. What it needs now is the ability to mass-produce ongoing experimentation that can bring that vision out into the cultural marketplace—to contest contemporary culture and create alternatives. Christianity no longer needs to build cathedrals, but it certainly needs to build alternative culture and cultural formations. If *The Daily Show* with Jon Stewart and *The Colbert Report* with Stephen Colbert has shown anything, it is the limitations of contesting dominant cultural and ideological formations through deconstruction. Certainly, contestation is important and valuable, but when it comes in the form of deconstruction, its fundamental limitation is that it does not build and create—it only, at best, limits power.

Institutional Christianity has not been effective at contesting the ideology of secular humanism, particularly the ideologies of militarism, materialism, and sexual hedonism. What the discussion of *Joyeux Noël* attempts to prove is that the most effective form of contestation is not necessarily deconstruction—as has long been assumed by postmodern theorists—but rather, the construction of alternative images—a positive hermeneutic.

In order to create more effective alternative cultural discourse, Christianity does not need to build more infrastructure, but to reorganize its existing infrastructure as more flexible, inventive, and productive. The current operational approach amounts to little more than maintaining an ineffective but costly system and hoping for more Christian alternatives to emerge from the margins of mainstream media. To contest dominant culture more effectively, to move further in its goal to transform the world, the church will have to do more: it will have to create a kingdom culture, one that can compete with secular humanism. The aesthetics that can deliver that level of effectiveness has not fully come into their own. If the church wants it to come into being, it will have to relinquish its obsession with an outmoded aesthetic built around power, obedience, and hierarchy and unleash the creative and critical potential of its people (and institutions).

The necessity for the church to create its own kingdom culture is not just a matter of confronting the increasing marginalization of the church within culture, but also, a way to address the continuing decline and deficiencies of secular humanism itself. The more secular humanism fails to provide for the spiritual needs of people, the greater the vacuum that must be filled. Nowhere is this more evident that the worldwide overvaluation of professional sports. Postmodern culture has not only undercut the vitality of traditional rituals, which had their roots in religion, but vanquished community on an epic scale. Professional sports like NFL football and NHL hockey have increasingly become sites of creating postmodern, virtual community, complete with ritual, as have college sports like football and basketball. The degree of postmodernity within sports communities is demonstrated by the profound insignificance geography exercises in creating the community. Team members can and do come from anywhere—they are virtual commodities that owners and institutions trade and compete for. In addition, television broadcasting and merchandising deals are more important than actual ticket sales at team stadiums. And the corollary of television broadcasting is that it increases the fan base transgeographically.

At its core, sports fandom creates allegiance to virtual community, belonging to a defined collective whose triumphs and travails the fan participates in as a core component of the community. The billions of dollars at stake in these virtual communities, however, testifies to the hunger that people have for community, while at the same time indicating the degree to which sports play an overvalued and yet ultimately unfulfilling role within culture. Few fans recognize the illusory quality of actually winning the big championship. The game is played, conquest is achieved, and players and fans bask in glory for an exceedingly short amount of time before they must transition into the quest for the next championship.

Comparatively speaking, Christianity offers profoundly superior opportunities for authentic community, but it has not yet quite imagined how to bring them into being. In general, Christianity offers a far more compelling, vital, and enriching mode of existence than secular humanism can ever hope to offer, but the church, fundamentally, does not know how to effectively convey that message, nor for the most part do its institutions. The corollary of this problem is that the church is performing incredible work throughout the world: alleviating hunger, ecological devastation, profound poverity, and inequality in several different places. For the most part, however, it fails to show its work because it does not know how to capitalize on the technological changes that make it possible, and because it does not have aesthetic experience.

A glimpse of what the possibilities could be like can be found with the *Fondazione Buon Pastore* (Good Shepherd Foundation) in Rome, Italy. The Good Shepherd Foundation works throughout the world to alleviate suffering. In 2014, it provided support to 332,504 people in twenty-one different countries. Organizationally, the Good Shepherd Foundation began to recognize that in order to continue and expand their work, they needed to inform people about their work. They not only looked to social media, but to video. In 2015, they completed production of *Maisha: A New Life Outside the Mines.* The documentary does more than just promote the work of the foundation, it explores the violent intersection between the global economy and the developing world—here, the Democratic Republic of Congo. As the film points out, "The raw materials that power our mobile phones, computers, and energy grids lie under your feet here in great abundance," but in doing so by creating ecological devastation. The film dramatically shows and explicitly states that "We saw scores of young children, pregnant women, and nursing mothers toiling in toxic pools" that the mining creates.

In addition to showing the staggering conditions under which the film's subjects live, *Maisha* also examines the grassroots project run by the Good Shepherd Sisters that attempts to provide an alternative life and alternative modes of production to the mines. As the film points out, there are no warlords or child soldiers, no coercive force, just the crushing power of the global, digital economy. What Good Shepherd Foundation, and the film itself recognize, however, is that despite the crucial role that Kolwezi plays in supplying this economy, it is virtually unseen and unheard of—not surprisingly, or even uniquely, given its exploitation. *Maisha* is an attempt to break that silence, to give image to how this underground part of the global economy operates. It is a bold step toward participating in construction of an alternative culture. The next step is to bring other institutional organizations of the church into the process, and to experiment with new forms and styles to create new ways of seeing and conceptualizing the alternatives.

In this respect, the church, as such, does not so much need to engage in "culture wars" as much as it needs to create alternative culture. If nothing else, it should recognize the irony in the phrase. Even if it fails to see the irony, it should recognize that the reason it loses so badly in "culture wars" is that, fundamentally, it does not know how to create culture. Rather than going to war or battling over culture, the church needs to be engaged in creating a kingdom culture. But to create culture, you need to know how to signify, and to signify compellingly, as Hollywood so clearly demonstrates, you need an aesthetic. This book has tried to demonstrate that a new aesthetic of Christianity has been forming within the margins of popular culture. The church needs to marshal this aesthetic, and bring it fully into being. The world can hardly wait.

Notes

1. See, for example, WGBH's *Frontline* coverage of Francis's introduction, http://www.wgbh.org/programs/Frontline-6/episodes/Secrets-of-the-Vatican-49783.

2. Pope Francis, "A Big Heart Open to God," interview with Antonio Spadaro, *America*, September 30, 2013, 6.

3. Ibid., 7.

4. Ibid.

5. Pope Francis, *Evangelii Gaudium*, November 26, 2013.

6. Gonzalez-Andrieu, *Bridge to Wonder*, 13.

7. Plate, *Walter Benjamin, Religion, and Aesthetics*, 2.

8. Gonzalez-Andrieu, *Bridge to Wonder*, 18.

9. Williams, *Marxism and Literature*, 132.

10. A vivid example of Williams's concept is women's "big hair" style of the 1980s. Within the period of the 1980s, the style exerted palpable pressure: a woman would not want to be caught dead without it. Outside the period, a woman would not be caught dead wearing it, demarcating a specific period. In terms of cultural analysis, the style itself can be located as a reaction against both the flower power style of the 1970s and the beehive style of the 1960s—in other words, it evolved stylistically. In addition, however, the style is also a result of social dynamics and processes: the evolving concept of femininity, the increasing role of women in the workplace, and the continuity of legitimizing the commodification of women's appearance.

11. Williams, *Marxism and Literature*, 133.

12. Carroll, *Christ, Actually*, 31.

13. Gonzalez-Andrieu, *Bridge to Wonder*, 18.

14. Hall, "Encoding, decoding," 513.

15. Ibid.

16. *A Christmas Miracle.*

17. Schulz, *A Charlie Brown Christmas*, 40.

18. Michelson, "Towards Snow" 175.

19. Brooks, *The Melodramatic Imagination*, 14.

20. One could argue that the group's appropriation of the Christmas decorations is the very kind of commercialism that Charlie Brown rejects, and in this manner, the plot contains the ideological threat that Charlie Brown has created throughout the story. I would counter, however, that the show is not, as argued previously, concerned with "rejection" as much as it is transformation. The children in the scene use the tools at hand both to symbolize and complete the process of transformation.

21. Brooks, *The Melodramatic Imagination*, 16.

22. See, for example, Jameson, *The Political Unconscious*, and Morris, "Banality in Cultural Studies."

23. Fiske, "Opening the Hallway," 212.

24. Hall, "Encoding, decoding," 513.

25. Couldry, *Listening Beyond the Echoes*, 60.

26. See, for example, "The Ivory Tower Comes to the Windy City," in Clapp, *Border Crossings*, 53–62.

27. Augustine of Hippo, *The Confessions*, book I, chapter 1.

28. This personal experience of the inability to satisfy unquenchable desire leads to a kind of "anti-physicality" bias in Augustine's theology. Drawing on classical Greek philosophy and the writings of Paul the Apostle, Augustine has a tendency to see sexuality as corruption. Nonetheless, his work strives to bring a dialogical understanding to Christian theology.

29. Hall, "Encoding, decoding," 513.

30. See, for example, Pope Francis's November 2013 Apostolic Exhortation, *Evangelii Gaudium*, and Pope Benedict's first book, *Jesus of Nazareth* and John Paul II's encyclical *Centesimus Annus*. Fred Kammer, SJ, points out that Pope John Paul II further clarified his criticism of capitalism in a 1993 address in Latvia, arguing, "the church, since Leo XIII's *Rerum Novarum*, has always distanced itself from capitalistic ideology, holding it responsible for grave social injustices (cf. *Rerum Novarum*, 2). In *Quadragesimo Anno* Pius XI, for his part, used clear and strong words to stigmatize the international imperialism of money (*Quadragesimo Anno*, 109). This line is also confirmed in the more recent magisterium, and I myself, after the historical failure

of communism, did not hesitate to raise serious doubts on the validity of capitalism" (http://www.loyno.edu/jsri/catholicism-and-capitalism).

31. Milbank, Žižek, and Davis, *Paul's New Moment,* 5.

32. Ibid., 1.

33. See, for example, Rocchio, "Attacking 'Support Our Troops.'"

34. Milbank, Žižek, and Davis, *Paul's New Moment,* 2.

35. Rocchio, "Patriarchy has Failed Us," *1.*

36. Bordwell, Staiger, and Thompson, *The Classical Hollywood Cinema,* 5.

37. John 8:7 (NABRE).

38. Hall, "Encoding, decoding," 513.

39. Hebrews 11:1 (NRSA).

40. Likewise, her pleading with Noah to spare the babies is reminiscent of the scene where she tells Harry that she will accompany him to confront Voldemort in *Harry Potter and the Deathly Hallows Part II.*

41. Hall, "Encoding, decoding," 515.

42. Ibid., 508.

43. Ibid., 509.

44. Mark 9:2–8 (NABRE).

45. Staiger, in Bordwell, Staiger, and Thompson, *The Classical Hollywood Cinema,* 332.

46. And indeed, a more detailed analysis than I can provide here can clearly delineate that the film offers pointed criticism of gender roles, keenly anticipating the women's rights movement that follows in a few short years, the marginalization of children, and the ethical deficiencies of modern empire and industrial capitalism.

47. See, for example, the argument on p. 276 in Bakhtin, *The Dialogic Imagination*, in which Bakhtin argues, "The word, directed toward its object, enters a dialogically agitated and tension-filled environment of alien words, value judgments and accents, weaves in and out of complex interrelationships, merges with some, recoils from others, intersects with yet a third group: and all this may crucially shape discourse, may leave a trace in all its semantic layers, may complicate its expression and influence its entire stylistic profile."

48. Hauerwas, *With the Grain of the Universe,* 216.

49. Bakhtin, *The Dialogic Imagination*, 286.

50. Frohlich, "Desolation and Doctrine in Therese of Lisieux," 274.

51. Belford Ulanov, "Religious Devotion or Masochism?," 191.

52. See, for example, Frohlich's argument that Therese's "'little way' . . . is not the saccharine piety of affecting the multiplication of good deeds (as it has often been portrayed). Nor is it a search for extraordinary positive or negative experiences. Rather, it is the most demanding ascesis of simply living neighborly charity in the very ordinary here and now. In the end, Therese no longer expects to encounter God in 'essence'; she simply trusts in the 'event of apophasis' as it occurs in the midst of her daily acts of love" ("Desolation and Doctrine in Therese of Lisieux," 274).

53. Le Goff, *St. Francis of Assisi*, 57.

54. Cunningham, *Francis of Assisi*, 130.

55. Ibid., 131.

56. Bakhtin, *The Dialogic Imagination*, 285.

57. Cunningham, *Francis of Assisi*, 132.

58. Dennis et al., *St. Francis and the Foolishness of God*, 18–19.

59. Myers, *Binding the Strong Man*, 10.

60. Ibid., 312.

61. Ibid.

62. Radford-Reuther, *Sexism and God-talk*, 69.

63. Plate, *Walter Benjamin, Religion, and Aesthetics*, 12.

64. Ibid., 121.

65. Martin, *How Can I Find God?*

66. Martin, *My Life with the Saints*, 171.

67. The one thing Christianity does seem to guarantee, at least as far as the writings in the Bible attest, is trial and suffering.

68. Eisenstein, *Film Sense*. See, for example, the discussion in "Form and Content: Practice" in which Eisenstein goes so far as to argue that in his film *Alexander Nevsky*, a line of music corresponds to a pictorial representation—at least figuratively.

69. Bentley Hart, *The Beauty of the Infinite*, 5.

70. Ibid., 4–5.

71. Ibid., 16.

72. Ibid., 17.

73. http://www.youtube.com/watch?v=8oiueRe14p8.

74. Bentley Hart, *The Beauty of the Infinite*, 21.

75. http://fbibler.chez.com/tvstats/nielsen_ratings_2.html.

76. See, for example, Feur, "HBO and the Concept of Quality TV," and Lane, "The White House Culture of Gender and Race in *The West Wing*."

77. Lane, "White House Culture," 32.

78. Gledhill, "Genre and Gender," 348.

79. Rocchio, *Reel Racism*.

80. Admittedly, the narration's criticism of Mookie's actions are nuanced and complex, but it is not asking too much for professional film critics to tease out the meaning of a film—it's not exactly brain surgery.

81. Eboo Patel, "Religious Extremists Have a Media Strategy," http://www.faithstreet.com/onfaith/2007/03/30/religious-extremists-have-a-me/5926.

82. See, for example, the specific discussion of the campaign urging MSNBC to stop giving airtime to the FRC on http://faithfulamerica.org/about/.

83. Michael Livingston, "Most Christians to Left of Far Right," http://www.faithstreet.com/onfaith/2007/10/24/most-christians-to-left-of-far/1969.

84. Fiske, *Television Culture*, 37.

85. Ibid., 45.

86. Williamson, "The Problems of Being Popular."

87. Hall, "Encoding, decoding," 101–3.

88. Ibid., 102.

89. In clarifying her point, C. J. states, "blanket the continent with highways." This, of course, is precisely what happened in America, wreaking ecological havoc by effectively cutting off migration routes for numerous forms of wildlife, including the grizzly bear, elk, and grey wolf (among numerous others).

90. http://www.csmonitor.com/USA/Latest-News-Wires/2014/1216/Nuns-on-a-bus-can-relax-Vatican-sings-new-tune-on-US-nuns.

91. See, for example, http://articles.latimes.com/2012/apr/19/nation/la-na-vatican-nuns-20120420, and http://www.seattletimes.com/seattle-news/praise-not-punishment-for-our-nuns/.

92. http://globalsistersreport.org/omalley-calls-vatican-investigation-lcwr-disaster-14971.

93. Gustav Niebuhr, "Spiritual Values Are In, But, Please, No Sermonizing," *New York Times,* September 1, 1996, http://www.nytimes.com/1996/09/01/movies/spiritual-values-are-in-but-please-no-sermonizing.html?pagewanted=all.

94. Caryn James, "*Losing Chase* (1996)," *New York Times,* February 4, 1996, http://www.nytimes.com/movie/review?res=9806E1DC103AF937A35751C0A960958260.

95. Brooks, *The Melodramatic Imagination,* 15.

96. Ibid.

97. Champagne, *Italian Masculinity as Queer Melodrama,* 14.

98. Horton, ed., *Comedy/Cinema/Theory*, 5.

99. Bakhtin, *Rabelais and His World.*

100. Palmer, *The Logic of the Absurd,* 42.

101. It also keeps secular humanists (who by and large have no great investment in the traditional church) engaged by siding with popular culture over the traditional church.

102. Peter Boullata, personal communication, retrieved September 8, 2013.

103. Keating, *Manifesting God*, 71.

104. Ibid., 74.

105. Casey, *Sacred Reading,* 6.

106. The only scene that comes close to this level of isolation and intimacy is the scene where God reveals to Evan how the valley he lives in looked in its natural state—before it was clear cut to make a massive subdivision.

107. See, for example, Bordwell, *Narration in the Fiction Film*, 54–55.

108. See for example ibid., 33–39.

109. Balthasar, *Prayer*, 27.

110. In addition, queer studies would point to the manner in which the film suggests that the film depends on heteronormativity to work through Evan's salvation.

111. Peter Boullata, "The Wrath of Jonah," sermon, http://fplex.org/index.php/component/content/article/614-the-wrath-of-jonah.

112. United States Conference of Catholic Bishops, *The Book of Jonah*, http://www.usccb.org/bible/jonah/.

113. DeConto, *This Littler Light*.

114. Žižek, *The Sublime Object of Ideology*, 123.

115. Carroll, *Constantine's Sword*.

116. Louf, *Tuning in to Grace*, 12.

117. Groome, *What Makes Us Catholic*, 60.

118. Ibid., 20.

119. Ibid., 21.

120. Hauerwas, *After Christendom?*, 37.

121. Ibid.

122. Ibid., 33.

123. Ibid.

124. Bloch, *Man on His Own*, 39.

125. Ibid., 49

126. Bordwell and Thompson, *Film Art*, 220.

127. Ibid., 221.

128. Brimlow, *What About Hitler?*, 9.

129. Ibid.

130. Ibid. For more information on Dietrich Bonhoeffer's participation in the plot to assassinate Adolf Hitler, see Metaxas, *Bonhoeffer*, and Bethge, *Dietrich Bonhoeffer*.

131. The disastrous Vietnam War and the social upheaval that followed in its wake foreclosed the opportunity. Hollywood was notably silent on Vietnam—unable to create patriotic films with the success it enjoyed with World War II and unwilling to gamble on antiwar sentiments and its potential backlash. The first wave of Vietnam War films—*The Boys in Company C* (1978), *The Deer Hunter* (1978), and *Apocalypse Now* (1979) are all notable for their willingness to display the insanity of the Vietnam War, while holding back on the kind of political and social analysis that would critique

militarism. If anything, Robert Altman's *M*A*S*H* (1970) delivered more sustained antiwar criticism. Set in the Korean War, *M*A*S*H* was understood by audiences as metaphorical critique of the Vietnam War.

132. Žižek, *Looking Awry*, 30.

133. Ibid.

134. Žižek, *The Sublime Object of Ideology*, 126.

135. Ibid.

136. The translation is my own from the film's dialogue, not the subtitles. The original Italian is: *Grasso, grasso, brutto brutto, tutto giallo in verita. Se mi cheidi, "dove sono?" ti rispondo "qua, qua, qua." Caminando faccio po po. Chi sono io? Dimmi.*

137. Brimlow, *What About Hitler?*, 167.

138. Toole, *Waiting for Godot in Sarajevo*, 262.

139. Pope Paul VI, *Humanae Vitae*, Section 9, http://www.vatican.va/holy_father/paul_vi/encyclicals/documents/hf_p-vi_enc_25071968_humanae-vitae_en.html.

140. Toole, *Waiting for Godot in Sarajevo*, 206.

141. Ibid.

142. Ibid., 210.

143. Lasansky, *The Renaissance Perfected.*

144. Yoder, "Armaments and Eschatology," 54.

145. Comolli and Narboni, "Cinema/Ideology/Criticism."

146. Significantly, the first theological writings of Christianity were not narratives, but theological tracts from the Apostle Paul. Christian narratives in the form of Gospels, however, supplanted these writings as the privileged discourses of Christianity.

147. Granger, *Harry Potter's Bookshelf.*

148. The popularity of the book is almost legion: over 450 million books sold and translated into sixty-seven languages, including Latin and ancient Greek. See, for example, http://entertainment.time.com/2013/07/31/because-its-his-birthday-harry-potter-by-the-numbers/. The BBC reports that the number of languages that the book has been translated into as sixty-seven, see http://news.bbc.co.uk/2/hi/entertainment/7649962.stm. That popularity translated into movie, video game, and merchandising success, with total movie sales topping $7 billion, and total merchandising sales reaching the same $7 billion level. See, for example, http://www.statisticbrain.com/total-harry-potter-franchise-revenue/. That level of economic activity is unequaled in the entertainment industry for a single franchise. The above referenced *Time* article

values the Harry Potter brand at $15 billion.

149. Granger, "Dumbing down American readers," The Boston Globe, September 24, 2003.

150. This is not to say that film adaptations are flawless in their interpretations of the literary text. Indeed, the Harry Potter franchise has several changes to the text that border on outright misinterpretations. Chief among these can be found in the concluding film, based on *Harry Potter and the Deathly Hallows*. In the book's version of the "Battle of Hogwarts" an armed collective of many different magical creatures and wizards comes to the aid of the defeated Hogwartians as the battle recommences. This collective uprising in the struggle against evil is critical to the narrative's symbolic meaning. The film, however, places the collective on the side of evil—as attached to Voldemort's forces. In general, however, as this chapter will discuss, the films consistently magnify discourses that are significant to the narrative.

151. Granger, *Harry Potter's Bookshelf*, xvi.

152. This is not to assert that the discourse of Christianity is the *only* social discourse weaving its way through the series. As Granger's work shows, there are several such discourses. Here I point specifically to the clever cultural discourse asserting the validity, and beauty, of the new, multiracial, multicultural England versus the old, class-based, socially hierarchical, imperial, and racist England that the book condemns via relationship and attitudes that characters display towards other magical creatures—centaurs, elves, and goblins—and about wizards and witches who, like Hermione, come from Muggle parents. This discourse is also articulated through character construction, as characters from former colonial territories populate the student body of Hogwarts: Cho Chang, the Patil sisters, Dean Thomas, and Seamus Finnigan to name a few.

153. Special thanks to Jack Rocchio for helping develop this point.

154. Jameson, *The Political Unconscious*, 76.

155. Several aspects of setting point to this analogical function. The first is Harry's gateway to the magical world: King's Cross. Named for a crossing point that formerly displayed a statue of George IV, it nonetheless operates dialogically within the narrative. Independent of the narrative, King's Cross references a culminating point in the Christian narrative—where the king of kings dies upon a cross. The narrative of Harry Potter makes use of this reference when Harry's self-sacrificial gesture (following the way of the cross) leads him to King's Cross—where he must decide between returning to life, or moving on to the afterlife. Another aspect of setting that points to its analogical role is the grave site of Harry's parents. Upon finding his parents' grave on Christmas Eve, Harry discovers that the inscription on the tombstone reads, "The last enemy that shall be destroyed is death," a quote from Paul's First Letter to the Corinthians (15:26). The plot draws attention to the dialogical meaning of the quote first by having Harry misinterpret it as a "Death Eater idea" and then having Hermione clarify with a secular interpretation that "It means . . . you know . . . living beyond death." Hermione's accurate interpretation serves as a model for the setting's analogical role: it creates a coherent whole, but points nonetheless to a master text that determines its actual meaning.

156. The plot even insists that the parallel between the two worlds operates in both directions—implicitly suggesting, for example, that World War II was caused by the Dark Wizard Grindelwald. In this manner, the parallelism serves another signifying function: unequivocally asserting through its narrative that the mystical world does indeed exist.

157. Thanks to Catherine Jacob-Dolan for pointing out that the text suggests the two worlds live diagonally through the creation of Diagon Alley—a designation that the plot underscores in book two when Harry mispronounces Diagon Alley.

158. The book makes this statement an indirect discourse of Voldemort by having it spoken by Quirrel as a lesson he learned from Voldemort.

159. Jones, *Dismissing Jesus*, 5.

160. Ibid., 12 and 13.

161. Clifford, *The Wisdom Literature*, 20.

162. Sawyer, "Missing from 'Harry Potter'—a real moral struggle," The Christian Science Monitor, July 25, 2007.

163. Ibid.

164. Ibid.

165. Bonhoeffer, *The Cost of Discipleship*, 47.

166. Ibid., 65.

167. Ibid., 89.

168. With its display of images and figures to direct secondary, or image-inary identification, deployment of camera and special effects, sounds and music to procure primary identification, and narrative organization that assigns social meanings and values to action that can secure symbolic identification, the cinematic experience readily mobilizes all three modes of identification, and privileges one in favor of another at any moment in ways that literature struggles to achieve. Nonetheless, it would be inaccurate to claim that these three modes of identification do not function within the literary experience, as the Harry Potter series demonstrates. Literary plots can certainly mobilize primary identification with its pacing, twists, or surprises. Plot descriptions provide an image internal to the reader's psyche that can create the analogous experiences of secondary/narcissistic identification. Finally, using narrative as a mode of organizing evaluation and meaning, literature readily mobilizes symbolic identification.

169. J. K. Rowling has subsequently said that the marriage of Ron and Hermione was a mistake, that Hermione should have married Harry in the end (see, for example, http://time.com/3680/j-k-rowling-says-hermione-should-have-ended-up-with-harry-potter-not-ron/.) Rowling thinks, in retrospect, that her decision to couple Ron and

Hermione only worked to please her, and was not done out of literary consideration. I argue, however, that the dance scene in *Harry Potter and the Deathly Hallows Part I* proves her "correction" to be wrong. In this scene, Ron has just abandoned Harry and Hermione, as well as the quest for Horcruxes. To compensate for this loss, Harry puts on music and begins to dance with Hermione. For Harry, the dance is a way to pull Hermione out of the loss and the strain of their quest, but begins to evolve into a metaphor for their own closeness, their own togetherness. Daniel Radcliffe's expressions, highlighted by camera placements and editing, then begin to show longing. They convey that Harry himself would like to escape Ron's betrayal and the strain of their quest by transferring his sacramental love for Hermione into romantic love. When he sees no such longing in Hermione's face, he abandons that desire. The literary consideration that Rowling is overlooking now is how she has so carefully constructed Harry and Hermione's relationship around sacramental love—and the ability of sacramental love to maintain itself without having to transfer into romantic love. Denying Harry and Hermione from eventually coupling was exactly the most literary consideration the author could have made: not giving into the standard conventions of romantic love and insisting instead on the vitality and richness of sacramental love. Moreover, while Ron can be considered a bit of a lout, Rowling clearly transforms his character in several places, nowhere more thoroughly than when Ron is the only one in the story who realizes the Hogwarts house elves are in danger and need to be warned. Rowling's correction downplays the potential of that transformation, not to mention the other transformations, which turn Ron into the more selfless, caring person who could fulfill and provide love for Hermione.

170. Perhaps the most notorious example of the entertainment industry failing to understand the intricacies of identification occurred when NBC replaced *Today* show anchor Jane Pauley with Debra Norville. Pauley was a beloved figure on the show, but the network's ratings demonstrated an inability to attract young female viewers. Norville lacked the intellectual gravitas of Pauley, but the network was confident that because she was young and attractive, young women would identify with her. The move was an unmitigated disaster and the ratings plummeted. NBC's error lay in the mistaken assumption that identification was a simple process of recognizing similarities.

171. Here too, Pope Francis has taken a leading role, installing showers for the homeless in St. Peter's Square and organizing local barbers to come and give haircuts to the homeless.

172. http://old.post-gazette.com/businessnews/20011008glass1008p2.asp.

173. http://old.post-gazette.com/businessnews/20011008glass1008p2.asp.

174. Institute for Sustainable Communities, "Case Study: Cleveland Ohio," 31.

175. Ibid.

176. Ibid., 36.

177. Ibid., 35.

178. http://community-wealth.org/strategies/panel/anchors/index.html.

179. http://www.thestar.com/news/gta/2015/04/18/anchored-in-hope-how-toronto-is-learning-from-clevelands-return-to-prosperity.html.

180. http://www.forbes.com/sites/steveodland/2012/03/24/college-costs-are-soaring/.

181. http://www.acenet.edu/the-presidency/columns-and-features/Pages/state-funding-a-race-to-the-bottom.aspx.

182. http://www.wsj.com/articles/SB10001424127887323316804578161490716042814.

183. http://chronicle.com/article/Rising-Pay-for-Presidents/230703?cid=megamenu.

184. "Executive Compensation at Public and Private Colleges," *The Chronicle of Higher Education,* June 8, 2015.

185. http://www.nytimes.com/2015/04/05/opinion/sunday/the-real-reason-college-tuition-costs-so-much.html?_r=1.

186. Thomas Frank, "Academy Fight Song," http://thebaffler.com/salvos/academy-fight-song.

187. For some institutions, like Georgetown, and to some degree Wake Forest, the elite quality of the education comes first, and religious heritage follows in its wake (no pun intended). For others, like Notre Dame and Boston College, identity gets resolved as being elite Catholic institutions: fundamentally a place where Catholics go to get an elite education, informed by Catholic values and spirituality, but all are welcome (especially elite athletes). The other side of the spectrum is Franciscan University, whose identity is that of a refuge for Catholics seeking orthodoxy as the answer to the liberal excesses of secular society.

188. http://www.businessinsider.com/nielsen-q4-total-audience-data-2015-3.

189. https://socialblade.com/youtube/top/100/mostsubscribed.

190. https://socialblade.com/youtube/user/jennamarbles.

191. Tate, "Disney's $1B YouTube Channel Investment Is the Future of TV," *Wired,* http://www.wired.com/2014/04/disney-maker-studios/.

192. Rocchio, "Video Education in the Net-casting Era: Towards A Critical Practice Pedagogy." Paper for the *Media in Transition 6* Conference, Cambridge, Massachusetts, April 2009.

Bibliography

A Christmas Miracle: The Making of a Charlie Brown Christmas. United Features Syndicate, 2008.

Agamben, Giorgio. *Homo Sacer: Sovereign Power and Bare Life.* Translated by Daniel Heller-Roazen. Stanford, CA: Stanford University Press, 1998.

Augustine of Hippo. *The Confessions.* Edited by David Vincent Meconi, S.J. Translated by Maria Boulding, OSB. San Francisco: Ignatius, 2012.

Bakhtin, Mikhail. *The Dialogic Imagination.* Austin, TX: University of Texas Press, 1981.

———. *Rabelais and His World.* Bloomington, IN: Indiana University Press, 2009.

Balthasar, Hans Urs von. *The Glory of the Lord: A Theological Aesthetics I: Seeing The Form.* Edited by John Riches. Translated by Erasmo Leiva-Merikakis. Edinburgh, Scotland: T & T Clark, 1998.

———. *Prayer.* New York: Sheed and Ward, 1961.

Belford Ulanov, Ann, "Religious Devotion or Masochism?: A Psychoanalyst Looks at Therese." In *Experiencing St. Therese Today*, edited by John Sullivan, 165–83. Carmelite Studies. Washington, DC: ICS, 1990.

Bentley Hart, David. *The Beauty of the Infinite.* Grand Rapids: Eerdmans, 2003.

Bethge, Eberhard. *Dietrich Bonhoeffer: A Biography.* Minneapolis: Fortress, 2000.

Bloch, Ernst. *Man on His Own: Essays in the Philosophy of Religion.* New York: Herder and Herder, 1970.

———. *The Principle of Hope*, vol. I. Translated by Neville Plaice et al. Cambridge, MA: MIT Press, 1986.

Bonhoeffer, Dietrich. *The Cost of Discipleship.* New York: Touchstone, 1995.

———. *Christology.* Translated by Edwin Robertson. London: William Collins Sons & Co., 1978.

Bordwell, David. *Narration in the Fiction Film.* Madison, WI: University of Wisconsin Press, 1985.

Bordwell, David, Janet Staiger, and Kristin Thompson. *The Classical Hollywood Cinema: Film Style and Modes of Production to 1960.* New York: Columbia University Press, 1985.

Bordwell, David, and Kristin Thompson. *Film Art: An Introduction.* 6th ed. New York: McGraw-Hill, 2001.

Borg, Marcus J., and John Dominic Crossan. *The First Paul: Reclaiming the Radical Visionary Behind the Church's Conservative Icon.* New York: HarperOne, 2009.

Boullata, Peter, "The Wrath of Jonah." Sermon. https://vimeo.com/74665187.

Brimlow, Robert. *What About Hitler? Wrestling with Jesus's Call to Nonviolence in an Evil World.* Grand Rapids: Brazos, 2006.

Brooks, Peter. *The Melodramatic Imagination.* New York: Columbia University Press, 1985.

Caputo, John D. *What Would Jesus Deconstruct? The Good News of Postmodernism for the Church.* Grand Rapids: Baker Academic, 2007.

Carroll, James. *Christ, Actually: The Son of God for the Secular Age.* New York: Penguin, 2015.

———. *Constantine's Sword: The Church and the Jews.* Boston: Houghton Mifflin, 2001.

Casey, Michael. *Sacred Reading: The Ancient Art of Lectio Divina.* Liguori, MO: Liguori, 1996.

Champagne, John. *Italian Masculinity as Queer Melodrama: Caravaggio, Puccini, Contemporary Cinema.* New York: Palgrave Macmillan, 2015.

Ciorra, Anthony J. *Beauty: A Path to God.* New York: Paulist, 2013.

Clapp, Rodney. *Border Crossings.* Grand Rapids: Brazos, 2000.

Clifford, Dick. *The Wisdom Literature.* Nashville: Abingdon, 1998.

Couldry, Nick. *Listening Beyond the Echoes: Media, Ethics, and Agency in an Uncertain World.* Boulder, CO: Paradigm, 2006.

Comolli, Jean-Luc, and Jean Paul Narboni. "Cinema/Ideology/Criticism." In *Movies and Methods,* vol. I, 22–30. Berkeley, CA: University of California Press, 1976.

Crossan, John Dominic. *God and Empire: Jesus Against Rome, Then and Now.* New York: HarperSanFrancisco, 2007.

Cunningham, Lawrence. *Francis of Assisi: Performing the Gospel Life.* Grand Rapids: Eerdmans, 2004.

DeConto, Jesse. *This Littler Light: Some Thoughts on NOT Changing the World.* Eugene, OR: Cascade, 2013.

Deacy, Christopher, and Gaye Williams Ortiz. *Theology and Film: Challenging the Sacred/Secular Divide.* London: Blackwell, 2008.

Dennis, Marie, et al. *St. Francis and the Foolishness of God.* Maryknoll, NY: Orbis, 1993.

Eisenstein, Sergei. *Film Sense.* Edited and translated by Jay Leyda. New York: Harcourt, Brace, Jovanovich, 1975.

Feur, Jane. "HBO and the Concept of Quality TV." In *Quality TV: Contemporary American Television and Beyond,* edited by Janet McCabe and Kim Akass, 145–57. London: I. B. Tauris, 2007.

Fiske, John. "Opening the Hallway: Some remarks on the fertility of Stuart Hall's contribution to critical theory." In *Stuart Hall: Critical Dialogues in Cultural Studies,* edited by David Morley and Kuan-Hsing Chen, 212–22. London: Routledge, 1996.

———. *Television Culture.* London: Routledge, 1994.

Frohlich, Mary. "Desolation and Doctrine in Therese of Lisieux." *Theological Studies* 61:2, 2000, 262–79.

Geertz, Clifford. *The Interpretation of Cultures.* New York: Basic, 1973.

Gledhill, Christine. "Genre and Gender: The Case of Soap Opera." In *Representation: Cultural Representations and Signifying Practices,* edited by Stuart Hall, 337–86. London: Sage, 2003.

Gonzalez-Andrieu, Cecilia. *Bridge to Wonder: Art as a Gospel of Beauty.* Waco, TX: Baylor University Press, 2012.

Granger, John. *Harry Potter's Bookshelf: The Great Books Behind the Hogwarts Adventures.* New York: Berkley, 2009.

Groome, Thomas. *What Makes Us Catholic: Eight Gifts for Life.* New York: Harper Collins, 2003.

Hall, Stuart. "Encoding, decoding." In *The Cultural Studies Reader*, edited by Simon During, 90–103. London: Routledge, 1993.

Hauerwas, Stanley. *After Christendom? How the Church is to behave if freedom, justice, and a Christian nation are bad ideas.* Nashville: Abingdon, 1991.

———. *With the Grain of the Universe: The Church's Witness and Natural Theology.* Grand Rapids: Brazos, 2001.

Horton, Andrew, ed. *Comedy/Cinema/Theory.* Berkeley, CA: University of California Press, 1991.

Institute for Sustainable Communities. "Case Study: Cleveland Ohio." In "Sustainable Economic Development: A Resource Guide for Local Leaders, Version 2.0. http:community-wealth.org/content/case-study-cleveland-oh-cleveland-evergreen-cooperatives.

Jameson, Fredric. *Late Marxism: Adorno or the Persistence of the Dialectic.* London: Verso, 1990.

———. *Postmodernism, or, The Cultural Logic of Late Capitalism.* Durham, NC: Duke University Press, 1991.

———. *The Political Unconscious: Narrative as a Socially Symbolic Act.* Ithaca, NY: Cornell University Press, 1981.

Jones, Douglas M. *Dismissing Jesus: How We Evade the Way of the Cross.* Eugene, OR: Cascade, 2013.

Kammer, Fred, S.J. "Catholicism and Capitalism." In *JustSouth E-Newsletter* 19, February, 2012.

Johnston, Robert K., ed. *Reframing Theology and Film: New Focus for an Emerging Discipline.* Grand Rapids: Baker Academic, 2007.

Keating, Thomas. *Manifesting God.* New York: Lantern, 2005.

Lacan, Jacques. *Anxiety, The Seminar of Jacques Lacan, Book X.* Edited by Jacques-Alain Miller. Translated by A. R. Price. Cambridge, UK: Polity, 2014.

———. *Identification, The Seminar of Jacques Lacan, Book IX.* Translated by Cormac Gallagher from unedited French manuscripts. London: Karnac, 2002.

———. *The Triumph of Religion* preceded by *Discourse to Catholics.* Translated by Bruce Fink. Cambridge, UK: Polity, 2013.

Lane, Christina. "The White House Culture of Gender and Race in *The West Wing*: Insights from the Margins." In *The West Wing: The American Presidency as Television Drama*, edited by Peter C. Rollins and John E. Conner, 32–41. New York: Syracuse University Press, 2003.

Lasansky, D. Medina. *The Renaissance Perfected: Architecture, Spectacle, and Tourism in Fascist Italy.* University Park, PA: The Pennsylvania University Press, 2005.

Le Goff, Jacques. *St. Francis of Assisi.* Translated by Christine Rhone. London: Routledge, 2004.

Louf, Andre. *Tuning in to Grace.* Translated by John Vriend. Kalamazoo, MI: Cistercian, 1992.

MacCabe, Colin. *Tracking the Signifier, Theoretical Essays: film, linguistics, literature.* Minneapolis: University of Minnesota Press, 1985.

Martin, James. *How Can I Find God?* Liguori, MO: Liguori, 1997.

———. *My Life with the Saints.* Chicago: Loyola, 2006.

Merton, Thomas. *Contemplative Prayer.* New York: Doubleday, 1996.

Metaxas, Eric. *Bonhoeffer: Pastor, Martyr, Prophet, Spy.* Nashville: Thomas Nelson, 2011.

Myers, Ched. *Binding the Strong Man: A Political Reading of Mark's Story of Jesus.* Maryknoll, NY: Orbis, 1997.

Michelson, Annette. "Towards Snow." In *The Avant-Garde Film: A Reader in Theory and Criticism*, edited by P. Adams Sitney, 172–83. New York: Anthology Film Archives, 1978.

Milbank, John, Slavoj Žižek, and Creston Davis. *Paul's New Moment: Continental Philosophy and the Future of Christian Theology.* Grand Rapids: Brazos, 2010.

Morris, Meaghan. "Banality in Cultural Studies." In *Logics of Television*, 119–44. Bloomington, IN: Indiana University Press, 1990.

Nolan, Albert. *Jesus Before Christianity.* Maryknoll, NY: Orbis, 1988.

Palmer, Jerry. *The Logic of the Absurd: On Film and Television Comedy.* London: British Film Institute, 1988.

Plate, S. Brent. *Religion and Film: Cinema and the Re-Creation of the World.* London: Wallflower, 2008.

———. *Walter Benjamin, Religion, and Aesthetics: Rethinking Religion Through the Arts.* New York: Routledge, 2005.

Pope Benedict XVI. *Jesus of Nazareth: From the Baptism in the Jordan to the Transfiguration.* New York: Doubleday, 2007.

Pope Francis. "A Big Heart Open to God." Interview with Antonio Spadaro. *America,* September 30, 2013, 14–38.

———. *Evangelii Gaudium.* Apostolic Exhortation, 2013.

Pope John Paul II. *Centesimus Annus.* Papal Encyclical, 1991.

Pope Paul VI. *Humanae Vitae.* Papal Encyclical, 1968.

Radford-Reuther, Rosemary. *Sexism and God-talk: Toward a Feminist Theology.* Boston: Beacon, 1983.

Rahner, Karl, S.J. *The Need and Blessing of Prayer.* Translated by Bruce W. Gillette. Collegeville, MN: Liturgical, 1997.

Rocchio, Vincent. "Attacking 'Support Our Troops': The Crisis of Cultural Studies in Confronting Militarism." http://culturalstudiesresearch.org/wp-content/uploads/2012/10/RicchioAttackingSupportourTroops1.pdf.

———. "Patriarchy has Failed Us: The Enduring Legacy of Neorealism in Contemporary Italian Cinema." *The Quarterly Review of Film and Television,* 29:1, 147–62.

———. *Reel Racism: Confronting Hollywood's Construction of Afro-American Culture.* Boulder, CO: Westview, 2000.

———. *"Video Education in the Net-casting Era: Towards A Critical Practice Pedagogy"* Paper for the Media in Transition 6 Conference, Cambridge, MA, April 2009.

Rowling, J. K. *Harry Potter and the Chamber of Secrets.* New York: Arthur A. Levine, 1999.

———. *Harry Potter and the Deathly Hallows.* New York: Arthur A. Levine, 2007.

———. *Harry Potter and the Goblet of Fire.* New York: Arthur A. Levine, 2000.

———. *Harry Potter and the Half-Blood Prince.* New York: Arthur A. Levine, 2005.

———. *Harry Potter and the Order of the Phoenix.* New York: Arthur A. Levine, 2003.

———. *Harry Potter and the Prisoner of Azkaban.* New York, NY: Arthur A. Levine, 1999.

———. *Harry Potter and the Sorcerer's Stone.* New York: Arthur A. Levine, 1998.

Schulz, Charles. *A Charlie Brown Christmas: The Making of a Tradition.* New York: Harper Collins, 2000.

Toole, David. *Waiting for Godot in Sarajevo.* Boulder, CO: Westview, 1999.

Vollmer, Ulrike. *Seeing Film and Reading Feminist Theology: A Dialogue.* New York: Palgrave Macmillan, 2007.

Williams, Raymond. *Marxism and Literature.* Oxford: Oxford University Press, 1977.

Williamson, Judith. "The Problems of Being Popular." *New Socialist,* September 1986, 14–15.

Woods, Robert H., and Paul D. Patton. *Prophetically Incorrect: A Christian Introduction to Media Criticism.* Grand Rapids: Brazos, 2010.

Yoder, John Howard. "Armaments and Eschatology." *Studies in Christian Ethics 1/1* (1988) 43–61.

———. *The Christian Witness to the State.* Newton, KS: Faith and Life, 1964.

———. *The Politics of Jesus.* Grand Rapids, MI: Eerdmans, 1972.

Žižek, Slavoj. *Looking Awry.* Cambridge, MA: MIT Press, 1992.

———. *The Sublime Object of Ideology.* London: Verso, 1989.

Index

B

C

D

F

G

H

S

www.ingramcontent.com/pod-product-compliance
Lightning Source LLC
LaVergne TN
LVHW041112080826
845145LV00007B/1786